Leading
Corporate
Citizens

Vision, Values, Value Added

Leading Corporate Citizens

Vision, Values, Value Added *Second Edition*

Sandra Waddock
*Boston College
Carroll School of
Management*

Boston   Burr Ridge, IL   Dubuque, IA   Madison, WI   New York
San Francisco   St. Louis   Bangkok   Bogotá   Caracas   Kuala Lumpur
Lisbon   London   Madrid   Mexico City   Milan   Montreal   New Delhi
Santiago   Seoul   Singapore   Sydney   Taipei   Toronto

The **McGraw·Hill** Companies

**Mc
Graw
Hill** **McGraw-Hill
Irwin**

LEADING CORPORATE CITIZENS: VISION, VALUES, VALUE ADDED

Published by McGraw-Hill/Irwin, a business unit of The McGraw-Hill Companies, Inc., 1221 Avenue of the Americas, New York, NY, 10020. Copyright © 2006, 2002 by The McGraw-Hill Companies, Inc. All rights reserved. No part of this publication may be reproduced or distributed in any form or by any means, or stored in a database or retrieval system, without the prior written consent of The McGraw-Hill Companies, Inc., including, but not limited to, in any network or other electronic storage or transmission, or broadcast for distance learning.

Some ancillaries, including electronic and print components, may not be available to customers outside the United States.

This book is printed on acid-free paper.

1 2 3 4 5 6 7 8 9 0 DOC/DOC 0 9 8 7 6 5

ISBN 0-07-287949-1

Editorial director: *John E. Biernat*
Senior sponsoring editor: *Kelly H. Lowery*
Editorial assistant: *Kirsten Guidero*
Associate marketing manager: *Margaret A. Beamer*
Project manager: *Kristin Bradley*
Production supervisor: *Debra R. Sylvester*
Design coordinator: *Cara David*
Senior media project manager: *Susan Lombardi*
Developer, Media technology: *Brian Nacik*
Cover design: *Cara David*
Typeface: *10/12 Times New Roman*
Compositor: *SR Nova Pvt Ltd., Bangalore, India*
Printer: *R. R. Donnelley*

Library of Congress Cataloging-in-Publication Data

Waddock, Sandra A.
    Leading corporate citizens : vision, values, value-added / Sandra Waddock.—2nd ed.
      p. cm.
    Includes bibliographical references and index.
    ISBN 0-07-287949-1 (alk. paper)
    1. Social responsibility of business. 2. Values. 3. Human ecology. 4. Common good.
    5. Citizenship. I. Title.
HD60.W33 2006
658.4'08—dc22

                2004063185

www.mhhe.com

For Ben
With love,
Mom
Boston 2005

Brief Table of Contents

Contents

Chapter 11
Values Added: Global Futures 329

Chapter 12
Leading Global Futures: The Emerging Paradigm of Leading Corporate Citizenship 357

Foreword

Take a look at the business press these days. It seems hard to escape a great deal of talk about companies becoming good corporate global citizens, especially in light of the wave of scandals that struck in the early 2000s. But just what is corporate global citizenship and how do corporations achieve it? *Leading Corporate Citizens* explores what it takes to make a company a leading corporate citizen as well as some of the pathways toward the type of personal leadership that such citizenship implies.

Leading Corporate Citizens is about corporate responsibility—what I call responsible practice—and is also much ado about stakeholders and the implicit and inextricable relationship that companies have with their stakeholders. The book uses a framework of vision, values, and value added to lead us into this exploration of corporate citizenship. Vision is personal, organizational, and even societal. Vision focuses on the ways in which our work together in an organization, a corporation, will make a difference in the world around us. Values are about what we want to stand for as individuals, as organizations, as society. The book illustrates how we can imbue our organization with constructive values to which stakeholders are willing to make a commitment. *Leading Corporate Citizens* is about the ways that having a positive and constructive vision supported by values contribute to productive sources of value added for the enterprise. It is about personal and organizational insight, vision, and learning as an on going activity that informs day-to-day practice. It is about balance in our lives, individual and organizational, and among what I call the spheres of activity in society, as well as in ways that are ecologically sustainable.

Leading Corporate Citizens is, in fact, about responsible practice and the associated bottom-line benefits. It is countercultural in the sense that it opposes a short-sighted, narrowly focused perspective on the purpose and roles of the firm and deliberately sets a difficult, long-range target that is in the interests of all—the common wealth. It is not necessarily about organizations that exist today as much as it is about organizations as they *need* to exist to build a better tomorrow. It is, however, about what does work and in that sense, it is intended to be a practical guide to action for leaders.

Leading Corporate Citizens is a book premised on working with what is best in capitalism, while preserving or enhancing a sense of the collective good that sustains us in our communities, families, and working lives. It is about integrated wholeness, rather than fragmentation, an attempt to focus on the truly big picture so that when leaders of the future make decisions, they will be well aware of the impacts of those decisions. It is also about paying attention to the soft stuff that is actually the hard stuff—to the qualitative as well as quantitative impacts and results of company actions, to the subjective as well as objective aspects of the lives we lead in organizations and societies today.

In *Leading Corporate Citizens* I try to present a positive vision of the corporation in society, in all its manifest roles, and with all of its impacts. Deliberately and even somewhat idealistically (my Pollyanna nature coming through full force), I intend to take us toward a new paradigm organization, one that does, in fact, take into account its responsibilities towards multiple stakeholders in the interest of achieving multiple positive bottom lines in the long term. At the same time, I will try to present some of the dominant critiques and problems of the modern corporation, particularly in chapter cases, so that management students are exposed to them and understand that there are two sides to the currently dominant paradigm of shareholder capitalism that might be somewhat (albeit not fully) alleviated by stakeholder capitalism.

Not all corporations today achieve this vision of responsible practice, of living vision and values that result in value and values added. In fact most probably don't, but many companies do show evidence of partially achieving it and some are working hard toward this vision. And, as *Leading Corporate Citizens* attempts to demonstrate, the rewards for those that do can be significant over the long term.

Structure of the Book

Leading Corporate Citizens is structured into four parts, the first of which provides "A Context for Leading Corporate Citizens." Chapter 1, Leading Corporate Citizenship: Vision, Values, Value Added, provides one of the core frameworks of the book: the idea that guided by inspirational vision and a set of principles or core values a company can add value. This chapter introduces the relational stakeholder perspective that guides much of the vision of the book itself. The chapter also introduces the concept of spheres of influence, focusing on the ecological underpinning, and focuses quite literally on the ground beneath our feet, the natural environment on which human civilization depends for its very existence and on which businesses depend for the raw materials used in the production of goods and services.

Users of the first edition will note that the original first and second chapters have been combined in this edition, that Chapter 7 on managing corporate responsibility is entirely new to this edition, and that Chapters 8 and 10 in particular have been extensively rewritten. Previous users will also note that there are now two cases included in each chapter, with discussion questions, and considerably more tension embedded in the cases to foster lively conversations.

Chapter 2, The Three Spheres of Human Civilization, rounds out the context in which businesses operate by arguing that human civilization, built upon the natural environment, can be described in three spheres: economic, political or governmental, and civil society. Each of these spheres has specific types of goals and a set of values that determines the nature and type of enterprise that tends to arise in that sphere.

The second part of the book tells us how to design and manage "Leading Corporate Citizens with Vision, Values, and Value Added." These chapters take the framework of vision, values, and value added sketched out in the first two chapters and elaborate each element of that framework, and a new chapter discusses how progressive companies are actually explicitly managing their responsibilities. Chapter 3, Personal and Organizational Vision, argues that vision that inspires meaning and commitment, both personally and organizationally, is necessary to bring out the best in all of us. This chapter further takes a developmental perspective on both individuals and organizations, making the case that relatively higher levels of cognitive, moral, and emotional development are needed to cope with the complexity and relative chaos of today's organizations if they are, in fact, to become leading corporate citizens.

Chapter 4, Values in Management Practice: Operating with Integrity, shows how integrity, in all senses of the word—honesty and forthrightness, operating from a principled base, and soundness and wholeness—is needed to bring vision to life in a way that engenders stakeholder commitment and the best possible performance. This chapter also argues for responsible practice as the basis of sound—and ultimately profitable—operations. The theme of Value Added: The Impact of Vision and Values is carried forward in Chapter 5, which tries to synthesize the evidence for linking vision, values, and value added, showing that not only is responsible practice the right thing to do but that ultimately it is the more effective—and profitable—way to go.

The third part of the book, "Leading Corporate Citizens and their Stakeholders," articulates the specific practices that leading corporate citizens can employ with respect to their stakeholders, the natural environment, and society at large to get to the value added discussed in the previous part of the book. Chapter 6, Stakeholders: The Relationship Key, discusses the boundary-spanning, stakeholder related functions found inside leading corporate citizens and highlights the specific practices that can be considered to be current "best practice" within each of the stakeholder arenas found in most companies.

Chapter 7, Managing Responsibility and Corporate Citizenship, is new to this edition. It specifically addresses the management systems that companies have begun to develop in the past few years to articulate and manage their stakeholder and environmental responsibilities. Chapter 8, Investment and Assessment for Corporate Citizenship, makes real the ways in which the nontraditional (non-financial) bottom lines associated with different stakeholders are being measured both by external research groups, analysts, and critics, and by companies themselves when they want to improve performance. This chapter, extensively revised, highlights the significant advances in measurement and reporting that have taken place in the early 2000s.

Chapter 9, Sustainability and the Global Village, focuses on ecology in two senses. First, the chapter provides some insight into the ways in which humans—and businesses in particular—impact the natural environment, and how the negative aspects of those impacts might be lessened and certainly need to be attended to. Then the chapter turns to the ecology of human civilization, addressing the ways in which cross- or multi-sector collaboration can be developed to address societal needs more holistically than they can be addressed from any one sphere of human civilization.

The final part of *Leading Corporate Citizens* is "Leading Corporate Citizens into the Future." This part moves us into the emerging norms and standards that are impacting business operations throughout the world today—and that are likely to have even more impact in the future. Chapter 10, Global Standards/Global Village, explicitly addresses the emergence of global standards for business practice, as well as human and labor rights, and illustrates some of the reasons why companies wishing to be leaders in corporate citizenship should set and live up to internal and external standards of responsibility.

Chapter 11, Values-Added: Global Futures, highlights some practical and creative ways in which leading corporate citizens can begin to think about—and anticipate—the future, making that future appear less chaotic and unpredictable. Finally, Chapter 12, Leading Global Futures: The Emerging Paradigm of Corporate Citizenship, attempts to pull all of this thinking together in what one reviewer said was certainly not the typical ending to a book such as this. Using Gareth Morgan's idea of "imaginization," this final chapter takes the reader on a tour of the new organization paradigm—the leading corporate citizen. In this tour, Chapter 12 attempts to illustrate what it would be like in such an entity, how it would feel, and why, in the end, it might be important to move in that direction.

In the end *Leading Corporate Citizens* is about leadership on multiple levels. First is the individual manager/executive's leadership and courage needed to take the long-term perspective implied in becoming a good citizen, attending to responsibilities and relationships inherent when interdependencies with stakeholders are acknowledged. A second level is that of the corporation, much maligned as a citizen in some parts of the world, but ultimately guided by individuals who must themselves live in the world created by these powerful organizations. Finally, there is a societal level of thinking and analysis that is critically important for moving us toward a better world. What I can hope is that some new awareness—mindfulness—of the need to be responsible for the impacts that corporate decisions have on multiple stakeholders is generated by this book. In the end, after all is said and done, it is our own integrity as human beings and as leaders of corporate citizens, it is knowing that we did our best, that will matter.

Acknowledgments

Thanks are in order, so many that I scarcely know where to begin and I know I will forget many important contributors to my ideas and knowledge.

For inspiration, community, and intellectual genesis of some of the ideas embedded in this book, I am grateful to my colleagues and friends in the Boston College Center for Responsible Leadership—as well as to our participants, now too numerous to name. The guides in the CRL's flagship program Leadership for Change to a positive vision of the corporation are many. From Sociology are Severyn Bruyn, Charlie Derber, Paul Gray, and Eve Spangler. From Boston College's Carroll School of Management (for LC and so much more) are Judy Clair, Joe Raelin (now at Northeastern University), and Bill Torbert; and our business partners over the years, Robert Leaver, Bill Joiner, Neil Smith, and, of course, LC founder and inspiration, Steve Waddell, and our director Rebecca Rowley.

I would like to thank my longtime co-author and colleague Sam Graves for his friendship, support, and our work together. It has been a source of much pleasure to work with him over the years. In many ways our work together provides the ultimate foundation for this book to the point where it probably could not have been written without the research partnership we have shared. In addition, I would like to thank Charlie Bodwell of the ILO for our collaboration on responsibility management.

Intellectual debts are much more difficult to repay. For all the authors cited in this book and so many more, I thank you for your ideas and vision. I hope your ideas have inspired mine in ways you find acceptable. Particular debts are owed to those who once taught and continue to teach me. From Boston University, where I did my graduate work (although most are now elsewhere), I thank mentor and now friend Jim Post, and John Mahon, Dave Brown, and Jerry Leader in particular. Stan Davis, who was at BU when I was there, also taught me the critical question: "so what?"

Other colleagues at Boston College have been supportive of our type of integrative thinking about teaching, community-collaborative relationships, and general integration of scholarship with the world about us: Mary Walsh from the School of Education, Fran Sherman from the Law School, Jean Mooney from the School of Education, Robbie Tourse from Graduate School of Social Work, Jim Fleming, School of Education, and Mary Brabeck, Dean of School of Education. Your work in outreach scholarship is truly an inspiration underpinning this book.

Leading
Corporate
Citizens

Vision, Values, Value Added

PART ONE

A Context for Leading Corporate Citizens

CHAPTER ONE

Leading Corporate Citizenship: Vision, Values, Value Added

I want to challenge you to join me in taking our relationship to a still higher level. I propose that you [corporate leaders] . . . and we, the United Nations, initiate a global compact of shared values and principles, which will give a human face to the global market.

Globalization is a fact of life. But I believe we have underestimated its fragility. The problem is this. The spread of markets outpaces the ability of societies and their political systems to adjust to them, let alone to guide the course they take. History teaches us that such an imbalance between the economic, social and political realms can never be sustained for very long. . . .

We have to choose between a global market driven only by calculations of short-term profit, and one which has a human face. Between a world which condemns a quarter of the human race to starvation and squalor, and one which offers everyone at least a chance of prosperity, in a healthy environment. Between a selfish free-for-all in which we ignore the fate of the losers, and a culture in which the strong and successful accept their responsibilities, showing global vision and leadership.

Kofi Annan, Secretary-General of the United Nations[1]

Corporations: Citizens of the (Natural and Human) World

Kofi Annan's words highlight an important and often forgotten reality: Business is integrally connected to both the social context in which it operates and the natural environment on which we all depend. With the statement above, Annan launched what has become the United Nations' Global Compact and signaled an important shift in the long-term relationships that businesses can expect to have with their many constituencies—their stakeholders as well as how they treat the natural environment.[2] As businesses have grown larger and more powerful, their attendant responsibilities to be good corporate citizens wherever they operate have also grown. Indeed, some argue that the rise of the very term *corporate citizenship* since the late 1990s came about in part because some companies in the process of globalization began to assume responsibilities formerly assigned solely to governments.[3]

Corporate citizenship is an integral part of the whole corporation as it exists in whole communities and whole societies, with whole people operating within. In this sense of wholes within other wholes, corporations are what Ken Wilber terms *holons*, that is, both wholes in and of themselves and parts of something larger. As holons, they are embedded in and affect the web of relationships that constitutes societies, just as biological systems are also interrelated webs.[4] In administering some of the responsibilities of citizenship, companies are increasingly finding themselves held accountable for their impacts on society and social rights (e.g., not polluting or otherwise contributing to deteriorating environmental conditions), on individual or civil rights (e.g., freedom from abusive working conditions), and on political rights (e.g., being held accountable when participating in countries whose governments do not uphold basic political and individual rights).[5]

The embeddedness of corporations in societies—that is, their existence as socially constructed holons in economic, political, and societal contexts—means that careful attention needs to be given to how they behave. Being or becoming a leading corporate citizen implies that companies must understand their relationships to both primary and secondary stakeholders in society, must learn to treat those stakeholders as well as the natural environment respectfully, and must understand the global context in which businesses operate. Sustainability depends on these systemic understandings, whether it is the ecological sustainability so in question today by many environmentalists, the sustainability of the societies and communities where businesses operate, or the longevity of the business itself.

If we conceive companies in terms of their relationships to stakeholders and the natural environment, then we come to the following definition of leading corporate citizenship:

> Leading corporate citizens are companies that live up to clear constructive visions and core values consistent with those of the broader societies within which they

operate, respect the natural environment, and treat well the entire range of stakeholders who risk capital in, have an interest in, or are linked to the firm through primary and secondary impacts. They operationalize their corporate citizenship in all of their strategies and business practices by developing respectful, mutually beneficial relationships with stakeholders and by working to maximize sustainability of the natural environment. They recognize that they are responsible for their impacts and are willing to be held accountable for them.

Corporate citizenship by this definition involves far more than meeting the discretionary responsibilities associated with philanthropy, volunteerism, community relations, and otherwise doing "social good," which some people think is sufficient[6] and which constitutes corporate *social* responsibility.[7] This broad understanding of citizenship means paying attention to how fundamental responsibilities—some of which are those traditionally assumed by governments, such as labor and human rights, environmental sustainability, and anticorruption measures—are being met in all of the company's strategies and operating practices, as well as to the outcomes and implications of corporate activities. For many companies, it means developing a "lived" set of policies, practices, and programs that help the company achieve its vision and values. The decision to be a *leading* corporate citizen is, of course, probably still voluntary on the part of companies; however, companies do bear responsibility for the ways in which they treat their stakeholders and nature—and can be judged on their impacts—whether they proactively or interactively assume the role of "good corporate citizen."

Given the preceding definition of *leading corporate citizens*, let's start with a proposition: The core purposes of the corporation include but go far beyond generating shareholder wealth. Indeed, wealth and profits are simply important by-products of the firm's efforts to create a product or service for customers that adds enough value that customers are willing to pay more than they would otherwise pay. Value-added goods and services are produced through the good offices of employees, managers, suppliers, and allies, using a wide range of forms of capital. Management thinker Charles Handy puts the issue straightforwardly:

> To turn shareholders' needs into a purpose is to be guilty of a logical confusion, to mistake a necessary condition for a sufficient one. We need to eat to live, food is a necessary condition of life. But if we lived mainly to eat, making food a sufficient or sole purpose of life, we would become gross. The purpose of a business, in other words, is not to make a profit, full stop. It is to make a profit so that the business can do something more or better. That "something" becomes the real justification for the business.[8]

Investments in businesses go way beyond those made by shareholders. Capital does, of course, include the important financial resources supplied by the owners or shareholders. Equally important, capital also encompasses the intellectual and human capital provided by employees, the trust and loyalty of customers that products or services will meet expectations and add value (for which they will pay), and various forms of social capital. Further, capital includes the infrastructure and social relations supplied by the communities and other levels of government in locations where the company has facilities. It includes interdependent relationships developed among its business partners, suppliers, and distributors, and it exists in the social contract written or unwritten by a range of local, state, and national governments, which have provided the social—and legal—contract and necessary physical infrastructure on which the firm's existence is premised.

All of these capitals are supplied to the firm by stakeholders. A stakeholder, generally, is any individual or group who is affected by or can affect an organization.[9] Companies exist in relationship to and because of their stakeholders. Simply stated, despite the prevailing idea that the purpose of the firm is to maximize shareholder wealth (and although it is absolutely essential that companies do produce wealth to survive), because of their numerous impacts, corporations are considerably more than profit-maximizing efficiency machines. Corporations are inherently and inextricably embedded in a web of relationships with stakeholders that create the very context in which they do business and that enable the enterprise to succeed. Without its core stakeholders, the corporation cannot survive, nor can it begin to make a profit, never mind maximize profits. Indeed, in many ways, the corporation is nothing more and nothing less than its primary relationships.

Therefore, we begin with this premise: Profits are essential to corporate success, and indeed corporate survival. Profits are critical to sustaining democratic capitalism, but they are in fact a by-product of the many relationships on which a corporation—or any other organization—depends for its legitimacy, power, resources, and various kinds of capital investments. This perspective, which differs from the traditional economics perspective on the firm (which says that the one and only purpose of the firm is to maximize profits or shareholder wealth), is called the *stakeholder capitalism concept of the firm.*

In this stakeholder view, stakeholder relationships and the operating practices (policies, processes, and procedures) that support those relationships are the basis of leading corporate citizenship.[10] Much is being written about global corporate citizenship these days. The neoclassical economics model, which dominates much business thinking, suggests that the corporation should maximize wealth for one set of stakeholders: the owners or shareholders. Conformance to existing law and meeting ethical responsibilities come next, especially in the view of economist Milton Friedman, who espouses the neoclassical economics perspective. In his classic article against the concept of social responsibility, entitled "The Social Responsibility of Business Is to Increase Its Profits," Friedman states:

> But the doctrine of "social responsibility" taken seriously would extend the scope of the political mechanism to every human activity. It does not differ in philosophy from the most explicitly collectivist doctrine. It differs only in professing to believe that collectivist ends can be attained without collectivist means. That is why in my book *Capitalism and Freedom,* I have called it a "fundamentally subversive doctrine" in a free society, and have said that in such a society, there is one and only one social responsibility of business—to use its resources and engage

in activities designed to increase its profits so long as it stays within the rules of the game, which is to say, engages in open and free competition without deception or fraud.[11]

The basis for Friedman's assertion, echoed by other economists as well, that shareholders are the only important stakeholder is that owners have taken a risk with their investments in the firm and are therefore owed a profit. But this view is too constricted to be useful in a world in which it is increasingly recognized that other stakeholders are equally important to the survival and success of the firm and that they too make significant investments in the welfare of the firm.

Recent thinking about corporate citizenship has significantly broadened the scope of its definition to recognize that citizenship inherently involves the rights and duties of membership. Chris Marsden and Jörg Andriof of the University of Warwick, United Kingdom, summarize this perspective:

> As Peter Drucker . . . says, however, citizenship is more than just a legal term, it is a political term. "As a political term citizenship means active commitment. It means responsibility. It means making a difference in one's community, one's society, one's country." Drucker might have added, in today's global economy, "one's world." Good corporate citizenship, therefore, is about understanding and managing an organisation's influences on and relationships with the rest of society in a way that minimises the negative and maximises the positive.[12]

Stakes and Stakeholders

Let's start this journey into leading corporate citizenship by considering the definition of a *stake* and therefore a *stakeholder* in more detail. The word *stake* can have one of three different general meanings, each representing a different type of relationship between the stakeholder and the entity in which a stake exists (see Table 1.1). A stake is a claim of some sort, for example, a claim of ownership based on a set of expectations related to principles of ethics, such as legal or moral rights, justice or fairness, the greatest good for the greatest number, or the principle of care.

Second, a stake can signify that a stakeholder has made an investment, thereby putting some sort of capital at risk.[13] In this usage, a stake is an interest or a share in some enterprise or activity, a prize (as in a horse race or other gamble) or perhaps a grubstake (for which the provider expects a return for the risk taken). Typically, the type of risk under consideration relates specifically to the type of capital invested. Thus, for example, owners invest financial capital in the firm, while communities may invest social capital—or relationships built on trust and association—in the firm's local presence or create infrastructure to support the firm's activities. Employees invest their human capital, their knowledge, and their intellectual energies—all forms of capital—in the firm. Customers invest their trust as part of the firm's franchise and hence their willingness to continue to purchase the goods and services produced by the firm. Suppliers may invest in specific technology, equipment, or infrastructure so that they can enhance their relationship to the firm over time and make the bonds tighter.

TABLE 1.1 The Types of Stakes

Stake As:	Stake Is Based On:
• Claim	• Legal or moral right
	• Consideration of justice/fairness
	• Utility (greatest good for the greatest number)
	• Care
• Risk	• Investment of capital, including:
1. Owner	1. Financial capital
2. Community	2. Social/infrastructure capital
3. Employee	3. Knowledge/intellectual/human capital
4. Customer	4. Franchise (trust) capital
5. Supplier	5. Technological, infrastructure capital
• Bonds (tether, tie)	• Identification (process)

Each type of stake creates a relationship that, when constructive and positive, is:
1. Mutual
2. Interactive
3. Consistent over time
4. Interdependent

The third meaning of *stake* is a bond, such as a tie or tether, something that creates links between two entities, including tangible links that bind the entities together (e.g., contracts or long-term relationships for purchasing supplies) as well as intangible relational links. Intangible bonds can come about because a stakeholder identifies in some way with the organization and therefore feels an association with the organization that potentially creates one of the other types of stakes, a claim or a risk.[14]

Stakeholder Relationships

Notice that each of the types of stakes identified in Table 1.1 creates a *relationship* between the stakeholder and the organization in which there is a stake.[15] For example, owners are clearly stakeholders. By making an investment, the stakeholder owner creates a relationship with the organization. Similarly, the stakeholder who puts something at risk for possible benefit through an enterprise creates a relationship with that enterprise, as communities do when they invest in local infrastructure that supports a firm's activities. Bonds of identity also create ongoing relationships. The important point, then, is that whichever meaning we use for *stake*, being a stakeholder creates an ongoing and interactive relationship between the stakeholder and the enterprise or activity.[16]

Stakeholder relationships also create a boundary around managerial responsibilities so that corporations are responsible not for all of the problems of society but only for those that they create or those that affect them. Thus, when we think about corporate responsibility, we can think in terms of the public responsibility of managers, which is limited to the areas of primary and secondary involvement of their enterprises. The principle of public responsibility, which was developed by scholars Lee Preston and James Post, comes about in part because companies are granted permission or charters (literally, incorporation papers) by the states in which they are established and in part as a result of the impacts that companies have on their various stakeholders and the natural environment, and for which society wishes to hold them accountable.[17]

The scope of managers' public responsibilities is quite wide given the resources that companies, particularly multinational companies, command and the resulting power they hold. According to Preston and Post, management's responsibilities are limited by the organization's primary and secondary involvements (see Figure 1.1). Primary involvement arenas are related to the main business mission and purpose of the firm as attempts to live out its vision in society. Thus, as Preston and Post state, "Primary involvement relationships, tested and mediated through the market mechanism, are essential to the existence of the organization over time."[18]

Primary involvement arenas are those that affect primary stakeholders, that is, those stakeholders without whom the company cannot stay in business.[19] For most companies, primary stakeholders include owners, customers, employees, suppliers, and allies. Although some people believe that the environment is a stakeholder, because it supplies the raw materials necessary to the company's existence,[20] we will take the perspective that the environment is not a

FIGURE 1.1 **Primary and Secondary Stakeholders of the Corporation**

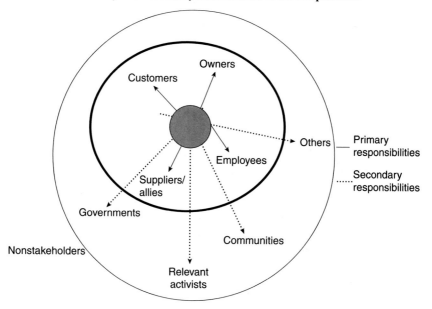

stakeholder but rather an essential underpinning to all human civilization, an underpinning that needs to be healthy for human civilization to survive.[21]

Managerial public responsibilities do not end with primary involvement arenas; they extend also to arenas of secondary involvement, which include those arenas and relationships that affect or are affected by the firm's activities. Secondary stakeholders are those who affect or are affected by the company's activities indirectly or as a by-product. Secondary stakeholders may not be in direct transactions with the corporation or necessary to its survival. Because they can impact the firm or are affected by the firm's activities, it is important that secondary stakeholders' needs and interests be taken into consideration in much the way that the needs and interests of primary stakeholders are.[22] Thus, the governments that create the rules of the game by which companies operate, as well as the communities that supply the local infrastructure on which companies depend, can be considered secondary stakeholders.

Stakeholders interact with—or in the case of primary stakeholders actually constitute—organizations; that is, they are in relationship to an organization or company. For example, activists may attempt to influence corporate environmental policy but may not be in a position to put the company out of business; thus, they are secondary stakeholders. Similarly, towns and cities located downstream from a company may feel the impact of its polluting a river that flows through and thus are secondary stakeholders. Firms ignore these impacts at their peril, because secondary stakeholders can be demanding or dangerous when their needs are urgent, when, for a variety of reasons, they have power or, if they are inactive, when they are awakened into action.[23]

Companies are typically started and financed by owners, who in the current thinking of many business leaders are considered to be the dominant (and sometimes only important) stakeholder. Other stakeholders are critical to the success of companies as corporate citizens because they too have placed various forms of their capital at risk, are invested in, or tied in relationship to companies. For example, *employees* as stakeholders develop, produce, and deliver the company's products and services. A company's existence is also contingent on the goodwill and continued purchases of *customers*. Companies also depend on the earth for raw materials (ultimately) and *suppliers and allies or partners*, who produce the raw materials necessary for the company to generate its own goods and services. Relationships with these stakeholder groups constitute any leading corporate citizen's *primary stakeholder relationships*.

There are also *critical secondary stakeholder relationships* without which most companies could not survive. For example, companies rely on *governments*—local, state/provincial, national, and increasingly international—to create rules of society that make trading, economic, and political relationships feasible over time. Corporate citizens rely on their local *communities* for an educated workforce and for the infrastructure that makes production of goods and services possible (e.g., roads, local services, and zoning regulations). And there are other critical secondary stakeholders depending on the particular circumstances of the company and the nature of its business (see Case 1.1).

In 1999, swine production contributed $1 billion to the North Carolina economy, surpassing tobacco. Swine production has experienced explosive growth under the stimulus of franchises offered by large meat-processing corporations, like Murphy Family Farms, which give growers a set price for the output of their mass-production operations. Many of the estimated 10 million porkers who populate North Carolina's eastern lowland counties spend their lives confined to pens in huge high-tech facilities that deliver food to the front and dispose of waste at the rear via conveyor belts. Since a hog produces four times as much waste as a human being, one corporate hog farm can generate a waste stream equivalent to that of a city of 250,000 people. A Web site titled Hog Watch posted by the Environmental Defense Fund notes that North Carolina's hogs "produce a mind-boggling amount of waste: 19 million tons of feces and urine a year, or over 50,000 tons every single day. That's more waste in one year than the entire human population of Charlotte, North Carolina, produces in 58 years! To make matters worse, almost all of North Carolina's hogs are concentrated in the eastern coastal plain, an economically important and ecologically sensitive network of wetlands, rivers, and coastline." The traditional method for dealing with this prodigious outflow has been to dig a waste lagoon, followed by spraying the liquefied waste on nearby fields as an organic fertilizer.

By the mid-1990s, the growth of these swine factories in North Carolina was generating a political backlash against the externalities imposed on neighboring communities by corporate hog farm practices. Beyond the obvious "public bad" of a downwind stench and the incremental impact of acid rain from evaporating ammonia, the waste lagoon and field spray system create a nitrogen-rich effluent carried by rain into nearby streams. Excessive nitrogen in the streams feeds the bloom of algae, turning the streams emerald green. When this algae collects in wetlands near the ocean, it dies and sinks to the bottom. Bacteria, feeding on the dead algae, rob the water of oxygen, causing periodic fish kills near fishing and tourist areas. The failure of one industry to recognize and internalize its externality costs imposes an economic burden on other industries, while also negatively impacting society and the ecological system.

In the summer of 1995, public concern about the negative environmental impacts of corporate pig farming reached new heights in the soggy, smelly aftermath of Hurricane Floyd. Torrential rains in June swelled the state's more than 3,600 waste lagoons to near overflowing, weakening their retaining walls and threatening a deluge of liquid waste on downstream fisheries and communities. Many hog farmers illegally drained excess lagoon waste into streams and swamps to prevent a breach in their dikes. In the end, Hurricane Floyd washed out 50 waste lagoons and drowned more than 30,000 hogs. Defenders of corporate hog farm practices sought to divert public blame and political retribution by claiming that this environmental calamity was an act of God. A critic in the state legislature countered that this was a sign from God that conventional methods for dealing with the industry's societal mess were inadequate and had to change.

State politicians, previously concerned with promoting economic development and highly sensitive to the political clout and campaign contributions of "Boss Hog," responded to public pressure for increased regulatory controls and oversight. In 1997, the general assembly imposed a temporary moratorium on new hog farms and stepped up regulatory oversight of swine operations. In 1999, Governor Jim Hunt decreed that existing waste lagoons must be phased out over 10 years. The following year, the Democratic state attorney general Mike Easley, in charge of the regulatory crackdown, ran for governor on a platform calling for more balance between the push for economic

growth and the pull for corporate accountability and environmental sustainability.

The search is on for a new, more sustainable swine waste processing technology, at an
estimated cost to taxpayers and hog farmers of
at least $400 million. One of the most promising
approaches is a bacterium that reduces the
waste to amino acids that can be reconstituted
as animal feed. In the end, the solution to this
problem will be political rather than scientific.
Some have called on the government to promote a "systems solution" by creating a market for the processed swine waste, whether as
compost, animal feed, or crab bait. This would
give farmers some added income to cover the
higher cost of managing manure. Many hog
farmers have borrowed heavily to finance
expansion at a time when overproduction has
driven the price of pork bellies below the
break-even point for many producers. A more
sustainable industry may also be a smaller
industry, with limits to growth to accompany
limits on waste.

DISCUSSION QUESTIONS

1. Take the perspective of different actors in
   this situation (e.g., farmers, local communities downriver and downwind of the hog
   farms, politicians, customers). How would
   being in these different situations shift your
   perspective on the viability and importance
   of keeping local pig farms operating?

2. What would be the best solution to this
   situation from each stakeholder's perspective? How can an overall solution be
   reached?

Sources: Jerry Calton, University of Hawaii, Hilo.
This case is based on the *Raleigh News-Observer*
investigative series entitled "Boss Hog," which won
the 1996 Pulitzer Prize for public service journalism.
For an in-depth look at this messy issue, go to
www.nando.net/sproject/hogs. See also
Environmental Defense Fund Web site titled Hog
Watch, www.environmentaldefense.org/
system/templates/page/subissue.cfm?subissue=10
(accessed March 16, 2004).

Corporate Responsibility and Citizenship

By defining *corporate citizenship* through the lens of a company's strategies
and operating practices, we are taking a practice-based stakeholder view of
the corporation, which significantly broadens understanding of the stakeholders to whom a firm is accountable. This view moves the conversation directly
toward the quality and nature of the relationships that companies develop
with stakeholders and assessment of the impacts of corporate activities on
those stakeholders, as well as on the natural environment, whose interests are
frequently represented by environmental activists though it is not itself a
stakeholder.[24] Such a perspective moves our thinking away from a largely
descriptive and even instrumental (or usefulness) perspective on stakeholder
relationships. We move, in this book, toward a more normative model, that is,
a model of how, in the best of worlds, stakeholder relationships *ought* to be,
as the opening quotation by Kofi Annan, secretary-general of the United
Nations, suggests.[25]

In support of this perspective, the Business Roundtable (BRT), a major association for business leaders, issued a document titled "Statement on Corporate
Responsibility" as long ago as 1980, even before the term *stakeholder* itself
became popularized.[26] In this statement, the BRT argued that "it is clear that a
large percentage of the public now measures corporations by a yardstick beyond

strictly economic objectives."[27] In the words of the BRT, which are even truer now that business impacts frequently have a global scope:

> [The corporation's] economic responsibility is by no means incompatible with other corporate responsibilities in society. In contemporary society all corporate responsibilities are so interrelated that they should not and cannot be separated.
>
> The issue is one of defining, and achieving, responsible corporate management which fully integrates into the entire corporate planning, management, and decision-making process consideration of the impacts of all operating and policy decisions on each of the corporation's constituents. Responsibility to all these constituents *in toto* constitutes responsibility to society, making the corporation both an economically and socially viable entity. Business and society have a symbiotic relationship: The long-term viability of the corporation depends upon its responsibility to the society of which it is a part. And the well-being of society depends upon profitable and responsible business enterprises.[28]

In other words, responsible leaders and managers cannot operate blindly with respect to the impacts that their actions have on any and all of their stakeholders or the natural environment, especially if they hope to do well over the long term. Gaining the respect and commitment of employees, customers, suppliers, communities, and relevant government officials, as well as owners, is essential to productivity and performance. Because corporations are part of and interdependent with the communities and societies in which they operate, they need to actively engage with their stakeholders. Maintaining positive stakeholder relationships involves establishing constructive and positive relationships with them, and being constantly aware of both the status and health of each stakeholder group. These relationships, then, are the essence of corporate global and local citizenship.

Stakeholder Relationship Management

Respect for others is at the heart of good stakeholder relations. While it is frequently true that companies have a great deal of power because they command significant resources, they need to recognize the importance of maintaining good relationships with their stakeholders to experience outstanding long-term performance. Recent research, for example, shows that when companies score highly in *Fortune* magazine's reputational ratings, they are also consistently high performers with respect to their primary stakeholders.[29] Further, companies that are more responsible also appear to perform better financially, thus creating a virtuous circle.[30]

Companies' stakeholder relationships can evolve in one of three ways: reactively, proactively, or interactively.[31] Good stakeholder relationships can be sustained only if the company takes an interactive stance.

Reactive Stance

When companies or their managers take a reactive stance, they may not be paying attention very much to what is going on outside the company's boundaries.

They may deny their responsibility for establishing and maintaining positive policies toward stakeholders, engage in legal battles to avoid responsibility, or do the bare minimum to meet the letter but not the spirit of the law.[32] Reaction puts the company and its managers on the defensive rather than in a more positive mode. Because managers have failed to anticipate problems from stakeholders, they may find themselves wondering how things evolved in such a negative fashion.

Proactive Stance

Better, but probably still insufficient to establish truly positive stakeholder relationships is the stance that companies sometimes take when they work to proactively anticipate issues arising from external stakeholders. They may do this by establishing one of any number of what are called boundary-spanning functions to cope with their external relations.

Boundary-spanning functions are those that cross organizational boundaries, either internally or externally, and attempt to develop and maintain relationships with one or more stakeholder groups. For example, modern multinational corporations typically will have at least some of the following functions: public affairs, community relations, public relations, media relations, investor relations, employee relations, government relations, lobbyists, union relations, environmental officers, issues management, and (in one recent instance) a vice president for corporate responsibility.

Interactive Stance

Even a proactive stance falls short of the ideal unless the company's boundary-spanning functions are managed interactively and with respect for the claims, risks, and bonds that stakeholders have. Because stakeholders exist in relationship to the firm, they are embedded in a network that makes them interdependent for their mutual success in activities where their interests overlap. Thus, arguably the best stance for showing ongoing respect for the firm's stakeholders is a mutual and interactive one that is consistent over time and that acknowledges both the mutuality of the relationship and the interdependence of the two entities.

Such constructive and positive relationships between organizations and their stakeholders are built on a framework of interaction, mutual respect, and dialogue, as opposed to management or dominance. That is, progressive companies no longer attempt to manage or dominate their stakeholders. Rather, they have recognized the importance of engaging with them in a relationship based on respect and dialogue or talking *with* each other rather than talking at each other, which is more one-sided. Building this relationship is not a one-time thing but rather an evolving long-term process that requires commitment, energy, a willingness to admit mistakes, and a capacity for both parties to change when necessary.

Understanding the Spheres of Influence: The Ecological Underpinning

Even at present population levels, nearly a billion people go to bed hungry each night. Yet the soils on which we depend for food are being depleted faster than nature can regenerate them, and one by one the world's once most productive fisheries are collapsing from overuse. Water shortages have become pervasive, not simply from temporary droughts but also from depleted water tables and rivers taxed beyond their ability to regenerate. We hear of communities devastated by the exhaustion of their forests and fisheries and of people much like ourselves discovering that they and their children are being poisoned by chemical and radioactive contamination in the food they eat, the water they drink, and the earth on which they live and play.

As we wait for a technological miracle to resolve these apparent limits on continued economic expansion, some 88 million people are added to the world's population every year. Each new member of the human family aspires to a secure and prosperous share the planet's dwindling bounty . . . Bear in mind that population projections are produced by demographers based only on assumptions about fertility rates. They take no account of what the planet can sustain. Given the environmental and social stresses created by current population levels, it is likely that if we do not voluntarily limit our numbers, famine, disease, and social breakdown will do it for us well before another doubling occurs.[33]

Modern business activities occur in an intensely competitive, even hypercompetitive, and relatively newly globalized environment.[34] Change is considered to be a constant, and there is ever-increasing pressure for enhanced productivity and performance. For many businesses, growth and efficiency come by way of dog-eat-dog competition in which the winner takes all in terms of market share and supposedly maximized profits for shareholders.

Without diminishing the importance of competition—and competitiveness—for corporate success, we can add another perspective. Consider that companies operate in a sphere or sector of activities we can call the economic sphere. This sphere has all of the imperatives of growth, efficiency, productivity, and competition inherent in the current capitalistic paradigm, which, with the fall of communism and the rapid evolution of e-commerce, now is operating at some level in most free societies in the world. We know, however, that the economic sector cannot operate independent of society. The economic system is a creature of society.

There is more to society than economics. Living well—that is, living the good life, by almost anyone's definition—has important elements of long-term sustainability with regard to community and ecological health, and also requires some form of governance, or government, to function well. Each of these spheres (which will sometimes be called sectors) intersects and overlaps to some extent with all the others; hence, they must be viewed together as a system, inextricably and unavoidably interwoven. The success of any one of these sectors requires that there be an appropriate balance of power and

FIGURE 1.2 **Spheres of Influence: Economic, Political, Social, Ecological**

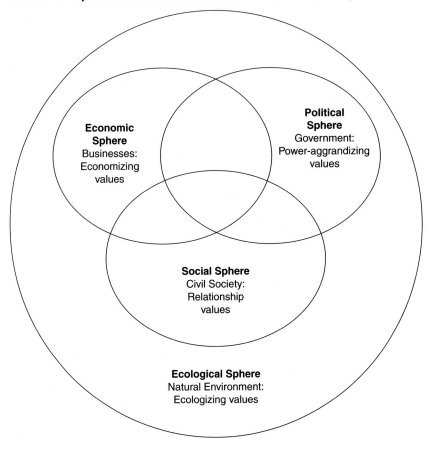

interests among all of them as well with the ecological surround on which they depend. To complete this picture and provide for an integrated view of what is frequently called the global village (i.e., the world of communities in which we all live and to which we are all connected), we must deeply understand the critical role of the ecological or natural environment. The ecological environment or sphere forms the essential foundation on which all else rests. Without the diversity inherent in the natural environment, without its sustaining resources (which provide raw materials for production), and without appropriate balance in human activities to protect those natural resources, industry and human society quite literally cannot sustain themselves. In that sense we are dependent on this foundation of ecology and the web of life that it supports for our very existence.[35] Leading corporate citizenship needs to be understood as a system characterized by ecological interdependence and mutuality among entities operating in the different spheres (see Figure 1.2). The following are definitions for each of the spheres that form a core structure for understanding leading corporate citizenship:

1. The *economic* sphere encompasses the businesses, profit-generating enterprises, and associated supplier/distributor relationships that produce the goods and services on which human civilization depends.

2. The *political* or *public policy* sphere encompasses government bodies at the local, state, regional, national, and global (international) levels that create the rules by which societies operate and establish what is meant (within and among societies) by the public interest.

3. The *civil society* or civilizing sphere encompasses all other organized forms of activity, such as nongovernmental organizations (NGOs), nonprofit enterprises, schools, religious organizations, political organizations, families, and civic and societal enterprises. This sphere generates the civilizing relationships and sense of community that characterize human society.

4. The *natural or ecological environment* underpins and supports all else, providing sources of raw materials for sustaining human civilization and healthy societies. A healthy ecology is essential to the long-term health of all of human civilization.

Understanding how these spheres intersect and influence each other necessitates a brief journey into system thinking, followed by a more in-depth look at the ecological sphere that underpins what we call society.

Systems Thinking: The Need to Integrate the Environment

Western philosophy and Western science underpin the capitalistic economic system in which we live today throughout much of the developed world. Western science, including the social science of economics, tends to approach its subjects by taking them apart and reducing them to their smallest elements. Once the smallest elements or fragments have been understood, the Western approach hopes to reintegrate the subject and thereby figure out how it works as an integrated whole. This approach derives from thinkers like Descartes, is premised on Newtonian physics, and is empiricist in its orientation in that it seeks observable evidence in coming to its conclusions.

But this approach, which essentially reduces things to their fundamental parts or atomistic elements, also separates the material elements (body) from nonmaterial aspects of the world like consciousness, emotions, aesthetic appreciation, and spirituality. In simple terms, Western thinking has largely separated and broken into fragmented parts the mind and body, with little mention at all of heart, spirit, community, or meaning, none of which are directly observable. It has, in some respects, done much the same thing to the environment, making some people forget (or ignore) our very human interdependency with nature. Additionally, technological advances have sometimes made progress seem inevitable, as if a solution to whatever problems arise is always just around the corner. The Western approach has a major drawback in that it tends to lessen people's ability to think about the system as a whole, which also reduces their ability to think about systemic and ecological impacts of business actions.

A cloud masses, the sky darkens, leaves twist upward, and we know that it will rain. We also know that after the storm, the runoff will feed into groundwater miles away, and the sky will grow clear by tomorrow. All these events are distant in time and space, and yet they are all connected within the same pattern. Each has an influence on the rest, an influence that is usually hidden from view. You can only understand the system of a rainstorm by contemplating the whole, not any individual part of the pattern.

Business and other human endeavors are also systems. They, too, are bound by invisible fabrics of interrelated actions, which often take years to fully play out their effects on each other. Since we are part of that lacework ourselves, it's doubly hard to see the whole pattern of change. Instead, we tend to focus on isolated parts of the system, and wonder why our deepest problems never seem to get solved.

Source: Peter Senge, *The Fifth Discipline: The Art and Practice of the Learning Organization* (New York: Double day, 1991), pp. 6–7.

The fragmented or atomistic approach has come under severe criticism in recent years, for reasons that management thinker Peter Senge highlights (see Note 1.1). Many people now believe that a more integrated approach, in part ecologically based and in part based on an integration of mind and body (or material and nonmaterial), better speaks to the long-term needs of human beings and the communities and organizations to which they belong. Such an approach will be particularly critical in the technologically complex and ecologically resource-constrained future, in which an understanding of the impacts of one part of the system on the other will be increasingly necessary.

This systemic approach to leading corporate citizenship has been fueled by the development of chaos and complexity theories, which are shedding greater light on the behavior of complex systems, a set to which human systems clearly belong. It has been further advanced by quantum physics, astrophysics, and biology's new understandings of the nature of matter and the interconnectedness among all living things, as well as between living and nonliving matter.[36]

Such developments have highlighted the need for a more integrated approach to understanding the impact of human beings, and the economic organizations they create, on the world and in particular on the natural environment. One seminal work emphasizing a systems approach to management is Peter Senge's influential book *The Fifth Discipline*. Systems thinking emphasizes wholes or, more accurately, holons—whole/parts—and the interrelationships and interdependencies among them.[37] As noted earlier in this chapter, a holon is anything that is itself whole and also a part of something else. Thus, for example, a neutron is an entity, a whole, and it is also a part of an atom. A hand is an entity in itself and also a part of an arm, which is part of a body, and so on. In social systems, an individual (whole) is part of a family (whole) that is part of a community, and so on. In organizations, individuals are part of departments, which are units of divisions, which are parts of the corporate entity, which are part of their industry whole, which in turn are part of society. Holons are integrally linked to the other holons of which they are a part. When something shifts in one holon, the other holons are affected as well because all holons in a given system are interdependent.

We can think of holons as being nested within each other. Each holon is nested within the next level of holon, assuring their interconnectedness and interdependence. What this means in system terms is that anything that affects one part of the system also affects (at some level and in some way) the whole system. Thinking about systems in this way changes our perspective on the corporation: No longer can we consider that a company operates independently of its impacts on stakeholders, society, or nature. Because the companies are part of the larger holon of the communities, societies, and the global village in which they are nested, these systems must, by this way of thinking, impact each other reciprocally.

For example, a company might think of itself as separate from a nonprofit organization to which it has given money in the past or a supplier in its supply chain. When the company withdraws funding—cuts the nonprofit off or decides to use another supplier—the company's leaders may believe that they have ended their impact and responsibility. But the withdrawal of funding creates shifts in the financial stability of the nonprofit or the supplier and has multiple ramifications both within these enterprises and the clients they serve. And while the company may believe that it is immune from these impacts, there may be subtle shifts in employee morale or important customer relationships that ultimately affect the business. All actions within holons have impacts.

The general approach in the Western world to support a given position has been to look for empirical evidence, that is, objective data. Rather than looking at subjectively (or in collective settings, intersubjectively) experienced realities, the typical Western approach is to focus on the material evidence that can be gathered to support the case. But thinkers like Senge (and ecologists like Gladwin, physicists like Capra, and theorists like Wheatley, among many others)[38] propose that it is important to incorporate not only the objective data but also the nonmaterial, that is, the elements of consciousness and conscience, of emotion and feelings, of meaning and meaningfulness, of spirit and indeed of spirituality, if the work of enterprise is to be approached holistically.

Philosopher Ken Wilber has worked to construct an integrative developmental framework for understanding the world's systems.[39] He notes that the Western tradition has focused almost exclusively on objective, empirically observable elements of individual and collective systems. Wilber generates a two-by-two matrix (see Figure 1.3) in which he places individual and collective exterior elements (i.e., what is objective) on what he terms the right-hand side. On the left-hand side, he places the individual and collective interior aspects of the world. Complete understanding of any system therefore encompasses (1) interior, or nonobservable, elements that we must ask about, such as thoughts, feelings, meanings, aesthetic appreciation, and (2) exterior, or observable, elements. Additionally, both interior elements and external elements also contain individual and collective aspects. Wilber names three categories of holons—*I, we,* and *it* (by collapsing both individual and collective exterior elements into the single category of observable behaviors—it/its).

FIGURE 1.3   **Wilber's Framework for Understanding Holons**

Left-hand Side	Right-hand Side

	Interior	**Exterior**
Individual	Subjective Intentional Realm of "I" experienced	Objective Behavioral Realm of "It" observed
Collective	Intersubjective Cultural Realm of "We" experienced	Interobjective Social Realm of "It(s)" observed

As you move through this book, try to keep in mind that really understanding anything, including business decisions, requires dealing with all four ways of viewing the world (interior/individual, interior/collective, exterior/individual, and exterior/collective). We are all familiar with traditional data-gathering efforts that focus on the importance of objective information, whether individual or group. For example, traditional financial measurement both for individuals (i.e., pay) and companies (i.e., profits) is a normal measure. At the same time, subjective individual aspects—that is, how individuals experience their organizations or what the group experiences—are also meaningful in creating visionary organizations.

By taking an integrative and holistic systems perspective, we can reshape how we see our impact on the world and the world's on us. In the words of Peter Senge:

> Systems thinking is a discipline for seeing the "structures" that underlie complex situations and for discerning high from low leverage change. That is, by seeing wholes we learn how to foster health . . . [Systems thinking and the related disciplines of personal mastery, mental models, shared vision, and team learning] are concerned with a shift of mind from seeing parts to seeing wholes, from seeing people as helpless reactors to seeing them as active participants in shaping their reality, from reacting to the present to creating the future.[40]

Starbucks (see Case 1.2) is one company that understands the importance of taking a systemic approach to its business and its many stakeholder—as well as one that recognizes the growing imperative of sustainability, which will be discussed in the next section of this chapter.

Can a huge company with enormous retail clout, a company that dominates its industry, gain credibility with consumers and critics alike by promoting more ecologically sensitive shade-grown coffee for the environment, supply chain management, and fair trade pricing for its suppliers? That is exactly what coffee giant Starbucks is trying to do, but not without criticism. By 2004, Starbucks had more than 7,500 retail locations in North America, Latin America, Europe, the Middle East and the Pacific Rim. It sells its coffee in a wide range of restaurants, businesses, airlines, hotels, and universities, as well as through mail-order and online catalogs. Ubiquitous as it has become, Starbucks seems well on its way to achieving its goal of establishing itself as the most recognized and respected brand in the world. So how does a company that has achieved such market dominance by selling coffee (and related) products move toward ecological sustainability and fair treatment of its suppliers and their workers in its growing operations?

In 1992 Starbucks established its first environmental mission statement (see Exhibit 1). After being roundly and publicly criticized for its labor and sourcing practices, the company had, by 1995, developed its Framework for a Code of Conduct, becoming the first coffee company to acknowledge its responsibility for working conditions, wages, and rights of coffee workers on the farms of its suppliers. By 1998 Starbucks had formed an ongoing partnership with Conservation International (CI) intended to support shade cultivation, which protects biodiversity, encourages use of environmentally sustainable agricultural practices, and helps the farmers earn more money. This partnership, which was renewed and upgraded in the summer of 2000, permits CI to work in five coffee-growing projects in Latin America, Asia, and Africa. Through a program called Conservation Coffee, Starbucks enables CI to help small farmers grow coffee in the buffer zone of the reserve under the shade of the forest canopy. Growing coffee in the shade helps protect the reserve's forests, streams, and wildlife, while providing substantial income benefits for the farmers.

In 2001 the company, still facing criticism about its percentage of purchased shade-grown coffee and increasing attacks on wages and working conditions on suppliers' farms, established a Preferred Supplier Program to "encourage continuous improvement in sustainable coffee production." This program

EXHIBIT 1 Starbucks' Environmental Mission Statement

Source: www.starbucks.com/aboutus/envapproach.asp (accessed February 24, 2004).

Starbucks is committed to a role of environmental leadership in all facets of our business. We will fulfill this mission by a commitment to:

- Understanding of environmental issues and sharing information with our partners (employees).
- Developing innovative and flexible solutions to bring about change.
- Striving to buy, sell and use environmentally friendly products.
- Recognizing that fiscal responsibility is essential to our environmental future.
- Instilling environmental responsibility values.
- Measuring and monitoring our progress for each project.
- Encouraging all partners to share in our mission.

EXHIBIT 2   **Starbucks' Supplier Code of Conduct**

Source: www.starbucks.com/aboutus/supplier_code.asp (accessed February 24, 2004).

Starbucks strives to be a great, enduring company by employing business standards and practices that produce social, environmental and economic benefits for the communities where we do business. We believe that conducting business responsibly benefits society as well as our various stakeholders, including employees, customers, suppliers, investors, and community members.

As a global company, Starbucks does business with suppliers from many countries of diverse cultural, social, and economic circumstances. We strive to work with suppliers that are committed to our universal principles of operating their business in a responsible and ethical manner, respecting the rights of individuals, and helping to protect the environment.

Our suppliers are required to sign an agreement pledging compliance with Starbucks' Supplier Code of Conduct and specific standards, which include the following:

- Demonstrating commitment to the welfare, economic improvement and sustainability of the people and places that produce our products and services
- Adherence to local laws and international standards regarding human rights, workplace safety, and worker compensation and treatment
- Meeting or exceeding national laws and international standards for environmental protection, and minimizing negative environmental impacts of suppliers' operations
- Commitment to measuring, monitoring, reporting and verification of compliance to this code
- Pursuing continuous improvement of these social and environmental principles

established a point system in which suppliers could become preferred suppliers not only by meeting certain quality standards (a given for the quality-conscious company) but also by focusing on environmental impacts (e.g., soil management, water reduction, and various waste management and conservation approaches); social conditions of workers (e.g., wages and benefits, health and safety, and living conditions); and economic issues, especially economic transparency. By late 2003 the company's experience with this program had evolved into its Supplier Code of Conduct, which required suppliers to live up to Starbucks' own standards (see Exhibit 2).

Since that time, the company has moved progressively forward in its efforts to establish a leadership position on environmental sustainability issues within the coffee industry. Using The Natural Step's sustainability framework (discussed in the next section of this chapter), Starbucks identified three primary areas of environmental impact on which to assess its ecological footprint: sourcing; transportation; and store design and operations,

including energy, water, recycling, and waste reduction. In 2002, Starbucks president and chief executive officer Orin Smith accepted a Humanitarian Medal of Merit for Starbucks' leadership on sustainability from the Coffee Quality Institute.

Still, critics were not satisfied with Starbucks' performance on human rights, labor, and ecological issues. The activist group Global Exchange, which has an ongoing campaign to pressure Starbucks to procure and promote more fair trade coffee, pointed out in 2004 that prices for coffee were at an all-time low (around 50 cents a pound) and that while some 235 million pounds of coffee were recorded by the Fair Trade Coffee Register in 2003, only some 32 million pounds were sold. The group further charged that Starbucks still does not offer brewed fair trade coffee in its stores, nor does it promote that coffee as the "coffee of the day." The activist group advocated that consumers exert pressure on Starbucks by requesting brewed fair trade coffee in retail shops and otherwise making their preferences known.

For Starbucks, the quest for credibility with its customers, activists, and investors presents a series of ever-new challenges around its supply chain management, environmental, and purchasing policies. These challenges over time have pushed the company in the direction of recognition of new and expanding responsibilities in line with society's changing expectations for large and powerful companies.

Sources: Bart Slob and Joris Oldenziel, "Coffee and Codes: Overview of Codes of Conduct and Ethical Trade Initiatives in the Coffee Sector," www.somo.nl/somo_ned/publicaties/Coffee%20&%20Codes,%20SO MO,%202003%20-%20Enhanced.pdf (accessed February 24, 2004); Elliot J. Schrage, "Promoting International Worker Rights through Private Voluntary Initiatives: Public Relations or Public Policy," Report to the U.S. Department of State (Iowa City: University of Iowa Center for Human Rights, 2004); and www.starbucks.com/aboutus/pressdesc.asp?id=380 (accessed February 24, 2004).

Natural Ecology: The Biological Basis of Citizenship

Why do companies like Starbucks move toward sustainable ecological practices in addition to recognizing the importance of stakeholders throughout their supply chains? Let us begin to understand the overall system in which businesses operate at the foundation: the natural environment. With the earth's population at more than 6 billion and projected to double within the next century (if trends don't change), there is an increasing imperative to understand the impact of human beings on the ecology that sustains them. One organization that has taken a creative and systemic approach to understanding ecological sustainability and business's role in it is the Swedish nonprofit organization The Natural Step (TNS).

Founded in 1989 by Dr. Karl-Henrik Robert, TNS works to develop a consensus about the ecological environment, the role of humans in that environment, and the ways in which humans are threatening not only other forms of life on earth but also themselves by engaging in activities that result in deteriorating natural conditions.[41] Robert, joined by a Swedish physicist, John Holmberg, defined a set of important system conditions based on the laws of thermodynamics and natural cycles that form TNS's framework for environmental sustainability.

Sustainability, as the biologist Humberto Maturana notes, is critical not just to the environment but also to human beings, and particularly to the natural environment's capacity to sustain human civilization. The environment, Maturana points out, will go on in one form or another, no matter what humans do to it. The real question is, Can human society survive major ecological changes?[42] TNS's framework is aimed at helping both individuals and organizations understand ecology systemically so that the use (and abuse) of natural resources can be reduced and newer sustainable approaches to production developed. In addition, TNS hopes to help focus the development of new, less resource-intensive technologies and to provide a common language and set of guiding principles for sustainable enterprise. TNS has relatively recently been introduced into the United States, Canada, the United Kingdom, Japan, and Australia; however, TNS is a household word in Sweden.

Thinking Systemically about Ecology: The Natural Step Framework[43]

TNS highlights some of the problematic aspects of human economic development on the ecology. Because of the impact of the 6 billion people currently alive on earth, multiple ecological systems—including croplands, wetlands, the ozone layer, rain forests, fisheries, and groundwater—are facing serious trouble. Visible garbage is filling up landfills, while various pollutants accumulate less visibly in the atmosphere. The ozone hole is increasing, with negative consequences for human life. Rain forests continue to be depleted with almost unimaginable impact on world ecology, for not only do rain forests provide fresh water but they also cleanse the atmosphere. Some ecologists believe that a sustainable number of people on earth would be between 1 and 2 billion, well below current population levels.

According to environmentalist Paul Hawken, "We are far better at making waste than at making products. For every 100 pounds of product we manufacture in the United States, we create at least 3,200 pounds of waste. In a decade, we transform 500 trillion pounds of molecules into nonproductive solids, liquids, and gases."[44] Clearly, if we believe that the earth's resources are limited and that demands on the system cannot be sustained at this rate of "progress," then a new approach to productivity is necessary. TNS's framework provides a set of system conditions that, according to the scientists who originally created the system in Sweden (and others where it is being replicated throughout the world), will be needed to prevent the world from hitting a wall of unsupportable demands on the natural environment. Note 1.2 lists the system conditions for sustainability as developed by TNS, which works with companies such as Home Depot, Bank of America, and McDonald's on implementing these conditions.

The TNS system is aimed at sustainable development. Sustainable development can be defined as "a process of achieving human development . . . in an inclusive, connected, equitable, prudent, and secure manner," according to ecological scholar Thomas Gladwin and his colleagues.[45] Gladwin has defined five elements that represent a set of constraints on human development, similar to those for the material world that TNS produced (see Table 1.2).

Inclusiveness connotes an expansive view of the space, time, and component parts of the observed ecology, embracing both ecological and human conditions in the present and the future. *Connectivity* means understanding the inherent interconnectedness and interdependence of elements of the world and problems in the world. *Equity* means a fair distribution of resources and property rights within and between generations. Putting connectivity and equity together suggests greater comprehension of the unavoidable links between, for example, creating better ecological health and efforts to reduce poverty or the gap between rich and poor.

Prudence means taking care of the resources of the world, as suggested by the TNS constraints. In practice, being prudent means keeping ecosystems and socioeconomic systems healthy and resilient; avoiding irreversible losses of

The Natural Step's Four System Conditions for Sustainability

The Natural Step system conditions, also called principles of sustainability, define the basic conditions that need to be met in a sustainable society. By looking at the three ways we are damaging nature, and then adding the word "not," The Natural Step has defined the three basic principles for an ecologically sustainable society. However, because we are talking about sustainability for people and for the planet, a basic social principle is also needed—that human needs are met worldwide. From this assessment, we articulate four basic principles for a sustainable society:

In a sustainable society, nature is not subject to systematically increasing:

1. concentrations of substances extracted from the earth's crust;
2. concentrations of substances produced by society;
3. degradation by physical means; and, in that society,
4. human needs are met worldwide.

Source: www.naturalstep.org/about/faq.php#system_conditions (accessed March 1, 2004).

ecological or other resources; and, again as the TNS constraints indicate, keeping human activities within the earth's regenerative capacity. Finally, *security* focuses on the sustainability of human life, that is, ensuring "a safe, healthy, high quality of life for current and future generations."[46]

Later in this book, we will consider some of the ecological problems that have arisen as a result of human and economic development, technological advances, and the process of industrialization as part of the systemic thinking process. For now, what is important is to recognize that systemic thinking fundamentally means thinking in new ways about the relationships that exist among human beings, the enterprises they create, and the rest of the natural world.

Indeed, thinking about ecological sustainability may mean complementing traditional (Western) ways of viewing human beings' relationship to the natural world with more holistic perspectives. It may even mean shifting our perspective away

TABLE 1.2 **Constraints on Sustainable Human Development**

Source: Thomas N. Gladwin, James J. Kennelly, and Tara-Shelomith Krause, "Shifting Paradigms for Sustainable Development: Implications for Management Theory and Research," *Academy of Management Review* 20, no. 4 (October 1995), pp. 847–907.

Inclusiveness	Expansive view of space, time, and elements of ecology (present and future)
Connectivity	Understanding inherent interconnectedness and interdependence of world's elements and problems
Equity	Fair distribution of resources and property rights (within and between generations)
Prudence	Taking care of world's resources so they are healthy and resilient
Security	Sustainability of health, high quality human life for present and future generations

form an anthropomorphic (human-centered) or technocentric (technologically oriented) worldview beyond even an ecocentric (ecological) worldview.[47] It may mean a wholly integrative approach to economic development focused on sustainability.

A fully integrative perspective would synthesize the three critical spheres of civilization (economic, political, and societal) with the ecological, and would also integrate the subjective and intersubjective elements of emotions, intuition, aesthetics, and culture, among others, into our perspective. The result would be better understanding of the values that underpin each sphere of activity and an integration of them into an ecologically sustainable and holistic worldview.

The Need for Balance

Just as nature requires a balance among elements to sustain any healthy ecological environment, we must think about corporate global citizenship as part of the social ecology. Balance among the interests of all three important sectors of human civilization is of paramount concern. In sustaining this balance among sectors and with the natural world, we must also marry competition and competitiveness with cooperation and collaboration, in the process that biologists call symbiosis. Competition *and* collaboration, with sustainability, are necessary and important to societal—and business—health and success. The physicist Fritjof Capra perhaps puts it best:

> The recognition of symbiosis as a major evolutionary force has profound philosophical implications. All larger organisms [and organizations], including ourselves, are living testimonies to the fact that destructive practices do not work in the long run. In the end the aggressors always destroy themselves, making way for others who know how to cooperate and get along. Life is much less a competitive struggle for survival than a triumph of cooperation and creativity. Indeed, since the creation of the first nucleated cells, evolution has proceeded through ever more intricate arrangements of cooperation and coevolution.[48]

Mastering systems thinking is a critical element of creating continually improving and learning enterprises.[49] An integrative systems approach is essential if we are to conceive of operating businesses, as well as governments and civil society enterprise, in sustainable ways, giving due consideration to the seventh generation out, as our Native American ancestors would have noted.

Leading Challenges: A New Paradigm for Corporate Citizenship

Fundamentally, leading corporate citizenship cannot evolve into constructive stakeholder relationships without the active participation of effective, aware, and progressive leaders. Aware leaders have thought deeply about their own values and vision, and as a result are prepared for the complex world they must face. Being prepared won't necessarily lessen the complexity or the difficulty of the decisions they must make, but awareness does help leaders make the right decisions when challenges are high, as they inevitably are in the complex social and political environment. Particularly in an era in which activists and other stakeholders can mobilize nearly instantaneously and globally, awareness of and response to the demands of leading a corporate citizen is a must. In effect, this mobilization is what happened in 1999 when activists prevented the World Trade Organization from meeting in Seattle, in 2001 when terrorists struck the World Trade Center and the Pentagon, and since that time in the increasing antiglobalization sentiments expressed by activists around the world.

In light of challenges like these, the goal of this book is to help those managers leading corporate citizens to understand the real world of complex dilemmas leaders face and the multiple perspectives embedded in every decision. The book also seeks to build awareness of the impacts and implications of those decisions on the people—the stakeholders—whom they affect. The book is organized as follows:

- Part 1, *A Context for Leading Corporate Citizens*: The first two chapters, including this one, explore the context in which businesses operate today. In this chapter, we explored the spheres of human civilization as they are built on a healthy ecological environment. In Chapter 2, we will continue to explore the interrelationship of the corporation (as it exists within the economic sphere) and the organizations and enterprises that exist in the political and civil or societal spheres.

- Part 2, *Leading Corporate Citizens with Vision, Values, and Value Added*: Mere understanding of the need for balance among the spheres is insufficient to guide organizations successfully. Both individuals and organizations need clear and constructive visions embedded with constructive end values to get the kinds of added value that sustain a business. Successful leaders develop personal and organizational vision and awareness, growing intellectually, emotionally, and morally so that they can cope with the complexity and challenges of the global business arena. Higher levels of individual and organizational awareness and development, ongoing learning, and empowerment are also necessary for organizations to succeed in the complexity of the modern world. We will explore the realities and links among vision (Chapter 3), values (Chapter 4), and value added (Chapter 5).

- Part 3, *Leading Corporate Citizens and Their Stakeholders*: Chapters 6 through 9 provide significant evidence that developing positive operating practices with respect to multiple stakeholders is likely to be the key to organizational success in the future. We will explore relationships with stakeholders directly by assessing the links companies create with their many stakeholders so that they can get to value added (Chapter 6). Then we will explore how an emphasis on multiple bottom lines rather than a single bottom line can be productive (Chapter 7). In taking this approach, we will learn that the "soft stuff" is really the "hard stuff," but that it can be and is being measured.

In Chapter 7, we will explicitly look at the ways in which corporate responsibility and citizenship can be managed internally. We will explore the ways in which operating with integrity adds value—and values—to business enterprises through living up to articulated visions as well as established codes promoting respect and human dignity (Chapter 8). In Chapter 9, we will assess the ecology of leading corporate citizenship, exploring both the natural environmental and sustainability implications of corporate activities, and moving toward an understanding of what a broader awareness of the impact of economic activities on the environment means for long-term economic development. The intersection of the knowledge economy, the blurring of boundaries with increased technological connectivity, and the need for respecting human dignity will serve as a foundation for this exploration.

- Part 4, *Leading Corporate Citizens into the Future*: The exploration of vision, values, and value added as ways of managing corporate responsibility provides a framework for businesses to operate with integrity amid complexity and change, that is, living up to codes of conduct and emerging global standards (Chapter 10) and operating with value added rather than in a value-neutral stance (Chapter 11). Finally, we will focus on developing an integrated vision of what a new paradigm corporation would look like if it were fully implemented (Chapter 12). How and where would individuals fit in? What does this new paradigm organization look, feel, and act like? How can we manage effectively and efficiently, doing the right thing and doing things right, for the future?

Endnotes

1. Kofi Annan, "Business and the U.N.: A Global Compact of Shared Values and Principles," World Economic Forum, Davos, Switzerland, January 31, 1999. Reprinted in *Vital Speeches of the Day* 65, no. 9 (February 15, 1999) pp. 260–61. For further information on the Global Compact, see www.unglobalcompact.org.

2. The classic references are R. Edward Freeman, *Strategic Management: A Stakeholder Approach* (New York: Basic Books, 1984), and William M. Evan and R. Edward Freeman, "A Stakeholder Theory of the Modern Corporation: Kantian Capitalism," in *Ethical Theory and Business*, ed. T. Beauchamp and N. Bowie (Englewood Cliffs, NJ: Prentice Hall, 1998). Max Clarkson identifies stakeholders as primary and secondary, depending on the level of risk they have taken with respect to the organization. See Max B. E. Clarkson, "A Stakeholder Framework for Analyzing and Evaluating Corporate Social Performance," *Academy of Management Review* 20, no. 1 (1995), pp. 92–117.

3. Dirk Matten and Andrew Crane, "Corporate Citizenship: Towards an Extended Theoretical Conceptualization," *Academy of Management Review* 29 (2004).

4. See the works of Ken Wilber, for example, *A Brief History of Everything* (Boston: Shambala, 1996); *Eye of the Spirit: An Integral Vision for a World Gone Slightly Mad* (Boston: Shambala, 1998); and *The Marriage of Sense and Soul: Integrating Science*

and Reason (New York: Random House, 1998). For a discussion of the web that constitutes life and the ways in which all matter is interrelated see Fritjof Capra, *The Web of Life* (New York: Anchor Doubleday, 1995).

5. Matten and Crane, "Corporate Citizenship."

6. Michael Porter's views on corporate (social) responsibility are characteristic of this perspective. See Michael Porter and Mark R. Kramer, "The Competitive Advantage of Philanthropy," *Harvard Business Review* 80, no. 12 (December 2002), pp. 56–69.

7. Sandra Waddock, "Companies, Academics, and the Progress of Corporate Citizenship," *Business and Society Review* 109 (March 2004), pp. 5–42.

8. Charles Handy, "What's a Business For?" *Harvard Business Review* (December 2002). Reprinted by permission of *Harvard Business Review*. Copyright 2002 by the Harvard Business School Publishing Corporation; all rights reserved.

9. Freeman, *Strategic Management*.

10. See, for example, James E. Post, Lee E. Preston, and Sybil Sachs, "Managing the Extended Enterprise: The New Stakeholder View," *California Management Review* 45, no. 1 (2002), pp. 6–29; and James E. Post, Lee E. Preston, and Sybil Sachs, *Redefining the Corporation* (New York: Oxford University Press, 2002).

11. Milton Friedman, "The Social Responsibility of a Business Is to Increase Its Profits," *New York Times Magazine*, September 13, 1970. Copyright © 1970. The New York Times Company. Reprinted with permission.

12. Chris Marsden and Jörg Andriof, "Towards an Understanding of Corporate Citizenship and How to Influence It," *Citizenship Studies* 2, no. 2 (1988), pp. 329–52.

13. See Clarkson, "A Stakeholder Framework," for an extended discussion of stakes. See also Ronald K. Mitchell, Bradley R. Agle, and Donna J. Wood, "Toward a Theory of Stakeholder Identification and Salience: Defining the Principle of Who and What Really Counts," *Academy of Management Review* 22, no. 4 (October 1997), pp. 853–86.

14. For a perspective on this, See Tammy MacLean, "Creating Stakeholder Relationships: A Model of Organizational Social Identification—How the Southern Baptist Convention Became Stakeholders of Walt Disney," paper presented at the annual meeting of the Academy of Management, San Diego, CA, 1998.

15. Thanks are owed to Max B. E. Clarkson for providing a basis for thinking about corporate social performance in terms of stakeholder relationships. See Clarkson, "A Stakeholder Framework."

16. See, for example, Freeman, *Strategic Management*, and Evan and Freeman, "A Stakeholder Theory of the Modern Corporation." See also Clarkson, "A Stakeholder Framework," and, more recently, Mitchell, Agle, and Wood, "Toward a Theory of Stakeholder Identification and Salience."

17. The concepts of primary and secondary involvement come from Lee E. Preston and James E. Post, *Private Management and Public Policy: The Principle of Public Responsibility* (Englewood Cliffs, NJ: Prentice Hall, 1975).

18. Ibid., p. 95.

19. This definition is from Clarkson, "A Stakeholder Framework," p. 106. However, the distinction goes back to Freeman, *Strategic Management*.

20. For example, Mark Starik, "Should Trees Have Managerial Standing? Toward Stakeholder Status for Non-Human Nature," *Journal of Business Ethics* 14 (1995), pp. 204–17.

21. See, for example, Robert A. Phillips and Joel Reichart, "The Environment as a Stakeholder? A Fairness Based Approach," *Journal of Business Ethics* 23 (January 2000), pp. 183–97.

22. Clarkson, "A Stakeholder Framework," p. 107.

23. Mitchell, Agle, and Wood, "Toward a Theory of Stakeholder Identification and Salience." Mitchell, Agle, and Wood's model has been somewhat modified by Steven L. Wartick and Donna J. Wood, *International Business and Society* (Malden, MA: Blackwell Press, 1998), in the fashion incorporated into this discussion.

24. See Duane Windsor, "Stakeholder Responsibilities: Lessons for Managers," in *Unfolding Stakeholder Thinking: Theory, Responsibility and Engagement*, ed. Jörg Andriof, Sandra Waddock, Bryan Husted, and Sandra Sutherland Rahman (Sheffield: Greenleaf, 2002), pp. 137–54.

25. For background on descriptive, instrumental, and normative branches of stakeholder theory, see Thomas Donaldson and Lee E. Preston, "The Stakeholder Theory of the Corporation: Concepts, Evidence, and Implications," *Academy of Management Review* 20 (January 1995), pp. 1, 65–91.

26. See Business Roundtable, "Statement on Corporate Responsibility," in *Business and Society: Economic, Moral, and Political Foundations*, ed. Thomas G. Marx (Englewood Cliffs, NJ: Prentice Hall, 1985), p. 152. The term *stakeholder* entered the popular parlance in 1984 with the issuance of Freeman, *Strategic Management*.

27. Business Round table, "Statement on Corporate Responsibility," p. 152.

28. Ibid., p. 157.

29. Note that this link is the basis of the instrumental argument for positive stakeholder relationships, as discussed by Donaldson and Preston, "The Stakeholder Theory of the Corporation."

30. See for example, Joshua D. Margolis and James P. Walsh, *People and Profits? The Search for a Link between a Company's Social and Financial Performance* (Mahwah, NJ: Erlbaum, 2001); Joshua D. Margolis and James P. Walsh, "Misery Loves Companies: Rethinking Social Initiatives by Business," *Administrative Science Quarterly* 48 (2003), pp. 268–305; S. A. Waddock and S. B. Graves, "Quality of Management and Quality of Stakeholder Relations: Are They Synonymous?" *Business and Society* 36, no. 3 (September 1979), pp. 250–79; and S. A. Waddock and S. B. Graves, "The Corporate Social Performance–Financial Performance Link," *Strategic Management Journal* 18, no. 4 (1997), pp. 303–19.

31. For a discussion of this framework, see Preston and Post, *Private Management and Public Policy*.

32. See also Clarkson, "A Stakeholder Framework," p. 109. Clarkson's "postures" are different from the stances outlined here.

33. David C. Korten, *When Corporations Rule the World* (San Francisco: Berrett-Koehler, 1995), p. 21.

34. See Richard D'Aveni, *Hyper-Competition: Managing the Dynamics of Strategic Maneuvering* (New York: Free Press, 1994).

35. For a marvelous and accessible description of the interconnectedness of living and material entities, see Capra, *The Web of Life*.

36. For some insight into these topics, you can start with James Gleick, *Chaos: Making a New Science* (New York: Viking, 1987); Stuart Kauffman, *At Home in the Universe: The Search for the Laws of Self-Organization and Complexity* (New York: Oxford University Press, 1995); Capra, *The Web of Life*; Humberto R. Maturana and Francisco J. Varela, *The Tree of Knowledge: The Biological Roots of Human Understanding*, rev. ed. (Boston: Shambala, 1998); and of course Peter Senge, *The Fifth Discipline: The Art and Practice of the Learning Organization* (New York: Doubleday, 1991).

37. The term *holon* is from Arthur Koestler and is extensively developed in Ken Wilber's work. Relevant works by Wilber include *Sex, Ecology, Spirituality: The Spirit of Evolution* (Boston: Shambala, 1995), *Eye of the Spirit*, and *A Brief History of Everything*.

38. Thomas N. Gladwin, James J. Kennelly, and Tara-Shelomith Krause, "Shifting Paradigms for Sustainable Development: Implications for Management Theory and Research," *Academy of Management Review* 20, no. 4 (October 1995), pp. 874–907; Fritjof Capra, *The Turning Point: Science, Society, and the Rising Culture* (New York: Bantam Books, 1983); and Margaret J. Wheatley, *Leadership and the New Science: Learning about Organization from an Orderly New Universe* (San Francisco: Berrett-Koehler, 1992).

39. See Wilber, *Sex, Ecology, Spirituality; Eye of the Spirit;* and *A Brief History of Everything*.

40. Senge, *The Fifth Discipline*, p. 69.

41. Information on The Natural Step can be found at www.naturalstep.org.

42. This paragraph is based on a talk by Humberto Maturana at the 1998 annual meeting of the Society for Organizational Learning (SoL). A version of this talk by Humberto Maturana Romesin and Pille Bunnell, entitled "Biosphere, Homosphere, and Robosphere: What Has That to Do with Business?" is available at www.solonline.org/res/wp/maturana/index.html (accessed June 29, 2004).

43. This section is based on The Natural Step Web site, www.naturalstep.org (accessed February 25, 2004).

44. Quoted in ibid.

45. Gladwin, Kennelly, and Krause, "Shifting Paradigms for Sustainable Development."

46. U.S. President's Council on Sustainable Development, quoted in Gladwin, Kennelly, and Krause "Shifting Paradigms for Sustainable Development." Much of the discussion in these paragraphs is based on this article.

47. These terms are developed in Gladwin, Kennelly, and Krause, "Shifting Paradigms for Sustainable Development."

48. Capra, *The Web of Life*, p. 243.

49. Senge, *The Fifth Discipline*.

The Three Spheres of Human Civilization

All human systems and ecosystems require balance: competition with cooperation, selfishness and individualism with community and social concern, material acquisitiveness with thirst for knowledge and understanding, rights with responsibilities and the striving for love, justice, and harmony. . . . Natural systems never maximize single variables, such as profit or efficiency. Thus, we can infer that maximizing behavior on the part of any individual or firm is shortsighted and destructive of the larger system . . .

Grassroots globalists and their organizations are often spurned by governments as amateurs, agitators, or troublemakers. Even the United Nations has warmed only slowly to citizen organizations. They are now emerging as a third, independent sector in world affairs—challenging the domination of global agendas by nation states and transnational corporations. The global civil society, newly interlinked on the Internet and by millions of newsletters, increasingly driving agendas of nations and corporations, which still refer to citizens groups as nongovernmental organizations (NGOs). Many grassroots globalist leaders retort that governments and corporations are NCOs (noncivil organizations). Global concerns have been on the agendas of grassroots civic groups, including churches and other organizations that have worked for food aid, peacemaking, education, culture, and youth exchange since the turn of the [20th] century.

Reprinted with permission of the publisher. From Building a Win-Win World, *copyright © 1996 by Hazel Henderson, Berrett-Koehler Publishers, Inc., San Francisco, CA. All rights reserved. www.bkconnection.com.*

[It] is clear that the large American corporation today is more rather than less responsive to the social demands of its external environment. But these exercises in social responsibility no longer represent managerial discretion—corporate executives' sharing of the fruits of market power with stakeholder groups in order to assure labor peace and enhance their position in the community and in society. Instead, they reflect the explicit demands made by government regulation, and firms' efforts to go beyond regulation in ways that integrate these requirements into their strategic and business planning so as to enhance competitiveness and profitability, rather than simply raising costs. Government regulations and court decisions have limited the scope of managerial decision making; today's managers are continuously seeking ways to convert these societal restrictions in to competitive opportunities.

Marina v.N. Whitman, New World, New Rules: The Changing Role of the American Corporation, *p. 140.*

Human civilization depends on a healthy ecological environment for its sustenance and maintenance; the environment or ecological system, as discussed in Chapter 1, underpins all we do and are, providing essential elements of earth, air, and water, not to mention the raw materials of productive processes. But human society is itself a complex system that requires balance among several competing sets of influences and activities, some of which today seem out of balance.

To understand human civilization from an integrated perspective, we will explore in this chapter the necessary balance among three spheres that encompass human activity: economic, political, and civil society. We recognize, as we discussed in Chapter 1, the need for a healthy ecology underpinning all. Figure 2.1 shows the spheres presented in Figure 1.2 and illustrates a balance among all of the spheres and within the ecological sphere. In this chapter we discuss in detail the three spheres of *human* civilization, the economic sphere, the political sphere, and the civil society sphere.

Each of these spheres of human activity has a dominant emphasis and an underlying values imperative (see Figure 2.2). In the economic sphere, the focus

FIGURE 2.1   **Balanced Spheres of Activity**

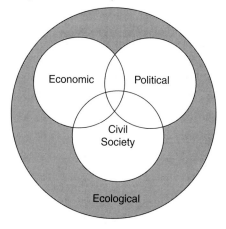

FIGURE 2.2   **The Three Spheres of Human Civilization in and out of Balance**

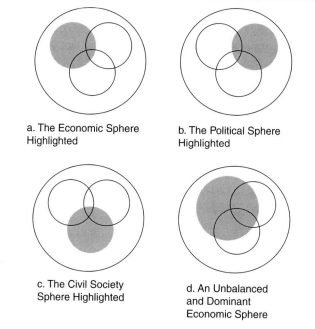

a. The Economic Sphere
Highlighted

b. The Political Sphere
Highlighted

c. The Civil Society
Sphere Highlighted

d. An Unbalanced
and Dominant
Economic Sphere

is on the production of goods and services, with a driving imperative of economizing, that is, making efficient use of resources. In the political sphere, the sphere of governments, the rules of societies are established and an infrastructure is created that sustains and governs each society, as well as the interactions among societies or nations. Because governments have the power to force—or coerce—people to do what the law demands, the political sphere is dominated by power aggrandizing values. Finally, the civil society sphere emphasizes the building and maintenance of community and is driven by values of relationship and civilizing.

Obviously, there is much more activity within each sphere than can be reasonably discussed here. This chapter will try to provide a synthesis of key features within each sphere as they relate to understanding how leading corporate citizens can provide goods and services efficiently using their imperative of economizing, while still operating with integrity and responsibly with respect to the other spheres. Because vast differences exist among nations, particularly regarding the national ideologies that guide political and cultural decisions, we will begin our exploration of the three spheres of human society by gaining an understanding of national ideologies. Then we will move to the discussion of the three spheres of human activity.

Intersecting Spheres of Human Civilization, Nature, and Associated Values

Chapter 1 highlighted the importance of taking a systemic view of the relationship between business institutions and their impact on the natural environment. Figure 2.1 illustrates the overlapping, connected, and interdependent relationship that exists among the economic, civil society, and political spheres of activity and influence, and the way in which all three are dependent on the natural environment.

Each sphere has a different imperative of goal, and each operates with a different set of values at its core. In a pioneering work relating business values to biophysics and biochemistry, William Frederick outlined three important "value clusters," two of which dominate business or economic activities in the economic sphere (see Note 2.1).[1] The first and probably most dominant value for business corporations is economizing, or the prudent and efficient use and processing of resources needed to live well. Economizing is the primary purpose—and indeed the imperative—of business, that is, creating goods and services as efficiently as possible. The second value cluster that Frederick says underpins business activity is power aggrandizing, or augmenting and preserving the power of managers and the organization itself.[2] Frederick notes that power-aggrandizing businesses (as well as other forms of organizations, like governments in particular) have a tendency to accumulate and control resources and power over time, making themselves more and more influential.

These two value clusters are in some significant degree of tension with the third value cluster of ecologizing. Ecologizing is the tendency of evolutionary and natural processes to "interweave the life activities of groups in ways conducive to the perpetuation of an entire community."[3] Ecologizing, effectively, means using resources in ways that sustain life and energy, meaning (as with nature) that nothing goes to waste. Viewed ecologically, what is waste to one part of the system becomes, in effect, food for another part of the system.

Economizing: The prudent and efficient use and processing of resources needed to live well.

Power aggrandizing: Augmenting and preserving the power of managers and the organization itself.

Ecologizing: The evolutionary and natural processes that interweave with life activities of groups so that they are conducive to the perpetuation of an entire community.

Source: William C. Frederick, *Values, Nature, and Culture in the American Corporation* (New York: Oxford University Press, 1995).

When we take a very broad perspective on the three spheres of human civilization, we can see that the values Frederick identifies may provide different guiding imperatives for the different spheres of activity. For example, Frederick notes that both economizing and power aggrandizing are central to economic sector activities. If, however, we look at the broader societal system, we note that the major form of currency in the political sector is power, probably even more so than in business, while the major emphasis of business is economizing. Thus, if we think about the value clusters Frederick has identified at the more macro level of human civilization viewed through the spheres systems lens, we note that each sphere of activity also has a dominant value cluster.

The dominant values of business cluster around economizing (with contributions from power aggrandizing). Businesses rightly focus on efficiency of production of the goods and services they are in business to generate. In contrast, the government or political sphere activities tend to focus on the garnering and use of power, since governments are in the business of setting the rules of the game for society. Thus, the dominant values of the political sphere or governments are those of power aggrandizing. Civil society, in contrast, tends to focus on developing organizations and institutions that "civilize" society, building relationships and community. Thus, the values of the civil society sphere, which is not addressed in Frederick's model, are more congruent with relationship and community building.

And, as we have seen above, natural processes tend to waste nothing, suggesting that nature, which provides ecological underpinning for all of this human activity, is dominated by ecologizing values in nature. Table 2.1 shows the major values associated with activities in each of the three spheres of human civilization plus nature, with what Frederick called X-factor values added. X-factor values are the values that individuals bring with them into any institutional or organizational setting; hence, they are related to individuals. Further, human society has developed a set of technological values that have fostered industrial development over the past centuries.

Economizing values, dominant within businesses, emphasize not only keeping the system whole, efficient, and economic but also growing continually.

TABLE 2.1 **Dominant Values within Each Sphere of Activity**

Source: Adapted from William C. Frederick, *Values, Nature, and Culture in the American Corporation* (New York: Oxford University Press, 1995).

Business Sphere	Political (and Business) Sphere	Civil Society Sphere	Nature (Ecology)
Economizing Values	**Power-Aggrandizing Values**	**Relationship Values**	**Ecologizing Values**
Economizing	Hierarchical (rank-order) organizing	Care	Linkage
(Efficiency)	Managerial decision power	Connectedness	Diversity
Growth	Power-system equilibrium	Community	Homeostatic succession
Systemic integrity	Power aggrandizement	Civility	Community
Technological Values		**X-Factor Values (Individual)**	
Instrumental pragmatics		Personal, idiosyncratic, role-conditioned values	
Cooperative-coordinative relations			
Technical expertise			
Public openness			
Participatory leveling			

Given these values, it is not surprising that businesses tend to focus on efficiency and growth at almost any cost. These emphases are the natural by-products of the business system that modern society has created.

Power-aggrandizing values, which are present in business and dominate the political (public policy) sphere, focus on maintaining hierarchy (bureaucracy) through a managerial decision-making capacity that helps to keep the power system stable or in equilibrium, and continued power enhancement. Given the importance of power-aggrandizing values in the public policy sphere, where governments at all levels operate, perhaps it is understandable that governments focus on the acquisition and use of power. Efficiency is not government's imperative; the product or output of governments has more to do with establishing the rules by which societies operate than with producing goods and services.

Civil society includes all of the social institutions other than business and government bodies that sustain the fabric of society. Civil society is dominated by values of relationship. These values emphasize the importance of building and sustaining relationships through what Nel Noddings terms an ethic of care—building connectedness and fostering civility through the building of community.[4]

Activists in the arena of the natural environment choose values of ecologizing, which focus on connectedness and maintenance of diversity as well as on the use of resources such that nothing is wasted. Natural processes consistently evolve while maintaining patterns.

X-factor values, as noted earlier, are those particular personal values that individuals bring to the enterprise with them to any organization. Technological values, which drive business activity, are pragmatic in that they use various instruments to achieve their ends. Additionally, according to Frederick, technologists learn to value "coordinative, integrative, and cooperative relationships among tool users." Also valued by technology users are technical expertise, honesty, and "participatory leveling," which is the tendency of advanced technology to create participatory and democratic environments.[5]

The dominant values form an imperative for organizations within each sphere that guides them. Thus, business organizations are justifiably driven toward economizing ends of efficiency, given the way human societies have to this point framed business activities, and much the same can be said of the imperatives driving organizations in other spheres.

The Role of National Ideology

National ideology is a shared system of beliefs, or as defined by George C. Lodge and Ezra F. Vogel, "the collection of ideas that a community uses to make values explicit in some relevant context."[6] *Values* are "timeless, universal, noncontroversial notions that virtually every community everywhere has always cherished."[7] In other words, at the core of every society are end values—such as justice, economizing, and respect—that participants in the society can believe in. When combined with the specific context or historical development of a community, these values constitute the community's unique identity, typically an identity that members of a given community or state want to preserve. Although ideology at its extreme can be a source of dissension or differences, in milder and healthier forms, ideology helps people to establish an important sense of place, identity, and community by creating common understandings.

According to Lodge and Vogel, ideology has five components, which are listed in Table 2.2. These components involve the ways in which people are perceived—in particular, how they are perceived in relation to the broader community, as well as what types formal and informal policies and culture exist to manifest those relationships. Ideology also involves perceptions of nature and reality, and determines what type of government is considered appropriate within a given culture or nation.

Lodge and Vogel identified two "ideal-type" ideologies, which can be placed at either end of a continuum, with most real-world ideologies somewhere in between the two ends. On the one end of the continuum is individualism, an ideology in which individuals are the ultimate source of value and meaning,

TABLE 2.2 **Components of Ideology**

1. The relationship between the human being and the community, the individual, and the group; and the means to individual fulfillment and self-respect;
2. The institutional guarantees and manifestations of that relationship, such as property rights;
3. The most appropriate means of controlling the production of goods and services;
4. The role of the state; and
5. The prevailing perception of reality and conception of nature, concerning, for example, the role of science and the functions of education.

with community interests defined through self-interested competition (i.e., what economist Adam Smith meant by free-market competition in its ideal state). On the other end of the continuum is communitarianism, a system in which community interests are considered more important and meaningful than those of individuals. These differences in ideology create significant impacts on how business can be done in different countries, and they have implications for how companies view their corporate citizenship.

Individualism

Individualism is the atomistic notion that a community is no more than the sum of the individuals in it.[8] Under an individualistic system property and other individual rights take precedence, and the best government is thought to be a limited government. Individualism also emphasizes competition and materialism, to the extent that it focuses on satisfaction of consumer desires. Newtonian science, with its fragmentation and atomization, undergirds thinking about nature in individualistic systems. The United States is probably the most individualistic country in the world, though there is considerable tension even in the United States between values of individualism and those that favor community.[9] Individuals holding more radical views on individualism tend to separate economic, political, and civil society spheres and want to keep them separate through a laissez-faire approach to government. They also celebrate free competition, limited government, and equality of opportunity. Ultimately, this individualism is captured in Thomas Jefferson's immortal phrase from the Declaration of Independence, "life, liberty, and the pursuit of happiness."[10]

Communitarianism

At the other end of the continuum of ideologies is communitarianism, which serves in many ways as a counterpoint to individualism. Communitarianism is characterized by an emphasis on community, with the belief that the community is something organic and whole in itself, comprised of more than the sum of its parts. Under communitarian systems, people believe that the needs and interests of the community take precedence over those of individuals, and that survival, justice, self-respect, and other human values depend on recognition of community needs. Communitarian cultures focus on equality of outcomes or results, frequently using hierarchy to achieve equitable outcomes. They also value consensus rather than the more contractual arrangements preferred in individualistic societies.

Rather than emphasizing property and individual rights, communitarian societies tend to emphasize the rights and duties of membership, placing community needs first in priority. Communitarian societies frequently have active, planning-oriented governments, which can be democratic or more authoritarian in form. Scientifically, communitarian societies tend to take a more holistic (rather than atomistic) view of nature and the world around them, seeing interdependence among societal elements rather than independence. Japan and many other Asian nations lean toward the communitarian end of the ideology continuum.

Impact of Ideology

Understanding where a nation falls on the ideology continuum is important for managers and leaders because the cultural differences that manifest themselves can determine the proper approach to business within a society. For example, managers in more communitarian countries may need to see a potential business partner as part of their community, developing a trusting relationship with future partners over an extended period, before they are able to work together successfully. Managers from more individualistic nations may want to immediately outline a contractual agreement, as soon as it can be signed by the lawyers. Such a tactic might well alienate communitarian managers who ordinarily build business on the relationship and trust that comes out of knowing each other over time.

Further, cultural differences that manifest themselves as a result of differing ideologies may be deeply valued by people within that society. Attempts by multinational corporations or intergovernmental organizations to do business in ways that contradict or subvert the prevailing ideology may be met with discontent and resistance at best and downright rebellion at worst. Most people care deeply about their own cultures and beliefs; they may well resent or even resist attempts by global superpowers or transnational corporations to impose one way of doing things. Embedded as they are within their own ideological perspective, most people find it difficult to accept a perspective radically different from their own unless they are capable of holding in their own heads multiple perspectives simultaneously. (See the discussion of cognitive development in Chapter 3 for more on holding multiple perspectives simultaneously.)

Without deep understanding of differences in ideology and their cultural manifestations, it is easy for leaders of corporate citizens to get themselves and their companies into trouble inadvertently, or to step on toes of actors in the political or civil society spheres unintentionally. Managers are constantly faced with the paradoxes and tension inherent in the individualism–communitarian continuum, especially in a world that is highly interconnected electronically and in which many companies operate globally. For example, although there are global standards about respecting human dignity and taking care of the natural environment, there is a natural "tension of the opposites" that requires careful balancing when dealing with communities other than one's own.

Further, attitudes toward government as a policymaker differ radically depending on whether one's country is based on individualistic or on communitarian values.[11] Individualistic countries like to keep government off the people's backs, as the saying goes in the United States. Government's role is to protect property and rights, enforce contracts, and ensure that markets are free so that competition can be fostered. Government intervention is frowned on, except when there is a crisis, and business–government relations are typically adversarial at best. Individualistic countries believe that public policy is best developed through the play of contesting parties in the public policy arena rather than through centralized control over policymaking.

Communitarian nations, in contrast, view government as prestigious and authoritative, at times even authoritarian.[12] Because the interests of community are placed over those of individuals, government's primary role is seen as defining and meeting community needs and interests. Such countries emphasize membership in the community, and governments play an important role in determining what constitutes membership as well as what duties and rights membership entails. Although communitarian countries believe that consensus is important, when the interest of the community as a whole is at stake, there may be little hesitation to force consensus either from an authoritarian central government or from a coercive grassroots movement. Relations between business and government in communitarian countries tend to be more collaborative and cooperative than they are in individualistic nations.

The Need for Both/And

Of course, no nation is fully individualistic or fully communitarian. There is always a tension of the opposites, because healthy societies require both individualism and community. The United States, for example, has struggled to sustain community over the years in the face of the dominant ideology of individualism. Economist Adam Smith's invisible hand of the free market, which will be discussed in more detail later in this chapter, is supposed to result in a better society, not in an amoral, cutthroat free-for-all where consequences are not taken into account. Smith, after all, was primarily a moral philosopher and only secondarily the progenitor of economic theory as we know it today.

Western philosophy and culture generally tend to be more rooted in individualism, while Eastern and Southern philosophies and cultures tend to be more communitarian, although there are vast differences among nations. The ideology and culture of the nation will greatly influence not only public policy but also what is considered acceptable corporate behavior. Applying thinking about ideology to leading corporate citizens, we can see that companies face a significant tension between the need for fostering entrepreneurial (and individualistic) efforts to innovate, while sustaining a community engaged in the common purposes of the firm. This tension can be healthy or problematic, depending on how far toward an individualistic or communitarian philosophy a company goes, because there is always some need to balance individualism.

This book argues, as does philosopher Robert Solomon, that excellent performance in companies requires a commitment to integrity and to balancing these types of tensions, as well as care and compassion for people in the company.[13] Being caring and compassionate inherently demands just this type of balance between the needs of individuals and the need for a community that works together toward some common goal.

The Economic Sphere

Many observers believe that business is the most powerful institution in society today. One report puts the point baldly: "Of the 100 largest economies in the world, 51 are corporations; only 49 are countries (based on a comparison of corporate sales and country GDPs)."[14] Think of these statistics, drawn from the same report: there are 82 U.S. companies in the top 200 (by size) and 41 Japanese companies; the annual income of these companies is 18 times more than that of the 1.2 billion people in the world who live in poverty; these companies' economic activities amount to 27.5 percent of the total; however, they employee only 0.78 percent of the workforce. Certainly, the modern corporation is today's dominant influence on human lives, as well as the ecology, particularly in industrialized parts of the world. This power makes some observers believe that the world is out of balance (see again Figure 2.2).

Corporate power inevitably leads to corresponding responsibility for leading corporate citizens, particularly because corporations in the United States have been granted rights similar to those granted to persons. Corporate decisions, after all, impact not only other businesses but also the other sectors that comprise society: the political sphere and the civil society sphere. The following paragraphs will explore the origins and nature of business enterprise as we know it today.

At the core of today's dominant economic model is the values cluster of economizing, that is, "prudent, careful, sometimes deliberately calculated, rational-where-possible actions of individuals, groups, and organizations that are intended to produce net outputs or benefits from a given amount of resource inputs."[15] Given these dominant values, it is not surprising that company leaders seek out ways to conserve precious resources and continue to grow, or that they use power-aggrandizing techniques to consolidate their resources and strengthen their influence on the markets they serve.

Economic development is an important contributor to the welfare of societies. The positive side of economic development is that it brings goods, services, and jobs to consumers throughout the developed world. Although some critics decry the materialism inherent in such a consumerist approach to the global economy (and imbalance in the social system, as Figure 2.2d suggests), the competitive dynamic on which it rests is undeniable. Rapid change, intensifying competition, multiple new competitors in most product and service domains, and global connectedness have reshaped the economic—and social—environment in which people in the developed world live today.

With all of the change implied by the globalization process, staying connected to stakeholders, fostering individual and corporate citizenship and civic engagement, and maintaining community, whether inside the organization or outside of it in society, would appear to be more important than ever. Without ties to local communities, and the relationships that sustain them, it is difficult for companies to be accountable for the decisions they make—to be leading corporate citizens.

The Capitalist Market System Today and in the Past

Corporate citizenship responsibilities derive directly from the origin of the corporate form itself, which is based in a legal charter granted wherever a company operates. This government-granted charter gives a company the right to do business and receive certain legal benefits. In particular, incorporation means that the corporation itself is treated as a person that can be sued. In addition to the corporation's being viewed as a person, individual managers are now increasingly being held liable for corporate acts. For example, in the wake of the numerous corporate scandals of the early 2000s, the U.S. government passed the Sarbanes-Oxley Act of 2002. This act requires chief executive officers (CEOs) to certify that audited financial statements of the company are accurate, provides for an oversight board and new rules for the accounting industry, imposes strict penalties on executives and companies committing fraud, and protects whistleblowers (i.e., those who make wrongdoing public). It also demands independence of public company audit committees on the board, requires companies to assume responsibility for their financial reports and avoid improper influence on audits, and creates a number of other conditions intended to hold companies accountable for their statements and internal practices, particularly as they relate to the governance of the company.[16]

In the United States, early corporations were granted charters through state legislatures, for only limited periods and with restricted powers. Charters were considered "legal fictions with no claim to a natural place in the order of things or in the spontaneous associations or contracts of private parties."[17] Over time, however, U.S. courts made decisions that granted to companies the rights of a legal person. These rights include the right to free speech, which is powerfully used not only in advertising and the media but also by corporate political action committees (PACs), entities established by corporations to lobby legislators and take other political actions on the organization's behalf. Prior to being granted the rights of a legal person, however, corporations were considered to be instruments to forward the public interest rather than instruments primarily operated for private gain. There is a significant movement today, which broke into public view at the end of the 20th century during protests against the World Trade Organization, to return the corporation to its roots and its public responsibilities. A lawsuit against Nike, for example, charged the company with misusing its free speech rights.

Neoclassical Economics

Today's market system, frequently termed free-market capitalism, is based on a number of assumptions. Derived from the ideas of Adam Smith, the concept of a free market is today expressed in the neoclassical economic system. The premise of neoclassical economics is that a multitude of small buyers will demand goods and services from a multitude of small producers. No one buyer or supplier will, under this model, be able to command a significant portion of the market or influence the market price. Over time, with many transactions, demand and supply will reach a point of equilibrium.[18]

Another assumption of the neoclassical model is that information is readily available to all participants in the market (i.e., there are no trade secrets or proprietary knowledge). Further, sellers bear all the costs of producing goods and services, that is, such costs are internalized rather than externalized. Full-cost accounting, which fully accounts for all of the costs associated with the production of goods and services—including those costs today not typically included, such as the cost of using up raw materials or creating pollution—would thus be employed. When costs are not included in a full costing system, they are typically externalized to society and paid for by the public through taxes or reduced quality of life. The costs remain in the system somewhere, even if they are borne not by the organization that produces them but by taxpayers.

Additionally, the free-market model of neoclassical economics assumes, following David Ricardo's theory of comparative advantage, that investment capital remains within national borders and international trade is balanced. Finally, the model assumes that savings are invested in productive capital.[19]

Failed Assumptions of Neoclassical Economics

The problem with the assumptions of neoclassical economics is that few of them actually apply to today's economies, which means that to some extent the balance implied in the term *free market* is mythical in the complex global economic arena. For one thing, most modern industries, rather than being made up of numerous small buyers and sellers, are oligopolies comprised of a few very large corporations, some of which are larger than whole countries' economies, as noted earlier. This reality means that some companies do, in fact, command significant portions of the market and are quite capable of influencing the market price.

Further, most large corporations have numerous trade secrets and much closely held proprietary information that they use to their competitive advantage. Indeed, trade secrets are often the very source of competitive advantage (in addition, of course, to the knowledge capital of employees). Many costs are externalized. In fact, the whole thrust of the economizing value that is the business imperative is to foster as much externalization of costs as possible in order to preserve efficiency and enhance productivity. But because "the costs are in the system somewhere,"[20] they must be paid for somewhere, typically by taxpayers.

Finally, since the early 1980s, there has been an almost obsessive attention to increasing shareholder wealth in the current system with little regard for other stakeholders, which in the United States, of course, is related to strong individualistic ideology. Most owners or shareholders in modern large corporations are distantly removed from any strategic or operational details because they own only a small fraction of the millions of company shares outstanding and have little voice in or impact on corporate affairs. They are, as iconoclastic management thinker Charles Handy points out, not really owners in any true sense of the word, but rather distanced investors who deserve a fair return.[21] Unfortunately, the emphasis on maximizing shareholder wealth means that too frequently corporate resources are used to generate short-term improvements in share price, while long-term and societal needs are put aside, bringing us back to the question of balancing societal—not just economic—needs. The shareholder wealth or finance capitalism model thus pays little regard to building productive assets in the underlying business, in part because accountability for corporate actions is limited and corporate power is high.[22]

The Public Responsibilities of the Corporation

There is an alternative perspective that suggests that companies have public as well as private responsibilities. While setting public policy is a part of the political sphere, corporations and their leaders, by virtue of the charter granted to them by the state, do have public responsibilities that need to be recognized explicitly. Public responsibilities revolve around understanding the impacts that companies have on their stakeholders, the natural environment, and the broader societies in which they operate. In return for the right or license to operate granted by states and nations, corporate citizens need to respect the rights of other stakeholders, treat them fairly and justly, and avoid harm wherever possible.

In a seminal book describing the "principle of public responsibility" for the private corporation, Lee Preston and James Post describe the scope of managerial responsibility based on the extent of impacts of corporate actions, decisions, and behavior.[23] Preston and Post describe two levels of managerial responsibility, primary and secondary. Primary responsibility has to do with the business of the organization, that is, "the role that defines its nature and social purpose and that provides the basis for exchange relationships between it and the rest of society."[24] Primary responsibilities, which can be considered private, have to do with the impacts and outcomes of corporate decisions and actions with respect to primary stakeholders (employees, customers, owners, suppliers, and allies) and direct effects on the natural environment. In addition, because of their close ties, key secondary responsibilities—business responsibilities—need to be met with respect to other important stakeholders, including local communities where the company has operations or does business and the governments that establish the rules of relevant societies.

The secondary responsibilities of an enterprise have to do with its historical and continuing public character. According to Preston and Post, the secondary responsibilities of the firm are "all those relationships, activities, and impacts of the organization that are ancillary or consequential to its primary involvement activities,"[25] including the use of its products or services, and the externalities associated with production processes. Thus, a company may have a responsibility for the social welfare of its retirees through operation of a decent pension plan that will support them. It may be responsible for the education of local school-children to the extent that they represent the workforce of the future on whom the company and its affiliates depend. It may be responsible for the sustainability of the ecological environment because the company itself depends on that environment for its own resources and because the health of the community is also intertwined with the ecology. Secondary—and public—responsibilities are those associated with the broader and less direct societal and ecological impacts of the firm's operations, that is, the by-products of business operations.

Together, primary and secondary responsibilities encompass all of the arenas and stakeholders that corporate leaders should pay attention to in their decision-making capacities. Stakeholder impacts, particularly secondary impacts, also determine the extent to which economic activities in our three-sphere model intersect with the political and civil society spheres. The more overlap in a given stakeholder arena, the more responsibility a company has for its actions with respect to that stakeholder. Of course, corporations, like all of human society, depend on an ecology that supports human life at their base. Case 2.1, on Wal-Mart, illustrates how a company's highly successful competitive strategy can have unintended consequences for stakeholders.

The business system itself can be viewed as an ecological system, without clear boundaries between one type of enterprise and the next, interconnected and interdependent, and working as much from collaboration as from competition.[26] Many business leaders recognize that their companies co-evolve with their competitors, suppliers, customers, and other stakeholders rather than operating independently. By taking a systems perspective on this co-evolution and recognizing their interdependency with stakeholders in the other spheres of society, leading corporate citizens can learn to tap new opportunities early because they are in constant dialogue with these key stakeholders, who frequently operate predominantly in the political and civil society spheres. But leading corporate citizens also need to recognize that these other stakeholders play important roles in the balancing act of sustaining human civilization in a natural world.

Rethinking Public Responsibilities

As noted earlier in this chapter, today in America and increasingly throughout the world, leaders believe they owe their primary allegiance to shareholders (owners). Many corporate leaders consider other stakeholders' needs and interests secondary, when they consider them at all. This narrowness of perspective, which derives from the ideology of individualism, has significant consequences for other important stakeholders, who are too frequently left out of consideration when companies take actions on behalf of shareholders/owners, and whose needs would be better considered in a communitarian logic. For example, when companies cut costs in the interest of achieving more profitability or when they acquire other companies simply because they desire more power, their executives may be thinking only of shareholder wealth without regard to the consequences for employees, customers, or local communities.

In its March 8, 2004, issue *Fortune* ranked Wal-Mart number one on its list of "most admired" corporations. Yet in the same issue, the magazine ran a story by Jerry Useem entitled "Should We Admire Wal-Mart?" Now the largest retailer in the world, with more than 3,500 stores globally (and plans for one new store a week), Wal-Mart has a well-known strategy of driving down prices for customers to achieve its strategic intent: products at the lowest possible prices. It accomplishes these ends by pressuring its suppliers for more efficiency (i.e., economizing) and squeezing out inefficiencies in all of its operations, creating both the stunning success of the retail giant and much of the controversy surrounding it. Useem's question put the controversy surrounding the retail giant's performance starkly:

> There is an evil company in Arkansas, some say. It's a discount store—a very, very big discount store—and it will do just about anything to get bigger. You've seen the headlines. Illegal immigrants mopping its floors. Workers locked inside overnight. A big gender discrimination suit. Wages low enough to make other companies' workers go on strike. And we know what it does to weaker suppliers and competitors. Crushing the dream of the independent proprietor—an ideal as American as Thomas Jefferson—it is the enemy of all that's good and right in our nation.
>
> There is another big discount store in Arkansas, yet this one couldn't be more different from the first. Founded by a folksy entrepreneur whose notions of thrift, industry, and the square deal were pure Ben Franklin, this company is not a tyrant but a servant. Passing along the gains of its brilliant distribution system to consumers, its farsighted managers have done nothing less than democratize the American dream. Its low prices are spurring productivity and

helping win the fight against inflation. It is America's most admired company.

> Weirdest part is, both these companies are named Wal-Mart Stores, Inc.

Jerry Useem, "Should We Admire Wal-Mart?" *Fortune,* March 8, 2004, p. 118.

As if doing business globally and dealing with communities that resent the negative impact of the huge retail chain with all of its scale economies on local retailers weren't difficult enough, the world's largest retailer, which itself employs 1.4 million people, faces significant criticism from labor and human rights activists on its sourcing practices from what Useem calls "squeezing its suppliers to death" on costs. At the same time, the company is known for its straightforwardness, with "none of the slotting fees, rebates, or other game playing that many merchants engage in." Useem details some of the pros and cons of Wal-Mart's highly successful strategy:

> If a company achieves its lower prices by finding better and smarter ways of doing things, then yes, everybody wins. But if it cuts costs by cutting pay and benefits—or by sending production to China—then not everybody wins. And here's where the story of Good-Wal-Mart starts to falter. Just as its Everyday Low Prices benefit shoppers who've never come near a Wal-Mart, there are mounting signs that its Everyday Low Pay (Wal-Mart's full-time hourly employees average $9.76 an hour) is hurting some workers who have never worked there . . . The $15 billion in goods that Wal-Mart and its suppliers imported from China in 2003 . . . accounted for nearly 11% of the US total— contributing, some economists argue, to further erosion of US wages.

Customers love Wal-Mart for its low prices, at least until it turns its back on the local communities where its stores operate, which it has been known to do, leaving, as Yale School Dean Jeffrey Garten points out in *Business Week*, the "local community with empty structures and huge shortfalls in public revenues." And that doesn't take into account decimated downtowns, where locally owned and managed stores typically fold because they are unable to compete against Wal-Mart's efficiency machine.

As if doing business globally and dealing with communities that resent the negative impact of the huge retail chain with all of its scale economies on local retailers weren't difficult enough, Wal-Mart faces significant criticism from labor and human rights activists on its sourcing practices. To prove the difficulty of implementing self-monitoring and auditing of suppliers located in far-flung locations such as China, Wal-Mart faced damaging allegations in a National Labor Committee (NLC) report issued in May 2000. The NLC is the same organization that exposed Wal-Mart's labor violations with respect to products that carried Kathie Lee Gifford's name in Central America in 1997. The real issue highlighted by the NLC report, in some respects, is the difficulty that auditors face in uncovering even dramatic worker exploitation and mistreatment.

Indeed, it was the Kathie Lee Gifford fiasco in 1997 and all of the ensuing negative publicity that pushed Wal-Mart to implement stringent accountability standards and an extensive self-policing supplier auditing system. To monitor suppliers, Wal-Mart hired PricewaterhouseCoopers (PWC) and Cal Safety Compliance Corporation to inspect and audit its overseas suppliers. But the auditors themselves had a tough time figuring out that severe abuses were going on. It was not until *Business Week* released the results of an intensive three-month investigation of a factory in China that significant ongoing abuses at the Chun Si Enterprise Handback Factory in Zhonghshan, a city in the Guangdong Province of southern China, were publicly exposed.

Then in 2003, the company, already facing more lawsuits than any other U.S. company (in part because of sheer size), was hit with a major sex-discrimination class action suit alleging systematic mistreatment of its female employees. Among other charges, the suit claims that Wal-Mart pays women less than men in the same jobs, prevents them from advancing by denying them training, and prevents them from applying for management positions by failing to post them. Bolstering the charges is the fact that the company has only around 10 percent female managers while 70 percent of hourly sales workers are women. All of these complexities have led Yale's Jeffrey Garten to query: "If Wal-Mart succeeds with its low-price-at-any cost strategy, what kind of message does this send about the ability of US companies to be good corporate citizens? What kind of backlash against international trade and investment would it eventually provoke?"

DISCUSSION QUESTIONS

1. Should we admire Wal-Mart? Why or why not?
2. What are Wal-Mart's public responsibilities, given its community, labor, and ecological impacts?
3. How does a company like Wal-Mart, with its successful strategy, contribute to our understanding of what corporate citizenship is?
4. Do you consider Wal-Mart to be a leading corporate citizen? Justify your answer.
5. Investigate current charges against Wal-Mart surrounding its labor practices, both domestically and abroad. What conclusion do you reach about the company's corporate citizenship?

Sources: Jeffrey E. Garten, "Wal-Mart Gives Globalism a Bad Name," *Business Week*, March 8, 2004; Debra McClinton, "The Next Big (Legal) Thing?" *FastCompany* 36 (April 2003), pp. 112–14; Jerry Useem, "Should We Admire Wal-Mart?" *Fortune*, March 8, 2004, pp. 118–20; and Dexter Roberts and Aaron Bernstein, "A Life of Fines and Beating," *Business Week*, October 2, 2000, pp. 122–28. See also the National Labor Committee Web site, www.nlcnet.org.

During the 1990s, numerous downsizings, restructurings, and reengineerings eroded employee loyalty, commitment, and morale and left resources stretched and change a constant. During the early 2000s, scandals left some corporations in bankruptcy and others with reputations so ruined that their futures were highly uncertain and their stakeholder loyalty questionable. This erosion of loyalty becomes critical when companies face, as they are facing now, personnel shortages. Communities suffer the consequences of companies moving long-standing facilities to lower-wage countries, leaving a wreckage of unemployed workers, devastated small businesses that relied on patronage from bigger businesses, and eroded community tax bases and infrastructure. One clear example involves the cost-cutting maneuvers, massive employee layoffs, and numerous failed acquisitions and subsequent divestitures of General Electric (GE) under the leadership of Jack Welch.[27] Welch is touted as the CEO of the 20th century because his leadership made GE's stock price soar; however, little attention is given to some of the by-products of the layoffs and other cost-cutting moves that accompanied this profitability. A balanced approach suggests that both types of issues need consideration.

Other indicators of problems with the current business model might be noted. Air and water pollution, toxic waste, and other negative by-products of production are created by a corporate system that finds it more efficient to gain competitive advantage through externalizing such costs rather than assuming them within product costs. With adequate regulator protections, such externalization may be the most efficient means of achieving certain types of productivity. In developing nations, transnational enterprises emphasize low-cost production in what some term a "race to the bottom"[28] that pits nation against nation and leaves too many people working in sweatshop conditions with little, if any, dignity or freedom.[29]

E-commerce, or dot-com, companies posed another whole set of issues related to corporate citizenship. Characterized by extremely rapid growth, immense wealth for relatively young entrepreneurs, intense competitive pressure, and little profit at least in early stages of their lives, dot-com companies needed to grow into better understanding of their responsibilities to stakeholders other than owners.[30] In addition, some dot-com companies were virtual companies, meaning that employees, customers, and suppliers meet only online rather than face-to-face. The citizenship implications of such virtual organizations have yet to be clarified.

Still, it is clear that leading corporate citizens today demands more rather than less of tomorrow's executives. Leaders must take into consideration the impacts of their decisions on the wide range of stakeholders interdependent with them in the societal holon, that is, incorporate at least a modicum of communitarian thinking into their individualistic and entrepreneurial efforts. Taking this perspective on the public responsibilities of the corporation seriously means that corporations are probably not responsible for, nor should they take responsibility for, arenas of political/public policy and civil life for which organizations operating in those spheres have and, to be in balance, should demand more responsibility. Because of the amount of power that transnational corporations have accrued in recent years, it is critically important that actors within each of the other two spheres of human civilization (as well as activists on behalf of the natural environment) have relatively equal access to shaping the future of societies. It is to these important other spheres, and the ways in which they can and should balance corporate power and resources, we now turn.

The Political Sphere

The political sphere is comprised of governments and governmental organizations (GOs) on multiple levels. Governments exist at multiple levels. They operate locally, administering towns and cities; they operate at a state, provincial, or regional level; and they operate at the level of nation-state. Increasingly, they operate between governments at the intergovernmental organization (IGO) level. Each of these levels has responsibility for setting the rules of society, which affect the economic and civil spheres (as well as the political) at their level.

Those who make public policy, whether elected or appointed to public office in democratic societies, are charged with responsibility for the public interest or the common good. In democratic societies, the public good is at least in theory determined either directly by the public or by elected officials chosen to represent the public.

The Common Good

The critical role of institutions in the political sphere is to determine what actions, policies, and rules are in the *public interest* or the *common good* and to set the rules of society that foster that common good. These rules are frequently called rules of the game or rules of society. Such rules are implemented through *public policy*, which is the combination of decisions and actions taken by elected and appointed public officials.[31] *Public interest* is defined as the particular standards and values that people in a society would generally agree are in the best interests of that society. In most democratic nations, the common good is underpinned by values such as social justice, equity and fairness, and human dignity.

The political or governmental sphere, as earlier noted, is dominated by values of power aggrandizing in developing its institutions, standards, and policies, since there is no currency that represents the bottom line as can be found in business. Governmental organizations, as a result, have a distinct tendency to organize themselves bureaucratically, following rules and procedures, creating hierarchies, and establishing sets of regulations for constituencies to follow, partly as a result of the underlying value of power aggrandizing. In spite of this tendency toward power aggrandizing, government leaders in most democratic nations are charged with determining and implementing the (current) view of the common good as defined by the contest of forces that result from the pluralistic interests inevitably found in any society.

Governments create and implement the rules of societies through what is called the public policy process. According to Preston and Post, "Public policy refers to widely shared and generally acknowledged principles directing and controlling actions that have broad implications for society at large or major portions thereof."[32] A nation's political structure and constitution determine the public policy process and its outcomes, which in turn dictate how laws, court rulings, and executive decisions are to be made. The issues that are dealt with through public policy decisions and rulings constitute the *public policy agenda*, which may or may not represent majority opinion at any given time even in democratic nations.[33]

In the United States, there are three branches of government—the executive, the legislative, and the judicial—which form a system of natural checks and balances in an effort to assure that no one branch gains too much power or gets out of control. The public policy arena is filled with competing interests and contested values from numerous different groups, each of which wants some say in setting the public policy agenda. All of these competing interests would like to have their point of view and their best interests represented in laws, regulations, and court decisions in a system that is called pluralism. But only some interests can actually be represented in laws and regulations at any given time. Thus, an important task in making public policy is to determine which, among the many competing interests at play at any given time, should receive attention and priority. And, as must be obvious, both the public policy agenda and public policy itself shift over time as societal interests and needs change.

Of course, in a pluralistic society, where there are many points of view and many interests that need to be represented, it is difficult to determine the public interest or the common good. This variety of interests creates a contest of sorts that the public policy process, when it works well, is meant to help sort out. Citizens who wish to have voice on a given matter tend to band together in associations, activist groups, or other organizations so that their voices become more powerful—and better able to be heard by government officials. The Internet and other forms of electronic communication are facilitating the formation of such civic and political associations, which can form voting blocs, create newsletters, form protest movements, generate lobbying activities, or engage in numerous other forms of political action.

Recognizing the value of such activities, many companies have banded together in industry, trade, and other economic associations. Some observers even claim that such associations can be a foundation for developing what is called a civil economy, that is, an economy in which free-market forces are regulated by the forces of community and self-interest that seeks the good of the whole. Indeed, in some respects, it is this seeking of the common good that Adam Smith sought in developing the theory of free markets. Although the reality of markets is that they are not entirely free, their power to produce goods and services that do benefit humanity is real. That power, however, needs to be tempered by active involvement from officials whose primary duty is to act on behalf of a public interest defined, ideally, by some sort of democratic process.

In most nations, there are at least three levels of government to which businesses need to pay attention: local community or municipal, state or provincial, and national. In the future, we can expect that intergovernmental agencies will play an increasingly important role in setting the rules of societies, particularly the rules that go across societal boundaries.

Why Government?

There is a good deal of cynicism in the world about government today, in part because of its power-aggrandizing tendencies, which can sometimes result in seemingly immovable bureaucracies, overly burdensome regulations, and excess spending without as much success in reaching national priorities as many consider desirable. In part, the cynicism exists because of what linguist Deborah Tannen calls the "argument culture," in which issues tend to be polarized and all aspects of public officials' lives and actions are closely scrutinized for flaws and inconsistencies.[34]

Whatever their problems, governments do play a socially essential role in creating the rules of the society that permit corporate and market activity to develop, that enable markets to be free, and that provide for trust in the system of trading relationships that constitutes world economics. In addition, they set the rules that govern society itself, including the social discourse, types of organizations and activities permitted in civil and economic realms, and national or state priorities. Governments, when they work on behalf of citizens (which is not always the case in dictatorships), protect citizens from harmful actions that might result if there were no socially accepted rules to follow. In addition, they have an important role in protecting public goods and dealing with externalities that impact or are created by business operations.

Public Goods

Public goods, as opposed to the more generic *public good* defined above, are shared, generally indivisible, and external benefits that accrue to all citizens from actions taken by others.[35] Typically, people cannot use goods or services unless they are willing to pay for them, but public goods are available to all whether or not they are willing or able to pay. For example, when a company installs pollution equipment, everyone in the neighborhood benefits, even though they have not paid for the installation. Thus, the company has generated a public good. It has, however, potentially also incurred a cost that other companies do not have and may possibly have put itself at somewhat of a competitive disadvantage in doing so. Typical public goods are clean air, clean water, parks, and highways.

Externalities

Externalities are the reverse of public goods; they are "public bads." If, say, a company refuses to install pollution control equipment, everyone downwind suffers from the pollution created. (See the Boss Hog Case in Chapter 1 for a dramatic example of externalities.) Externalities, then, are the shared and usually indivisible costs that accrue to people or organizations even when they do not take the deleterious actions themselves. Common forms of externalities include most forms of pollution, which are shared by all in the form of undrinkable water or dirty air. The problem with externalities is that the costs do not disappear because they are externalized. These costs remain somewhere in the system—typically in the public arena. The general public, rather than the customers of the polluting business, has to pay.

The Prisoner's Dilemma

To illustrate externalities and public goods, we can examine a well-known problem from game theory called the prisoner's dilemma, which makes obvious why rulings and regulations are sometimes necessary. In a typical framing of the dilemma, a dictator captures two of the "regular suspects" for a heinous crime that has been committed. The dictator does not know which, if either, prisoner committed the crime. Separating them, the dictator tells one prisoner that if she implicates the other, that the dictator will be able to set her free, while the other will face hanging or life in prison. If neither confesses or squeals, then both will face, say, three years in prison. If only one confesses, then that prisoner faces 20 years in prison. Then the dictator goes to the other prisoner with the same message. Neither prisoner is allowed to talk with the other.

Obviously, the best system outcome is that neither prisoner confesses. In this case, both receive the reduced three-year sentences only. But clearly, the incentive for each prisoner individually is to maximize her "good"—and go completely free—by implicating the other.

Many business situations resemble prisoner's dilemmas. For example, the airline industry constantly finds itself engaging in price wars in which no company wins. The best outcome for the industry (the system) would be to avoid the price war. Individual companies, however, at least in the short term, find it hard to resist the potential gains in market share and revenue that come from starting to reduce prices. But once one company has reduced prices, others find it necessary to follow, thereby reducing overall industry revenues (and possibly benefiting consumers at least in the short run).

Companies that are proactive in incurring costs that others do not incur at the same time may also find themselves in a form of prisoner's dilemma. Going back to our pollution example above, we can see that the company that installs the pollution equipment proactively to be responsible places itself at a competitive disadvantage relative to others who may not choose to take such actions voluntarily, despite the environmental public goods that result.

Avoiding prisoner's dilemma situations is difficult unless there are rules of society in place that create the same standards, policies, and regulations for all companies in an industry, providing some justification for creating the rules of society. Another way of dealing with prisoner's dilemmas involves creating a set of shared values that establish the same expectations for all players in a situation. Shared values and expectations can help corporate citizens establish a higher ground—or a common good—on which those involved in a situation agree.

The Tragedy of the Commons

Similar to the prisoner's dilemma in its implications is what biologist Garret Hardin called the tragedy of the commons.[36] Such situations arise when there are commons—public goods that are available to all that can be consumed, or destroyed if overused. Individuals have incentives to overuse the common in an effort to gain advantage for themselves, thereby destroying the resource for all.

Imagine a lake, for example. Many people who enjoy the serenity and beauty of the lake build houses with docks and then put motorboats into the water. Soon, there are too many houses, the lake becomes polluted, and the noise of constant motorboating has destroyed the very serenity that people sought out. The planet Earth is a global commons. Because of the tendency that biological systems of all sorts have to overuse commons, protecting them is an imperative for the natural environment as well as the future of human civilization. Thus, there is a critical role for laws and regulations to protect the commons that we all share.

Free Riders

When there is a common good to be gained, or when an externality can be avoided through the actions of some, there is a tendency toward free ridership.[37] Free riding occurs when it is difficult or impractical to exclude people or organizations from a benefit or public good. When such goods are available, there is little incentive for any one individual or organization to pay for them, which gives rise to a tendency to free-ride to gain the benefits without paying the costs.

Trade or industry associations, for example, can give rise to free ridership when they seek out benefits for the industry as a whole. Members in the association pay dues that support the seeking of benefits, but all members of the industry, whether or not they join the association, will benefit from the association's efforts. Thus, there is a tendency to let others join and pay dues, while avoiding membership in the association. The costs of membership are imposed on members, while free riders gain the benefits without incurring associated costs.

As with protecting the commons, avoiding free ridership means leveling the playing field by creating rules and regulations that all must follow. Another way to deal with free ridership is by creating associations that establish industry, trade, or market standards that pressure both companies and individuals to live up to expectations and standards of what one observer calls a civil market.[38]

Laws, Regulations, and Court Rulings

Legal systems help governments balance public goods and externalities, avoid the tragedy of the commons, and reduce free ridership. Laws, regulations, and court rulings can provide an equitable outcome or demand equitable inputs. All companies following a court decision or regulatory decree need to either internalize similar costs or incur the same costs to avoid the externalities, placing no one of them at a competitive disadvantage relative to others following the same guidelines. Thus, in the example of public goods, if all companies are required to install pollution equipment, the costs are the same for all competitors. In the case of externalities, laws can reduce the incentives companies have to externalize as many costs as possible.

The Shifting Public Policy Agenda

Over time, the rules of societies shift. Shifts occur in part because of techno-logical changes, such as those that made it necessary to break down regula-tory barriers among financial institutions. They also occur because societies recognize formerly unmet needs—for example, for public or worker safety, consumer protection, or environmental protection, which were some of the arenas that generated activist movements during the 1960s that resulted in the passing of protective laws and regulations in the United States. And they occur because information availability raises consciousness about issues of public concern.

In democratic societies, public policy is shaped by a number of forces that are often contesting with each other to gain dominance and to have their positions represented in whatever rules are created. Among the factors that shape the public policy agenda are public opinion. Public opinion includes the ideas of opinion leaders, that is, key leaders to whom others listen, and also by what is reported in the media about surveys, case studies, and other research undertaken by various polling groups and social researchers. Public opinion is shaped by the experiences that people have within their communities and at work, as well as by what is reported in the media. For example, in Woburn, Massachusetts, an increase in the number of children dying of leukemia—ostensibly from pollution generated by the W. R. Grace Company—became a public issue. The events that followed are chronicled in the book and movie *A Civil Action*. A similar situa-tion occurred in California with Pacific Gas & Electric company and was made into the popular movie *Erin Brokovitch*. Clearly, leading corporate citizens would prefer to have their reputations publicized for more positive reasons than community outrage.

Political and social activists also help to shape public policy through interest and pressure groups that bring public attention to an issue. Activists use boy-cotts, protests, publicity, and media relations to try to frame issues in ways that meet their needs and interests, while those groups opposing the activists attempt to frame the issues differently. One such issue is smoking, which health activists have framed as an issue about health and addiction, while cigarette company officials have framed as an issue about personal rights. Policymakers are fre-quently caught in the middle of such competing interests. In the case of tobacco, states and the federal government rely on the jobs and taxes generated by ciga-rette sales, yet they also are burdened by the health-related costs of smoking. Sorting out what is actually in the public interest in such a contested situation is, fundamentally, what the policymaker's job is all about.

Company leaders in the United States also help to shape public issues by framing the debate, testifying before Congress, making speeches, and issuing reports that garner media and public attention. Elected officials can use the bully pulpit created by their elective office to frame issues. Many business organizations attempting to shape the public policy agenda send leaders to testify before the U.S. Congress. They also hire lobbyists to represent the company's perspective to legislatures at the national and state levels, and create political action committees (PACs) to supply information and expertise about the company's industry to elected officials that may be deciding on a law that will affect the company.

One of the problems associated with corporate political activism relates to the fact that companies have significant economic resources and therefore power with which to have their positions represented. This power becomes especially apparent when companies create PACs, hire lobbyists, or provide public officials with industry-biased information. Communities, activists, and individuals may have significantly fewer resources at their disposal. Some people raise questions about whether sufficient public voice is available to less powerful or less-resource-rich parties in the public policy arena to assure equitable outcomes. In 2002, in an effort to end some of the worst abuses of the system, President George W. Bush signed the McCain-Feingold bill, which limits the size of political contributions.

Shifting Public Issues

Attention and activity in the public policy arena shift over time with the shifting of competing interests, as well as with the relative amount of power and voice different contesting parties have. Social problems exist in all societies, but they become public issues when sufficient public attention is devoted to them (see Case 2.2).

A public issue has a number of elements.[39] First, public issues are in the public arena, possibly subject to public policy or nonpublic resolution. An issue develops for stakeholders when something becomes problematic for at least one stakeholder and when it is controversial, that is, when it is contested in the public arena. The contest arises particularly when there are multiple opinions (often of people or groups of equal goodwill) on what the best resolution of that issue should be. Further, issues develop when, for at least one stakeholder, there is a gap between what "is" and what "ought to be." Further, unless that gap creates some significant perceived present or future impact on the organization, society, or stakeholder, it is unlikely to become an issue. Frequently, issues arise when there is a question of legitimacy or when there is controversy about what the costs and benefits of issue resolution are.

Issue Life Cycle

Public issues tend to go through a generalized life cycle as they emerge from obscurity, indifference, or simple inattention and make their way onto the public policy agenda (see Figure 2.3). Not all issues follow exactly the same cycle, and not all are resolved through the public policy process. In fact, many companies have established issue management, public relations, and public affairs units in the hope that they can work cooperatively with government and community stakeholders or forestall actions before issues are resolved legislatively or in the court system.

FIGURE 2.3 Issue Life Cycle

Sources: Adapted from James E. Post, *Corporate Behavior and Social Change* (Reston, VA: Reston Publishing, 1978); and H. A. Tombari, *Business and Society: Strategies for the Environment and Public Policy* (New York: Dryden Press, 1984).

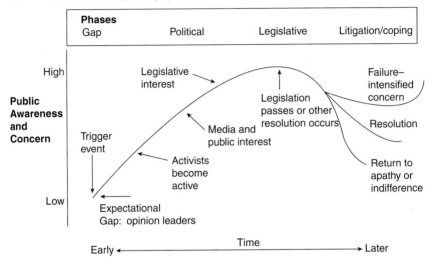

Public issues generally begin in unmet expectation.[40] The gap between what is and what ought to be draws attention to the issue from one or more stakeholders, who begin to (at least try to) shape or frame the issue in ways that meet their interests and perceptions. Often this gap develops when society is changing with resulting changes in public expectations.

For example, use of DDT as a pesticide was largely uncontroversial until the 1963 publication of Rachael Carson's *Silent Spring*, which galvanized environmentalists into action.[41] Similar trigger events include the publication of the surgeon general's report on smoking and health in the 1960s, which generated a great deal of antismoking activism. More recently, sweatshop conditions in less developed countries from which clothing and shoes are sourced have drawn outrage from the general public when publicized by activists such as the International Labour Organization (ILO). During the first, or gap, stage, only a few people or groups, typically activists or opinion leaders, may be interested in the issue, but once their activities begin to draw concern and attention, the issue enters the second stage of its life cycle.

The second, or political, stage of the issue life cycle occurs when the issue, as framed by one or more of the interested stakeholders, begins to draw public attention and concern, typically through the media or through various forms of activism. In this stage, the new expectations have become more widely known and accepted and the issue itself may become politicized.[42] As Figure 2.3 suggests, public awareness of the issue increases rather dramatically during this stage and more stakeholders are likely to become involved in the effort to frame the issue in a way that benefits their particular point of view. In this stage, the contest of different values is in full swing.

Governmental or political actors become involved as the issue progresses to the third, or legislative, stage of the life cycle. These actors begin to try to figure out how and where the issue should be dealt with legislatively, if that is to be the actual outcome. Once an issue has entered the legislative phase of its life cycle, public debate and contested framings of the issue are likely. It is during this phase that business leaders and others may be called to testify before the relevant legislative body. Also in this stage lobbyists become proactive in getting information to legislators or other decision makers in the hope of influencing the outcome in favor of a company or industry stakeholder group.

Assuming legislation is passed, the issue enters a fourth stage, called litigation or coping, in which stakeholders are expected to comply with the new legislation. If they continue to disagree with the outcome, they might fight it through the court system by means of litigation. If legislation does not pass or is unsatisfactory to some powerful stakeholders, the issue can take on new life. This is what happened with the environmental movement when in the 1980s it became clear that existing regulations were insufficient to solve newly recognized ecological problems like acid rain, rain forest depletion, and the shrinking of the ozone layer. Renewed environmental activism ensued in an effort to pass stricter laws protecting the environment. In 1992 the United Nations sponsored the first conference set up to deal with the increasingly global nature of environmental problems generated by population growth and processes of industrialization.

Generally speaking, the government is one of at least three primary stakeholders in any public issue that affects business. (Not all public issues impact businesses.) The other two are corporations or the economic community, and the particular activist or issues group interested in pursuing the issue to resolution.[43] Gaining a rich and comprehensive understanding of any issue therefore requires a capacity to hold the multiple perspectives of at least these stakeholders simultaneously and to see where their interests diverge and where they converge. This, generally, is the task of policymakers as they attempt to determine what outcome at a given time would be in the public interest. And, in their quest to determine the public interest, policymakers' ideas and perceived solutions are shaped, as are all members of a culture, by the national or community ideology.

Economic Development and the Political Sphere

Many people hold that developing countries need to progress through the same stages of industrialization today that Western industrialized nations passed through in their own development. During their industrialization, many Western and Eastern European nations gave little regard to respecting people or their needs and rights; workers, for example, were viewed as tools to be used and discarded when used up, rather than as full human beings. Additionally, respect for the environment and its resources was generally lacking as corporations aimed at economizing by externalizing as many costs and problems as possible. As can be seen in many parts of the world today, the costs of such externalizing and disregard for the human spirit are manifold. Evidence can be seen in the burning of rain forests in South America with the consequent problems for the ozone layer and presence of carbon dioxide in the atmosphere. It exists in the prevalence of sweatshop conditions and child labor in less developed countries to which much business is outsourced. And, among other places, it exists in the general disregard for human rights in some developing nations.

Such lack of respect for people and ecology, which is permitted in some parts of the world even today, encourages companies to act, in the interests of economizing and power aggrandizing, with disregard for the impacts of their actions. Many corporate actions affect not only nature but also civil society, where the relations generating civility and community are developed. Because governments in less developed countries do not always have the resources or indeed the incentives to create appropriate infrastructures or regulations to protect their people, abuses do occur. As a result, people work in sweatshop conditions, where they are allowed little freedom of movement, even to go to the bathroom. In some places, pay is less than a living wage even for local conditions and workers make mere pennies an hour. Some workers in such situations are punished physically for not meeting production schedules. And they are not permitted to associate or to unionize to gain some power and voice so that efforts can be made to improve conditions.

In developing countries desperately in need of economic development, some governments are willing to permit companies to engage in practices that they might otherwise wish to avoid. Too frequently in less developed nations, many of the factory workers are young children who should by international standards be in school, or young women whose only other employment opportunities may be even worse than the sweatshop conditions in which they work. For example, when Bangladesh forbade the employment of children in factories, many young workers seeking substitutes found themselves in prostitution or doing the burdensome manual labor of breaking bricks.[44]

Just as sustaining a healthy body requires eating a balanced diet and dividing time properly among work, play, exercise, and family/friends, so a healthy social system—at the most macro of levels, the planet—also demands *balance*. For companies to be able to succeed in the long term, corporate power must be balanced with that of governments, which establish the rules of the game by which economies exist and businesses compete. And, as will be discussed in the next section of this chapter, corporate power must also be balanced with human needs for the civilizing relationships, meaningful work and life, and community that are found in civil society.

The Civil Society Sphere

Civil society is fundamentally associational society. Civil society comprises entities and organizations that develop civility and coherence through the long-term building of civilized community and social capital, the capital of relationships. The organizations and associations of a civil society constitute community at whatever level of analysis is being considered. Civil society includes families, religious institutions, nonprofit organizations and other nongovernmental organizations (NGOs), educational institutions, health care institutions, voluntary organizations, civic and political organizations, and associations of all types.

In one sense, civil society is everything outside the economic and political spheres of activity, or as political scientist Alan Wolfe puts it, "those forms of communal and associational life which are organized neither by the self-interest of the market nor by the coercive potential of the state."[45] In its positive and constructive sense, civil society includes those enterprises and associations that promote what is thought to be the common or collective good in societies. That is, we would like to be able to exclude from our definition of *civil society* any negative associational entities, such as terrorist organizations or radical groups bent on destroying society, since these entities' purposes are decidedly and determinedly uncivil in their intent and impact. Such uncivil groups would include the terrorists who used airplanes to attack the World Trade Center and the Pentagon on September 11, 2001.

The fundamental purposes of civil society are to construct relationships among social institutions and peoples that give meaning to the terms *civility* and *community*. Hence, the fundamental values of civil society are those of relationship, civility, and community. As Alan Wolfe notes in his seminal book *Whose Keeper?* the basic values of any society, in a sense, are those values that comprise its ideology as discussed above.[46] In contrast to the economizing or power-aggrandizing values of the economic and political spheres, these are the values that are encompassed in friendships, loyalties, love, and personal values and that build relationships. These values are the X-factor values that individuals and some groups bring to all of their activities and they are also deeply embedded in the meanings that we associate with community.[47]

Just as there is a need for a healthy ecosystem to support human civilization, so there is a need for a working civil society to provide the values and social capital to support economic and political activities. As the structure and rules that government constructs provide a foundation for enterprise, so the relationships of trust and civility allow the economic system to operate effectively. Civil society provides a foundation of connectedness that gives people a sense of place and community. Civil society is where shared norms and values (the ideology that shapes political and governmental activities) emerge in the first place. Civil society provides the human in human civilization.

The humanization that comes from positive social capital occurs because links within a given community create a network of reciprocal relationships and mutual obligations among individual members of that community. Community members also exchange information, which helps them build a shared sense of identity and common set of values. In turn, these values generate norms of behavior and appropriate practices that provide sanctions where appropriate and rewards where feasible.[48]

Bowling Alone

In research spanning some 20 years, scholar Robert D. Putnam found that those Italian provinces where associational ties, civil society, was strongest were also the most prosperous and politically successful regions.[49] Those regions where associational ties were fewer and people were generally less engaged in society were substantially less healthy and productive.

One reason that the decline in civil engagement would be problematic is that civil engagement and social capital bolster democratic institutions and norms, making declines in social capital problematic. A symptom of decreased association is that fewer people vote or become actively involved in public life and discourse. Some of the other symptoms Putnam uncovered include fewer people participating in public meetings on town or school affairs, less attendance at political events, and overall less political participation. Other symptoms of less associational activity include fewer people reporting themselves as religiously affiliated, falling union membership, less involvement in parent–teacher associations, and reduced membership and volunteering in civic and fraternal organizations.[50]

Putnam entitled his widely cited article "Bowling Alone" because one of the "whimsical yet discomfiting" data sources for his conclusion that civic engagement in America may be decreasing had to do with the number of people bowling in leagues, that is, in association with each other. While he found that the total number of people bowling in the United States increased by 10 percent between 1980 and 1993, the number of bowling leagues decreased by 40 percent, perhaps evidence of the country's individualistic orientation. As Putnam points out, bowling alone by itself may not be problematic, but the "broader social significance . . . lies in the social interaction and even occasionally civic conversations over beer and pizza that solo bowlers forgo."[51]

Putnam attributes the declines in civic engagement and consequent social capital to a number of possible factors.[52] One is the pressure of time and money. A second possible factor is the changing role of women—as women entered the workforce, they had less time available for associational and volunteer activities. A third possible factor is the breakdown of the family resulting from higher divorce rates and increases in single-parent families and one-person households. Putnam also notes that there is circumstantial evidence that the rise of the welfare state may have crowded out private initiative, decreasing social capital in its wake. One other factor is the generational effect—older people tend to be more civically engaged than younger people.

But Putnam, fully satisfied by none of these possible explanations, comes up with another likely culprit: television. He believes television may be a disruptive force for civil society for a number of reasons. The timing is right. TV viewing is associated with low social capital because it takes the place of other activities in which people might be with others generating social capital. TV affects viewers' outlooks, particularly with respect to the benevolence of others, and it takes the place of hobbies, clubs, and outdoor activities, visiting, and (for children) just hanging out.

Putnam's work has generated a great deal of controversy and debate. Not everyone agrees that social capital in the United States is diminishing, though there is significant evidence that high social capital is indeed an important element of healthy societies. Maria Poarch, for example, found that many people in America today form their associational ties through work rather than within their communities, as was more common in the past.[53]

Civility and Society

Overall, when social capital diminishes there is less sense of community, less common good, because people have less in common and less of a sense of shared identity. Clearly, healthy societies need healthy social institutions that build strong and vibrant communities. The institutions—family, civic and nonprofit organizations, religious and educational institutions, and membership organizations of all sorts—bring people into contact with each other to develop a sense of what it means to be part of that particular community.

Strong families (however we define the word *family*) are at the base of healthy communities, along with many types of associational activities that help people to be actively involved with their communities. Among these activities are voluntary and nonprofit organizations that meet needs that political and economic enterprises do not meet. These needs might be spiritual or affiliative (having to do with loving, trusting, and caring relationships), health-related, intellectual (as with educational enterprises), or physical and structural (as with groups formed to meet the needs of disadvantaged people).

Through their development of trust, shared identity, and sense of community, healthy civil societies develop proactive and capable citizens.[54] In democracies, an active citizenry is capable of solving its own political and economic problems. Active citizens are also capable of placing restraints they believe appropriate on enterprises and activities in both of the other spheres of activity, as well as in civil society itself. These restraints occur through political action as well as through the activism associated with a range of causes of concern to different citizen groups when they share a common set of values and goals. Active citizens are capable of mobilizing themselves and the other spheres to deal with problems as they arise, while passive citizens, who feel little connectedness to or shared interest with the communities they are in, may remain passive, with problems going unresolved.

Globalization's Impacts

The dominance of multinational corporations in the world has created a significant degree of controversy about globalization and its impacts on civil society. One important critique of globalization (specifically, corporate globalization or neoliberalism) identifies several problematic aspects for many nations, particularly those that are still developing, which are listed in Table 2.3. Pointing out that modern globalization is not inevitable, but rather a system designed by human beings, the 19 authors of the critique note that the current global system promotes free trade and consumerism over other possible societal values,

TABLE 2.3 **Key Ingredients of the Globalization Model**

Source: John Cavanagh, Jerry Mander, and others from the International Forum on Globalization, *Alternatives to Economic Globalization: A Better World Is Possible* (San Francisco: Berrett-Koehler, 2002).

- Promotion of hypergrowth and unrestricted exploitation of environmental resources to fuel that growth.
- Privatization and commodification of public services and of remaining aspects of the global and community commons.
- Global cultural and economic homogenization and the intense promotion of consumerism.
- Integration and conversion of national economies, including some that were largely self-reliant, to environmentally and socially harmful export-oriented production.
- Corporate deregulation and unrestricted movement of capital across borders.
- Dramatically increased corporate concentration.
- Dismantling of public health, social, and environmental programs already in place.
- Replacement of traditional powers of democratic nation-states and local communities by global corporate bureaucracies.

including protecting the citizens of one's own country, in the belief that benefits will ultimately trickle down to the poor. Promoted by the so-called Bretton Woods organizations formed after World War II to create economic stability (e.g., the World Bank, the World Trade Organization, and the International Monetary Fund), free trade is seen in this view to benefit largely the already-rich and corporations, leaving behind the poor as well as developing nations.[55]

Today, we face further ambiguities with respect to the impact of economic sphere activities, particularly globalization, on civil society. These ambiguities have probably been best articulated by Benjamin Barber in his book *Jihad versus McWorld*.[56] Barber tells of a world torn between the forces of tribalism and parochial ethnicity (which he calls Jihad) and those of globalizing market forces (McWorld). Whereas Jihad fosters what Barber calls a tyrannical paternalism, McWorld has a corporate-centric focus on consumption, markets, and profits that encourages companies to satisfy what seems to be unmitigated self-interest in a world without boundaries. Neither Jihad nor McWorld in its extreme form is conducive, Barber suggests, to democracy, to responsibility (individual or corporate), or to civil society.

When there are problems, strong civil ties or larger amounts of social capital generally enable citizens to challenge governments and corporations so that communities' needs, aspirations, and ideas about the common good can be met.[57] In its more negative connotations, however, and when taken to extremes, as in Barber's notion of Jihad, too much social capital can be exclusionary and quite negative, even fanatical, creating tribalism and an us-versus-them attitude, such as that found in groups of terrorists. However, critics of globalization charge that it has a tendency to break down civil society locally by forcing countries to stop protecting local and regional economies in favor of the global economy. This happens because globalization fosters growth and environmental exploitation, typically in the form of monocultures (single crops), and supports export-oriented industries as opposed to locally sustainable industries that might be somewhat less efficient.[58]

Corporate citizens, like ordinary citizens, may need to be rooted in the identity of the localities in which they operate if they hope to be successful in the long run, because that is where values and norms develop and where meaning is generated. A strong civil sphere provides a necessary counterpoint to the otherwise dominating power of the multinational corporation with its individualistically oriented values focused on material goods and consumerism. In a sense, having a strong civil society creates numerous public goods that can then be shared by all members of the relevant communities.

Organizing Enterprise in the Three Spheres

Each of the three spheres of activity is associated not only with a distinct values basis but also with a specific organizational type and primary purpose.

Business Organization in the Economic Sphere

In the economic sphere, the organizational type is the business organization. Businesses are usually private, in that they are privately owned, either by a sole proprietor or family, through a partnership arrangement, or through legal incorporation, which grants them certain rights and responsibilities. In some nations, of course, businesses have been nationalized and are government owned, and increasingly, businesses have become employee-owned, at least in part. These complications aside, if the organization in question is a company that is driven by economizing, its purposes should revolve around production of goods and services truly needed by customers. Generally, all companies will have as primary stakeholders their owners, employees, customers, and (to the extent that the company is a virtual company relying on specific providers of services and goods that have been outsourced) suppliers, as well as allies and partners.

Governmental Organization in the Political Sphere

Governmental organizations (GOs), in contrast to business enterprises, are formed to serve the public interest or the public good within the political sphere, and their major underlying value is power aggrandizing, particularly emphasizing the use of political capital. GOs thus have as their primary stakeholders a set of quite different stakeholders than do companies.

GOs' stakeholders include the political or governmental body that established them. (In the United States, this might be the legislative, executive, or judicial branch of government.) Stakeholders also include the general public for their franchise and because public opinion sways governmental bodies to act (at least in democratic societies), employees, the clients or customers served. In addition, society or the local community is a primary stakeholder for governmental organizations because a GO's fundamental purpose is serving the public interest and

TABLE 2.4 Primary Stakeholders of Organizations in Different Spheres

Dominant Type of Organization	Sphere of Influence	Primary Purpose	Dominant Values	Key Stakeholders
Business (private sector) Proprietorship Partnership Corporation	Economic	Produce goods and services	Economizing	**Primary** Owners Customers Employees Suppliers Allies/partners **Critical Secondary** Community Governments
Governmental Organization (GO) Executive officers (elected officials, regulatory agencies) Legislative officials Judiciary	Political	Serve public good/interest	Power aggrandizing	Government General public Employees Clients/ customers Society
Nongovernmental Organization (NGO) Nonprofit Religious organizations Health care organizations Educational institutions Civil and civic organizations Political, trade, and industry associations	Civil society	Build/maintain society and community	Civilizing Building and maintaining relationships	Funder(s) Clients Employees Suppliers Society

because its operating expenses are paid for by taxes garnered from the public. Some of the key differences in the organizations found within each sphere of activity are noted in Table 2.4.

Nongovernmental Organizations (NGOs) in the Civil Society Sphere

Another common type of organization, particularly in the United States, is the nonprofit or not-for-profit organization, which is the most popular organizational form in the civil society sphere. In most countries, such entities are called nongovernmental organizations (NGOs). The primary form of capital in NGOs is social capital. NGOs tend to be helping or service organizations that accomplish humanizing-oriented goals rather than being moneymaking or for-profit enterprises, though sometimes they are also activists. Their typical goals have to do with social or public good, at least by their own definitions. There are many types of organizations in this sphere as well, including religious institutions, educational institutions, associations, and political organizing bodies, as well as families. Although families are part of civil society, for purposes of this discussion, we will consider only formally organized entities rather than the less formally structured relationships among families.

Many if not most NGOs are not-for-profit organizations in that they attempt to break even rather than to make profits. We might note that the status of not-for-profit does not mean that NGOs lose money or even necessarily that they do not seek profits (or at least break even). Rather, the financial bottom line is not their most important bottom line. Instead, NGOs tend to focus on ecology, health, associational, spiritual, social, and so on, which we can summarize as social capital in its broadest sense. NGOs, unlike companies, have no owner. Rather, they tend to be funded by individuals, governments, or foundations to pursue particular, typically social or common-good-related, purposes.

Lack of ownership makes NGOs' primary stakeholders different from those of private firms. NGO stakeholders include employees, clients (instead of customers), and funders, as well as those interest groups or activists in society that have a stake in the particular domain and activities of the NGO. Funders can be individuals, foundations, or government entities. In some cases, we may want to include suppliers as NGO stakeholders, although those suppliers may be other agencies that make a necessary link between clients needing services and the nonprofit organization hoping to provide the service or product.

Blurring Boundaries

Although we have described activities within each of the spheres of activity as if they were easily separable, it is clear today that some of the boundaries among these different types of enterprises are blurry at best. For example, there has been a considerable rise in the number, focus, and extent of intersector collaborations or partnerships since the early 1980s, when they first became popular. Among these are school–business partnerships and multisector partnerships that integrate all three sectors.[59] Strategic alliances of all sorts have become commonplace among and between businesses, as well as between businesses and other social institutions such as schools and job training programs.

Additionally, many companies are blurring the relationships among stakeholders through, for example, employee stock ownership plans (ESOPs). ESOPs typically offer employees stock and some degree of participation as owners in the company, thereby converting them into owner-employees. Further blurring occurs as a result of the huge proportion of retirement money invested in equity funds, which gives many employees an often unrecognized ownership stake in long-term corporate performance.

After years of accusations that sweatshops and other abusive practices existed in its supply chain factories in developing nations, footwear giant Nike began implementing extensive controls on the companies in its supply chain in the late 1990s. But the very effort to be proactive ultimately got the company in trouble with some of its stakeholders. In 1997 Nike issued a print advertisement that stated that the company paid "on average, double the minimum wage" in developing nations and that its workers were "protected from physical and sexual abuse." The ad and related statements were a partial response to accusations that had been thrown at the company by human and labor rights activists during the early and mid-1990s.

In 1980 Marc Kasky sued Nike in the California courts, accusing the company of false advertising under California's consumer protection legislation. The suit raised serious questions about whether corporations can publicly defend themselves using ads or public relations, and in the long term may raise serious questions both about the personhood of corporations and the future of triple-bottom-line (social, ecological, and economic) reporting. The case made its way to the U.S. Supreme Court, where it was dismissed on a technicality in mid-2003 and sent back to the California Supreme Court. In the meantime, the lawsuit raised a firestorm of concerns from companies supporting Nike's rights to free speech, from those concerned about giving too many powers to powerful (and nonhuman) corporations, and from activists concerned about the future of social reporting (see Exhibit 1 for some commentary). One group critical of corporate personhood, ReclaimDemocracy.org, stated, "The notion that corporations—entities unmentioned in our Constitution—should enjoy protections created for living human beings is a concept deserving burial deep in the same dark closet as the legal precedents of slavery and 'separate but equal.' "

According to Adam Kanzer and Cynthia Williams, writing in *Business Ethics Magazine*,

> The case hinges on whether Nike's statements are commercial or political speech, because the former is subject to greater regulation. Nike maintains its statements were political because they touched on matters of public concern. The California Supreme Court disagreed, reasoning that when a commercial entity states facts about its products or operations to influence consumer decisions, that is commercial speech.
>
> Even Nike concedes that social issues have financial impact—since labor controversies affected Nike's stock price and financial performance in the late 1990s. Yet Nike defines any commercial speech that also touches upon matters of public concern as "political speech," which makes it more difficult to regulate. That definition is alarmingly broad, affecting nearly every aspect of a corporation's business. After all, the financial performance of a publicly traded corporation can be considered a matter of "public concern."

Rather than live with the uncertainty of many more years of litigation, in September 2003, Nike and Kasky issued a joint press release announcing that a settlement had been reached. In the settlement, Nike made a $1.5 investment in workplace-related program investments by contributing the funds to Washington, D.C.–based Fair Labor Association (FLA) for program operations and worker development programs focused on education and economic opportunity. The expectation was that the funds would be used by FLA for three major initiatives: (1) increased training and local capacity building to improve the quality of independent monitoring in manufacturing countries, (2) worker development programs focused on education and economic opportunity, and (3) multisector collaboration to advance a

EXHIBIT 1   **Commentary about *Kasky* v. *Nike* When the U.S. Supreme Court Sent the Decision Back to California's Supreme Court**

"The decision is devastating. It has a chilling effect for corporate communications."

Reed Bolton Byrum, President and CEO of the Public Relations Society of America

"I don't believe that a company responding to public allegations that have become the focus of a major international debate should have to face . . . the possibility of severe financial penalties because some of its assertions in the course of that debate turn out to be false . . . If the ruling stands, it will almost certainly make some companies reluctant to vigorously defend themselves in the court of public opinion. That is not a good thing."

Bob Herbert, Op-Ed, *New York Times*; May 6, 2002. Originally published in the *New York Times*, August 26, 2002.

"[I]n areas of voluntary disclosure—like publishing environmental and social reports—there will still be great incentive for companies to remain silent. There's no doubt that under the California ruling, a social report would qualify as commercial speech, thus losing its Constitutional protection . . . Since most still view social reporting as something nice, rather than something necessary, it's hard to imagine they'll put themselves in legal jeopardy."

Paul Holmes, *PR Week*, August 26, 2002. Reprinted with permission.

"While Nike's critics have taken full advantage of their right to 'uninhibited, robust, and wide open' debate, the same cannot be said of Nike, the object of their ire [solely because] Nike competes not only in the marketplace of ideas, but also in the marketplace of manufactured goods."

Kasky v. Nike, Dissenting Justice Chin, Justice Baxter

"Factual errors are part of any robust back-and-forth and do not generally nullify the constitutional protection afforded to speech. That must be as true of Nike as it is of its critics."

Washington Post editorial, August 25, 2002

"The California ruling means all public utterances (including PR) by companies will be treated as if they were advertising and will therefore be bound by the far more stringent advertising laws. Companies falling foul of these may forfeit the profits from their Californian operations."

Alex Benady, *Financial Times*, August 14, 2002

"Nike's campaign was not close to any reasonable line. The purpose of its communications was not merely to sell shoes but to change minds. And the protection of efforts to change minds is the very essence of free speech. Under the California court's standard, many of the letters this page receives every day would be grist for lawsuits—not against *The Post*, but against the companies whose representatives sent the letters. That cannot be right. The Supreme Court should clarify that it isn't."

Washington Post editorial, August 25, 2002

---

common global standard to measure and report on corporate responsibility performance among companies. Nike admitted no liability in the settlement, nor did any of the court decisions ever address the accuracy of statements made by the company.

A Nike press release stated,

Jim Carter, Nike's Vice President and General Counsel, indicated that although an amicable settlement was reached in this case, the company has heard from many other corporations, media organizations and non-government organizations, who remain concerned about the impact of the California Supreme Court ruling on transparency—specifically companies who wish to report publicly on their progress in the areas of corporate responsibility. Because of the potential difficulties posed by the application of California Statute section 17200, Nike decided not to issue its corporate responsibility report externally for its fiscal year 2002 and will continue to limit its participation in public events and media engagement in California.

However, Nike will continue to advocate for corporate transparency and both parties agreed that a portion of the settlement should explore supporting a multi-sector collaboration on the further evolution of a common global reporting standard and a universally applied process for corporate accountability. The FLA will dedicate a portion of the settlement funds to this purpose that will hopefully address the consumer's desire for better information to measure company performance and public policy concerns regarding uniform standards.

DISCUSSION QUESTIONS

1. Did Nike do the right thing in settling? What are the implications of leaving the question of freedom of speech for companies open with respect to the future of social and ecological statements and reports?

2. Should companies have the right to free speech the way persons do?

3. What are the implications of allowing companies, even leading corporate citizens, the same rights as people? Why might this be a reasonable thing to do? Why might it be problematic?

Sources: Adam M. Kanzer and Cynthia A. Williams, "The Future of Social Reporting Is on the Line," *Business Ethics*, Summer 2003, www.business-ethics.com/nike_vs_kasky.htm (accessed March 12, 2004). Reprinted with permission from *Business Ethics*; P.O. Box 8439; Minneapolis, MN 55408. Phone 612-879-0695; Nike, "Nike, Inc. and Kasky Announce Settlement of *Kasky* v. *Nike* First Amendment Case," www.nike.com/nikebiz/news/pressrelease.jhtml?year=2003&month=09&letter=f (accessed September 12, 2003); William Blaue, "The Implications of the Nike and Kasky Settlement on SCR Reporting," SocialFunds.com, September 18, 2003, www.socialfunds.com/news/article/cgi/1222.html (accessed March 12, 2004); Sandy Brown, "For Corporate Speech, the Other Shoe Is Yet to Drop," *Adweek* 44, no. 2 (June 30, 2003); and "*Nike* vs. *Kasky*: Corporations Are Not Persons," *Truthout*, June 11, 2003, www.corpwatch.org/bulletins/PBD.jsp?articleid=7110 (accessed March 12, 2004).

Further, the pace of change and the link created by the electronic revolution, which permit people and organizations to be connected at all times, wherever they are, have created what authors Stan Davis and Christopher Meyer have called the blur of a connected economy.[60] Combine the blurring of boundaries with the need to build and maintain ongoing positive relationships with the many stakeholders that both comprise and connect the business enterprise today, and what you get is a need to construct business (and other) enterprises as networks rather than as traditional hierarchical organizations.

Network organizing does not mean that hierarchy disappears, for hierarchy is still necessary within many of business's functions, particularly as part of the control system. The roles of hierarchy and dominance, however, diminish in the network enterprise, as companies attempt to treat key stakeholders with respect and dignity and work in the collaborative mode more appropriate to the network form. In networks, as in biological systems, collaboration and cooperation assume greater importance than or at least as much importance as competition. Solutions in networks tend to converge toward win–win solutions rather than win–lose competition because network members recognize their interdependence with others as key to their own success.

Leading Challenges: Ecology, Competition, and Collaboration

For management thinking, the implications of the integrated perspective we have been developing in Chapters 1 and 2 are profound. Fundamentally, such a perspective means that interdependence, collaboration, cooperation, and partnership—as many companies are now discovering though their numerous alliances—are (ironically enough) at the heart of competitive success. Just as such a vision of a more collaborative approach to management changes our perspective on what it is important to foster in organizations, so does it influence our view of society.

Partnership and collaborative approaches in the midst of intense competition are necessary elements of leading corporate citizenship today. The paradox implied by the tension of opposites—competition and collaboration—operating simultaneously places many demands on leaders and their corporate citizens. New leadership skills are needed to work in a wide range of global contexts with differing ideologies and consequently differing cultures, as well as in different spheres, include the capacity to work with people different than oneself. Not only do leading corporate citizens need to understand how to operate responsibly and with integrity within the context of their own company and industry, but increasingly they need to understand how their work fits in the network of relationships that constitutes the broader system. The ability to understand where others are coming from, and to value differences, a capacity to hold multiple perspectives in one's own head simultaneously, and to understand values that go well beyond economic values, will hold leading corporate citizens in good stead as they attempt to accomplish their own work. Just what is necessary to begin these important tasks will be the subject of the next part of this book: Leading Corporate Citizens with Vision, Values, and Value Added.

Endnotes

1. William C. Frederick, *Values, Nature, and Culture in the American Corporation* (New York: Oxford University Press, 1995). Much of the discussion in this section is adapted from Frederick; however, the application to other spheres is the present author's.

2. Ibid., p. 92.

3. Ibid., p. 9.

4. Nel Noddings, *Caring: A Feminine Approach to Ethics and Moral Education* (Berkeley: University of California Press, 1984).

5. Frederick, *Values, Nature, and Culture*, pp. 201–3.

6. George C. Lodge and Ezra F. Vogel, *Ideology and National Competitiveness: An Analysis of Nine Countries* (Boston: Harvard Business School Press, 1987).

7. Ibid., pp. 2–3. Much of this discussion of ideology is based on Lodge and Vogel's book.

8. See ibid., pp. 12–23, for these definitions. This section is derived from Lodge and Vogel's work.

9. For a good illustration of this tension, see Robert N. Bellah, Richard Madsen, William M. Sullivan, Ann Swidler, and Steven M. Tipton, *Habits of the Heart: Individualism and Commitment in American Life* (New York: Harper & Row, 1985).

10. Thanks to Jerry Calton, University of Hawaii, Hilo, for suggesting the ideas in this paragraph.

11. The following discussion is based on George Cabot Lodge, *Comparative Business-Government Relations* (Englewood Cliffs, NJ: Prentice Hall, 1990).

12. Ibid., p. 4.

13. See, for example, Robert C. Solomon, "The Moral Psychology of Business: Care and Compassion in the Corporation," *Business Ethics Quarterly* 8, no. 3 (July 1998), pp. 515–33.

14. Sarah Anderson and John Cavanagh, *Top 200: The Rise of Corporate Global Power* (Washington, DC: Institute for Policy Studies, 2000). Posted at www.corpwatch.org/upload/document/top200.pdf (accessed March 12, 2004).

15. Frederick, *Values, Nature, and Culture*, p. 28.

16. Ibrahim M. Badawi and Adrian P. Fitzsimons, "Sarbanes-Oxley Act and SEC Proposals Address Corporate Responsibility," *Bank Accounting and Finance* (October 2002), pp. 30–35.

17. Charles Derber, *Corporation Nation: How Corporations Are Taking Over Our Lives and What We Can Do About It* (New York: St. Martin's Press, 1998), p. 122. Derber's ideas are used in this paragraph.

18. Cogent and articulate explanations of free-market capitalism and critiques of neoclassical assumptions can be found in a number of sources, including Derber, *Corporation Nation*; David C. Korten, *When Corporations Rule the World* (San Francisco: Berrett-Koehler, 1995), and *The Post-Corporate World: Life After Capitalism* (San Francisco: Berrett-Koehler, 1999); and Lee E. Preston and James E. Post, *Private Management and Public Policy* (New York: Prentice Hall, 1975). This section is consolidated from these texts and general understanding.

19. See Korten, *The Post-Corporate World*, pp. 37–63; and Derber, *Corporation Nation*, pp. 118–36.

20. Robert Leaver, president of New Commons, personal communication.

21. Charles Handy, "What's a Business For?" *Harvard Business Review* (December 2002), pp. 49–55.

22. Korten, *The Post-Corporate World*, pp. 51–59.

23. Preston and Post, *Private Management and Public Policy.*

24. Ibid., p. 95.

25. Ibid., p. 96.

26. One very interesting perspective on this is found in James Moore, *The Death of Competition: Leadership and Strategy in the Age of Business Ecosystems* (New York: HarperBusiness, 1996).

27. For an insightful and stimulating set of insights into the history of General Electric during Welch's tenure, see Thomas F. Boyle, *At Any Cost: Jack Welch, General Electric, and the Pursuit of Profits* (New York: Random House, 1998).

28. See, for example, Hazel Henderson, *Building a Win-Win World: Life Beyond Global Economic Warfare* (San Francisco: Berrett-Koehler, 1996); and William Greider, *One World, Ready or Not: The Manic Logic of Global Capitalism* (New York: Touchstone Books, 1998).

29. Issues of sweatshops are explored in detail in Pamela Varley, ed., *The Sweatshop Quandary: Corporate Responsibility on the Global Frontier* (Washington, DC: Investor Responsibility Research Center, 1998).

30. See, for example, James E. Post, "Meeting the Challenge of Global Corporate Citizenship," Boston College Carroll School of Management, Center for Corporate Community Relations, Series on Corporate Citizenship, 2000; see also James E. Post, "Moving from Geographic to Virtual Communities: Corporate Citizenship in a Dot.Com World," *Business and Society Review* 105, no. 1, pp. 27–46.

31. Preston and Post, *Private Management and Public Policy*, p. 56.

32. Ibid.

33. Ibid.

34. Deborah Tannen, *The Argument Culture: Stopping America's War of Words* (New York: Ballantine Books, 1999).

35. Richard Zeckhauser and Elmer Schaefer, "Public Policy and Normative Economic Theory," in *The Study of Policy Formation*, ed. Raymond A. Bauer and Kenneth J. Gergen (New York: Free Press, 1968), pp. 27–101.

36. Garrett Hardin, "The Tragedy of the Commons," *Science* 162 (1969), pp. 1243–48.

37. Mancur Olsen Jr. developed the concept of free riders in *The Logic of Collective Action* (Cambridge, MA: Harvard University Press, 1965).

38. See Severin T. Bruyn, *A Civil Economy: Transforming the Market in the Twenty-First Century* (Ann Arbor: University of Michigan Press, 2000).

39. This definition is adapted from Steven L. Wartick and John F. Mahon, "Toward a Substantive Definition of the Corporate Issue Construct: A Review and Synthesis of the Literature," *Business and Society* 33, no. 3 (December 1994), pp. 293–311. Wartick and Mahon discuss a corporate issue, while the discussion here focuses on public issues more generally and a broad range of stakeholder interests.

40. The public issue life cycle as outlined here is discussed in James E. Post, *Corporate Behavior and Social Change* (Reston, VA: Reston Publishing, 1978); and John F. Mahon and Sandra A. Waddock, "Strategic Issues Management: An Integration of Issue Life Cycle Perspectives," Business & Society 31, no. 1 (Spring 1992), pp. 19–32. See also H. A. Tombari, *Business and Society: Strategies for the Environment and Public Policy* (New York: Dryden Press, 1984), for an original discussion of the public issue life cycle used in Mahon and Waddock's article.

41. This example is used in Post, *Corporate Behavior and Social Change*.

42. Ibid., p. 23.

43. See Mahon and Waddock, "Strategic Issues Management."

44. Sandra Rahman, "The Global Stakeholder's Message, the Firm's Response, and an Interpretation of the Ensuing International Dilemma." PhD Dissertation, Nova Southeastern University, 2000.

45. Alan Wolfe, "Is Civil Society Obsolete? Revisiting Predictions of the Decline of Civil Society in *Whose Keeper?*" *Brookings Review* 15, no. 4 (Fall 1997), pp. 9–12.

46. Alan Wolfe, *Whose Keeper? Social Science and Moral Obligation* (Berkeley: University of California Press, 1989).

47. Frederick, *Values, Nature, and Culture.*

48. This paragraph is based in part on Karen Penner, "The Ties That Lead to Prosperity," *Business Week*, December 15, 1997, pp. 153–55.

49. Robert D. Putnam, *Making Democracy Work: Civic Traditions in Modern Italy* (Princeton, NJ: Princeton University Press, 1993).

50. See Robert D. Putnam, "Bowling Alone: America's Declining Social Capital," *Journal of Democracy* 6, no. 1 (January 1995), pp. 65–78, and "The Strange Disappearance of Civic America," *American Prospect* 24 (Winter 1996), http://epn.org/prospect/24/24putn.html. The discussion that follows is derived from these two articles.

51. Putnam, "Bowling Alone," p. 69.

52. Putnam, "The Strange Disappearance of Civic America."

53. Maria Poarch, "Civic Life and Work: A Qualitative Study of Changing Patterns of Sociability and Civic Engagement in Everyday Life," doctoral dissertation, Boston University, 1997.

54. Jean Bethke Elshtain, "Not a Cure-All," *Brookings Review* 15, no. 4 (Fall 1997), pp. 13–15.

55. John Cavanagh, Jerry Mander, and others from the International Forum on Globalization, *Alternatives to Economic Globalization: A Better World Is Possible* (San Francisco: Berrett-Koehler, 2002).

56. Benjamin Barber, *Jihad vs. McWorld* (New York: Times Books, Random House, 1995).

57. See Michael W. Foley and Bob Edwards, "The Paradox of Civil Society," *Journal of Democracy* 7, no. 3 (1996), pp. 38–52.

58. Cavanagh et al., *Alternatives to Economic Globalization.*

59. See, for example, Sandra A. Waddock, *Not By Schools Alone: Sharing Responsibility for America's Education Reform* (Greenwich, CT: Praeger, 1995); and Steve Waddell, "Market-Civil Society Partnership Formation: A Status Report on Activity, Strategies, and Tools," *IDR Reports* 13, no. 5 (1998); and Steve Waddell and L. David Brown, "Fostering Intersectoral Partnering: A Guide to Promoting Cooperation among Government, Business, and Civil Society Actors," *IDR Reports* 13, no. 5 (1997).

60. Stan Davis and Christopher Meyer, *Blur: The Speed of Change in the Connected Economy* (Reading, MA: Addison-Wesley, 1998).

PART TWO

Leading Corporate Citizens with Vision, Values, and Value Added

CHAPTER THREE

Personal and Organizational Vision

The organizing tendency of life is always a creative act. We reach out to others to create a new being. We reach out to grow the world into new possibilities.

Every self is visionary. It wants to create a world where it can thrive. So it is with organizations. Every organization calls itself into being as a belief that something more can be accomplished by joining with others. At the heart of every organization is a self reaching out to new possibilities.

This does not mean that all intents to organize are good or healthy . . . But every act of organizing is the expression of a self that has realized it cannot succeed alone. We organize to make our lives more purposeful. We organize always to affirm and enrich our identity.

It is strange perhaps to realize that most people have a desire to love their organizations. They love the purpose of their school, their community agency, their business. They fall in love with the identity that is trying to be expressed. They connect to the founding vision. They organize to create a different world . . .

Identity is the source of organization. Every organization is an identity in motion, moving through the world, trying to make a difference. Therefore, the most important work we can do at the beginning of an organizing effort is to engage one another in exploring our purpose. We need to explore why we have come together. How does the purpose of this effort connect with the organization? Does it connect to our individual hopes and desires? Is the purpose big enough to welcome the contributions of all of us?

Reprinted with permission of the publisher. From A Simpler Way, *copyright* © *1996 by Margaret J. Wheatley and Myron Kellner-Robers, Berrett-Koehler Publishers, Inc., San Francisco, CA. All rights reserved. www.bkconnection.com*

Vision, Values, Value Added

Successful companies achieve value added—or profitability for shareholders—by a sustained effort to develop excellent products and services that meet the needs and interests of their customers. Such companies achieve a vision underpinned by values that result in value added. This and the following two chapters will build the case for that statement. Vision, as the quote from Meg Wheatley above indicates, provides a way for stakeholders to identify with an enterpriser—and thereby creates the potential for a lasting, productive bond.

What Is Vision?

The word *vision* has connotations that provide helpful insights in understanding the links that we must make among the spheres of society. Of course, vision means to see with the eye, but it means more than that: a vision is also a power to perceive what is not actually present, a form of imagining the possibilities and potentials, of anticipating what could be. Used constructively and positively, visions provide a picture, an image that taps into the imagination and allows it to soar.

In his seminal work on the learning organization, *The Fifth Discipline*, Peter Senge defines *vision* as a picture of the future that you seek to create.[1] To the extent that a vision is a picture, it helps us to quite literally see where we want to go and make choices about how to get there.

Visions, of course, can be negative, oppressive, or autocratic, as were those of Hitler and Stalin. Thus, it is important to leading corporate citizenship that the values that support a company's vision be positive and inspiring—constructive. Values that are constructive aim toward enhancing human spirit and building a better world, in contrast to being destructive of the human spirit and the ecology that sustains us. We will discuss values underpinning successful corporate global citizenship extensively in Chapter 4, once we have a clearer understanding of the role of vision at both the individual and organizational levels.

Visions are created by visionary individuals or in organizations by managers or groups working collaboratively to achieve some higher purpose. In the past visionaries were considered to be impractical dreamers out of touch with reality. Today, however, it is well recognized that successful organizations need visionaries who can help them dream about higher purposes that inspire action, commitment, and connection, especially among critical stakeholders like employees. In this positive sense, visionaries are, first of all, those who see what is clearly and unrelentingly. They are realists, willing to grapple with the hard facts, figures, and relationships that constitute organizational life. But second, and equally important, visionaries are those who are able to imagine a possible or hoped-for future—and to represent that future to others in ways that capture their imaginations and help guide them toward the realization of the vision.

Visions Create Meaning and Foster Purpose

Visions help create meaning within corporate citizens and help others to make the connections between actions, values, and the purposes of the enterprises in which they are involved. Visions become organizationally real when they are widely held and widely shared, not when they are housed solely in one individual's mind. Visions tap people's spirit and soul, they draw out feelings and emotions; in short, visions inspire. A shared vision, one not foisted on people, draws out individuals' own personal visions and creates meaning for the group. Shared visions provide opportunities for each individual to live out a dream through productive organizational work that calls for personal commitment and engagement and allows the individual to see that she or he is really making a difference, making a contribution. As Senge comments:

> A shared vision is not an idea. It is not even an important idea such as freedom. It is, rather, a force in people's hearts, a force of impressive power. It may be inspired by an idea, but once it goes further—if it is compelling enough to acquire the support of more than one person—then it is no longer an abstraction. It is palpable. People begin to see it as if it exists. Few, if any, forces in human affairs are as powerful as shared vision.[2]

Clear visions in organizations are created by developing, implementing, and sustaining what scholars James Collins and Jerry Porras term *core ideology*, which consists of the vision or company purpose and a set of core values that sustain so-called visionary companies even through bad times.[3] And all companies face bad times. The key to having vision and values guide action or practice is to hold true to the underlying core ideology and to make sure that it is a positive and inspiring vision that helps create sustaining meaning for everyone involved with the firm. Simultaneously, companies need to make the changes that are necessary to sustain the company strategically and competitively and work on those elements of strategy that need to change as the internal and external context changes. The same dynamic holds true for individuals.

Visions are necessarily implemented through practices that operationalize core values in day-to-day initiatives that corporate citizens undertake to get the work done. Values are demonstrated in how relationships are developed with stakeholders, including employees, customers, community members, owners, and local authorities. In other words, visions are implemented through the processes, policies, and procedures—in sum, the practices—that organizations develop.

By creating visions that inspire commitment, loyalty, meaning, and a sense of community among primary stakeholders—and by implementing practices that sustain positive interaction with key stakeholders—corporate citizens can achieve high levels of performance over time. Inspiration can take place at the individual, group or unit, and organizational levels, particularly as successful organizations interact with stakeholders. This chapter will focus on what vision is, how it inspires individuals and organizations, and what its implications are for society.

Why Vision?

Clearly articulated visions serve as guides to action and decisions. Vision delineates for individuals and organizations just what actions and decisions make sense. Further, clear and constructive visions help determine what kinds of actions should *not* be taken, because those actions either are unnecessary, will deter achievement of the vision, or are inconsistent with the vision or its associated values. When they are positive and constructive, visions guide participants in a common enterprise toward the achievement of shared goals and toward productive ways of interacting. Visions are enacted through organizational norms and cultures, that is, the shared set of practices and beliefs that tell people "how things are done here," as well as what the company stands for. Visions provide, both figuratively and literally, a picture of where the company is going and how it is going to get there.

Vision inspires in multiple ways, not least of which is getting people to make a (positive) difference in the world. It is this sense of making a difference that creates meaningfulness. Vision can create aspirations; it can enhance the pursuit of a larger purpose, something outside of and bigger than oneself or one's own purposes. Constructive and positive visions can exhilarate, encourage, and connect people in their pursuit of common purpose. Visions help to create a sense of "we" rather than "us versus them" in an organization, as well as a sense of belonging to a community doing important work together. Shared visions can also foster creative risk taking and experimentation, which are necessary for innovation and entrepreneurship even within large corporations. And vision helps managers overcome the notorious short-term orientation by focusing their attention on the long-term achievement.[4] These outcomes of vision, suggested by Peter Senge, are critical if companies are to become leading corporate citizens and their managers are to be perceived as responsible and trustworthy.

Both individuals and organizations can have visions. Entrepreneurs, founders of organizations, and individuals who lead change in difficult situations are desirable leaders, particularly when they can help others visualize new ways of doing things. An organization can establish a vision that helps it gain commitment from both members and external stakeholders to move the organization toward success.

In some respects, most corporations operating today are not visionary in the sense that we have been describing, nor is their citizenship exemplary. And even among those that are visionary, vision alone is insufficient to guide corporate citizenship, especially as we have defined it in the context of developing positive stakeholder relationships. Relationships inherently require a capacity to see into another person's position and understand his or her perspective. This capacity is at the heart of building successful stakeholder relationships, and it makes significant demands on leaders of corporate citizens.

This chapter argues that, in addition to vision, mindfulness is one of the foundations of leading corporate citizenship, along with integrity, which will be the subject of Chapter 4. For corporate leaders, being mindful means thinking through the consequences of their actions, a capacity that Russell Ackoff has called wisdom.[5] Wisdom in turn demands that leaders achieve relatively high cognitive, moral, and emotional levels of development in order to be able to take the perspectives of different stakeholders into account simultaneously and think about decisions and actions systemically rather than only linearly. Thus, one emphasis is to determine what kinds of individual and organizational vision combined with other capabilities need to be developed in leaders and organizations. Ultimately, the goal is transform both individuals and business enterprises into leading corporate citizens, so they can act mindfully with respect to the impacts they necessarily have on their stakeholders.

Visionary Leaders

Some individuals can see what others cannot. They make links that others do not necessarily make. They are aware of their surroundings. They are systems thinkers who understand the relationships among different facts, events, and opportunities. They see underneath the chaos of daily life to find possibilities, potentials, and meaning—and they can articulate those possibilities in ways that make sense to others. It is the awareness of those possibilities, potentials, and meanings that inspires others to join in efforts that link people in common efforts, whether those are community efforts, businesses, or social change agendas. We all know some of these people. We call them visionary leaders.

Leadership, even visionary leadership, is not some arcane undertaking available only to the select few. Through exploration of what is important in his or her life, any person can develop awareness of self and others, awareness of impacts, and awareness of the profound values that underpin actions and decisions. Such awareness helps the person understand his or her impact on a given context, know where significant changes can be made either internally or with others, and develop personal vision that can, in turn, inspire organizational vision. Personal and organizational visions inspire work, life, and play. Visions that inspire organizations and even whole societies create an internal sense of meaning and purposefulness in the people who belong to them. Inspirational organizational visions embed responsibility, higher purpose, and significant meaning in the enterprise to provide a basis for working together on something.

Crafting a positive and inspirational vision, whether personal or organizational, therefore involves determining what is meaningful, what provides purpose, and what goals will inspire self or others to action. As Abraham Zaleznik points out in his important article "Managers and Leaders: Are They Different?" leaders "are active instead of reactive, shaping ideas instead of responding to them. Leaders adopt a personal and active attitude toward goals. The influence a leader exerts can alter moods, evoke images and expectations, and establish specific objectives that determine the direction an enterprise takes. The net result of this influence changes the way people think about what is desirable, possible, and necessary."[6]

Zaleznik, whose original article was reprinted in 1992 as a classic in the *Harvard Business Review*, points out further that modern organizations, operating in the chaos of change and ever-increasing competition, need real—visionary—leadership more than ever. "Vision," he says in his retrospective commentary, is "the hallmark of leadership, is less a derivative of spreadsheets and more a product of the mind called imagination." Zaleznik urges that business leaders learn to cope with the chaos of uncertain change, rapid technological evolution, and rapid evolution by using their imaginations. He further suggests that opportunities for vision can potentially be found in anomalies such as customer complaints, necessary process improvements, or new applications of technology as much as in smooth operations.[7]

Developing that visionary imagination and awareness—and translating it to the organization—is a critical part of leading corporate citizens as opposed to ordinary or nonmindful corporate citizens. The next sections of this chapter will focus on three domains of human development that are important for individual leaders to be able to act mindfully with respect to their decisions. We will argue that higher rather than lower levels of cognitive, moral, and emotional development are necessary among the leaders of corporate citizens today if they are to lead mindfully and operate with consciousness of the impacts of their actions on stakeholders. In fact, a stakeholder-based approach to leading corporate citizens requires leaders not only to be aware (self-aware and "other-aware") but also to imbue their organizations with a set of values and operating principles that guide actions toward mindfulness at all levels of the enterprise.

Individual Awareness and Reflection: Development in Multiple Domains

Consciousness or awareness, particularly self-consciousness, is what distinguishes human beings from other sentient beings.[8] Humans are the only beings (that we yet know of) that are truly conscious of their own existence.[9] This awareness results in a capacity to reflect. Reflection provides the significant capacity for humans to continue to learn and develop cognitively.[10] But there is more. The capacity to reflect also provides for growth and maturing processes in other domains. In organizational life, moral and emotional development is also essential for good citizenship. Such development is, in particular, a necessary condition for working effectively with stakeholders, the key ingredient of corporate citizenship.

Consciousness is intricately tied to language, as the biologists Humberto Maturana and Francisco Varela point out.[11] The close link between the development of consciousness and awareness of language suggests that human beings are inherently social creatures, creating through their interactions not only individual meaning and purposes but also communities. Communities are shaped by cultural, spiritual, and economic bonds that result from human interactions. Because humans are social creatures necessarily embedded in communities, and because "self-awareness is at the core of being human,"[12] creating shared meanings through awareness, vision, and reflection is part of the human experience and, when generatively embedded in organizations, a core of citizenship.

The communal nature of human society, which Frans de Waal has documented among our primate progenitors, gives rise not only to language and meaning, to common purpose and shared identity, but also to notions of right and wrong, that is, to ethics.[13] Organizations in the economic and other spheres are a part of this communal nature; hence, their modes of operation and the shared meanings that their purposes allow them to fulfill are inherently and fundamentally premised on ethics and values as well. Individuals in key decision-making capacities within organizations—leaders and managers—need to understand how to create purpose and shared meaning through the visions they engender. Only then can they develop organizations that embody positive visions that contribute constructively to society in ways that enhance work in the other spheres and treat the natural environment respectfully.

Creating shared purpose—creating meaning—is a primary function of leaders. Creating meaning is not limited in time or space; in a modern networked organization, meaning can be found throughout the enterprise. Meaning exists not only in the top echelons but wherever a leader works with others to create it.

Transformation: From Managers into Leaders

There is a long-standing debate about whether leaders are born or made. We believe that a capacity for leadership can be nurtured as an individual matures, particularly as his or her cognitive, moral, and emotional capacities develop. Higher development in these three critical arenas means that leaders are more aware of their impacts and can think through and develop better relationships, all skills critical to leading corporate citizenship.

Wisdom, management scholar Russell Ackoff says, "is the ability to perceive and evaluate the long-run consequences of behavior."[14] This capacity of what we shall call mindfulness is "associated with a willingness to make short-run sacrifices for long-term gains."[15] The notorious short-sightedness of corporations, not to mention the sorry state of relationships that many companies have with some of their stakeholders, suggests that mindfulness may be in woefully short supply among corporate leaders.

Certainly, mindfulness—wisdom—requires a degree of maturity and insight that not every leader finds easy to attain. Being mindful demands that individual decision makers who are acting on a company's behalf function at relatively high developmental levels, not only cognitively but also morally and emotionally. If corporate citizenship demands building relationships with stakeholders, it also demands insightful understanding of these stakeholders' perspectives—and taking that perspective requires a fairly high cognitive capacity as a starting point.

Seeing the consequences and implications of actions, one of the requisites of integrity as described above, marries cognitive with moral development, also at a relatively high level. Not only does thinking through consequences demand systemic thinking, but it also means that leaders have to be well aware of the ways that others stakeholders will perceive and understand their actions and practices. Additionally, leaders have to be willing to reflect honestly about their understanding, about their relationship with other stakeholders, and about their own roles within the company.

Developing this level of understanding and reflection means that leaders not only need the cognitive capacity to "perspective-take" but also the moral capacity to understand how their decisions affect others (which is the essence, after all, of ethics). Further, because sound relationships are key to the stakeholder-based definition of corporate citizenship, leaders also need emotional maturity sufficient to build lasting relationships with critical stakeholders. Emotional maturity means that leaders can engage in good conversations with stakeholders and take actions that respect stakeholders' interests, while still achieving their own interests.

While it might be ideal for an individual to be as mature morally and emotionally as she or he is cognitively, there is ample evidence that some individuals who achieve very high levels of one type of development may be significantly less developed in other areas. For example, a scientist who has a highly developed cognitive capacity may be emotionally immature or morally undeveloped, which can result in an inability to get along well with others or think through the ethical consequences of developing a new technology. Cognitive development appears to be a necessary (but not sufficient) precondition for other types of development, such as moral and emotional development, all of which we view as essential to leading corporate citizens today.[16]

Highly developed cognitive, moral, and emotional capacities allow people to understand issues that stakeholders raise from other stakeholders' perspectives as well as their own. The way issues are raised has to do with the way an individual or institution frames it. *Frames* are the underlying structure of beliefs and perceptions.[17] All issues, policies, and perceptions are necessarily viewed through some sort of lens or frame. Understanding this reality means that one has acquired the ability to understand others' points of view. Particularly in contentious arenas, such as those involving stakeholder relationships studded with controversial and contested issues, it is important to be able to understand where others are coming from. Having the reflective capacity to be able to understand that most of the frames that people use are tacit—that is, unarticulated rather than explicit—can help in analyzing a situation more incisively and coming to a reasonable and agreeable resolution among all parties when multiple frames are at play.

The consequences of lack of maturity in an important domain, such as cognitive, moral, or emotional, may include significant harm to an organization's relationship with key stakeholders as well as to its capacity to develop a shared sense of meaning and responsibility for its own actions. Thus, the definition of *leadership* used here relates to both vision and a capacity to take varying perspectives into account, while taking responsible action:

> Leaders are individuals who achieve personal vision, work effectively in
> organizations to create shared meaning and constructive vision/values, and are able
> to reflect on and understand the perspectives of a range of stakeholders and the
> implications of their actions and do the right things in the circumstances.

Development and Leading Corporate Citizens

Understanding the frames that others bring to a situation and developing strategies for dealing with the civil society, political, and ecological spheres that intersect with the economic requires significant cognitive development. Leading corporate citizenship also means carefully reflecting on policy and strategic decisions and their long- and short-term implications for the company, the industry, and the broader set of stakeholders who are affected. Since these decisions necessarily affect others, and hence have inherent ethical content, leading corporate citizenship also demands a high level of moral development. Finally, working with others to actually develop and implement effective policies and make good decisions necessitates high levels of emotional development. To fully understand these arenas of development requires a brief foray into developmental theory.

Developmental Theories

Research on personality, cognitive, moral, emotional, and even spiritual development suggests that individuals go through a variety of stages as they mature. Developmental theorists now believe that there are, in fact, numerous different domains of development[18] and that generally individuals move through these stages in order, progressing from the less to the more developed—and typically more encompassing—stage, without regressing. Individuals may, of course, be only partially in the next stage at any given time. Although the stages of these different types of development are associated with physical maturing that comes with the aging process, they are not invariably either concurrent or necessarily associated with any given age.

Developmental theorists believe that development has certain characteristics. Stages are considered to be invariant (at least by some researchers) in that all individuals go through them in the same progression as they mature. Howard Gardner (who researches multiple intelligences), Lawrence Kohlberg (who studied moral development), and Jean Piaget (who studied child development) have all claimed that there are three waves or stages that constitute a generic stage framework:[19] preconventional, conventional, and postconventional.[20]

Ken Wilber suggests that there are further stages of development—stages he terms post-postconventional—that are relevant to spiritual growth,[21] but the three generic stages will serve as our guiding framework below. Many developmental theorists agree on these three general stages of development, which have analogs in multiple arenas.

Preconventional reasoning generally means that a person does not yet understand society's expectations and rules but rather operates from a fear of punishment if rules are broken or when there is self-interest to do something.[22]

Conventional reasoning means "conforming to and upholding the rules and expectations and conventions of society or authority just because they are society's rules, expectations or conventions."[23]

Postconventional reasoning individuals understand and accept that society has rules but realize that there are general principles that underlie those rules and can apply those principles in different situations.[24] To the extent that these generic stages apply for many forms of development, they represent a useful framework for understanding cognitive, moral, and emotional development.

Further, many developmental theorists argue that stages are, in a sense, nested. In effect, they consider each stage a holon, a whole/part, that is subsumed within and surpassed by the next stage or holon, as we discussed in Chapter 1. With each stage comes a greater degree of capacity and depth of understanding because earlier understandings are encompassed by the greater capacity exhibited in the later stage. Many developmental theorists believe that once an individual has moved from one stage to the next, it is unlikely that he or she will regress. The new ways of understanding (i.e., a capacity to take another's point of view versus believing that there is only one's point of view) become incorporated into the new stage.

With these basic tenets of developmental theory in mind, we can begin our exploration of three specific arenas of development especially critical to the development of reflective and aware leaders able to interact responsibly with stakeholders. These are cognitive development (which is linked to social and personality development), moral development, and emotional development.

Cognitive Development in Adults

Robert Kegan and others, like William Torbert, have pursued adult developmental theory.[25] Kegan builds on the work of Piaget, by considering the frames that an individual is capable of using at any given developmental stage.[26] Kegan's work is helpful in generating understanding of the ways in which individuals develop a capacity to take the position of the "other," that is, to view things from another's (e.g., a stakeholder's) perspective. Children at the preconventional stage are cognitively capable of perceiving only their own point of view. From their perspective, there *is* only self. Actions result from fantasy (magic) or impulses. As they enter the stage of concrete reasoning, children begin to appreciate the fact that others are out there and can begin to make cause-and-effect inferences, typically based on roles in a tit-for-tat kind of reasoning, or reciprocity. Kegan shows these dispositions using simple figures that illustrate clearly the perceptual and cognitive capacity of the individual at each stage (see Figure 3.1).

FIGURE 3.1   Kegan's Developmental Stages

Source: Robert Kegan, *The Evolving Self: Problem and Process in Human Development* (Cambridge, MA: Harvard University Press, 1982).

	Subject	Object
Stage 1		
PERCEPTIONS: Fantasy	Movement	Single point/
Social Perceptions		Immediate/
Impulses	Sensation	Atomistic
Stage 2		
CONCRETE: Actuality, Cause-effect, Data	Perceptions	
Point of view: Role-concept **Simple reciprocity**	Social perceptions	
Enduring Dispositions Needs, Preferences Self-concept	Impulses	Durable category
Stage 3: Traditionalism		
ABSTRACTIONS Ideality, Inference, Generalization Hypothesis, Proposition, Ideals, Values	Concrete	
Mutuality/Interpersonalism **Role consciousness** **Mutual reciprocity**	Point of view	Cross-categorical Trans-categorical
Inner States Subjectivity, self-consciousness	Enduring dispositions Needs, Preferences	
Stage 4: Modernism	Abstractions	
ABSTRACT SYSTEMS Ideology Formulation, Authorization Relations between abstractions		
Institution **Relationship-regulating forms** **Multiple-Role Consciousness**	Mutuality Interpersonalism	
Self-Authorship Self-regulation, Self-formation Identity, Autonomy, Individuation	Inner states Subjectivity Self-consciousness	System/Complex
Stage 5: Post-Modernism	Abstract system	
DIALECTICAL Trans-ideological/post-ideological Testing formulation, Paradox Contradiction, Oppositeness	Ideology	
Inter-institutional **Relationship between forms** **Interpenetration of self and other**	Institution Relationship regulating forms Self-authorship, -regulation, -formation	Trans-System Trans-Complex
Interpenetration of selves *Inter-individuation*		

In Kegan's third stage, traditionalism, individuals can make inferences, generalizations, hypotheses, and propositions because they are able to reason abstractly. (Note that this stage is Piaget's formal operational stage.) In this stage, individuals become conscious of the roles they take and interact with expectations of reciprocity from others. They are aware of their own subjectivity and are self-conscious; they can realize that others also have these capabilities. Many adults stay in this stage for most of their adult lives.

The fourth stage Kegan calls modernism. Here individuals have the capacity to do systems thinking, and they begin to understand that there are relationships among the abstractions they make, as well as that institutions also have roles. They not only can see themselves within a number of institutions but also begin to understand that they can be self-regulating or self-forming in the application of ideas and principles.

Kegan's final stage is postmodernism, which few individuals actually reach. According to Kegan's research, the complexity of modern life increasingly requires more people to reach this stage of development if they are to cope effectively with the competing demands imposed on them. This assessment seems particularly relevant to leaders of corporate citizens, who by necessity must contend with the demands, pressures, and perspectives of many different types of stakeholders.

In the postmodern stage, individuals are capable of understanding and holding multiple systems or paradigms in their heads simultaneously. Individuals in the postmodern stage understand that systems interact, just as individuals in the traditionalism stage understand that people have different perspectives that can interact. Individuals at this stage of development are comfortable with paradox and contradiction. Further, they are probably not tied in to any particular ideology because they can understand and hold in their heads multiple ways of viewing the world at once. Thus, postmodern-stage people can grasp multiple perspectives simultaneously. They tend to view other institutions and individuals as self-regulating, self-forming, and self-authoring.

Note that if leaders are to work well with multiple stakeholders in developing their companies' corporate citizenship, they will very likely need to have achieved at least the systems capacities of modernism and, better, will have developed to the postmodernist level of understanding. As Kegan points out, it takes time (maturity that comes with age) as well as real work to develop these capacities. Not many individuals, as yet, reach the fifth stage. But that level of development is, in fact, what the modern world demands of us cognitively. Dealing with complex problems, testing assumptions, inquiring about rationales behind decisions, and engaging in dialogue with others, including stakeholders very different from corporate leaders, can be helpful ways of developing these capacities.

Advancing Cognitive Capacity in Corporate Citizens

If leading corporate citizenship is based on developing stakeholder relationships, then understanding multiple stakeholders' perspectives cognitively is a key to success. One way to advance cognitive development is through techniques that involve various forms of conversation and dialogue, that is, the type of conversation in which different parties to an argument or issue express their point of view.

Cognitive development can also potentially be advanced, as Chris Argyris argues, by having individuals explore the reasoning behind behaviors and decisions, both their own and others'. Other scholars, such as Torbert and Fisher,[27] suggest that individuals should undertake personal experiments involving new behaviors focused in inquiry, for example, seeking out the perspectives of others, in order to move from one stage of development to another. Torbert has developed a framework of what he terms "action inquiry," in which managers enter into difficult conversations or conversations where perspective taking is needed. Action inquiry can be undertaken by first framing the situation; illustrating the other person's point; advocating a position; and finally (and perhaps most important) by openly inquiring about the perspective, position, and rationale of the other person.[28]

Action inquiry, as well as the dialogue processes recommended by William Isaacs can be helpful in developing leading corporate citizenships.[29] Companies can help their leaders develop these cognitive capacities through appropriate training and development programs, not just for top managers but for individuals throughout the organization.

Moral Development

The second developmental arena critical to leading corporate citizenship is moral development. After all, corporate citizenship is about responsible practice. To operate responsibly and with integrity, corporate citizens need leaders who understand how to reason from principles rather than simply assuming that "everything goes" because "it all depends."

Lawrence Kohlberg, who studied moral reasoning in males, found that there is a clear link between the development of the capacity to reason abstractly at the level Piaget terms formal operational thinking and the capacity to think in moral terms. Moral development, in fact, depends on the development of sufficient cognitive capacity to reason in more advanced ways, that is, at least at the third stage of Kegan's framework. According to Kohlberg, an individual who is at any given stage of cognitive development cannot reason morally at a higher stage of development.[30]

Kohlberg identifies six stages of moral development, two within each of the generic developmental levels (see Table 3.1). Individuals in the preconventional level reason through what Kohlberg calls heteronomous morality at stage 1 and individualism, instrumental purpose, and exchange at stage 2 (see Table 3.2).

Stage 1 (preconventional, heteronomous) individuals focus on obedience and punishment. They reason that it is wrong to break rules because rule breakers are likely to be punished. The motivation for doing the right thing from this stage is to avoid being punished or because higher authorities say you should. The general perspective in this stage is egocentric, in that the person at this stage quite literally does not recognize that other people may have a different perspective from their own.

Stage 2 (preconventional, instrumental purpose and exchange) individuals act morally to further their own interest. Stage 2 individuals focus on individualism, instrumental purpose, and exchange, following rules because it is in their self-interest to do so. They view what is right as what is fair and emphasize agreements, deals, and exchanges as ways of determining what is fair. The

TABLE 3.1   **Stages of Cognitive/Social and Moral Development**

Stage	Social Perspective	Moral Perspective
1	Concrete individual perspective	Preconventional
2	Member of society perspective	Conventional
3	Prior-to-society perspective	Postconventional or principled

TABLE 3.2   **Kohlberg's Stages of Moral Reasoning**

Source: Adapted from Lawrence Kohlberg, "Moral Stages and Moralization: The Cognitive-Developmental Approach," in *Moral Development and Behavior: Theory, Research, and Social Issues,* ed. Thomas Lickona, Gilbert Geis, and Lawrence Kohlberg (New York: Holt, Rinehart, and Winston, 1976) pp. 34–35; and Jeanne M. Logsdon and Kristi Yuthas, "Corporate Social Performance Stakeholder Orientation and Organizational Moral Development," *Journal of Business Ethics* 16 (1997), pp. 1213–16.

Level 1: Preconventional

What Is Right	Reasons for Doing Right	Social Perspective of Stage
Stage 1: Heteronomous Morality		
Obedience and punishment. Avoid breaking rules, fear of punishment, obedience, avoid physical property/personal damage.	*Act to avoid punishment or painful consequences to oneself.* Superior power of authorities.	*Egocentric point of view.* Doesn't consider others' interests or recognize differences in points of view. Actions based in physical reality not psychological interests. Confusion of authority and own perspective.
Stage 2: Individualism, Instrumental Purpose and Exchange		
Instrumental purpose and exchange. Follow rules when in immediate interest, act in own interest and needs (others do the same). Right is fair, equal exchange, a deal, an agreement.	*Act to further one's interests.* Serve one's needs or interests in a world where you recognize that others have interests too.	*Concrete individualistic perspective.* Aware that everyone has his own interest to pursue and conflicts exist among these. Right is relative (in concrete individualistic sense).

continued

continued

Level 2: Conventional

What Is Right	Reasons for Doing Right	Social Perspective of Stage

Stage 3: Mutual Interpersonal Expectations, Relationships, and Interpersonal Conformity (Interpersonal Concordance)

Interpersonal accord, conformity to group norms. Live up to others' expectations within your role(s). Being good is important, means having good motives, showing concern for others, keeping mutual relationships like trust, loyalty, respect, and gratitude.	*Act to meet expectations of immediate peers.* Need to be a good person in your own and others' eyes. Caring for others, believe in the Golden Rule, desire to maintain rules and authority that support good behavior.	*Perspective of the individual in relationships with other individuals.* Aware of shared feelings, agreements, expectations that take primacy over individual interest. Concrete golden rule relates points of view, puts self in others shoes. No generalized systems perspective.

Stage 4: Social System and Conscience

Social accord and system maintenance. Fulfill actual duties you agree to. Laws to be upheld except when they conflict with other social duties. Right means contributing to society, the group, or institution.	*Act to meet societal expectations stated in law.* Keep the institution going as a whole; avoid breakdown. Imperative of conscience to meet defined obligations.	*Differentiates societal point of view from interpersonal agreement or motives.* Takes point of view of system that defines the roles and the rules. Considers individual in relationship to the system.

Level 3: Postconventional or Principled

What Is Right	Reasons for Doing Right	Social Perspective of Stage

Stage 5: Social Contract or Utility and Individual Rights

Social contract. Aware that people hold variety of values and opinions, most are relative to group and should usually be upheld in interest of impartiality because they are the social contract. Some nonrelative values and rights exist that should be upheld regardless of majority opinion.	*Act to achieve social consensus and tolerance on conflicting issues.* Sense of obligation to law because of social contract to make and abide by laws for the welfare of all. Contractual commitment, freely entered upon, to family, friendship, trust, work duties. Laws, duties based on rational calculation of overall utility, "greatest good for the greatest number."	*Prior-to-society perspective.* Perspective of rational individual aware of values and rights prior to social attachments and contracts. Integrates perspectives by formal mechanisms of agreement, contract, objective impartiality, and due process. Considers moral and legal points of view (sometimes conflict).

continued

concluded

Stage 6: Universal Ethical Principles

Universal ethical principles. Follows self-chosen ethical principles. Particular laws or social agreements usually valid because they rest on principles. When laws violate principles, act in accordance with the principle, which are universal: justice, equality of human rights, and respect for dignity of human beings as individual persons.	*Act consistently with self-selected moral principles.* Belief as rational person in validity of universal moral principles and sense of personal commitment to them.	*Perspective of a moral point of view from which social arrangements derive.* Any rational individual recognizes the nature of morality or fact that persons are ends in themselves and must be treated as such.

rationale for being ethical from this stage's point of view is that it will be in one's self-interest to do so, especially since there is some recognition that others also have self-interests. The reasoning in this stage is based on concrete individualism, which means that the person is aware that others have a point of view and set of interests and may therefore have a different sense of what they need.

Stage 3 (conventional, interpersonal concordance) individuals act to meet the expectations of their immediate peers and close groups. Teenagers who conform to peer-group norms and expectations are at this stage. Individuals in this stage believe that what is right is what some important reference group expects. Individuals at this stage also understand the need to develop ongoing relationships through trust, loyalty, respect, and gratitude. Stereotypes and reference to the Golden Rule (i.e., "Do unto others as you would have them do unto you") dominate this type of reasoning. The perspective is one of the individual in relationship to other individuals, with an emerging capacity to take the other's point of view.

Stage 4 (conventional, social concordance and system maintenance) individuals act to meet social expectations that are articulated in the laws and rules of society. At this stage individuals begin to understand the system as a whole. They believe in doing what is right by fulfilling the duties that society (or an institution) has imposed but can see that there are times when doing so conflicts with other duties. They recognize the importance of the system as a whole and the need for rules and obligations to keep the system healthy. They can differentiate their own point of view from that of society as a whole and can place themselves within the larger context. Most adults are at this stage of development.

Postconventional stages emphasize principled reasoning, which may well be the type of reasoning most useful in the global economy, where corporate citizens have to contend with multiple cultures and their varying moral frameworks. At lower stages of development, managers are likely to engage in what is called ethical relativism, which can get them in trouble if they happen to believe that varying cultural practices are all acceptable. A prime example is bribery, which is against the law in virtually every country in the world. Reasoning from relativism (conventional stage), a leader might suggest that the fact that bribery happens in a culture makes it acceptable. Reasoning from principles (postconventional stage), however, makes it much harder to justify paying bribes, because principles of fairness, rights, or care can be used to show the problems associated with bribery for the whole system.

Stage 5 (postconventional, social contract) individuals act to achieve social consensus and tolerance on conflicting issues with system integrity in mind. Individuals at this stage are aware that people hold numerous values and opinions relevant to their own groups. But they also begin to recognize that there may be some nonrelative values or principles, like life and liberty, which should be upheld under any circumstances. Doing right in this stage means respecting the law because the social contract exists for the benefit of all. The dominant form of ethical reasoning (see Chapter 5) in this stage is utilitarian analysis, or "the greatest good for the greatest number."

Stage 6 (postconventional, universal ethical principles) individuals act consistently with self-selected moral principles. At this stage, individuals emphasize universal ethical principles, following self-chosen guidelines. They recognize that the social contract may be valid because it generally rests on valid principles, such as justice, equality of human rights, and human dignity. Doing right here means living up to one's own principles. The moral point of view in this stage recognizes that all persons should be treated not as means to some end but as ends in themselves. (See Chapter 5 for further discussion of ethical principles.)

As with the psychosocial and cognitive development discussed in the previous section of this chapter, moral development brings with it an increasing capacity to take the perspective of others and think through decisions and their implications systemically, which we have argued is essential for developing good stakeholder relationships and ultimately leading corporate citizenship. The later stages of development, because they encompass earlier stages, represent more advanced ways of reasoning that take increasing amounts of information and complexity into consideration and allow people to think more systemically and in a longer time frame.

Relationships, Care, and Moral Development

Kohlberg's research has been criticized because it was done entirely on men. Carol Gilligan studied moral development in women (though, unfortunately for the scientific validity of her work, only in women) to see if they reasoned morally using the same principles that men at later developmental stages do.

TABLE 3.3   **Gilligan's Stages of Moral Development in an Ethic of Care**

Developmental Stage	Focus	Implications
Preconventional	Caring for self	Good is ensuring survival.
Transition stage		Caring for self is considered selfish. Perspective of other is considered.
Conventional	Self and other	Connection between self and other is developed by concept of responsibility to ensure care for the dependent and unequal. Good equals caring for others. Conform to expectations of others, self-sacrifice.
Transition stage		Illogic of inequality between self and other results in reconsideration of relationships.
Postconventional	Dynamics of relationship	New understanding of interconnectedness between other and self. Care is self-chosen principle of judgment about relationships, universal in condemning hurt and exploitation.

Gilligan found that, in contrast to men who reason (at the higher levels) from principles, women perceive themselves—and their moral obligations—as embedded within a *network* of relationships, a perception that Gilligan called an "ethic of care."[31] Interestingly, Gilligan's work also suggests that individuals move through the same generic developmental stages of preconventional, conventional, and postconventional thinking identified above (see Table 3.3).

Gilligan's stages of moral development indicate that the women she studied based their reasoning on how decisions would affect the relationships in which they were embedded. Strikingly, however (yet not always well recognized), the women studied went through developmental phases in their capacity to role-take that were similar to the phases men went through in Kohlberg's studies. During the preconventional stage, women reason from caring about self, thinking about survival; that is, they do not take the perspective of others. They begin questioning their self-emphasis when they begin to develop a capacity to role-take, or see the perspective of others, which translates into the conventional stage as caring for others regardless of concern for the self. The transition stage into postconventional reasoning is characterized by a recognition that it is illogical to care only for others without regard for self, thus precipitating a need for reconciling these competing views for the good of the system as a whole.

The postconventional stage, as with other forms of postconventional development, is one in which multiple perspectives are held simultaneously, in this case from an understanding of the interconnectedness of those embedded in the relevant relationship web. Note that Gilligan suggests that there is principled reasoning going on at this stage. Even though the set of principles tends to focus on condemnation of exploitation and hurt versus the principles of justice and rights that the men in Kohlberg's studies used, the capacity to role-take provides a basis for thinking in more universal, complex, and generalizable terms than in earlier stages.

In looking at the studies of the moral development of women and men, it is important to note that the findings represent norms but not absolutes. Such studies suggest that men *tend to* reason from principles at the higher stages of development, while women *tend to* reason from an ethic of care or relationships. But these tendencies do not mean that men never reason from care or that women never reason from principles, merely that the genders have tendencies in these directions.

Kohlberg suggests that one important means of enhancing moral development is through social interaction, the opportunity for dialogue and exchange, which helps an individual gain insight into the perspective of others. Such role-taking is essential to moral development at the higher levels.[32] Role-taking is particularly important for understanding corporate citizenship in the multiplicity of contexts and issues that stakeholders bring to managers' attention for action. But, as we shall see next, a third set of developmental capacities—based on emotional maturity—is also necessary for effective leaders of corporate citizens.

Emotional Development

Writer Daniel Goleman has highlighted the third arena of critical importance to leaders who need to work interactively with stakeholders: emotional intelligence.[33] Goleman documents that individuals mature emotionally as they age, though he does not use the same kind of developmental theory we have been discussing above. Nonetheless, emotional intelligence (or development) is essential in the process of working with others, as well as in gaining a realistic perspective on the self.

Emotional intelligence encompasses five critical skills:

1. *Knowing one's emotions*: Self-awareness, or the capacity to recognize feelings as they happen, is the cornerstone of emotional intelligence.
2. *Managing emotions*: Handling feelings appropriately builds on self-awareness.
3. *Motivating oneself*: Marshaling emotions in the service of a goal is essential to paying attention.
4. *Recognizing emotions in others*: Empathy is attunement to the subtle social signals that indicate what others need or want.
5. *Handling relationships*: Managing emotions in others is key to maintaining relationships.

Clearly, all of the skills of emotional intelligence are crucial to successful leaders and, ultimately, to the success of the enterprises they manage. We have already discussed the importance of self-awareness. Awareness is the key to developing a vision that is personally meaningful and, when tied with the other skills of emotional intelligence, can result in visionary organizations whose purpose and meaning are widely shared. When meaning is not developed and shared, people can get stuck in meaningless jobs doing work that is of no value to anyone and that makes no contribution to anything other then putting bread on the table and shelter overhead. (Of course, in some circumstances, this is enough, but for individuals and organizations operating at higher levels of development, it is probably not sufficient. Nor, as we shall see in the chapter on stakeholders, does such treatment embody the necessary respect for human dignity.)

Managing emotions successfully provides a sense of self-mastery, or what Peter Senge calls personal mastery.[34] As Senge expresses it, personal mastery involves "approaching one's life as a creative work, living life from a creative as opposed to a reactive viewpoint."[35] Individuals who can manage their own emotions are in balance and harmony with themselves and the rest of the world, able to express their feelings appropriately to the circumstances.

Motivating oneself means taking initiative when appropriate opportunities arise and working toward goals. Obviously, leaders need this capacity to energize themselves before they will be able to help energize others toward pursuit of common goals. Research in cognitive psychology suggests that optimism—setting high but achievable goals—and thinking positively (i.e., visioning) can be powerful tools of motivating, not only to oneself but also to others. A feeling of self-efficacy, or the belief that one can control events in one's own life, is another key to self-motivation.

Although one would never know it from many headlines and cover stories in the business press that glamorize the tough boss, truly successful leaders have a great capacity to empathize with others. Empathy means putting oneself in others' places and understanding what they are feeling. As we noted above, the cognitive capacity to role-take is obviously essential to developing this emotional capacity.

Corporate citizenship means developing positive relationships with the many stakeholders who influence or are influenced by a company's activities. Doing this well means developing the capacity to effectively manage interpersonal relationships. Goleman notes that there are four distinct abilities that add up to the capacity to manage relationships effectively. These competencies are organizing groups, negotiating solutions, maintaining personal connection, and conducting social analysis (Table 3.4).

If we think about what is really needed to humanize modern organizations and make then stakeholder-friendly, it is the capacity to "manage with heart," as Goleman puts it.[36] Managing with heart means taking a positive—and visionary—approach to managing. It is inspirational and aspirational and helps others to become inspired and to aspire themselves.

Developing Personal Vision

The keys to emotional health are confidence, curiosity, intentionality (wishing and having the capacity to have an impact), self-control, relatedness (ability to engage with others), communication skills, and cooperation.[37] These are capacities that very young children who are treated well have. Such attributes are also

TABLE 3.4   **Emotional Development: Competencies**

Emotional intelligence entails:

- Knowing one's emotions
- Managing emotions
- Motivating oneself (self-efficacy)
- Recognizing emotions in others (empathy)
- Handling relationships

Capabilities needed:

- Organizing groups
- Negotiating solutions
- Maintaining personal connections
- Conducting social analysis

critical in organizational life today. They can be enhanced by the development of personal vision.

Developing a personal vision—and translating it to a shared organizational vision—is one way to begin to understand what is really important in life. It is also important for building collaborative relationships with stakeholders that are based on a sense of common purpose or meaning in the enterprise. Having a sense of purpose, what is meaningful, is one of Steven Covey's seven habits of highly effective people, and also an essential element of what Senge terms personal mastery.[38] How, after all, can someone effectively lead an organization or group, or build effective relationships with stakeholders whose perspectives are very different, if she is unaware of herself and what she stands for? We will see in Chapter 4 how important self-knowledge is to the types of constructive values that underpin successful corporate citizens and generate a sense of shared meaning in an organization.

In *The Fifth Discipline Fieldbook*, the authors suggest writing a personal vision statement, one that has been seriously considered, as a good starting point for developing personal mastery, personal vision, and ultimately organizational vision. As they say in the fieldbook, "Wherever you are, start here."[39] It is with self-aware individuals who achieve personal mastery that corporations can become the visionary corporate citizens needed to lead in the economic sphere tomorrow (see Case 3.1). Only through working on developing maturity in all of the domains discussed above can individuals avoid becoming what one of my former students called "instruments of the corporation."

Visionary Corporate Citizens

Developing mutually beneficial relationships with stakeholders is underpinned by corporate vision and values in leading corporate citizens, as James Collins and Jerry Porras, in their important book *Built to Last*, clearly show.[40] Collins and Porras demonstrated that what makes companies great is a well-conceived

Who is the greenest chief executive officer in America? By some accounts, that designation goes to Ray Anderson, CEO of Interface, Inc., a manufacturer of carpets, carpet tiles, fabrics, and related interior design products based in Atlanta, Georgia. Winner of the 2001 George and Cynthia Mitchell International Prize for Sustainable Development, Anderson exemplifies that a link can be made between personal and organizational vision. Let Anderson's words about his journey from typical CEO to environmental sustainability advocate speak for themselves:

> I am an industrialist, but I changed my view of the world in the summer of 1994. After 21 years of unwittingly plundering the earth, I read Paul Hawken's book *The Ecology of Commerce* (Harper, 1993). It came for me at a propitious moment. Our customers, especially interior designers, had begun to ask, "What's Interface doing for the environment?" So I had agreed, reluctantly, to speak to a newly assembled environmental task force of Interface people to address this awkward question. Awkward, because I could not get beyond, "We obey the law; we comply."

Hawken's book revolutionized Anderson's thinking. In his own words:

> I began to understand, reading Hawken, things I never learned in college: that there is red ink everywhere—that every life support system and every living system that make up the biosphere (where we and the other creatures live), the spherical shell that is 8,000 miles in diameter . . . and only about 10 miles thick . . . that every life support system and all the living systems that together comprise the biosphere are stressed and in long-term decline, and the rate of decline is accelerating: Where is the red ink coming from?
>
> - Polluted rivers and streams from municipal, industrial, agricultural, and construction sources.
> - Polluted and over-fished oceans. PCBs accumulating in orcas. Fish stocks collapsing, coral reefs dying . . .
> - Lakes polluted, many dead from acid raid, industrial pollution, and agricultural runoff; forests, too, dead and dying from acid raid and atmospheric ozone . . .
> - Disappearing wetlands—the beginning of the food chain, that leads to us at the other end.
> - Devastated rainforests, a critical lobe of Earth's lungs; old growth forests (haven for bio-diversity) almost gone, mostly clear cut, destroying habitat for countless species.
> - Depleted and polluted aquifers . . .
> - Spreading deserts.
> - Farmlands, denuded of topsoil, increasing in salinity from irrigation, and toxified by pesticides, turning into deserts.
> - Atmosphere, polluted by countless toxins, CO_2 and other greenhouse gases building up, inexorably to create climate aberrations—global warming . . .

Anderson took the insights he gleaned from Hawken's book and built them right into the fabric of his carpet business, focusing the business not only on profits but also on ecological sustainability. His vision is to make Interface a sustainable company and ultimately convert it into a restorative company—that is, one that contributes positively to the natural environment (see Exhibit 1). In a 2003 speech to the Third National Conference on Science, Policy, and the Environment, Anderson detailed the Master Plan that eventually evolved at Interface:

- *Waste elimination*, emulating nature in our industrial processes, nature where one organism's waste is another's food. This means revolutionary redesign and reengineering of processes.
- *Benign emissions*, to do no further harm to the biosphere. This means reshaping inputs to our factories. What comes in

EXHIBIT 1   Interface, Inc.

Source: www.interfacesustainability.com/visi.html (accessed March 17, 2004).

Our Goals, Our Vision

To be the first company that, by its deeds, shows the entire industrial world what sustainability is in all its dimensions: People, process, product, place and profits—by 2020—and in doing so we will become restorative through the power of influence.

Mission Statement

Interface will become the first name in commercial and institutional interiors worldwide through its commitment to **people, process, product, place** and **profits**. We will strive to create an organization wherein all **people** are accorded unconditional respect and dignity; one that allows each person to continuously learn and develop. We will focus on **product** (which includes service) through constant emphasis on **process** quality and engineering, which we will combine with careful attention to our customers' needs so as always to deliver superior value to our customers, thereby maximizing all stakeholders' satisfaction. We will honor the **places** where we do business by endeavoring to become the first name in industrial ecology, a corporation that cherishes nature and restores the environment. Interface will lead by example and validate by results, including **profits**, leaving the world a better place than when we began, and we will be restorative through the power of our influence in the world.

---

will go out—as product, waste, or emissions.

- *Renewable energy*, energy efficiency first, then harnessing sunlight, wind, bio-mass, and hydrogen—to cut the fossil fuel umbilical cord to Earth.

- *Closed-loop materials flows*, to cut the material umbilical cord to Earth for virgin materials.

- *Resource-efficient transportation*, to achieve carbon neutrality by eliminating or offsetting greenhouse gases generated in moving people and products from Point A to Point B.

- *Sensitivity hook-up. This is the cultural shift, the mind-set shift*, to sensitize and educate everyone—customers, suppliers, employees, communities—to the plight of Earth and to inspire environmentally responsible actions.

According to an article in *Environmental Design and Construction*, although the word *zealot* might reasonably be applied to Anderson, still he "has not lost sight of the more traditional business priorities needed to manage the world's largest manufacturer

of modular carpet and office textiles. If anything, his pursuit of sustainability has increased profits and sharpened his business acumen—no small order for a man who grew a 1.3 billion dollar-a-year multinational from his life savings and borrowed money."

Pushing concepts into middle management is also important in driving concepts of ecological sustainability deep into the enterprise, according to Joey Milford, a manufacturing engineer for Interface in West Point, Georgia. The following excerpt is based on an interview with Milford:

" We started with the simple things," Milford says. "We started by putting the right trash in the right receptacles for recycling, then evolved to look at how we make our products, what we put in our products, to even taking our concerns to our suppliers and our customers." Milford uses Interface's portable creels as an example of one of many innovations that grew from the sustainability quest. Traditionally, carpet yarn would be wound onto beams—large spools that feed the carpet tufting machines but that would, because of their design, leave as much as sixty pounds of scrap yarn behind after each run. By replacing the beams with portable creels, the waste was eliminated, resulting in savings that Milford believes amount to more than one million dollars per year. Would this have occurred without the sustainability program? Perhaps not, because it was the sustainability program's call for waste reduction that inspired the new design and encouraged development of the portable creels even though the process required more labor and an investment in new equipment.

Environmental performance, like other aspects of business, has to be measured to be managed effectively. In a prominently placed display in the plant, colorful charts plot progress toward specific environmental goals, tracking such things as carpet scrap, energy use, solid waste, and recycling, with most of the measurements based on per yard of carpet produced to account for fluctuating plant production. The charts grew from ISO 14001 certification, an environmental certification from the International Standardization Organization; tellingly, and in what many would consider an unusual move, Interface sought ISO environmental certification before seeking ISO quality certification, a point that Milford presents with measured pride.

Anderson himself takes pride in another aspect of reduced waste that he categorizes as "dematerialization." The idea is simple: to the extent that a product is overbuilt, waste is incorporated into the product. Interface researchers discovered that they could reduce the amount of yarn used in carpet from twenty-eight ounces to twenty-two ounces per square yard without a change in appearance or durability. Anderson talks frequently of planning on a "cradle-to-cradle"

basis; he wants Interface products designed so that, when they become worn, they can be easily and completely reused as raw material for new products. For example, redesigned carpet backings that Interface is developing will allow easy removal of carpet yarn, so that both yarn and backing can be recycled. And Anderson's vision extends beyond his own company's practices to those of his suppliers. "You are your supply chain," he says, and with that philosophy in mind he pressures his suppliers, including giants like Dupont, to think carefully about the processes that go into creating yarn and backing.

DISCUSSION QUESTIONS

1. Is Anderson's vision for Interface realistic?

2. How does Anderson link his personal vision to that of his company? Is this the right thing to do? Why or why not?

3. Can the company be profitable while adhering to its principles of sustainability and renewability?

Sources: Ray Anderson, "A Call for Systemic Change," plenary lecture, Third National Conference on Science, Policy, and the Environment: Education for a Sustainable and Secure Future, January 31, 2003, www.efswest.org/resource_center/articles_readings/Call_for_Systemic_Change.pdf (accessed March 19, 2004); Bill Streever, "Green Carpet," *Environmental Design and Construction*, March 11, 2003, www.edcmag.com/CDA/ArticleInformation/features/BNP_Features_Item/0.14120.101726.00.html (accessed March 19, 2004), iCopyright Clearance License 3.5223.588809-64097; Interface, Inc. Web site; www.interfaceinc.com/goals/vision.html (accessed March 17, 2004); Houston Advanced Research Center, "Carpet Magnate Ray Anderson Wins $100,000 Environmental Prize," January 15, 2003, http://www.hare.edu/hare/Content/NewsEvents/ShowNews.aspx/123 (accessed March 17, 2004).

and shared vision. Vision consists of articulated core values and core purposes that guide the corporation through its many hurdles. Vision and values, which Collins and Porras call "core ideology," are combined with clear descriptions of how to achieve the vision or strategies, which these authors term envisioned future and big, hairy, audacious goals (BHAGs). Core ideology remains relatively immutable and stable over time in the visionary companies, while the strategies underpinning BHAGs change as conditions warrant.

Collins and Porras's work is particularly rigorous in identifying the factors that have resulted in dramatically successful results for their visionary companies. Visionary companies, it seems, have successfully made the link between rhetoric and reality, closing the gap between what they say they are going to do and what they actually do in day-to-day practice. In other words, they are like individuals who are cognitively, morally, and emotionally mature; are self-aware and self-reflective; and are willing to acknowledge their faults and work to improve performance.

Collins and Porras compared the visionary companies to a second group of companies about the same age and in similar industries. By most measures also highly successful, these comparison companies nonetheless dramatically underperform the visionary companies as measured by their long-term financial and stock market performance. Despite the success of the less visionary companies, many if not most companies fail to create and implement visions and may be hard-pressed to live up to their potential for financial, market, and other measures of success. Most companies have a long way to go to create alignment between vision and values and their day-to-day operating practices, particularly with respect to treating stakeholders well.

Additionally, even when companies are classified as excellent, as were those studied in the early 1980s by T. J. Peters and R. H. Waterman,[41] it is clear from the many problems those very companies faced as time went by that sustaining excellence, no easy task, requires constant managerial attention and leadership.[42] Thus, not only do gaps exist between rhetoric and reality with respect to making vision real, but even when rhetoric and reality are brought into alignment, sustaining that alignment clearly requires constant attention.

Like individuals, then, leading corporate citizens need to develop a shared vision through a capacity for self-awareness and reflection on the implications and impacts of their actions and decisions. They need to be conscious of the decisions they make—and the impacts that those decisions will have on other stakeholders. This consciousness comes about through dialogue and interaction, through sharing of assumptions and rationales, and through efforts to work collaboratively toward common goals. Such development in organizations is a constant process, but it may not be a process of stages in quite the same way as it is with individuals.

Vision and Change: Transforming Organizations

Organizations do develop, much as people do. One important aspect of organizational development is structural. Corporations tend to be shaped by four key dimensions: age, size, industry growth rate, and stage of "evolution or

FIGURE 3.2 Greiner's Five Phases of Organizational Growth

Source: Larry E. Greiner, "Evolution and Revolution as Organizations Grow," *Harvard Business Review*, July–August 1972, pp. 37–46. Reprinted, with comments from the author, as HBR Classic, May–June 1998.

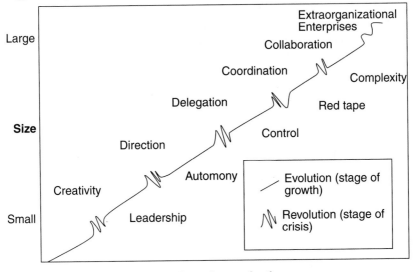

Age of organization

revolution."[43] And unlike people, organizations can and do regress from more advanced stages to less advanced stages, depending on their circumstances. Organizational structures represent one form of organizational (corporate) development. For example, downsizing, acquisitions, and other forms of restructuring can quickly change an organization's structure and associated developmental stage backward or forward, with significant implications for the company's interactions with key stakeholders.

In a classic *Harvard Business Review* article, Larry Greiner argues that organizations become increasingly institutionalized as they age and grow, and that the rapidity of their growth depends on industry dynamics. Organizations go through both evolutionary, or relatively stable, periods of development and revolutionary periods when change and turbulence are constant. With each developmental phase comes a crisis with which the organization must cope if it hopes to continue to be successful in the future (see Figure 3.2).

Greiner listed the phases of evolutionary organizational development as creativity, direction, delegation, coordination, collaboration—and we can add a new one of complexity. These relatively stable phases are punctuated by periods of crisis, a particular type of which is associated with each phase of growth. Thus, as the young and entrepreneurial organization in its creativity phase matures, it enters a crisis of leadership. Sometimes founders leave or are replaced during this crisis, because the organization requires more formalized management systems than are typically found in small creative enterprises. The crisis of leadership involves determining who will lead the organization out of its crisis.

The second evolutionary phase is one of direction. During this period the organization has typically hired a manager to establish a formalized organizational structure (frequently a functional structure) and accounting systems, budgets, reward and communication systems, and so on are generally formalized and installed. At the end of this phase, the company enters a second revolution—it is facing the crisis of autonomy. People lower in the organization feel too controlled and become ineffective because things have gotten overly centralized; they desire more autonomy.

The next evolutionary phase is one of delegation, in which the organization deals with the crisis of autonomy. Responsibility tends to be decentralized through structures such as profit centers and "divisionalization" may occur to create new incentives for innovation and entrepreneurial activities. The seeds of the crisis of control are planted in this decentralization, however, as communication within the organization falters because managers are autonomously running their own units. This creates a need for more coordination and integration across units.

Facing the need to reintegrate the organization, the next evolutionary phase the organization enters is that of coordination. In coordination, units tend to be merged into new groupings, formal communication and review procedures are established across units, and the headquarters begins to exert more control to bring things into line.

Of course, this coordinating activity generates the crisis of red tape. Hamstrung by all the bureaucratic coordinating mechanisms, the organization now begins to emphasize collaboration in its fifth stage. This stage is built around becoming more flexible through teamwork and collaborative problem-solving measures, flexible organizational arrangements, and experimentation. Greiner now posits that the crisis after this stage, which is the one in which organizations have become weblike structures, will be one of recognizing that the solution to the problem is not internal, but may be external.

Indeed, Greiner suggests that a sixth phase may now be evolving in which growth depends on the design of extraorganizational solutions (e.g., alliances, networks, and stakeholder relationships) rather than internal solutions. The crisis facing organizations at this highly developed stage is likely to be one of coping with change and complexity, something that many networked and virtual organizations face today.[44]

At each stage of structural development, companies are faced with the need to explain their actions and decisions to their stakeholders. Primary stakeholders like employees, customers, and allies are clearly affected by the organizational structure and practices that a company has generated to cope with the changes. In addition, as companies change shape by acquiring and divesting other companies (moving toward or away from centralized, decentralized, or network structures), not only can employees be retained or let go, but also communities and supplier networks are impacted. Leading corporate citizens at whatever stage of structural development need to have leaders who maintain awareness of these stakeholder impacts and relationships so that companies' reputations, which are increasingly critical to their success, are maintained positive and intact. Only by pushing the company to maintain a relatively high level of moral development, no matter what its stage of structural development, can leaders rest assured that stakeholders will be treated well.

Organizations and Moral Development

At the same time as its structure represents one type of development, a company's level of awareness or consciousness represents a wholly different domain of development, which can generally be characterized as how progressive the company is. Like structure, the level of progressiveness or consciousness about how the company's decisions impact stakeholders can quickly change (toward more *or* less progressive) in a company depending on a number of factors related to leadership, corporate culture, competitive circumstances, and internal dynamics. At the same time, it is clear that leading corporate citizens strive toward more aware cultures built on constructive values, where all stakeholders are respected and valued, where dialogue is possible, and where assumptions and actions can be questioned and, if need be, reversed.

In an interesting application of moral development theory to organizations, Jeanne Logsdon and Kristi Yuthas propose that organizations' approaches to guiding values and stakeholders relationships can be compared to (though obviously do not completely parallel) individual development.[45] Organizations, unlike people, however, can (and do) regress from more complex and advanced stage of development to less developed stages as structure, leadership and the management team, the reward system, industry dynamics, competition, performance, or internal culture changes. Stages in organization development are neither necessarily invariant (same-sequenced), nor are they necessarily always moving in a positive direction. Nonetheless, organizations do exhibit differences in moral climate that suggest that some companies are more or less progressive than others.

Logsdon and Yuthas compare the motivations and rationales for organizational actions to the moral reasoning stages of individual development, which we will suggest here are not exactly stages (as organizations need not progress through them) but rather states of being or cultural frames. Organizations in an obedience-and-punishment cultural frame, similar to the preconventional reasoning stage of individual development, act only to avoid painful consequences to the organization. Thus, organizations operating in this state will obey the law in order to avoid being punished but not really think about right or wrong from any other perspective. They are reactive toward stakeholders and largely unresponsive to stakeholder interests, other than perhaps those of owners to whom they are financially accountable. Under Al Dunlap, known popularly as Chainsaw Al, Sunbeam Corporation may well have been in this state. Dunlap aggressively restructured Sunbeam, shutting down factories and outsourcing jobs with little regard for stakeholders other than owners. Ultimately, the harshness backfired and Dunlap was fired by the board of directors when the company consistently failed to meet its financial targets. In a slightly more progressive state, instrumental purpose and exchange, companies act more proactively to further their own interests, that is, perhaps to achieve benefits from acting responsibly or at least appearing to do so.

In the conventional stages, companies are acting for reasons of interpersonal concordance. Such companies conform (as do teenagers) to the interests of their peer group, in this case to meet expectations of industry competitors, trade associations, or business community norms. In the social-accord-and-system-maintenance state, they begin to recognize the need to meet societal expectations as articulated in the law and therefore act with a compliance mentality. Most U.S. companies are likely operating from this type of cultural frame today.

Companies can also operate from a principled set of reasoning when they achieve a postconventional stage cultural frame. In this state, they focus proactively on their corporate citizenship so they can achieve social consensus and tolerance on conflicting issues. From this state, companies may act to achieve social consensus on issues that go beyond mere legal standards and constraints. Such companies recognize that some things need to be done because they are simply the right thing to do. Johnson & Johnson seems to have achieved and consistently maintained at least this stage of development, as was evidenced many years ago by its response to the Tylenol crisis. At that time the company used the values expressed in its "credo" to guide its response to poisoned capsules—and withdrew the product for a period in the interest of public safety. This values-based response allowed the company to later reintroduce the product and regain market share.

The most progressive state is when self-defined universal principles come fully into operation. Companies operating from universal principles act to identify, communicate, and apply universal moral principles in their organizational decision making, and are likely to do so in collaboration with their stakeholders, taking multiple perspectives into account.[46] It is these companies that achieve the status of visionary companies, as defined by Collins and Porras, and may be exemplified by the type of forward thinking on issues of environmental sustainability that interface is attempting to achieve. It is highly developed, progressive companies that have the possibility to begin to treat their stakeholders well through the practices they develop.

Note that Table 3.5 also highlights the posture that an organization is likely to take given its state of development. Using a preconventional cultural frame, companies are acting primarily to avoid punishment or further their own interests; they are likely to be fairly reactive in their posture toward stakeholders, acceding to demands and pressures only when necessary to avoid punishment.[47] Because their perspective is primarily one of self-interest (as with people), the best they can do is act to avoid consequences that they believe their actions might generate.

More progressive firms using conventional reasoning are more proactive with their stakeholders. Such companies would likely be active in trade and industry associations that attempt to establish and work with recognized standards; they recognize the importance of sustaining the peer group's identity and the social system more generally. From conventional reasoning, a company can go outside of itself enough to recognize that some stakeholder-related actions are needed to maintain the structure and well-being of the industry. They can thus move beyond mere reaction to proaction.

TABLE 3.5 **Organizational Cultural Frames**

Sources: Adapted from Jeanne M. Logsdon and Kristi Yuthas, "Corporate Social Performance, Stakeholder Orientation, and Organizational Moral Development," *Journal of Business Ethics* 16 (1997), pp. 1213–16; and Lee E. Preston and James E. Post, *Private Management and Public Policy* (New York: Prentice Hall, 1975).

Developmental State (Kohlberg)	Rationale and Motivation Applied	Operating Posture with Stakeholders
Preconventional		
1. Obedience and punishment	Act to avoid painful organizational consequences	Reactive
2. Instrumental purpose and exchange	Act to further one's interests	Reactive
Conventional		
3. Interpersonal accord, conformity to group norms	Act to meet expectations of peer companies, industry, or local business community norms	Proactive
4. Social accord and system maintenance	Act to comply with current laws and regulations	Proactive
Postconventional		
5. Social contract	Act to achieve social consensus on issues not fully addressed by legal standards	Interactive
6. Universal ethical principles	Act to identify, communicate, and apply universal moral principles in organizational decision-making	Interactive

From postconventional reasoning, a company's leaders recognize the need for doing the right thing inherently as a part of their position in society. They act from principles that help to build and sustain the necessary relationships that they have with stakeholders (as Gilligan's work would suggest) and they also clearly articulate the values on which their enterprise is built (see Case 3.2).

As noted, such clarity helps to guide decision-making processes and also helps a company build ways of engaging interactively in dialogue and conversation with stakeholders to determine their needs and interests, rather than assuming that they already know what the needs and interests of those stakeholders are. In this interactive mode of engagement, mutual learning and mutual change and accommodation can take place, bringing about the type of balance of interests demonstrated to be necessary among the three spheres of activity in human societies.

Leading Challenges: Development and the Vision Thing

Leading corporate citizens with vision is no easy task, particularly in a world that places such complex demands on both the company and its leaders. Yet thinking about the role of vision, individual and corporate, in creating the type

The odds are against companies in today's highly competitive, cutthroat airline industry, where price competition is rampant and fare wares are the name of the game, and where terrorist threats frequently stall operations. Southwest Airlines, however, has beaten the odds. How? The company's success has much to do with successful implementation of the original Southwest vision—and subsequent care (or, in the company's terminology, from its ticker symbol on the New York Stock Exchange, "LUV") for its core stakeholders by delivering "positively outrageous service":

> More than 30 years ago, Rollin King and Herb Kelleher got together and decided to start a different kind of airline. They began with one simple notion: If you get your passengers to their destinations when they want to get there, on time, at the lowest possible fares, and make darn sure they have a good time doing it, people will fly your airline. And you know what? They were right.
>
> Southwest Airlines has become the fourth largest major airline in America. We fly more than 64 million passengers a year to 58 great cities (59 airports) all over the Southwest and beyond. And we do it more than 2,700 times a day.

Southwest has implemented its vision—and achieved its long-term performance results (it was the only profitable airline after the September 11, 2001, terrorist attacks)—by valuing three important stakeholders: employees, passengers, and shareholders (see Exhibit 1). In the words of Colleen Barrett, president and chief operating officer of Southwest, who worked for years with founder Herb Kelleher to build the corporate culture and is credited with building the company's reputation for "LUV": "[The culture at Southwest is] fun, spirited, zesty, hard-working, and filled with love. Love is a word that isn't used too often in corporate America, but we've used it at Southwest from the beginning."

With respect to Southwest's attention to stakeholders—and particularly the concept of putting employees first—Barrett states:

> If senior leaders regularly communicate with employees, if we're truthful and factual, if we show them that we care, and we do our best to respond to their needs, they'll feel good about their work environment and they'll be better at serving the passengers. If employees pay attention to passengers, then passengers are going to like our service. If passengers think the price is right, if we deliver them on time, if their bags get there, and they get a smile and maybe even a little fun thrown in once in a while, they're going to come back. If they come back, we make money; then our shareholders are happy. You don't have to be a genius to figure all that out.

In 2004 Southwest placed in the top 10 of *Fortune* magazine's most admired corporations for the sixth year in a row. That ranking is not surprising given Southwest's performance—based on the way the company treats its primary stakeholders, commitments reflected in the company's mission and message to employees. As *Fortune* states:

> Last year the company earned $42 million—more than all the other US airlines combined. Its market capitalization of $11.7 billion is bigger than that of all its competitors combined, too. And last May, for the first time, Southwest boarded more domestic customers than any other airline, according to the Department of Transportation. Sure, the majors still have more revenue—Southwest, with about $6 billion in sales in 2003, ranks only No. 7 in that department—and they have more planes and carry more passengers when you include their overseas routes. And yes, some analysts question whether Southwest's amazing growth trajectory can continue. But, bottom line: is there any question which company is the leader of this industry?

EXHIBIT 1   The Mission of Southwest Airlines

Source: www.southwest.com/about_swa/mission.html (accessed March 23, 2004).

The mission of Southwest Airlines is dedication to the highest quality of Customer Service delivered with a sense of warmth, friendliness, individual pride, and Company Spirit.

To Our Employees

We are committed to provide our Employees a stable work environment with equal opportunity for learning and personal growth. Creativity and innovation are encouraged for improving the effectiveness of Southwest Airlines. Above all, Employees will be provided the same concern, respect, and caring attitude within the organization that they are expected to share externally with every Southwest Customer.

Southwest continues to offer its famous no-frills service—along with a little fun—to passengers: no meals (only peanuts), no fees to change tickets (all tickets are the same price), no assigned seats, no entertainment except for that provided by flight attendants. Focused on markets dominated by other airlines, the company offers very low fares and flies point to point (no hub-and-spoke system for Southwest). It remains financially conservative and struggles to keep costs in control (including pilots' salaries, which have risen as the company has grown).

The key to success for Southwest has been sticking to its low-fare strategy over the years and knowing that, in Barrett's words, "What we do is very simple, but it's not simplistic. We really do everything with passion. We scream at each other and we hug each other." As *Fortune* comments, "There's no question that the other airlines practice the screaming part. They haven't been so good at the hugging."

The challenges facing Southwest involve keeping costs under control and sustaining its unique employee-oriented culture as it continues to grow. Further, new competitors like JetBlue and AirTran have come online with much the same strategies, and the bigger competitors, not to be totally left behind, are developing subsidiaries like Delta's Song and United's Ted, which are directly targeting Southwest's passengers with low-fare strategies.

DISCUSSION QUESTIONS

1. Why does the concept "LUV" work so well at Southwest?

2. How important to Southwest's strategic success is the company's giving employees priority as primary stakeholders?

3. How should Southwest deal with the challenges now facing it?

Sources: Sharon Shinn, "Luv, Colleen," *BizEd*, March/April 2003, pp. 18–23; Andy Serve and Kate Bonamici, "The Hottest Thing in the Sky," *Fortune*, March 8, 2004, p. 86; and Southwest Web site; www.southwest.com/about_swa/mission.html (accessed March 23, 2004).

---

of world that we can all live in may be essential to building a better future. In this chapter we have looked at three types of development that leaders need to work on if they hope to create corporate visions that enhance, rather than harm, societies. By consciously choosing visions that create common and inspirational purposes that focus on building a better world, leaders can begin the long-term process of working productively and interactively with stakeholders. This interaction is necessary to building the successful stakeholder relationships required in our complex world.

And to do it well, leaders need to work on knowing themselves and their own purposes—visions—well, as well as building in learning opportunities for themselves and others in their organizations. Only by constantly working to enhance both individual and corporate awareness can we provide a necessary grounding of mindfulness and wisdom, necessary not just for corporate success but for the well-being of society and nature. Developing higher levels of awareness and mindfulness, which are keys to leading corporate citizens successfully, means taking time for *reflection* on the implications of decisions for the company's many stakeholders. It also means making time for *dialogue* with those stakeholders to ensure that their points of view are understood and incorporated into the company's plans. It is these activities that can heighten and advance development in the leaders of corporate citizens so that they will be able to avoid getting in over their heads, to use Robert Kegan's term. Such development is also needed for leaders to think systemically about their companies' actions and their own, understanding the implications of those actions on communities, employees, customers, and others who rely on and trust the company to act in good faith.

The argument made above suggests that it is better for a company to be interactively engaged with stakeholders in a dialogue than in mere compliance—that is, to be more rather than less progressive in its attitudes and posture toward stakeholders than to merely comply with the laws at the conventional stage of development or assume that it is the only actor that matters. Such interaction helps companies and stakeholders determine the best ways to meet their *mutual* needs and interests.

Progressive companies—leading corporate citizens—not only understand the visions and values on which their activities are built but also work toward the higher stages of interacting. In this way they are not only adding value for relevant stakeholders but also upholding the values that they have articulated and thereby doing the right thing with respect to all stakeholders. The link between vision and values—and the necessary link to value added—will be the topics of the next two chapters.

Endnotes

1. Peter M. Senge, *The Fifth Discipline: The Art and Practice of the Learning Organization* (New York: Doubleday, 1991). Further definitions and multiple exercises to help develop vision can be found in Peter M. Senge, Charlotte Roberts, Richard B. Ross, Bryan J. Smith, and Art Kleiner, *The Fifth Discipline Fieldbook: Strategies and Tools for Building a Learning Organization* (New York: Currency Doubleday, 1994).

2. Senge, *The Fifth Discipline*, p. 207. See also R. Edward Freeman and Daniel R. Gilbert Jr., *Corporate Strategy and the Search for Ethics* (Englewood Cliffs, NJ: Prentice Hall, 1988), for discussion of personal projects; and Sandra A. Waddock,

"Linking Community and Spirit: A Commentary and Some Propositions." *Journal of Organizational Change Management*, 1999, 12(4): 332–334.

3. See James C. Collins and Jerry I. Porras, *Built to Last: Successful Habits of Visionary Companies* (New York: HarperBusiness, 1994). See also James C. Collins and Jerry I. Porras, "Building Your Company's Vision," *Harvard Business Review*, September–October 1996, pp. 65–77.

4. These outcomes of vision are derived from Senge, *The Fifth Discipline*, pp. 207–11.

5. See Russell L. Ackoff, "On Learning and the Systems That Facilitate It," *Reflections* 1, no. 1 (1999), pp. 14–24, reprinted from the Center for Quality of Management, Cambridge, MA, 1996.

6. Reprinted from *Harvard Business Review*. From "Managers and Leaders: Are They Different?" by Abraham Zaleznik, March–April 1992, p. 4. Copyright © 1992 by the Harvard Business School Publishing Company; all rights reserved.

7. Ibid., p. 7.

8. See Ken Wilber, *Sex, Ecology, Spirituality: The Spirit of Evolution* (Boston: Shambala, 1995); Frans de Waal, *Good Natured: The Origins of Right and Wrong in Humans and Other Animals* (Cambridge, MA: Harvard University Press, 1996).

9. This said, de Waal, *Good Natured*, does present some evidence that some members of the primate group other than humans may have a degree of self-consciousness.

10. See, for example, Edward O. Wilson, *Consilience: The Unity of Knowledge* (New York: Alfred A. Knopf, 1998); and de Waal, *Good Natured*.

11. Humberto R. Maturana and Francisco J. Varela, *The Tree of Knowledge: The Biological Roots of Human Understanding*, rev. ed. (Boston: Shambala, 1998).

12. de Waal, *Good Natured*, p. 67.

13. Ibid. See also William C. Frederick, *Values, Nature, and Culture in the American Corporation* (New York: Oxford University Press, 1995).

14. See Ackoff, "On Learning," p. 14.

15. Ibid.

16. Lawrence Kohlberg, "Moral Stages and Moralization: The Cognitive-Developmental Approach," in *Moral Development and Behavior: Theory, Research, and Social Issues*, ed. Thomas Lickona, Gilbert Geis, and Lawrence Kohlberg (New York: Holt, Rinehart and Winston, 1976).

17. Frame analysis is elaborated in Donald A. Schön and Martin Rein, *Frame Reflection: Toward the Resolution of Intractable Policy Controversies* (New York: Basic Books, 1994).

18. We will focus here mainly on the three domains of cognitive (personality and social), moral, and emotional development.

19. Howard Gardner, *Frames of Mind* (New York: Basic Books, 1983) and *Creating Minds* (New York: Basic Books, 1994); Jean Piaget, *The Psychology of the Child* (New York: Wiley, 1969); Kohlberg, "Moral Stages"; Wilber, *Sex, Ecology, Spirituality*; and numerous other theorists.

20. Some people criticize developmental theories because they appear to be elitist in that the later stages are "better" than earlier stages. In the sense that later stages supersede and encompass the earlier stages in the nesting fashion described in the text, this criticism appears to be well founded. The text does not engage in a debate about developmental theory, but there is significant evidence that such nesting in fact

occurs. Each developmental stage incorporates a richer and more complex under-standing than the previous stages, with more perspectives able to be considered simultaneously. It is in that sense that there is a higher state of consciousness among human beings than animals that humans are considered to be morally superior to animals. There is, as Wilber points out in *Sex, Ecology, Spirituality*, more "depth" of understanding (or complexity) at later stages of development, while there is more "span" or breadth in lower stages.

21. Gardner, *Frames of Mind*; and Ken Wilber, *The Eye of Spirit: An Integral Vision for a World Gone Slightly Mad* (Boston: Shambala, 1998).

22. Kohlberg, "Moral Stages," p. 34.

23. Ibid., p. 33.

24. Ibid.

25. See William R. Torbert and Associates. *Action Inquiry: The Secret of Timely and Transforming Leadership* (San Francisco: Berrett: Koehder, 2004).

26. See, for example, Robert Kegan, *The Evolving Self: Problem and Process in Human Development* (Cambridge, MA: Harvard University Press, 1982), and *In Over Our Heads: The Mental Demands of Modern Life* (Cambridge, MA: Harvard University Press, 1994).

27. Torbert, *Action Inquiry*.

28. See ibid. See also William R. Torbert, *The Power of Balance: Transforming Self, Society, and Scientific Inquiry* (Newbury Park, CA: Sage, 1991).

29. William Isaacs, *Dialogue and the Art of Thinking Together* (New York: Doubleday Currency, 1999).

30. Kohlberg, "Moral Stages." Much of this section is derived from this article.

31. Carol Gilligan, *In a Different Voice: Psychological Theory and Women's Development* (Cambridge, MA: Harvard University Press, 1982).

32. Kohlberg, "Moral Stages," pp. 48–50.

33. Daniel Goleman, *Emotional Intelligence* (New York: Bantam Books, 1995). See also Daniel Goleman, *Working with Emotional Intelligence* (New York: Bantam Books, 1998). This section is drawn largely from Goleman's writings.

34. Goleman, *Emotional Intelligence*, p. 56; Senge, *The Fifth Discipline*, pp. 139 ff.

35. Senge, *The Fifth Discipline*, p. 141.

36. Goleman, *Emotional Intelligence*, chap. 10.

37. Ibid., p. 194.

38. Senge, *The Fifth Discipline*; Stephen R. Covey, *The 7 Habits of Highly Effective People* (New York: Free Press, 1990).

39. Senge, et al., *The Fifth Discipline Fieldbook*.

40. Collins and Porras, *Built to Last*.

41. T. J. Peters and R. H. Waterman, *In Search of Excellence: Lessons from America's Best Run Companies* (New York: Harper & Row, 1982).

42. For example, see James O'Toole, *Leading Change: The Argument for Values-Based Leadership* (New York: Ballantine Books, 1996).

43. See Larry E. Greiner, "Evolution and Revolution as Organizations Grow," *Harvard Business Review*, July–August 1972, pp. 37–46; reprinted, with comments from the author, as HBR Classic, May–June 1998. Greiner's model is developed in this section.

44. This latter point is the present author's.

45. Jeanne M. Logsdon and Kristi Yuthas, "Corporate Social Performance, Stakeholder Orientation, and Organizational Moral Development," *Journal of Business Ethics* 16 (1997), pp. 1213–26.

46. Much of this framework is provided in ibid.

47. The reactive, proactive, interactive framework can be found in Lee E. Preston and James E. Post, *Private Management and Public Policy* (New York: Prentice Hall, 1975). However, the application to states or cultural frames relative to moral development is the present author's.

CHAPTER FOUR

Values in Management Practice: Operating with Integrity

The social imperative is to think anew rather than retreat inward. Like it or not, this will require people to reimagine themselves as social beings on a larger stage, not helpless cogs in an awesome market system, and to glimpse the all-encompassing possibilities that the global revolution has put before them. The challenge is not to abandon old identities and deeply held values, but to enlarge them. If capitalism is now truly global, what are the global social obligations that accompany it? The wrenching economic changes will be understood in time as a great new opening in history—an invitation to social invention and human advancement—but only when people learn how to think expansively again about their own ideals . . .

A revolutionary principle is embedded in the global economic system, awaiting broader recognition: Human dignity is indivisible. Across the distances of culture and nations, across vast gulfs of wealth and poverty, even the least among us are entitled to their dignity and no justification exists for brutalizing them in the pursuit of commerce. Anyone who claims to hold human values cannot escape these new connections.

Reprinted with the permission of Simon & Schuster Adult Publishing Group, from One World, Ready or Not: The Manic Logic of Global Capitalism *by William Greider. Copyright © 1997 by William Greider. All rights reserved.*

Integrity: Honesty and Wholeness

We have all known people we admire because they have great integrity. We also know companies that we admire for their integrity as corporate citizens. Companies that are leading corporate citizens know that the key to their citizenship is operating with integrity and avoiding the ethical scandals and responsibility problems that plagued numerous companies during the early years of the new millennium. Integrity means that you know who and what you are. People and organizations of integrity know what they stand for, and their actions are consistent with that knowledge. Integrity also means sticking with your established principles and values over time. One company that ran into problems in this regard was General Mills, which in 2003 was ranked number two among *Business Ethics* magazine's "100 Best Corporate Citizens." By 2004, the company was responding to a Wells notice, which means that it was being investigated by the Securities and Exchange Commission (SEC) for problems related to its accounting and disclosure of sales. Despite its past record of good corporate citizenship, the company was being accused of overstating its earnings by some $500 million.[1] If the accusation proves accurate, something has clearly gone wrong.

Leading corporate citizens have values that are clear and compelling enough to influence their decisions and actions. Companies, especially those that are most successful over the long run, do in fact act with integrity in both good and bad times. This chapter will explore the meaning of operating with integrity, particularly in organizations but also in individual terms, in the belief that such integrity is at the core of long-term success and leading corporate citizenship.

It is important to be clear about the meanings of *integrity*. There are two primary definitions. First is soundness of moral principle or character: *honesty*. People—and organizations—have integrity when they are honest. They mean what they say, and their behavior reflects their intentions. Companies with integrity work hard to live up to the principles and values they articulate (assuming they do this at all); they are trustworthy, and they respect others.

The second meaning of integrity is *wholeness* or completeness. People and organizations, by this definition, have integrity when they are whole rather than when they are fragmented or atomized. Companies operating with this second meaning of integrity in mind recognize that they represent a system within society; they are holons, that is, both whole within themselves and also a part of something larger and more developed than themselves (see Chapter 1).[2]

As wholes, companies are complete *systems*. In a system, what happens in one arena impacts what happens in other arenas. By implication, the way that one stakeholder is treated not only affects the way that stakeholder perceives and interacts with the companies but also has ripple effects to other stakeholders within the system. As parts, or embedded elements of a larger structure, companies recognize their interdependence with society. Therefore, they recognize that what they do has numerous impacts, both expected and unexpected. Thus, they are careful in developing the practices that constitute their day-to-day activities, recognizing that whatever they do and however they treat their stakeholders will have long-term ripple effects, not only on the company but also on society.

Companies that recognize integrity as wholeness also know that they exist in the multiple domains of both individual and collectivity, and subjective and objective—and they find ways to bring these domains into all that they do. Organizations with integrity find ways to treat their stakeholders according to the principles they have established so that they too can remain successful and healthy. They engage not only the traditional bottom line but also the softer bottom lines associated with other stakeholders. Additionally, they inspire meaningful relationships that tap both the hard, or quantitative, aspects of performance and the "left-hand-side" aspects of emotion, meaning making, belonging, and commitment (see Chapter 1, Figure 1.3).[3] Leaders of such companies act mindfully, aware of the impacts their decisions have on many constituencies. They take the time to step back and reflect about their values and about the ways in which their actions reflect—or do not reflect—those values.

The definition of integrity as wholeness also speaks to the inclusion of all four of the domains that Ken Wilber has identified. That is, it is not enough for an enterprise to be successful only in the material or objective sense, or only for an individual or specific group. The subjective aspects of life—meaning making, emotional, even inspirational and spiritual—must also be satisfied if an organization is to operate with integrity, that is, as a principled whole. Integrity also speaks to the recognition of the need for the whole/partness of society, that is, the integration (integrity) of companies into the three-sphere system, with its ecological underpinning.

Values and Integrity

Values are the basis of any organization's ability to operate with integrity. Companies that wish to operate with integrity must articulate a set of positive and constructive values to guide their behavior. The best vision and mission statements embody what leadership theorist James MacGregor Burns terms *end values*, while simultaneously establishing a series of modal values to guide practice. End values describe desirable *end states*, or collective goals or explicit purposes, establishing standards for making choices among a set of alternatives. Thus, end values combine two meanings: goals and the standards by which those goals will be met.[4]

Modal values, in contrast, define modes of conduct or, in the corporate context we are describing, managerial practice. Burns describes modes as the means by which human enterprise should be conducted, although they are sometimes goals in themselves. Modal values include such things as honor, courage, civility, honesty, and fairness. Some modal values are *intrinsic*, in that they are ends in themselves (i.e., worth achieving simply because they are worth something), thus serving as both ends and means. Others are *extrinsic* or *instrumental*, in that they help us achieve a goal or end value.[5]

Operating with integrity means consistently operating with end values clearly in mind. And operating with integrity requires leaders who are highly developed cognitively, emotionally, and morally so that they can serve this transformational leadership role, inspiring others to join in the enterprise's worthy goals.[6] Achieving such end values helps all stakeholders involved in the enterprise develop their own meaning about the purposes of their work and their involvement in that work. If implemented properly, core values provide a means for identification with the broader and higher purposes articulated by the company, thus sustaining individual growth and development, as well as enhancing development of a collective spirit among stakeholders, particularly employees, who see themselves as a part of the firm.

Organizations with positive core values that guide their decision making can, in fact, succeed by operating with integrity, even when tough decisions have to be made—or perhaps especially when tough decisions have to be made. While sometimes such enterprises may suffer negative short-term consequences, say, from refusing to do business in countries where corruption is rampant, there is mounting evidence that they achieve lasting long-term success.

The downside risk, of course, of having inspiring and meaningful end values, with their associated visions, that generate commitment and loyalty from employees is the risk of creating a cult. Indeed, researchers James Collins and Jerry Porras have pointed out that the visionary companies they studied do indeed have cultlike cultures.[7] In addition, organizations with too-powerful cultures can override individuals in their effort to have everyone conform to the organization's vision. Thus, in creating the core values by which an enterprise is to be guided, it is critically important that leaders consider the implications of those values with regard to behavior. Such end values are likely to influence people's behavior within the system that constitutes the company in significant ways. Looking specifically at the kinds of values that good corporate citizenship inspires, as we will do below, will help companies avoid this problem and empower their stakeholders, while sustaining their own profitability.

Citizenship: Vision and Process

Leading corporate citizenship fundamentally involves developing a constructive, positive vision that inspires and connects people to it and the enterprise. To be fully lived, the vision needs to be thoroughly underpinned by a set of positive end values that guide policy development and implementation, as well as the ways in which stakeholders are treated every day, that is, the stakeholder relationships on which a company is built.[8] Being a good citizen is *not* about becoming a paragon of virtue, as some proponents of corporate social responsibility might argue. All companies, as human systems, get in trouble at times. For example, controversy about The Body Shop, which has pursued an overtly socially responsible strategy linked to its business purposes and yet has had problems with its franchisees and environmental practices, clearly illustrates the tension facing corporations trying to act as leading corporate citizens.

Rather than aiming to be a paragon of virtue, becoming a good organizational citizen is about honestly committing to and engaging in the ongoing *struggle* to live up to a set of core values. This struggle is both a process and an end in itself, just as modal values can be both means (processes) and ends.

The end values embedded in core ideology are typically articulated in a mission, vision, or values statement and sometimes in a code of conduct. The "living up to" is done through the development and implementation of operating policies, procedures, and programs, that is, the practices that define "the way business is done here." Implementing values through managerial, employee, and other stakeholder-related practices, such as customer relations, supplier relations, or governmental relations, is ongoing in that new developments and conflicts will inevitably arise as the external context changes, as new decisions are made internally, as new competitors arise, and as technology changes.

All of this suggests that one key to leading corporate citizenship, particularly at the global level, is finding a set of core values that are both constructive and truly meaningful within the internal and external context of the firm. Additionally, this meaningfulness must be expressed alongside and in some degree of congruence with the dominant value set of business—economizing—as discussed in Chapter 3. Corporations are in the business of doing something well for someone and making a profit as a result. Their natural and rightful tendencies toward economizing need to be balanced by constructive values that place weight on other important aspects of citizenship in society. Unfortunately, far too many corporate mission, vision, and values statements are left to molder in drawers or are hung on walls where few people ever glance. Perhaps they go unnoticed—and not lived up to—because they have been developed without significant thought as to whether the values they embody are actually alive within the corporation, through the practices and strategies that constitute the way the organization implements its business model.

A second key to leading corporate citizenship at the global level is having managers, leaders, and employees who are highly personally developed intellectually or cognitively, emotionally, and morally/spiritually. Individual development, when shared across an organization and incorporated into reward and other management systems, creates a climate or culture that allows for ongoing learning and expanding awareness. Learning involves not repeating problems because there is awareness of the impacts that actions have; understanding the interconnectedness among the organization, its stakeholders, and the natural environment; and growing the capacity to do what is necessary even in changing circumstances. Learning is essential to an organization that has any hope of succeeding in today's rapidly changing competitive environment.

Enterprise Strategy: What Do We Stand For?

Leading corporate citizens, in articulating their values and their fundamental purposes in society, clearly indicate what they stand for. In contrast to a company that buries its code of conduct, business principles, or vision statement in someone's drawer, a company whose values are alive lets all its members know what those values are, and how (and how well) they are being implemented. Such values, essential to leading corporate citizenship, become a critical part of what authors R. Edward Freeman and Dan Gilbert call "enterprise strategy," in which the organization and the individuals within it ask the fundamental question, "What do we stand for?"[9] Freeman and Gilbert suggest that the "What do we stand for?" question should be asked right alongside the fundamental strategy question, "What business are we in?"

In this questioning process, values become an integral (integrated) part of the practice of daily management. Rather than merely being added on to practices that already exist, they become an essential aspect of the practices: They *are* the system that the company develops to operationalize its vision, implement its values, and act with integrity. The enterprise strategy question focuses on the ways the company and its participating stakeholders will operate and how they will treat each other in doing business. In articulating and implementing core values through their day-to-day operating practices, particularly those that support a systemic and well-integrated management approach, companies can help create a meaningful context for stakeholders and build a values base right into strategies and operating practices.

Business success is built on constructive values that generate a sense of community and a context of meaning within the corporation. Contrary to some people's beliefs, corporations are more than profit-generating machines: To succeed, they require community, integrity, and the trust of stakeholders. To think otherwise is simply short-sighted and ignores the fact that companies exist in societies, which depend on them for jobs, tax payments, and key elements of the social structure.[10]

Freeman and Gilbert argue that one possible outcome of fully implementing enterprise strategy would be to allow people to achieve their individual purposes through pursuit of personal projects. Individuals could pursue their project, while simultaneously operating in the context of a community within a corporation, assuming that the project does not interfere with the rights and dignity of others and achieves company purposes in a meaningful way. If a company is generating an inspirational vision and corresponding set of values, then stakeholders, particularly employees, might find ways to achieve their own personal projects in the context of the company's goals.

Values That Enhance Internal Operations

Business scholars and managers alike have developed numerous management techniques likely to help organizations succeed in the turbulent global arena. Starting with the participative management theories of the 1970s, and including more recent corporate innovations—such as collaboration, strategic thinking, reengineering, total quality management, and the learning organization—corporations have adopted new approaches to managing in the hopes that at least one such approach will improve performance.[11]

Management scholar Jeanne Liedtka has proposed that many well-known management concepts have a common set of values that, if fully implemented, would constitute a progressive and constructive "ethic of practice." These common values allow companies to develop their unique and individual strategies to compete effectively, while treating internal stakeholders fairly.[12] Work by Collins and Porras on "built to last" or visionary companies supports Liedtka's argument, since it is to these companies' capacity to sustain and implement their visions and associated core values that Collins and Porras attribute their success. Remember that Collins and Porras said that visionary companies have both sustaining and relatively immutable core ideologies, comprised of vision and values, combined with the vivid descriptions that enable strategies to change as the situation warrants.[13]

Liedtka, drawing on the work of Alisdair MacIntyre,[14] defines the essential elements of a practice. A practice is (1) a cooperative human activity, (2) with intrinsic goods or outcomes related to the performance of the activity itself, (3) and a striving toward excellence both in the ends and the means, providing (4) a sense of ongoing extension and transformation of goals.[15]

We are all familiar with management fads or new approaches to improving performance that many companies have adopted in recent years.[16] Liedtka uncovers the common threads—the similarities in intent and values among these different theories that serve as fads for managers unwilling to look deeply within and make serious transformational, or systemic, changes across the whole enterprise. Using Senge's learning organization,[17] Deming's total quality management,[18] and Hammer and Champy's reengineering,[19] Liedtka finds that such approaches to improving organizational performance are best applied *systemically* as a means of transforming the entire enterprise so that the goals of economizing can be achieved fruitfully and within the constraints of ecology.[20]

When an approach is simply laid over existing management systems, elements like organizational structure, rewards, culture, and power relationships can remain essentially unchanged. Liedtka's insight is that management fads are founded on similar values that, if taken seriously, would allow for transformational change that could foster leading corporate citizenship. Any one of these approaches, applied systemically by embedding it fully into the operating practices of the firm, might dramatically enhance performance. Table 4.1 illustrates the values common to these approaches.

The first value common to the various recent management approaches is creating shared meaning. The effort to create a shared meaning, and its

TABLE 4.1 Values-Based Management Practices in Systems Approaches to Managing

Source: Adapted from Jeanne Liedtka, "Constructing an Ethic for Business Practice: Competing Effectively and Doing Good," *Business and Society* 37, no. 3 (September 1998), pp. 254–80.

Convergent Themes	Relevant Values-Based Practices
Create a shared sense of meaning, vision, and purpose that connects the personal to the organizational.	• Values community without subordinating the individual • Sees community purpose as flowing from individuals
Develop a systems perspective, a views individuals hold of themselves as embedded within a larger system.	• Seeks to serve other community members and ecosystem partners
Emphasize business processes rather than hierarchy or structure.	• Believes work itself has intrinsic value • Believes in quality of both ends and means
Localize decision making around work processes.	• Emphasizes responsibility for actions • Gives primacy to reach, with needed support
Leverage information within the system.	• Values truth telling (honesty, integrity) • Provides full access to accurate and complete information
Focus on development, at both personal and organizational levels.	• Values the individual as an end • Focuses on learning and growth, at both individual and organizational levels
Encourage dialogue.	• Allows freedom and responsibility to speak and to listen • Encourages commitment to find higher ground through exchange of diverse views
Foster the capacity to take multiple perspectives simultaneously.	• Strives to understand and work with the perspectives of others, rather than imposing own views
Create a sense of commitment and ownership.	• Emphasizes promise keeping • Instills a sense of urgency • Encourages engagement rather than detachment

accompanying vision, links the individual to the organization. Meaning and vision tap into the soft (or even spiritually significant) side of business. It is the inspiration provided by vision and related values that can make working in an organization not just a job, but a calling.[21] Meaning making focuses on people's needs to identify with an organization, to find personal meaning (or personal projects that allow individuals to develop their own work-related meanings)[22] in the larger context of doing something to make the world a better place, which arguably all individuals desire.[23] Of course, as anyone who has ever managed would indicate, the so-called soft stuff is really the hard stuff. Bringing the systemic and meaning-making elements of management into reality is among the hardest—and most important—managerial tasks.

The common value is developing a systems perspective among organizational participants, highlighting the place of the individual or group within the larger system and even within the spheres discussed in Chapter 2. This perspective helps participants see the system as a whole and develop an ability to see it from the perspective of different stakeholders. This capacity, which Mintzberg terms strategic thinking[24] and Senge terms systems thinking,[25] is a critical element of creating a stakeholder-friendly environment.

The third commonality is that these theories all emphasize processes rather than hierarchy or structure. Process approaches allow for continual learning, growth, and development, which is necessary because organizational and social change is a constant today.[26] Companies that value processes as well as products or outcomes do not tend to get stuck on issues of power and politics and can move forward when circumstances warrant without being threatened by the process of change itself. As Liedtka notes, such a system requires—and develops—a sense of commitment and ownership among members of the organization, and sometimes even engages interactively external stakeholders.

Localizing decision making around work processes allows for participants in an organization to "own" their work and its associated outcomes. Ownership creates pride in a job well done, as well as fostering organizational commitment, loyalty, and a sense of place or belonging, which is essential to fostering community and spirit.[27] Leveraging information within the system is particularly important in today's knowledge-based enterprises, where knowledge is a, if not the, critical source of competitive advantage.[28] If organizations are to change continually, if individuals are to grow within them, and if stakeholder relationships are to be developed positively, then they must share information honestly and with integrity.

Constant attention to personal and organizational development is another value common across the recent approaches to management. Only if people—and the organizations they exist in—can achieve higher levels of development will they be able to engage in the difficult struggle that implementing these values systemically entails. Only then can they continue to adapt and change as necessary in the complex environments within which they exist.

Both external and internal stakeholders continually pressure companies to perform better for a variety of reasons, in part because organizations are human systems imbued with human failings. Stakeholder dialogue helps create good conversations that can result in new solutions to intractable problems, unearth ethical issues that might otherwise go unnoticed, and create innovations that help everyone involved.[29] In general, good conversations or stakeholder engagements make room for the articulation of assumptions, the discussion of issues that might otherwise be undiscussable,[30] and help move understanding toward what Buddhists call third-way thinking, that is, new understandings that evolve in dialectical fashion from preexisting understandings of participants in the conversation. The capacity to understand multiple perspectives, another common characteristic of the systems Liedtka discusses, is essential to generating such new understandings and innovative potential.

As Liedtka notes, openness is the key to encouraging dialogue. In an open conversation, people are free to speak their minds and are also willing to challenge their own thinking. With this openness comes the potential for new ideas, innovations, and new relationships that create entirely new possibilities for the organization that would otherwise be missed. Combined with a capacity to make decisions locally, especially those decisions that affect employees' own work, openness generates, finally, a sense of ownership and commitment to the enterprise.

The combination of the themes and practices highlighted in Table 4.1 creates an internal management system with integrity in all meanings of the word. Such systemic approaches, properly implemented through values-based managerial practices, provide the basis for the articulation of enterprise strategy, that is, answering the "What do we stand for?" question. As we discuss in the next section of this chapter, the rise of global enterprise has made understanding common values across cultures an imperative for external relations as well as internal practices.

Values That Enhance Integrity[31]

To cope successfully with external stakeholders from the different spheres of influence and vastly different parts of the world, companies need to understand the values that are held in common across cultures. To be leading corporate citizens, they need to make strong efforts to actually live up to foundational values in the global arena as well as at home. Foundational values form a baseline for business activities; going below that baseline creates significant ethical problems. The concept of foundational values, or what business ethicists Thomas Donaldson and Thomas Dunfee term "hypernorms," suggests that, contrary to what some people believe, ethics are *not* all relative to one's culture or belief system.[32] In fact, Donaldson and Dunfee suggest that businesses exist in society because of a basic social contract, underlying which there are some core principles common across the world's many belief systems and cultures.

Determining what these foundational values or hypernorms are has proved a bit elusive; however, some possibilities can be derived from international documents and treaties, especially those generated by the United Nations. Hypernorms "entail principles so fundamental to human existence that they serve as a guide in evaluating lower level moral norms."[33] As demands for greater accountability and responsibility grow, corporations are increasingly being held accountable for the implementation of such agreements and foundational values.[34] Table 4.2 summarizes the links of spheres to foundational values, and Table 4.3 summarizes the values within each sphere.

Foundational values are built on the need for system integrity, trust, and mutual respect. According to Donaldson and Dunfee, three basic principles of

TABLE 4.2   Sphere System Goals and Their Implications for Foundation Values

Sources: System goals adapted from William C. Frederick, *Values, Nature, and Culture in the American Corporation* (New York: Oxford University Press, 1995). Core values of human dignity, basic rights, and community (good citizenship) adapted from Thomas Donaldson, "Values in Tension: Ethics Away from Home," *Harvard Business Review*, September–October 1996, pp. 1–12.

Sphere	System Goal	Area of Respect	Implications
Economic	Economizing	Human dignity	Respect for employees, labor standards, product/service integrity
Government	Power aggrandizing	Basic rights	Respect for system integrity, transparency and the rule of law
Civil society	Relationship	Community	Respect for local traditions, context, and basic human values
Environment	Ecologizing	Future generations	Respect for ecological sustainability that supports human civilization

respect are useful in determining foundational values: respect for core human values, including the absolute moral threshold for business activities; respect for local traditions; and respect for the belief that context matters in deciding right and wrong.[35] These guiding principles result in three core values:

- Human dignity.
- Basic rights.
- Good citizenship (working together to support and improve institutions on which the community depends).[36]

In the global community, several major treaties form the basis of a guiding set of principles articulated in 1999 by Kofi Annan, secretary-general of the United Nations (UN). These principles, known as the Global Compact, represent an agreement between the UN and businesses to live up to 10 core principles. Drawn from documents and agencies such as the UN Declaration on Human Rights and the Environment; the fundamental conventions of the International Labor Organization (ILO); and the 1992 Rio agreement, called Agenda 21, these principles cover all of the four spheres of influence discussed in Chapter 1 (economic, civil society, and ecological).

Labor standards are particularly relevant to the economic sphere. Foundational values in this domain include just and favorable working conditions, laws regarding minimum age and working conditions for child labor, nondiscrimination requirements regarding relative pay amounts and the right to equal pay for equal work, freedom from forced labor, and freedom of association (e.g., to form a union and bargain collectively).[37] Most of these can be found in the ILO's fundamental or core conventions, signed by most nations of the world.

The civil society sphere's foundation principles are mostly related to human rights and are largely based on the UN Declaration on Human Rights, first signed in 1948. These values include rights to freedom of physical movement, ownership of property, freedom from torture, a fair trial, nondiscriminatory treatment, physical security, freedom of speech and association, minimal education (at least), political participation, and subsistence.[38]

The ecological sphere is, of course, nature, whose fundamental principle of operation is that of sustainability or ecologizing: what is waste in one system is food in another.[39] The UN's Agenda 21 and Declaration on Human Rights and Environment emphasizes the following foundational values: taking a precautionary or preventive approach to environmental challenges (i.e., being cautious even when the scientific evidence does not yet fully confirm that something is problematic); responsible and ethical management of products and processes; and development and diffusion of environmentally sound technologies.[40]

TABLE 4.3 Foundation Values in the Spheres of Human Civilization and Natural Environment

Economic Sphere	Governmental Sphere	Civil Society Sphere	Ecological Sphere
• Just and favorable working conditions • Minimum age and working conditions for child labor • Nondiscrimination • Freedom from forced labor • Free association	• Participation • Decentralization • Diversity • Accountability • Transparency	• Freedom of physical movement • Ownership of property • Freedom from torture • Right to a fair trial • Nondiscriminatory treatment • Physical security • Freedom of speech and association • Right to at least a minimal education • Right to political participation • Right to subsistence	• Sustainability • Precautionary (preventive) approach to environmental challenges • Responsible and ethical management of products and processes • Development and diffusion of environmentally sound technologies

The political sphere is covered by a new tenth principle, based on global understanding of the problems of corruption and the anticorruption work of Transparency International, an organization founded in 1996 to fight corruption internationally, which now issues an annual country corruption index. It is also important to note that in 2003 the Organization for Economic Cooperation and Development (OECD) Convention on Combating Bribery of Foreign Officials in International Business Transactions was ratified by 34 signatory countries, accounting for three-fourths of global trade. Core foundational principles related to government are participation; decentralization (or what some people call subsidiarity, which means moving things to the lowest level where they can be effectively handled); diversity; accountability; and transparency.

Stakeholder Relationships as Practice: Implementing Constructive Values

Corporate global (or local) citizenship integrates the needs and interests of a range of stakeholders into the core purposes of a company and engages their commitment through the ongoing strategies and practices core to managing the enterprise. As Chapter 5 will detail, these practices can positively influence the traditional objective bottom-line indicators related to financial performance. They *also* engage the spirit and hearts of stakeholders in constructive ways that help to build a positive and proactive corporate culture and set of operating practices through which a company interacts with its numerous stakeholders. That is, they are integrative of the whole person.

Specific practice-related values (see again Table 4.1) underpin each of the themes common across the multiple managerial approaches that Liedtka discussed.[41] Further, these values support all of the definitions of integrity given earlier in this chapter. Developing shared meanings is supported by valuing community without subordinating the individual, developing community purposes from individual purposes, much as the individual projects approach articulated by Freeman and Gilbert.

Embedded within the implementation of practices associated with this theme, as well as in numerous of the others, is the type of "both/and" logic that Collins and Porras discovered in their visionary companies.[42] Good corporate citizens value *both* individuals *and* communities, *both* internally *and* externally. Similarly, individuals embedded in such systems show strong evidence of reciprocity rather than one-sided self-interest.

The focus on business processes, rather than simply products or outcomes, suggests the need for companies and their managers to pay attention to the structuring of work itself so that individuals within the firm can see the inherent or intrinsic value of their work. People in visionary companies or leading corporate citizens tend to be motivated by the nature of the work and the achievement of the core purpose itself, and only partially by extrinsic factors such as money or other rewards.

Key ethical practices associated with the common themes are respect and human dignity. These ideas can be operationalized as valuing the individual as an end rather than as a means to an end, which the philosopher Immanual Kant has proposed as a foundation for ethical behavior.[43] One should always value human beings as ends in themselves, not as mere instruments for achieving other ends. If companies take this practice and the values that underpin it seriously, then they will treat all of their human resources—that is, people who interact with them in whatever capacity—with dignity and respect. This respect extends to customers, who deserve good products that serve useful and necessary purposes. It also extends to employees, including laborers in less developed countries who, despite differences in standards, still deserve fair wages, labor rights, and adequate and safe working conditions. We will return to this aspect of stakeholder relationships later in the book when we discuss corporate relationships with different stakeholder groups.

Other aspects of the practices involved in generating integrity within firms include fostering higher levels of human and organizational development. Highly developed firms can encourage freedom and responsibility because they know that engaged stakeholders are committed to the purposes of the firm and will work toward them. They also encourage freedom of speech and association (fundamental labor rights according to the International Labor Organization)—and the responsibility to listen as well as to speak out when things go wrong (and when things go right, so that they are noted and appreciated). The capacity to take multiple perspectives, which is necessary to hold the multiple viewpoints of different stakeholders simultaneously, as noted in Chapter 3, demands a postconventional level of cognitive and possibly moral development. Companies pursuing the path of integrity foster such development among employees, managers, and other stakeholders. They are not threatened by the questioning of assumptions or the need to take full responsibility for actions. Such individual responsibility is the basis for solid long-term organizational performance.

Responsibility at all levels—the individual, the group, and the organization as a whole—is characteristic of the good corporate citizen. If companies are to expect that employees, for example, will be responsible for entrepreneurial and innovative efforts within their own domains, as many do these days, then they need to foster a supportive environment for doing so. Among the supportive elements in such an environment are devolving of responsibility to the appropriate level where action can be taken, access to complete and accurate information, consistency of word and deed (honesty or promise keeping), and serious engagement in the work of the enterprise rather than detachment. Further, and this is a critical point, the reward system must support the actual behaviors that are desired—because behaviors that are rewarded are the ones that happen!

Note that such enterprises can foster an emotional commitment, a loyalty, and sense of connection and community among stakeholders engaged with the enterprise. Thus, one implication of fully implementing the type of system that generates corporate integrity and good citizenship is that such companies are willing to acknowledge the importance of the human, or soft, investments in companies as well as the harder, more objectively measurable results.

Living Values

The combination of the enterprise strategy question, "What do we stand for?" with the articulation and implementation of values helps companies to step back from problematic situations and ask an important question. That question is not just "What can we do?"—which really asks what can feasibly be accomplished—but, more fundamentally, "What *should* we do?"

Not all situations facing companies are ethically easy to resolve. Many times managers face ethical dilemmas, that is, situations for which there is no clear or ready answer and in which any decision presents a tension or a conflict. A dilemma, by its very nature, puts the decision maker into a quandary. How can individuals and organizations operate with integrity in the face of such difficulties? Unless the decision maker—as well as the organization—has some guiding principles and values, decision making becomes even tougher. Hewlett-Packard is one company that has a clear set of values, called the HP Way, that guide its actions, even during tough and highly competitive times (see Case 4.1). Note two things about the HP Way: It articulates implicit goals and inspiration for members of the company, and it does not guarantee perfection. What it does do is provide important guidance for decisions and help the company get back on track when mistakes are made, as they inevitably will be, or when, as the next section discusses, decision makers face dilemmas.

Negotiating Dilemmas

When a dilemma arises, something more is needed than a vision or values statement. There is nothing quite as difficult to cope with as an ethical dilemma. By definition, a dilemma requires making a choice among sometimes equally undesirable alternatives, including those that have negative consequences for one or more stakeholders. Sometimes, despite the presence of clear vision and values, companies must make difficult choices. How do managers work through dilemmas and still feel good about their decisions?

One way to solve a dilemma is to reframe it so that it is not an either/or proposition with negative consequences. Managers should strive to see whether, using "third-way thinking," they can formulate a win–win proposition. Sometimes win–win propositions can be developed by moving the thinking at least one level of analysis higher than where the problem seems to reside. Other times, the difficult decision actually has to be made despite the dilemma.

For just such situations business ethicists Gerald F. Cavanagh, Manuel Valasquez, and Dennis Moberg have provided a helpful framework based on four major philosophical traditions in ethics.[44] This framework lays out four sets of values and a decision-making framework that together help guide the decision maker through the difficult situation toward the best possible answer, even when it is clear that no answer is perfect.

When one is confronted with an ethical dilemma, as Cavanagh and colleagues note, it is not enough to use only one type of reasoning. Although complexity remains, the best decision can be made by using all four of the following bases

Computer giant Hewlett-Packard (HP) has long been known for its corporate culture and particularly for the set of values that guide its operations, the HP Way (see Exhibit 1). Cited as an excellent company by Thomas Peters and Robert Waterman, in their 1982 book *In Search of Excellence*, HP also found its way into James Collins and Jerry Porras's 1995 *Built to Last* category of visionary companies. The HP Way plays no small role in the company's consistency of performance over the years and has guided the company's corporate citizenship since 1939, when the company's cofounders Bill Hewlett and David Packard gave some of their first-year profits to philanthropic organizations, all the way through a major merger with Compaq in 2002. One of the first U.S. signatories to the UN Global Compact, HP signals a broad commitment to leading corporate citizenship on its Web site:

CSR [corporate social responsibility], in our opinion, starts with a company's own employees and expands outward to business partners and suppliers. Our company is guided by a core set of ethics that drives progressive work-life programs, competitive pay and other programs internally and good citizenship externally. We expect all of HP's business partners, including our suppliers, to comply with all applicable laws and regulations as well as basic international principles relating to labor standards, occupational health and safety requirements and environmental protection. We are working with our top suppliers to establish a common set of expectations for improvement in their products, practices and programs.

Besides giving preference to suppliers that are proactively addressing their environmental impacts, we are dedicated to investigating questionable practices and taking corrective actions when necessary and appropriate. In the future, we expect suppliers to have policies on health and safety, labor and human rights, to establish common expectations, including continual improvement and innovation in their products, practices and programs.

Source: http://www.hp.com/hpinfo/globalcitizenship/csr/commitment.html (accessed 3/1/04).

Despite some rocky recent times, HP continues to work productively with a variety of stakeholders, including its communities, having contributed more than $1 billion in cash and equipment to schools, universities, community organizations, and other nonprofit organizations globally over a 20-year period. HP's most innovative program, called e-Inclusion, has direct potential business benefits as well as benefits to people affected by the digital divide—the growing technological gap between rich and poor people and nations. The vision of e-Inclusion is "of the future where technology is accessible to everyone in the world as a means to learn, work and benefit from information." E-Inclusion aims to close the digital divide between what HP calls the "technologically-empowered and the technologically-excluded" by creating inclusion communities (i-communities), digital villages in places as far flung as Ghana, South Africa, and Ireland. By collaborating with local institutions, HP creates core and satellite computing centers in villages, providing printers, cables, and support to generate local Internet access. The ultimate goal is to create whole communities that have wide Internet access with supporting technology.

Digital village programs and i-communities, as HP calls them, are already under way in places as far apart as East Palo Alto, California; Kumasi, Ghana; Dikhtole, South Africa; and Paris, France. The company committed $5 million to the program for a three-year period to support the digital villages, as well as to support other i-communities in places like Andra Pradesh, India; Mogalakwena

EXHIBIT 1   Organizational Values: The HP Way

Source: www.hp.com/hpinfo/globalcitizenship/gcreport/businessprac.html (accessed February 27, 2004).

A company cannot claim to be a good global citizen without running its daily business responsibly. This involves a commitment to corporate governance and business ethics, and putting that commitment into practice.

HP's core values have shaped our history and will continue to define our future. Following the merger with Compaq in 2002, we communicated these values throughout the new company. Our core values are:

- We are passionate about customers
- We have trust and respect for individuals
- We perform at a high level of achievement and contribution
- We achieve our results through teamwork
- We act with speed and agility
- We deliver meaningful innovation

We conduct our business with uncompromising integrity

Municipality of Limpopo Province, South Africa; and Houston, Texas.

One example of e-inclusion can be found close to home in San Diego's neighboring Native American reservations, which have long had problems with long-distance communications, even by telephone. By creating a tribal digital village—a wireless network among the 18 tribes that live on the reservations—HP and other local institutions hope to bring new economic and cultural development to the area. Because HP insists that community members collaborate with the company, the ways in which the e-inclusion programs are actually implemented are based on the community's own definition of its needs and interests, rather than imposed by HP.

Another i-community is being created in Mogalakwena Municipality in Limpopo Province, South Africa, a 6,000-square-kilometer area with 117 villages, where some 360,000 people live. Despite rich agricultural reserves and mineral resources, this area faces enormous challenges as it attempts to build its economy, with 65 percent of the population below the "bread line," and 30 percent of villages lacking access to basic services (including clean water, electricity, and health care). With a goal of being a

catalyst in creating economic sustainability, the i-community project brings HP's professionals together with local companies, governmental officials, and community leaders to link the 117 towns, villages, organizations, and citizens in an electronic communications network. This project began with community engagement, with HP sharing its vision with local stakeholders, and moved on toward development of local infrastructure to meet two key challenges—the provision of high-speed communication from headquarters to two satellite centers, and public access to the Internet. In the opening ceremonies in 2002, HP's CEO, Carly Fiorina, clearly expressed HP's long-term commitment to the project and emphasized the goal was long-term sustainable development, not altruism, with the ultimate goal of a global rollout.

Despite the orientation toward global replicability of the e-inclusion projects, as reported in HP's online magazine, *Cooltown*, "Each Digital Village has a separate set of needs, separate challenges, and requires a separate and customized solution. The flexibility to create these solutions—with the help of the community and with the ongoing support of Hewlett-Packard through the designation of an HP representative who remains closely involved with the community for the duration of the project—is what the Digital Village program offers the reservationists in Southern California." The hope is that eventually this connectivity will provide better access to health care, government services, and other services, helping communities in remote areas of developing nations enter the modern era.

DISCUSSION QUESTIONS

1. Is the e-inclusion program a smart move for Hewlett-Packard strategically? Why or why not?

2. What potential do i-community and e-inclusion initiatives have to bridge the digital divide?

3. Should a company like HP get involved in changing society in these ways? What are the implications of doing so? Of not doing so?

Sources: HP philanthropy and education, www.hp.com/e-inclusion/en/project/baltimore/ philanthropybackgrounderl.pdf, HP core values, www.hp.com/hpinfo/globalcitizenship/csr/ commitment.html, and HP e-inclusion, www.hp.com/e-inclusion/en (accessed February 27, 2004); International Conference Volunteers, "Bridging the Divide: Where Do We Start?" www.icvolunteers.org/en/projects/2002/2002_19_ wsim_08.01.cfm (accessed February 27, 2004) and Amy Cohen, "Blazing a Trail Across the Digital Divide," *Impulse: A Cooltown Magazine*, February 27, 2004, http://cooltown.hp.com/mpulse/ 1001-digitalvillage.asp (accessed March 1, 2004).

for ethical decision making: the norm of rights and duties, the norm of justice, the norm of utilitarianism (or the greatest good for the greatest number), and the norm of caring (see Figure 4.1).

Rights and Duties

Rights are important, normative, justifiable claims or entitlements. A right, as we saw earlier, is one of the bases of becoming a stakeholder. Rights derive out of the basic premise that each person is a unique individual deserving of human dignity. According to Cavanagh, moral rights have the following characteristics: Individuals using them can pursue their own interests, and rights impose duties, obligations, requirements or prohibitions on others. Legal rights are those written into specific laws, judicial decisions, or a constitution.[45]

In the United States, for example, the Bill of Rights (the first 10 amendments to the Constitution) spells out what are considered to be the essential rights of a U.S. citizen, including freedom of speech and freedom of religion. In the international arena, the International Labor Organization has spelled out rights and principles for individuals at work that include freedom of association (i.e., freedom to practice collective bargaining), freedom from forced labor, the abolition of child labor, and freedom from discrimination in labor. Most nations of the world have agreed to uphold these rights.

If we think of rights as one side of a coin, then we know that there is another side: duties or obligations. All rights come with a set of corresponding duties that need to be upheld if the right itself is to be sustained and societies are to be kept healthy. Individual freedoms unfettered by obligations would allow one person living out his or her rights to trample on the rights of others. Examples of duties are a responsibility to tell the truth and a duty to respect the privacy of others.

FIGURE 4.1 **Flow Diagram of Ethical Decision Making**

Source: Gerald F. Cavanagh, *American Business Values with International Perspectives*, 4th ed. (Upper Saddle River, NJ: Prentice Hall, 1998). Used with permission.

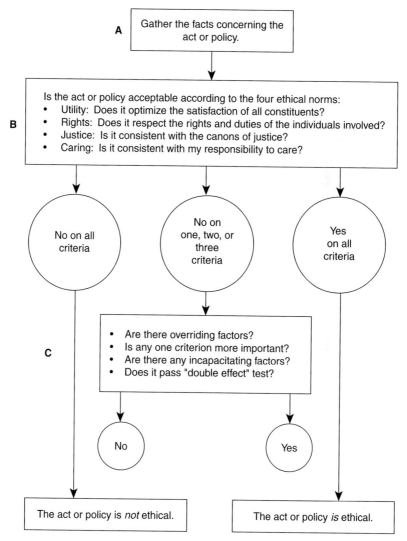

Some rights and duties are written into the law or other codes, while others are fundamental moral rights that enable communities and organizations to be viable over time. On the one hand, a problem with the rights perspective is that too much emphasis on rights can result in selfish and overly individualistic behavior. On the other hand, attention to rights assures respect for individual freedom and property.

In using the framework in Figure 4.1, one question to ask, then, is "Does this act respect the rights and duties of the individuals involved?"

Justice

In addition to considering whether rights are abrogated or supported in making a decision, the decision maker also has to consider the implications of the decision for justice. Justice, according to Cavanagh and his colleagues, requires that people be guided by fairness, equity, and impartiality, emphasizing in particular a fair distribution of societal benefits and burdens, fairness in the administration of laws and regulations, and fairness in sanctioning wrongdoing or compensating for wrongs suffered.[46]

Standards of justice, for example, prohibit discrimination and enormous inequalities in the distribution of goods and services within a society. In doing this, justice speaks to the issue of what philosopher John Rawls calls "distributive justice," which has as its fundamental principle that "equals should be treated equally and that unequals should be treated in accord with their inequality."[47] Rawls also suggests that societies and the distribution of goods and services within them should be constructed using a "veil of ignorance." That is, when we are responsible for a decision that will affect a system, we should make that decision as if we did not know where in the system we would end up. By doing this, we will make a decision that is fairest to all and allows us to overcome our own biases.

Philosopher Immanual Kant's "categorical imperative" gives us one way to identify the constraints on justice. One formulation of the categorical imperative is: I ought never to act except in such a way that I can also will that my principle should become a universal law. The second formulation of the categorical imperative states: An action is morally right for a person in a certain situation if and only if the person's reason for carrying out the action is a reason that he or she would be willing to have every person act on, in any similar situation.[48]

In using the analytical framework in Figure 4.1 for ethical decision making, Cavanagh and his colleagues suggest we need to think about justice as well as rights: Is this decision consistent with the canons of justice? Would I make the same decision if I could end up anywhere in the system after its impact has been felt?

Utilitarianism

The third basis for making ethical decisions is called utilitarianism, which is generally expressed as "the greatest good for the greatest number." Utilitarianism, which is the reasoning used in systems of cost–benefit analysis, is the most common kind of managerial reasoning. It does not necessarily mean that majority rules but rather that the harms and benefits of an action need to be considered from all perspectives. Some kind of calculation as to the degree of both harm and benefit is needed in decision making. As noted above, however, utilitarian outcomes need to be considered along with both justice and rights.

The concept of the greatest good for the greatest number, while difficult to operationalize quantitatively, proposes that the best action is the one that results in the best overall good, that is, for the most people affected by that decision. Thus, when weighing a decision that has both positive consequences for some groups and negative ones for others, it is important to consider where the most good is to be accomplished as well as where the most harm will be done. Decision makers need to weigh such considerations as how many people will be affected either positively or negatively, and the extent of the good or the harm done to each group (assuming these can be known in advance and quantified, which are two of the problems with utilitarian analysis). For example, a decision that would kill one person should never be made simply because, say, a large group will benefit financially.

Further, as Cavanagh points out, utilitarian norms emphasize the good of the group—the common good or the collectivity—over and above the good of any given individual, particularly the decision maker. Such a norm avoids the problems of self-interest that might otherwise arise in utilitarian analysis.[49] And, to enhance utilitarian analysis, it is necessary to incorporate consideration of rights, justice, and caring.

Caring

As noted in Chapter 3, some research suggests that women's moral development may proceed somewhat differently than men's and that women (as well as many men) may use a different basis for making ethical judgments than the principles of rights, justice, or utility. Women are, according to Carol Gilligan and Mary Field Belenky and colleagues, among others, focused more explicitly on what has been termed an ethic of care.[50] In business situations, as well as in life situations according to this ethic, emphasis on principles can be balanced effectively by consideration of how the decision will affect people and the relationships among people.

The ethic of care proposes that we exist within a network of relationships that are affected by the implications of ethical decisions. In making decisions according to an ethic of care, we take into account the effects on those relationships and the people who are in the network. As Cavanagh points out, the definition of *care* is left somewhat vague in feminist ethicists' writings, but it can be delineated by noting that the obligation to care varies according to the closeness of the relationship and the particular roles embedded in the relationship. That is, a mother has a clear and strong obligation to care for her child, whereas she has less of an obligation to care for an acquaintance. The obligation to care also exists only in accordance with one's capacity to give it.

It is interesting to note that an ethic of care seems to be more common in countries that have a more collectivist—or communitarian—orientation than do individualistic countries like the United States. Thus, in business situations in Japan and Korea, for example, this ethic seems to be at the basis for extended networks of companies, known as Keiretsu in Japan and Chaebol in Korea, that share mutual obligations to help and support each other before doing business with "outsiders." Indeed, in some Asian countries, the concepts of rights, justice, and utilitarianism as the basis of ethical thinking might seem strange indeed; the far more important consideration would be the impact of any given decision on important relationships.

Thus, an ethic of care suggests that when weighing a decision, one needs to ask, "How will this affect the people that I care about?" in addition to the other questions and, as the next section suggests, "What does this decision say about me as a person (or as an organization)?"

Virtue and Character for Leading Corporate Citizens

Robert Solomon, a consultant, ethicist, and scholar, argues passionately that there is a "better way to think about business" than in the typical "greed is good" way promulgated by the media and by Wall Street financiers like Ivan Boesky, who got in trouble for financial misdealing during the 1980s. (See also Case 4.2 for a discussion of a company with questionable values.) Solomon argues that good companies not only provide profits to shareholders but also develop a morally rewarding climate where good people can develop their skills and their virtue.

Solomon argues, from a virtue ethics perspective, that companies need to develop a culture that promotes integrity and virtue—or good character—among manager and employees. Companies are themselves communities, or social entities.[51] To be successful and enhance their own employees' commitment and personal integrity, they need to build trust, a sense of community, and other civilizing influences that help the business rise above pure self-interest. The best corporate citizens are built on a set of values that build trust, community, cooperative effort, and integrity (see again Table 4.1).

Managing: Ethical at the Core

All managing and leading is ethical at the core, because leadership inherently involves making decisions that affect stakeholders. Acting on the basis of principles, with care, and with the virtues associated with developing successful communities constantly kept in mind is what it means to operate with integrity. The flow diagram in Figure 4.1 can help when there is a difficult decision to be made, although it is critical that decisions be made from a position that honors personal integrity as well as common sense as well as the ethic of care. And of course dilemmas by their nature are difficult to resolve. The first step is to gather data and make a determination about the decision according to the four norms of ethics discussed above. Cavanagh and his colleagues then suggest that four additional questions need to be addressed before the ethics of the decision can be determined.

First, "Are there any overriding factors?" Overriding factors would be issues that justify, in a given case, one of the types of ethics. For example, commission of a heinous crime may, for some people, justify a decision to use the death penalty on a criminal. The second question that needs to be asked is, "Is one criterion more important than the others?" Third, we need to ask, "Are there any incapacitating factors, such as physical force or violence that overrule other considerations?"

Finally, we need to ask, "Is a 'double effect' present in the decision? That is, do different principles suggest different decisions?" When such a double

Is it possible for a company's vision and related values to be so powerful that they create cultlike cultures that actually create reputation-damaging difficulties for the firm, damaging its relationships with some of its important stakeholders? It seems as though Abercrombie & Fitch (A&F), which was accused of discrimination in late 2003 by several current and former employees, may be experiencing just that problem.

In an article called "Saving Face," reporter Jim Edwards emphasizes the "lock-step conformity" of A&F's "breathlessly enthusiastic 25-year-old" staff members, largely attractive young whites. A&F's vision focuses on selling upscale youth-oriented clothing to college-age young adults, using explicit sexually oriented advertising; provocative photographs in its advertisements, in its quarterly catalog (which was sold in plastic wrap in the stores), and on the walls of its stores; and attractive in-store models as salespeople. The latter practice was the source of the problem. In 2003 the company was hit by a discrimination lawsuit, filed by "a handful of former Asian and Mexican store employees—'brand representatives' in company parlance—who alleged that A&F refuses to hire Asians and Latinos, and banishes African Americans to behind-the-scenes jobs in the stock room, in order to make its staff mirror the overwhelmingly white models in its quarterly catalog."

Reporter Edwards notes

On one level, the lawsuit can be seen as yet another legal shakedown of the type that large competitors routinely attract. But a closer examination reveals a company going through a grinding crisis: A&F's business has matured; its same-store sales are in a two-year decline; its dirty laundry is being aired in court; and, amid new questions about its advertising, it is struggling to reassure the public that it is not racist. In short, A&F's troubles are a tangled mess of staffing policies, marketing issues, and old-fashioned hubris—all of which threaten to unravel the "class American" brand image it has worked so hard to preserve.

Illustrating the impact of negative publicity on corporate reputation is the emergence of a Web site called AFjustice.com, which provides extensive details about the discrimination lawsuit. Even though A&F's strategic goal is to be "edgy" with respect to popular culture as a way of attracting prosperous college students into its stores, some argue that in its approach to employee recruitment and job placement, as well as with respect to some of its provocative and sexually explicit ads and product lines (e.g., thongs targeted toward girls ages 10–16), it may sometimes go too far.

A&F denies that its policies are discriminatory; its lawyers suggest how its in-store brand representatives (salespeople) dress is what matters—not their race. In a very real way, A&F's strategic vision is in play as a result of the questions raised by the lawsuit. Edwards writes, "The issue . . . is not whether A&F or any other brand has the 'right' to market itself to any ethnic audience it wants—it does—but rather whether that marketing has encouraged a culture that is oblivious to racial discrimination. If the courts say it has, then A&F may be forced to rethink how it uses its store employees as brand ambassadors. And, ultimately, its entire approach to marketing."

A&F discontinued its quarterly magazine in the fall of 2003 and by 2004 had removed much of the nudity. Some observers suggest that A&F acted in response to criticisms, while others believe that the company was actually responding to softening in sales—an ineffective marketing strategy. A look at the mostly unclothed models on the A&F Web site suggests that it is likely the company's basic strategy remains intact. As *60 Minutes* reporter Morley Safer reported in December 2003:

Abercrombie's image is now party-loving jocks and bare-naked ladies living fantasy lives. Nubile young store "greeters" stripped down during the holidays to boost up sales. Flipping through their catalogs, you now might wonder what Abercrombie is selling. Could it be clothes? . . .

But Abercrombie & Fitch, the reputation that it once had was a very classical, classy look. That's long gone. Now, the provocative strategy aimed at teens and twenties has done wonders for Abercrombie's bottom line. And of course, the more parents are outraged, the bigger the sales. And now with more than 600 stores and annual revenues well over $1 billion, Abercrombie & Fitch has become just about the largest teen retailer on the block—and a mainstay of "Generation Y" couture, and even its music.

DISCUSSION QUESTIONS

1. Do A&F's policies have the potential to alienate the very customer base that it is trying to attract?

2. What do A&F's actual values seem to be? Do you think that these values are helpful or hurtful to A&F's reputation as a corporate citizen? Why?

3. What roles do A&F's vision and values play in fostering the inbred climate and possible racism that has created problems for the company? What needs to change to improve the situation?

4. What shifts in strategy would you recommend to A&F so that it can reshape itself as a leading corporate citizen?

Sources: Jim Edwards, "Saving Face," *Brandweek* 44, no. 36 (October 6, 2003) pp. 16–20; Morley Safer, "The Look of Ambercrombie & Fitch," *60 Minutes*, December 5, 2003, www.cbsnews.com/stories/2003/12/05/60minutes/main587099.shtml (accessed April 1, 2004), reprinted with permission from CBS News; and Daniel Gross, "Abercrombie & Fitch's Blue Christmas: The Dirty Little Secret Behind the Racy Catalog: Lousy Sales," *Slate*, December 8, 2003, http://slate.msn.com/id/2092175/ (accessed April 1, 2004).

effect is present, the act is considered ethical under three circumstances: (1) when there is no direct intent to produce a bad effect; (2) when the bad effect is simply a side effect of the decision and not a means to the end; and (3) when the good effect sufficiently outweighs the bad one that the good effect becomes an overriding factor.[52]

Note that the analysis of principles and effects using this model allows for conflicts among the principles and for making the inherently difficult determination about the extent to which those conflicts should affect the decision and in what direction. And that decision becomes even more complex when one also needs to consider how others will be affected by the decision in terms of care, and how one's own character—or that of the organization—will be affected by the decision.

Cultural Difference: Leading Corporate Citizens around the World

Cultural differences, like the differences in national ideology discussed in Chapter 3, also make a difference in terms of how companies can and do operate with integrity in different nations around the world. All of this, of course, complicates the difficulty of doing an analysis of the ethics of a given situation; however, understanding the bases of some of these differences can make life a lot easier.

Many of the models of corporate responsibility have been developed in the United States, although concepts of corporate citizenship and the triple bottom line are now current in England and the rest of the European Union. Businesses in Japan tend to view their citizenship less in the social and more fragmented ways that are popular in the United States, and more holistically as we are advocating with the stakeholder lens developed in this book. In other words, Japanese companies tend to view their citizenship as part and parcel of the way they do business day-to-day, the way they treat customers and employees, and how they relate to their government and the public interest defined by government.[53]

Operating with integrity in different cultures certainly means understanding important differences (see Table 4.4). These cultural differences exist along several dimensions that are critical for leading corporate citizens to understand. Readily recognizable, of course, are differences in language, including different structures, vocabularies, and word meaning.[54] Other relevant differences, discussed by Mary O'Hara Devereaux and Robert Johansen in their book *GlobalWork*, are the differences in context, perceptions of time, equality/power, and information flow. Even when individuals from two companies each view themselves as operating with integrity, misunderstandings can easily arise in global settings where deeply seated cultural differences based on different languages, context, power, time, or information flow are not understood.

TABLE 4.4   **Five Important Sources of Cultural Differences**

Source: Slightly adapted from Mary O'Hara-Devereaux and Robert Johansen, *GlobalWork: Bridging Distance, Culture and Time* (San Francisco: Jossey-Bass, 1994).

Language	Language includes the agreed-on structure, vocabulary, and meanings of written or oral communications, and the specialized dialects or jargons adopted by subcultures (including professions).
Context	The elements that surround and give meaning to a communication event are its context. In a scale of high to low, low-context communications hold information. In the single message or event, high-context communications are more subjective and distribute the information in person. The meaning of the event in the high-context culture is deeply colored by relationships, history, status, and other elements.
Time	Cultural attitudes toward time are generally *monochronic* (one event at a time) or *polychronic* (many events at once). Polychronic time is a state of being; monochronic time is a resource to be measured and managed. Concepts of time differ in interrelationships between past, present, and future.
Equality/power	Relationships between people and groups differ with respect to degree of equality, status, and authority.
Information flow	Messages flow between people and levels in organizations, and action chains move toward communication and task completion. The general flow patterns can be sequenced or looped.

One key type of difference involves what sociologists call *context*. Context involves the elements that surround and give meaning to communication. People in low-context cultures, such as those of the United States, Germany, and the Scandinavian nations, are focused on objective communication (i.e., the words or physical gestures). In contrast, people in high-context cultures, such as Japan, China, and Mexico, take their cues about the meaning of a communication as much from the situation and the relationships of all the people involved as from the words themselves. That is, words have little meaning without understanding the context in which they were said.

Relationships are significantly more important in high-context cultures than they are in low-context cultures, which helps to explain why it takes longer to develop business opportunities in, say, Japan, than in the United States, where relationships among the players do not matter as much as they do in Japan. For U.S. executives, having a written contract may be enough to establish an alliance that can successfully operate in a way that pleases both partners. In Japan, however, long-term relationships are essential to building trust, connection, and a shared sense of what is needed to make the alliance work. Anyone trying to establish a contract in a first meeting would be likely to be viewed as untrustworthy, that is, operating without the necessary context of relationships and therefore as without integrity.

Other cultural differences can be found in the perception of time. Some cultures are essentially monochronic, where people pursue one event, action, or activity at a time. Others are polychronic, where people may be simultaneously pursuing multiple activities. For people in polychronic cultures, time is a state of being and things are viewed as cyclical and iterative, while for monochronic cultures time is considered a scarce resource to be measured and managed carefully. Thus, for a monochronic U.S. manager, dealing with a one customer at a time means treating him or her respectfully and with integrity. In contrast, a polychronic Mexican manager or employee dealing with a customer from the same culture would be surprised if a customer were insulted because she or he was answering the phone, writing out one customer's order, and simultaneously waiting on a third customer. Handling multiple activities at once is what is expected in Mexico.

Cultures also differ in the ways people handle power and equality across organizational and social levels. For example countries like the United States and those in Northern Europe have lower power distance and are relatively accepting of the idea that all people are created equal (at least in principle). Most nations of the world, however, have more hierarchical power relationships; they accept inequalities and hierarchical arrangements more readily, including uneven application of rules, as a way of life. Clearly, misunderstanding of these differences in the way power is handled and people are treated can lead to conflicts and concerns about whether corporations with operations in different cultures are actually living up to their values or operating with integrity.

The final area that has been identified as creating important cultural differences has to do with information flow, specifically, whether information is sequenced or looped in more cyclical fashion. Generally speaking, low-context cultures like the United States tend to try to get straight to the point when there are issues of information flow. Information flow involves both the path and speed of communication, which US managers like to be both direct and speedy. Managers from many other cultures, in contrast, especially high context cultures where relationships matter, and polychronic cultures where time is viewed more cyclically and less linearly, tend to see information as more looped and connected with other processes not immediately involved in any given situation.

Leading Challenges: Operating with Integrity

We have seen how important it is for companies (and individuals!) to have a clear and inspiring vision embedded with positive values if they hope to operate with integrity. The challenges of operating with integrity are many, and leaders clearly need to develop personal awareness and mindfulness of the impacts of their decisions on other stakeholders.

Mindfulness demands personal presence.[55] Leaders must recognize that the same person who makes business decisions is the one they must face in the mirror in the morning. There can be no disconnect between business judgments and personal integrity if managers are aware, conscientious, and ethical. And, of course, common sense is paramount, especially in applying the simple rule of "What would I do if I knew this decision were going to be broadcast on TV tomorrow?" At the same time, while it is important to base decisions impacting stakeholders on principles, it is also clear that leading corporate citizens need to take fundamental cultural differences in attitudes toward time, relationships, and information into account or problems will needlessly multiply.

It is because of the very complexity of making corporate decisions with integrity, particularly in the complex global arena, that the capacity to take other stakeholders' perspectives into account is key. So too is the ability to think critically—and systemically—about the implications of a decision about to be made. Leading corporate citizens know this and provide plenty of safe spaces in the company for reflection, for questioning of actions, for critical thinking, and for stakeholder input—before and not after major decisions are made.

In Chapter 5, we will explore the ways in which operating practices can be assessed for companies operating both domestically and globally in an ecologically sustainable way.

Endnotes

1. See, for example, Seth Jayson, "General Mills' Slow Grind," Motley Fool.com, March 16, 2004, www.fool.com/News/mft/2004/mft04031612.htm (accessed March 31, 2004); and Tara Murphy, "General Mills Says SEC Wants Info," *Forbes*, March 3, 2003, www.forbes.com/2003/04/03/cx_tm_0403video2.html (accessed March 31, 2004).

2. See, for example, Ken Wilber, *A Brief History of Everything* (Boston: Shambala, 1996).

3. Ibid.

4. James McGregor Burns, *Leadership* (New York: Harper Torchbooks, 1978), pp. 74–76.

5. Ibid., p. 75.

6. A downside risk is that such inspiration creates cults.

7. James C. Collins, and Jerry I. Porras, *Built to Last: Successful Habits of Visionary Companies* (New York: HarperBusiness, 1997).

8. Burns, *Leadership*.

9. See R. Edward Freeman and Daniel R. Gilbert Jr., *Corporate Strategy and the Search for Ethics* (Englewood Cliffs, NJ: Prentice Hall, 1988).

10. See, for example, Robert C. Solomon, *A Better Way to Think about Business: How Personal Integrity Leads to Corporate Success* (New York: Oxford, 1999).

11. The thinking in this section is largely derived from an article by Jeanne Liedtka, "Constructing an Ethic for Business Practice: Competing Effectively and Doing Good," *Business and Society* 37, no. 3 (September 1998), pp. 254–80.

12. Ibid.

13. See Collins and Porras, *Built to Last*.

14. Alisdair MacIntyre, *After Virtue* (Notre Dame, IN: University of Notre Dame Press, 1981).

15. Liedtka, "Constructing an Ethic for Business Practice," p. 260.

16. For an interesting analysis, see Jane Whitney Gibson and Dana V. Tesone, "Management Fads: Emergence, Evolution, and Implications for Managers," *Academy of Management Executive* 15, no. 4 (2001), pp. 122–33.

17. The learning organization concept was popularized by Peter M. Senge, *The Fifth Discipline: The Art and Practice of the Learning Organization* (New York: Doubleday, 1991).

18. The seminal book is W. Edwards Deming, *Out of the Crisis* (Cambridge, MA: MIT Center for Advanced Engineering Study, 1982). Numerous books exist on total quality management.

19. The popular book on this topic is Michael Hammer and James Champy, *Re-Engineering the Corporation: A Manifesto for Business Revolution* (New York: HarperBusiness, 1993).

20. William C. Frederick, *Values, Nature, and Culture in the American Corporation* (New York: Oxford University Press, 1995).

21. See Michael Novak, *Business as a Calling: Work and the Examined Life* (New York: Free Press, 1996).

22. See Freeman and Gilbert, *Corporate Strategy and the Search for Ethics*.

23. See Sandra A. Waddock, "Linking Community and Spirit: A Commentary and Some Propositions," *Journal of Organizational Change Management*, 1999, 12(4): 332–344.

24. See Henry Mintzberg, *The Rise and Fall of Strategic Planning* (New York: Free Press, 1994), or "The Fall and Rise of Strategic Planning," *Harvard Business Review*, January–February 1994, pp. 107–14.

25. See Senge, *The Fifth Discipline*.

26. For a discussion of continual, as opposed to continuous, improvement in the context of quality management and personal growth, see Dalmar Fisher and William R. Torbert, *Personal and Organizational Transformations: The True Challenge of Continual Quality Improvement* (London: McGraw-Hill, 1995).

27. See Waddock, "Linking Community and Spirit."

28. Stan Davis and Christopher Meyer discuss this at some length in *Blur: The Speed of Change in the Connected Economy* (Reading, MA: Addison-Wesley, 1998).

29. The term *good conversation* was developed by James A. Waters and published in Frederic R. Bird and James A. Waters, "The Moral Muteness of Managers," *California Management Review*, Fall 1989, pp. 73–88.

30. Chris Argyris focuses on "undiscussability" in *Knowledge for Action: A Guide to Overcoming Barriers to Organizational Change* (San Francisco: Jossey-Bass, 1993). See also Bird and Waters, "The Moral Muteness of Managers."

31. This section is based on Sandra Waddock, "Creating Corporate Accountability: Foundational Principles to Make Corporate Citizenship Real," *Journal of Business Ethics* 50 (2004), pp. 313–27.

32. Thomas Donaldson began developing these ideas in *The Ethics of International Business* (New York: Oxford University Press, 1992), and moved them forward in "Values in Tension: Ethics Away from Home," *Harvard Business Review*, September–October 1996, pp. 1–12. He wrote explicitly about hypernorms with Thomas W. Dunfee in "Toward a Unified Conception of Social Contracts Theory," *Academy of Management Review* 19, no. 2 (1994), pp. 252–84, and *Ties That Bind: A Social Contracts Approach to Business Ethics* (Boston: Harvard Business School Press, 1999).

33. Donaldson and Dunfee, "Toward a Unified Conception of Social Contracts Theory," p. 265.

34. S. Prakash Sethi, "Globalization and the Good Corporation: A Need for Proactive Co-existence," *Journal of Business Ethics* 43, no. 1/2 (2003), pp. 21–31.

35. Donaldson, "Values in Tension," p. 6.

36. Ibid., pp. 7–8.

37. Lara P. Hartman, Bill Shaw, and Rodney Stevenson, "Exploring the Ethics and Economics of Global Labor Standards: A Challenge to Integrated Social Contract Theory," *Business Ethics Quarterly* 13, no. 2 (April 2003), pp. 193–225.

38. Donaldson and Dunfee, *Ties That Bind*, p. 68.

39. Frederick, *Values, Nature, and Culture.*

40. UN Global Compact Web site, www.unglobalcompact.org (accessed April 14, 2004).

41. Liedtka, "Constructing an Ethic for Business Practice." The practices discussed in this section are from Liedkta's article.

42. Collins and Porras, *Built to Last.*

43. Kant, Immanual, *Groundwork of the Metaphysics of Morals.* NY: H. J. Paton, 1964.

44. The decision-making framework is summarized in Gerald F. Cavanagh, *American Business Values with International Perspectives*, 4th ed. (Upper Saddle River, NJ: Prentice Hall, 1998). Much of the discussion in this section is adapted from either this book or one of the following articles: Manuel Velasquez, Dennis J. Moberg, and Gerald F. Cavanagh, "Organizational Statesmanship and Dirty Politics: Ethical

Guidelines for the Organizational Politician," *Organizational Dynamics*, Autumn 1983, pp. 65–80; Gerald F. Cavanagh, Dennis J. Moberg, and Manuel Velasquez, "The Ethics of Organizational Politics," *Academy of Management Review* 6, no. 3 (1981), pp. 363–74; and Gerald F. Cavanagh, Dennis J. Moberg, and Manuel Velasquez, "Making Business Ethics Practical," *Business Ethics Quarterly* 5, no. 3 (July 1995), pp. 399–418.

45. Cavanagh, *American Business Values*, p. 75.

46. Ibid., pp. 78–79.

47. Ibid., p. 79; and John Rawls, *A Theory of Justice* (Cambridge, MA: Harvard University Press, 1971).

48. Immanual Kant, *Groundwork of the Metaphysics of Morals*, trans. H. J. Paton (New York: Harper & Row, 1964); cited in Cavanagh, *American Business Values*, p. 78. Much of this discussion is adapted from Cavanagh.

49. Cavanagh, *American Business Values*, p. 81.

50. See Carol Gilligan, *In a Different Voice: Psychological Theory and Women's Development* (Cambridge. MA: Harvard University Press, 1982). For an extension of this work into cognitive domains, see also Mary Field Belenky, Blythe McVicker Clinchy, Nancy Rule Goldberg, and Jill Mattuck Tarule, *Women's Ways of Knowing: The Development of Self, Voice, and Mind* (New York: Basic Books, 1986).

51. Robert C. Solomon, *A Better Way to Think about Business: How Personal Integrity Leads to Corporate Success* (New York: Oxford, 1999).

52. Cavanagh, *American Business Values*, pp. 83–87.

53. This difference became clear on a visit to the Boston College Center for Corporate Citizenship by a contingent of Japanese businessmen representing the Kaneiren, the Kansai Economic Federation, of Japan in September 2000.

54. The five cultural differences discussed here are based on Mary O'Hara-Devereaux and Robert Johansen, *GlobalWork: Bridging Distance, Culture and Time* (San Francisco: Jossey-Bass, 1994). O'Hara-Devereaux and Johansen in turn draw from Edward T. Hall and Mildred Reed Hall, *Understanding Cultural Differences: Germans, French, and Americans* (Yarmouth, ME: Intercultural Press, 1990), and Geert Hofstede, *Cultures and Organizations: Software of the Mind* (London: McGraw-Hill, 1991).

55. For an interesting perspective on the concept of presence, see Peter Senge, Otto Scharmer, Joseph Jaworski, and Betty Sue Flowers, *Presence: Human Purpose and the Field of the Future* (Boston: Society for Organizational Learning, 2004).

CHAPTER FIVE

Value Added: The Impact of Vision and Values

Our understanding of both investment and return is founded upon a traditional separation in the creation of social versus economic value. It is logical. It is the common understanding of the world. It is also inherently wrong.

The fundamental challenge to be addressed is that even a child knows the value of a quarter is the same, yet different from the value of a lollipop one has bought with that same quarter. The tension experienced by communities attempting to trade economic vitality for environmental health is the same as that balanced by the conscientious investor pursuing both financial rationality and social sense. Yet historic definitions of investment and return ask us to somehow choose between the two. It is a dissonance that rings in our ears because all know it to be a false dichotomy, a *non*-Faustian bargain we are being asked to make, since we know only half the investment is on the table and only half its true value under consideration.

The buzzing in our ears is the *Zero-Sum Dissonance* of a traditional artificial market that only considers and values financial returns . . . In truth, the core nature of investment and return is not a trade-off between social and financial interest but rather the pursuit of an embedded value proposition composed of both.

Jed Emerson, "The Blended Value Proposition: Integrating Social and Financial Returns"[1]

143

Value Added

Companies are in the business of adding value through their economizing efforts. Most of the time we measure that value solely in terms of added financial value or shareholder wealth; however, recent attention to what is called the triple bottom line of economic, social, and ecological returns has highlighted the reality that there is more than one type of value—and multiple *values* supporting the generation of value added. It is the merging of these values that Jed Emerson calls the blended value proposition.[2] Consider the following examples:

> FedEx boasts a large fleet of trucks to carry out its package delivery services. In May 2003, the company agreed to purchase 20 hybrid delivery trucks with the long-term intention of entirely replacing its 30,000 medium-duty express delivery vans with hybrids. In pioneering the use of hybrid trucks, which combine high-efficiency diesel or gas engines with electric motors to save on fuel usage, the company expects significant savings, according to a report by the Global Environmental Management Initiative (GEMI). Cost savings are expected to accrue from reduced maintenance expenditures because the engines run cleaner, longer-lasting brake systems, and fuel savings. FedEx is collaborating with the Environmental Defense Fund's Alliance for Environmental Innovation on performance specifications for the new trucks.[3]

> Dow Chemical collaborated with the Natural Resources Defense Council and five activist groups to voluntarily reduce wastes and emissions in its Michigan Operations site. Results included 43% reduction in emissions and 37% reduction in targeted wastes (totaling over 10 million pounds of waste and 1.5 million pounds of emissions per year). Accompanying process improvements translated to a return of 180% or more than $5.4 million annually on a one-time capital expenditure of $3.1 million. Because the project was developed collaboratively through a stakeholder-engagement process, relations among key stakeholders, including activists, improved dramatically.[4]

These examples help illustrate the close relationship between good stakeholder-related practices, environmental sustainability, and value added, in a blended value orientation to performance. In addition, they highlight the need to consider the full costs of doing business from what some observers call cradle to cradle (rather than cradle to grave, implying waste and loss).[5] They further highlight the waste involved in problematic stakeholder relationships and environmental practices, not just the obvious ones that are typically measured.

Thinking about value added beyond traditional financial measures is critically important in an era when social activists, community leaders, and politicians are demanding more transparency, accountability, and responsibility from businesses for their impacts on stakeholders and the natural environment than ever. Broadening the definition of value also matters in a knowledge-and information-based economy, where the sources of value added and wealth generation are shifting dramatically. As a report on what the European Commission calls the "intangibles economy" points out:

> Intangibles such as R&D, proprietary know-how, intellectual property and workforce skills, world-class supply networks and brands are now the key drivers of wealth production while physical and financial assets are increasingly regarded as commodities.[6]

The word *intangibles* covers a multitude of nonfinancial but highly valuable resources in any modern organization: human, intellectual, social, and structural capital. Stakeholder relationships (including those with employees), organizational culture, innovations that come from committed stakeholders who trust the enterprise enough to share them, and the human assets and abilities that people bring with them are all part of this mix. Developing the basis of trust that allows these intangible forms of capital to develop is the very essence of good stakeholder relationships. Social capital, as scholars call these forms, is a core ingredient of leading corporate citizenship. Intangible assets are built on trust, and as the scandals of the early 2000s demonstrated, trust is lost when companies and other types of organizations fail to operate with integrity. In contrast, when trust is present, there is great potential for excellent productivity and performance; for contributions from a multitude of stakeholders; and (no small thing), for the avoidance of fines, regulations, and other hindrances to doing business. And these gains do not even take into account the retention of customers and employees, and investments from all types of investors, including those interested in corporate responsibility. It is building strong relationships through constructive stakeholder and environmental practices—and their link to value added—that will be the focus of this chapter.

Making a Decision to Operate with Integrity

There is a long-standing debate among scholars about whether it pays to be responsible; that is, is there a positive relationship between responsibility and financial performance? This question, focused around making a business case for being responsible, has caused scholars, social investors, and skeptics alike to seek out a profitability rationale for companies' being responsible and accountable. While evidence has been mounting to show that this relationship is, in fact, a positive one, it is clear that leading corporate citizens—and their managers— have a fundamental choice to make: to operate responsibly or not. And that decision about integrity should be independent of bottom-line results. As Matthew Kiernan, CEO of Innovest Strategic Value Advisors, states: "Why on earth should one need to make a 'business case' for doing the right thing?"[7]

Fortunately (at least for those who believe that companies should be doing the right thing whatever the consequences), there is significant and growing evidence that the "both/and" of effectiveness and efficiency, integrity and economizing, doing things right and doing the right thing brings about long-term success. This so-called business case can be found along a number of critical stakeholder and natural environment dimensions, but these dimensions do highlight the stark choice executives face. Companies' leaders can choose to operate with only the interests of economizing and power aggrandizing in mind. Or they can articulate their own values, understand what they stand for in a positive and constructive way, and operate with integrity, sometimes even when there is a short-term cost to doing so. Either way, they will be held responsible—and increasingly accountable—for their actions by a growing array of interested stakeholders.

The choice is thus fundamentally a moral one that involves an important distinction between the concepts of *effectiveness* and *efficiency*. In the words of management theorist Russell Ackoff, quoting Peter Drucker:

> Peter Drucker once made *a distinction between doing things right and doing the right thing. This distinction in the same as that between efficiency and effectiveness.* Information, knowledge, and understanding contribute primarily to efficiency but provide little assurance of effectiveness. For effectiveness, wisdom is required.[8]

Leading corporate citizens seek wisdom in their choices and the impacts of those choices. Thus they have to be efficient *and* effective, do things right, economize appropriately so that little is wasted and their activities and the communities that support them are sustainable. *And* they need to do the right thing so that they can operate with integrity and respect for the dignity of their stakeholders, as well as the health of the natural environment. Once again we are faced with implementing decisions using the logic of both/and rather than the less progressive logic of either/or.

Companies that know what they stand for and operate within their stated values will—and do—choose to operate with integrity and treat stakeholders well. Companies that operate without integrity lose the trust of important stakeholders, including investors, customers, and employees—and sometimes find themselves in major difficulties when misdeeds are found out, as happened with Enron Corporation, Tyco, WorldCom, Arthur Andersen, and numerous other companies embroiled in scandals in the early 2000s. Operating with integrity and respect can sometimes mean internalizing costs that might otherwise be externalized. Sometimes it means putting a code of conduct or set of operating principles in place—and sticking to them even when there is temptation to lapse, even when governments fail to enforce local regulations and laws. It is in this sense that companies in particular are acting to ensure the rights of citizens, sometimes in the place of governments.[9] Sometimes it simply means thinking through the consequences of operating practices and choosing those that do the least harm or help stakeholders the most, using the type of decision framework presented in Chapter 4.

For example, companies can develop hurtful employee policies that make recruitment difficult and turnover high, that essentially treat employees as cogs in the machine of business rather than as people, discarding them through layoffs when the going gets rough. Or they can choose policies that retain highly skilled and knowledgeable workers to improve productivity in the long term, even when times are tight. They can be careless about product and packaging design, generating waste and harmful by-products, or they can carefully design products to minimize packaging and waste and move toward sustainabililiy. They can develop shoddy products that may sell quickly but ultimately destroy goodwill among customers, leading to fewer repeat sales, or they can pay attention to quality and value added for the customer, leaving customers satisfied and willing to purchase again. They can seek the materials from suppliers at the lowest possible cost, stretching the suppliers' resources to the maximum and inhibiting their survival. Or companies can work in alliance with their suppliers to build a healthy network of relationships and allow the supplier enough in profits to make appropriate and adequate investments in R&D, infrastructure, human resources, and equipment to meet long-term demand.

Further, companies can treat their local communities and the natural environment as temporary stopping (or, more accurately, stomping) grounds, grabbing tax breaks and infrastructure development from the community, or externalizing pollution, without recognizing the long-term costs to the community. Or they can recognize the mutuality of the corporate–community relationship and become a neighbor of choice, instilling goodwill and positive long-term commitment that enhances the well-being of community and natural environment.[10] Leading corporate citizenship happens when companies do this simply because it is the right thing to do, not when they are forced to do so by public or stakeholder pressures, laws and regulations, or media scrutiny.

There seem to be few negative by-products of operating responsibly, at least when many companies are studied together and, increasingly, a fiduciary responsibility case is being made for responsible practices—as a part of a company's normal risk management activities. More important, much of the research suggests that there may be positive benefits to acting responsibly. The rest of the chapter will explore some of the evidence for the link between effectiveness and efficiency, doing the right thing and doing things right—and, ultimately, operating with integrity.

Responsibility and Performance

There is a long tradition of research on the relationship between financial performance and corporate social responsibility, which we have simply termed *responsibility* or *responsible practice*.

Vision and Value Added

One of the more striking studies of the impact of vision can be found in the work of James Collins and Jerry Porras, which was discussed in Chapter 4. In their book *Built to Last,* Collins and Porras report on studies of 36 companies, 18 classified as visionary and 18 runners-up, which were not necessarily unvisionary companies but did exhibit fewer of the qualities of visionary companies.[11] Although the comparison companies are good companies, matched in size, industry, and longevity to the visionary companies, Collins and Porras compared them to the silver or bronze medal winners versus gold medal winners.

The critical element of Collins and Porras's study, however, is determining the impact of vision on long-term performance. And that impact is dramatic! Despite the fact that the visionary companies exhibit elements of their human (and therefore fallible) origins in some of the strategic and performance bumps and hurdles they have crossed in their years (and they are all long-lived companies), the visionary companies markedly outperform the comparison companies. In doing so, the visionary companies, guided by their core ideology and meaningful sense of purpose, display what Collins and Porras term "remarkable resiliency," or the ability to bounce back from adversity.[12] Let Collins and Porras's findings speak for themselves:

> Visionary companies attain extraordinary *long-term* performance. Suppose you made equal $1 investments in a general-market stock fund, a comparison company stock fund, and a visionary company stock fund on January 1, 1926. If you reinvested all dividends and made appropriate adjustments for when the companies became available on the Stock Exchange, your $1 in the general market fund would have grown to $415 on December 31,1990—not bad. But your $1 in the visionary companies' stock fund would have grown to $6,356—over six times the comparison fund and over fifteen times the general market.[13]

Collins and Porras draw several conclusions that debunk management myths:

> Contrary to business school doctrine, "maximizing shareholder wealth" or "profit maximization" has not been the dominant driving force or primary objective through the history of the visionary companies. Visionary companies pursue a cluster of objectives, of which making money is only one—and not necessarily the primary one. Yes, they seek profits, but they're equally guided by a core ideology—core values and sense of purpose beyond just making money. Yet, paradoxically, the visionary companies make more money than the more purely profit-driven comparison companies.[14]

The key to understanding Collins and Porras's findings is to understand that *profitability is a by-product of doing something well, not the end in itself.* Unlike Collins and Porras, however, we have argued here that the most successful visions are those driven by end values that add meaning and meaningfulness to the sets of relationships embedded in an organization. If constructive values and respect for stakeholders really underpin effective visions, then it would make sense that visionary companies outperform nonvisionary companies in practices they have evolved in their relationships to their stakeholders. In fact, my own research with my colleague Sam Graves on this very topic, using the same companies that Collins and Porras studied, indicates that visionary companies *do* treat their primary stakeholders better than do the nonvisionary companies.

Visionary companies outperform the nonvisionary companies in their treatment not only of owners (through financial performance, which Collins and Porras addressed), but also of customers, employees, and communities. Although our study showed no statistically significant difference in the treatment of the environment between the two groups of companies, the difference was nearly statistically significant and positive. When treatment of stakeholders

FIGURE 5.1   Corporate Social Performance: Overall Average Comparison

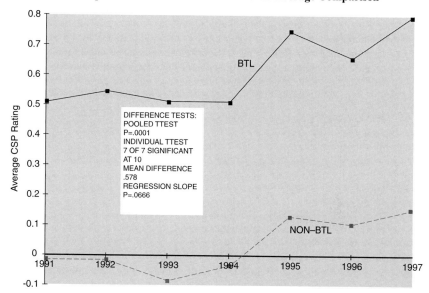

was combined into a single measure, the difference between the gold medal visionary companies and silver medal comparison group was significant in every year we studied.[15] Figure 5.1 shows the overall social performance of the built-to-last companies against the comparison group in our study.

Social and Financial Performance

The typical assumption, particularly in financial circles, is that there is a necessary trade-off between social and financial performance. This assumption suggests that social and ecological responsibilities are discretionary, which we have argued they are not. Instead, we argue that such responsibilities are integral to determining a company's overall performance—in a blended value sense. The fear embedded in this assumption is that the more responsible companies will place themselves at a competitive disadvantage because they are incurring more costs than other companies. Certainly, some responsibilities do require investment; however, there is significant evidence that—when viewed as investments—they show returns much like any other type of investment.

In 2003 Joshua Margolis and James Walsh published a metastudy examining all 127 studies between 1972 and 2002 that addressed the relationship between social and financial performance. Let the results of this metastudy speak for themselves:

Corporate social performance has been treated as an independent variable,
predicting financial performance, in 109 of the 127 studies. In these studies, almost

half of the results (54) pointed to a positive relationship between corporate social performance and financial performance. Only seven studies found a negative relationship; 28 studies reported non-significant relationships, while 20 reported a mixed set of findings. Corporate social performance has been treated as a dependent variable, predicted by financial performance, in 22 of the 127 studies. In these studies, the majority of results (16 studies) pointed to a positive relationship between corporate financial performance and social performance. Four studies investigated the relationships in both directions, which explains why there are more results than studies . . .

A clear signal emerges from these 127 studies. A simple compilation of the findings suggests there is a positive association, and certainly very little evidence of a negative association, between a company's social performance and its financial performance. A recent meta-analysis of 52 CSP-CFP studies reached this same substantive conclusion.[16]

Despite the strong evidence of the relationship between social and financial performance—and the suggestion in some studies that more responsible companies may simply be better managed and hence more profitable—many analysts and CEOs still are skeptical.[17] They seem to believe in the either/or logic of trade-offs, rather than the both/and logic that suggests you will get better long-term results from treating your stakeholders better. Given the accumulating evidence, however, it becomes harder and harder to believe that there are necessary drawbacks to behaving more responsibly.

Stakeholder Relationships and Performance

Leading corporate citizenship is fundamentally about integrity, responsibility, and accountability for the company's impacts on stakeholders and nature. One fundamental proposition of this book is that the better an organization's relationships with its stakeholders and the natural environment, the better its long-term performance—the company's capacity to add value. There is a growing literature to suggest the truth of this proposition. Moreover, whether or not integrity and responsibility are profitable, companies should uphold them for simple ethical reasons.

Responsible Investing

We have already seen that companies with better overall social performance seem to also do better financially. One question that investors, considered as owners, seek answers to (in the old either/or logic) is whether there is a penalty for investing in more responsible businesses. Socially responsible (or just responsible) investors care about the uses to which their money is put. Three strategies are used: Investors (1) screen companies against certain criteria, (2) use their shareholder resolutions to actively seek changes from management, or (3) accept lower returns for specific types of community-based investments aimed at doing social good. The Social Investment Forum estimates that some $2.16 trillion is now invested in professionally managed portfolios that use one or more of those criteria.[18] This means that in the United States one out of every nine investment dollars, or about 11.3 percent of the total, is now socially invested in one way or another.[19] Of this investment, $1.99 trillion is in privately managed portfolios, while $151 billion is in mutual funds.[20] Also notable is that during the major downturn in the general stock market during the early 2000s, socially screened mutual funds continued to grow even when the rest of the market was in decline, suggesting greater investor confidence in companies rated more responsible than others.

As with financial performance discussed above, it appears that market performance of socially screened funds (i.e., the stock price) is either about the same as or slightly better than traditional funds, with possibly somewhat higher volatility. Scholars studied the performance of screened companies for five years and found that the mean financial performance of large responsible companies is significantly better than that of other large companies.[21] Results of the 2003 study using a metric called market value added (MVA), which measures long-term value added for shareholders since the inception of the company, demonstrate that responsible corporations generate two to four times more long-term wealth for shareholders than the remaining companies in the Standard & Poor's (S&P) 500. To do the study, authors Stephen Barlas, Alfred King, Peter Leitner, and Curtis Verschoor compared companies rated as the "100 Best Corporate Citizens" by *Business Ethics* magazine,[22] whose ratings are based on data from the prominent social research firm KLD Research and Analytics,[23] and compared their performance to the rest of the S&P 500. Data from ratings for 2001, 2002, and 2003 showed that the mean MVA for responsible companies was nearly three times that of less responsible companies, that is, those in the S&P 500 not included on the best 100 corporate citizens ranking.[24] Further, despite the market decline of the early 2000s, the return on responsible companies outpaced that of the rest of the companies by a greater amount each year.[25]

The Domini Social Index (DSI) is a set of socially screened companies weighted by market capitalization; it was begun in 1990 to be tracked against the S&P 500 and is based on data from KLD Research and Analytics. In the years since its initiation, the DSI has outperformed the S&P 500 consistently on the basis of total returns, as well as on a risk-adjusted basis, providing further evidence that doing well and doing good may go hand in hand. Figure 5.2 shows the results of the DSI's performance as compared to the S&P 500 and the Russell 1000 index of the 1000 largest US companies from the DSI's inception up to 2004. Notably, the top line, the DSI, consistently outperforms both of the other indexes.

In the Barlas et al. study discussed above, several other analyses were undertaken. These researchers determined that the mean MVA of responsible companies listed in the FTSE4Good Index in the United Kingdom in 2002 was 3.67 times and in 2003 was 3.33 times the rest of the S&P 500 companies. The added wealth creation by responsible companies for 2003 was $10.7 billion, with similar results demonstrated for the U.S. Dow Jones Sustainability Index, a collection of large companies meeting environmental and social screens. Similar

FIGURE 5.2 **Domini Social Index Compared to the Standard & Poor's 500 and Russell 1000 Indexes**

Source: Copyright © 2004 by KLD Research and Analytics, Inc.

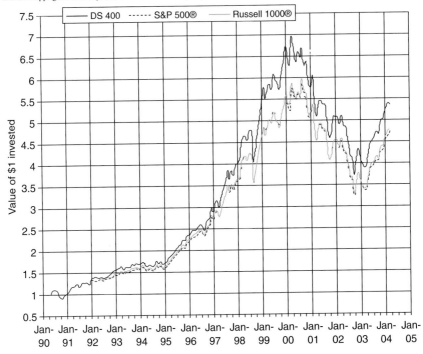

results were found for companies that had instituted codes of conduct as compared to those that had not.[26] The authors conclude: "This new study provides powerful new evidence supporting the belief of many investors that firms that have a strong ethical culture and effectively address social and environmental issues also deliver excellent financial results to their shareholders. Study results are also consistent with the fact that socially and environmental managed mutual funds have reported better-than-average results."[27]

Overall, the research on whether investors earn as much on their investments in responsible as compared to less responsible companies suggests that there is no apparent trade-off in financial performance. In fact, one result of better responsibility may be to reduce overall risk for investors. Further, the results indicate that investors may actually benefit from the better management practices and stakeholder relationships associated with greater levels of responsibility. Minimally, it appears, the relationship is a neutral one. Since there is a choice to be made—and the choice is fundamentally, as we pointed out above, a moral one—then it makes sense to invest in more responsible companies.

Employee Relations and Performance

The impact of treating employees well is far from trivial. Jeffrey Pfeffer and John Veiga summarized a good deal of research on the relationship between firm economic performance and employee relations.[28] Quoting from two major studies, they note:

> According to an award-winning study of the high performance work practices of 968 firms representing all major industries, "a one standard deviation increase in use of such practices is associated with a ... 7.05 percent decrease in turnover and, on a per employee basis, $27,044 more in sales and $18,641 and $3,814 more in market value and profits, respectively." Yes, you read those results correctly. That's an $18,000 increase in stock market value *per employee*! A subsequent study conducted on 702 firms in 1996 found even larger economic benefits: "A one standard deviation improvement in the human resources system was associated with an increase in shareholder wealth of $41,000 per employee"— about a 14 percent market value premium.[29]

Turnover costs are estimated by *Fortune* magazine to be on the order of $50,000 and $100,000 for top talent in the United States,[30] while the Saratoga Institute suggests that turnover costs for employees below top management are about the average cost of the employee's salary and benefits.[31] Greater employee satisfaction can result in decreased turnover, reduced recruitment costs, and less absenteeism. Although such costs are not typically treated in financial statements, they are considerable and progressive companies do what they can to ensure that their employees like working in the company. The Work Foundation and Future Foundation examined the impact of corporate responsibility directly on how employees viewed the company. The findings demonstrated that younger employees (18–24) and older employees (45+) took corporate social responsibility into account more than others. Employee loyalty was significantly correlated with the company's corporate social responsibility rating.[32]

In an exciting book, Pfeffer also shows the value of "putting people first," in terms of both company profitability, and other ways of assessing organizational performance.[33] After looking at the five-year survival rates of initial public offerings, studies of profitability and stock price in numerous industries, and research on specific industries, Pfeffer concluded that gains on the order of 40 percent can be achieved when high-performance management practices are implemented. (Managing responsibility will be discussed in Chapter 7.) The analysis showed that survival rates were associated with the real value placed on people, as well as the reward system in the company. For example, policies such as employee stock ownership plans and profit sharing significantly improved survival rates. (See Case 5.1 for a description of Costco's efforts to treat employees well.)

Pfeffer and Veiga, in their summary of research on employee policies and organizational performance, conclude that progressive employee practices help companies improve their performance because:

> Simply put, people work harder because of the increased involvement and commitment that comes from having more control and say in their work; people

Even though Wall Street analysts don't like to believe it, treating employees well can be a winning strategy, and Costco offers living proof. Touted as "The Only Company Wal-Mart Fears" by *Fortune,* Costco is 20 percent of Wal-Mart's size, but in *Fortune*'s words "has made a monkey of the 800-pound gorilla" in the warehouse club niche. Despite having 312 stores to Wal-Mart's Sam's Club's 532, Costco made $34.4 billion to Sam's Club's $32.9 billion, nearly double the revenue per store. An analysis by *BusinessWeek* shows that in 2003 Costco's profits per employee averaged $13,647 to Wal-Mart's $11,039, with sales per square foot at $795 for Costco and $516 for Wal-Mart.

Despite these figures, and a 25 percent gain in profits announced in the first quarter of 2004, Costco's stock price dropped by 4 percent. *Business Week,* taking the analysts to task, stated:

> The market's view of Costco speaks volumes about the so-called Wal-Martization of the U.S. economy. True, the Bentonville (Ark.) retailer has taken a public relations pounding recently for paying poverty- level wages and shouldering health insurance for fewer than half of its 1.2 million U.S. workers. Still, it remains the darling of the Street, which, like Wal-Mart and many other companies believes that shareholders are best served if employers do all they can to hold down costs, including the cost of labor.

What gets Costco in trouble with Wall Street analysts is the fact that its pay is considerably higher than Wal-Mart's. Costco pays on average $15.97 to Wal-Mart's $11.52, and provides health care coverage to 82 percent of workers to the retail giant's 47 percent; it also includes 9l percent of workers in retirement plans to its competitor's 64 percent. According to *BusinessWeek,* the strategy of paying employees well has multiple benefits:

> We found that by compensating employees generously to motivate and retain good workers, one-fifth of whom are unionized. Costco gets lower turnover [6% to Wal-Mart's 21%] and higher productivity. Combined with a smart business strategy that sells a mix of higher-margin products to more affluent customers, Costco actually keeps its labor costs lower than Wal-Mart's as a percentage of sales [9.8% to 17%], and its 68,000 hourly workers in the U.S. sell more per square foot.

Fortune notes that Costco lives by four key axioms:

1. Obey the law.
2. Take care of your customers.
3. Take care of your employees.
4. Practice the intelligent loss of sales.

These axioms are echoed by James D. Sinegal, CEO and president of Costco, who is philosophical about Wall Street's pressures: "We think that when you take care of your customers and your employees, your shareholders are going to be rewarded in the long run. And I'm one of them [the shareholders]; I care about the stock price. But we're not going to do something for the sake of one quarter that's going to destroy the fabric of our company and what we stand for."

Unfortunately, as *Business Week* noted, "Most of Wall Street doesn't see the broader picture . . . and only focuses on the upfront savings [that would come from reducing pay levels and benefits]." From the perspective of the economic and social systems as a whole, the implications are profound, as *BusinessWeek* points out:

> The cheap-labor model turns out to be costly in many ways. It can fuel poverty and related social issues and dump costs on

other companies and taxpayers, who indirectly pick up the healthcare tab for all the workers not insured by their parsimonious employers. What's more, the low-wage approach cuts into consumer spending and, potentially, economic growth.

CEO Sinegal says, "Paying your employees well is not only the right thing to do but it makes for good business." Elsewhere, he noted, "They're entitled to buy homes and live in reasonably nice neighborhoods and send their children to school."

DISCUSSION QUESTIONS

1. Why does Costco have such high employee retention rates? What are the performance implications of treating employees the way Costco does compared to the way Wal-Mart does?
2. Is there something wrong with the way that analysts are assessing Costco's

performance or are they right to think that Costco should reduce what it pays employees?
3. What does Costco's stand on pay and benefits say about its corporate citizenship?
4. Have the progressive pay scales and policies actually affected performance? What might these policies do for long-term shareholder value?

Sources: Christine Frey, "Costco's Love of Labor: Employees' Well-Being Key to Its Success," *Seattle Post-Intelligence*, March 29, 2004, http://seattlepi.nwsource.com/business/166680costco29.html; John Helyer, "The Only Company Wal-Mart Fears," *Fortune*, November 24, 2003; and Stanley Holmes and Wendy Zellner, "The Costco Way: Higher Wages Mean Higher Profits. But Try Telling Wall Street," *Business Week*, April 12, 2004, pp. 76–77.

work smarter because they are encouraged to build skills and competence; and people work more responsibly because more responsibility is placed in hands of employees further down in the organization.[34]

In 2004, the Global Environmental Management Initiative (GEMI) reported the results of a number of studies related to managing human resources. One study of 404 publicly traded companies found that up to 30 percent of a company's market value derives from how the company manages its workforce.[35] Another study found that among professional service firms in 15 different countries, if employee morale is boosted by 20 percent financial performance rises by 40 percent.[36] Training employees also has been found to contribute positively to profitability.[37] The links between investing in employees in various ways and profitability seem clear and unambiguous.

Given this strong relationship between the ways employees are treated and organizational performance, it makes sense to ask, "What kinds of company practices produce such results?" In some respects, the policies are easily determined and might be identified by anyone using common sense about the way he or she would like to he treated. Going back to our discussion of values in Chapter 4, we can argue that developing such policies really means operating with integrity and implementing constructive rather than debilitating practices with respect to employees.

Implementation is difficult in part because of the basic values driving the economic sector, which were discussed in Chapter 1: economizing (which emphasizes efficiency as a first priority) and power aggrandizing (which drives

managers to want to accumulate ever-increasing amounts of power for themselves). Perhaps by recognizing these driving values underlying some of the
more negative practices of corporate life, leaders can overcome their short-term
tendencies to want to acquire more power or cut costs in the near term and
develop better practices that help the company achieve long-term success. Doing
so and implementing positive employee policies can result in significant performance improvement, as demonstrated by many companies with excellent
employee policies, including Starbucks, Southwest Airlines, and Patagonia.

Diversity Management, Work/Family Policies, and Performance

Another approach to assessing the relationship between the way that companies
treat employees and financial performance is to assess their approach to diversity management and the work/family relationship. There is considerable belief
among management scholars that greater levels of diversity will result in better
performance because more and different points of view will be represented in
decisions, which should improve performance. This assumption rests on the
resource-based view of the firm, which says that the more resources that are
used, and the better those resources are, the better the firm will perform strategically and in other ways.[38]

The advocacy group Catalyst studied whether companies that aggressively
recruit and retain women do better than those that do not. Those companies with
greater gender diversity (measured as the highest percentage of women among
top officers) had 35.1 percent higher return on equity and 34 percent higher total
return to shareholders than those with fewer women.[39] Another study attempted
to study whether companies that had more women in their management ranks, as
well as on the board of directors, outperformed those with less diversity in management. Although the study found no relationship between the number of
women on the board and performance, the researchers did find that there was a
significant positive relationship between the percentage of managers who were
women and financial performance.[40]

Similarly, in a series of studies reported in *The Wall Street Journal*, the
reporter concludes, "A growing number of employers suspect improving
employee satisfaction will have an indirect but important effect on profit."[41]
Because intellectual and human capital are becoming increasingly important
sources of competitive advantage, and because there are structural changes in the
economy that have caused a scarcity of skilled and knowledgeable employees,
many companies have begun to find new ways to treat their employees with
respect and integrity. For example, Sears Roebuck found that employee attitudes
impacted not only revenues but also customer satisfaction: "If employee attitudes on 10 essential counts improve by 5%, Sears found, customer satisfaction
will jump 1.3%, driving a one-half percentage point rise in revenue."[42]

Northern Telecom of Toronto found similar relationships among employee
attitudes and satisfaction, customer loyalty, and profitability, and MCI
Communications find links between employee attitudes and turnover. In part,
this relationship exists because experienced employees are more efficient and

knowledgeable than newer employees, and because retention reduces turnover and recruitment costs.[43] As must be obvious, companies' treatment of one group of primary stakeholders is critically related to the way it is perceived—and the way it treats—other stakeholders as well. We will continue to explore these important interrelationships in the next couple of sections.

Customers and Responsibility

In addition to investors and employees, many customers too are seeking responsible practices at the companies from which they purchase goods and services. Customer loyalty, gained through providing high-quality products and services, is increasingly important to gaining status as a leading corporate citizen. Also, the reputation of the firm with customers is critical. One other aspect of developing positive relationships with customers has to do with customer's perception of a company's overall level of responsibility, which, increasingly, is being seen as influencing their propensity to purchase from that company.

Satisfied customers are a tremendous source of long-term business. Happy customers tell 6 others of their experience, while unhappy customers tell 22, potentially costing significant business over a period of time.[44] Companies that operate with integrity want to assure that their customers are satisfied not only with the quality of products but also with their usefulness. Further, customer surveys consistently indicate that many customers intend to make purchasing decisions with the company's responsibility reputation in mind, although there is yet no clear evidence that these attitudes actually translate into purchasing behavior.[45] Indeed, one study found that by far the best predictor of growth for companies in most industries is the percentage of customers who can be classified as "promoters," that is, customers who will tell others positive things about the company.[46]

Research by Susan Mohrman, Edwin Lawler, and Gerald Ledford Jr. demonstrates links between employee involvement and total quality management programs, which appear to work together in an integrated way to contribute to overall corporate performance, measured in financial terms. Generally speaking, these researchers found that these two types of systems-oriented programs, which provide a meaningful relationship between the employees and the work in ways that improve the product (so that customers are better served), are significantly related to better financial performance. In this study, financial performance was measured by return on sales, return on assets, return on investment, and return on equity.[47]

Another study links employee satisfaction with ensuring customer loyalty and long-term growth. Because customers typically relate to a company through a specific employee, the loss of that employee tends to reduce the customer's loyalty and commitment to the company, thereby reducing growth potential. Rob Duboff and Carla Heaton, the authors of the study, suggest very straightforwardly that "engendering loyalty among valuable employees is imperative" because "To develop effective, long-term relationships with profitable customers, . . . firms must also develop effective, long-term relationships with valuable employees who are able and willing to serve those customers."[48]

In another approach to looking at customer relationships, an innovative marketing company studies what consumers say about corporate citizenship with respect to their purchase intentions. In a 2003 study about holiday purchases, for example, Cone, Inc., a Boston-based marketing research firm, found that 60 percent of consumers intended to purchase a product where a percentage of the price was donated to a cause and 55 percent intended to purchase from a retailer that supported a cause.[49] Cone also found that, in the aftermath of the scandals that struck corporate America in the early 2000s, customers and employees are increasingly willing to punish companies whose values they do not respect. In this survey more than 1,000 adults were asked how they would respond to a company's negative corporate citizenship practices. The findings are striking: 91 percent would consider switching to another company's product or services, 85 percent would speak out against that company (creating reputational problems and, possibly, as the research cited above suggests, reduced growth), and 83 percent would refuse to invest in that company. Beyond that, 78 percent say they would boycott the company, 80 percent would refuse to work there, and 68 percent would find their loyalty reduced.[50]

It is becoming increasingly clear to marketers as well as corporate citizens interested in establishing good customer relationships through relationship marketing that they need to pay attention to many factors, especially those associated with product quality and corporate reputation, not to mention employee policies that impact attitudes, to maintain customer loyalty.

Supplier Relationships

Many companies, particularly those using suppliers in developing nations, have found that the practices of their suppliers, when problematic, can get them in trouble with consumers and activists. Buying from suppliers accused of using child labor, fostering abusive or sweatshop working conditions, or abrogating global labor standards can create significant reputational problems—and even consumer boycotts or overt anticompany campaigns. To cope with this issue, many companies that outsource manufacturing have found it necessary to develop a code of conduct for themselves—and require that their suppliers adhere to it as well. Increasingly, companies in the clothing, footwear, toy, and sports equipment industries find it necessary not only to have their codes of conduct in place for their suppliers, lest they lose customer and employee loyalty, but also to actively monitor their suppliers, often using outside monitors, to ensure adherence to those codes.

Supplier relationships need to be considered as part of the essential social capital that enhances the ultimate results or performance of the purchasing company. Long-term suppliers can sometimes develop new production methods that help a company meet its quality or productivity targets, but will do so only if they have a good relationship with the company. This form of social capital, which is built on stable and trusting relationships, can increase efficiency through greater information diffusion and may also decrease opportunism, which can reduce monitoring costs as well as enhance efficiency.[51]

Overall Stakeholder Relations and Performance

Throughout this book, we have defined corporate responsibility as being the way that a company treats its stakeholders through its day-to-day operating practices. Using this definition, my colleague Sam Graves and I performed another study that assessed the link between the overall quality of management in firms and their stakeholder relations (including their relationship to owners, measured in terms of financial performance).[52]

In this study, we used the *Fortune* reputational rating for quality of management (and the overall reputational rating as well) to assess the perceived quality of management of companies. We compared that rating to the ratings companies received for specific primary stakeholder categories that included the owners (financial performance), employee relations, and customer relations (a product and quality measure), as well as for society through a community relations measure and for environmental management through a measure related to environment.

What we found was that higher quality of management was strongly associated with better treatment of owners through financial performance, employee relations, and customers (through the product variable), and significantly associated with treatment of society through the community relations variable. In this particular study, treatment of the environment had no apparent relationship to improved perception of quality of management by outside observers, such as the CEOs and analysts who contribute to the *Fortune* quality-of-management and overall reputational ratings.

Overall, however, the findings indicate that quality of management and quality of stakeholder relationships are highly interrelated, providing further support for the idea that good management is the same thing as good stakeholder relationships. Since positive financial and social performance are also related, it would appear that there is mounting evidence that treating stakeholders respectfully and from a basis of integrity can contribute to corporate success.

This argument is somewhat problematic, according to social auditor Simon Zadek, because "it often is not right in practice in the short run, and the short run (as John Maynard Keynes pointed out) can last a hell of a long time."[53] Instead, as Zadek argues, this relationship really matters when stakeholders gain sufficient voice over corporate affairs that they are heard by management and can influence practice. As we have seen from the studies cited above, such stakeholder voice is an increasingly important part of the corporate landscape.

Environmental Management, Sustainability, and Performance

Environment management and the increasingly apparent need to move toward sustainable development poses another set of questions for leading corporate citizens. This question focuses on whether incorporating good environmental practice can result in better profits. We have already seen that value can be added through improved relationships with investors (owners), customers, and employees, and through overall responsible practice. We have also noted the better performance of the Dow Jones Sustainability Index over the general market. According to Innovest, a strategic value adviser focused on responsible investing, its proprietary environmental weights help create an ecology-enhanced index fund that outperformed the S&P 500 by about 15 basis points during 2002–2003.[54] Although the difference is modest, it does, once again, suggest that there need be no trade-off for investing in more environmentally responsible companies.

There is further evidence. The German research firm Oekom Research undertook a study with Morgan Stanley Dean Witter in 2003 that showed that companies receiving higher environmental ratings outperformed those with lesser ratings in the stock market. Companies rated as sustainability leaders (186 leaders in multiple sectors) were compared with 416 companies that received lower ratings. The results: the best-in-class companies outperformed the rest by more than 23 percent.[55]

What about environmental management? Does it too result in better profitability? The emerging evidence suggests that, while there can be some costs associated with implementing environmental management systems, in general reducing waste, reducing pollution, recycling, and related environmental management approaches are cost-effective. Research increasingly suggests that more environmentally responsible companies are, in fact, more profitable.[56]

Furthermore, recent research on the links between environmental management and stock price suggests that, like other constructive practices for building positive stakeholder relationships discussed above, better environmental policies actually improve financial performance for owners in terms of share prices. Companies can not only achieve direct cost reductions through programs like 3M's Pollution Prevention Pays (see Case 5.2), but such programs also have "a significant and favorable impact on the firm's perceived riskiness to investors and, accordingly, its cost of equity capital and value in the marketplace."[57] Indeed, improved environmental performance and management systems contribute as much as 5 percent to stock price.

Social Capital and Performance

Leading corporate citizens know that relationships with primary and secondary stakeholders matter now more than ever. The research on social capital (which we will discuss in Chapter 8) bolsters this argument and enhances our understanding of why these relationships matter. Social capital can be viewed as the trust and alliances generated by the relationships that people in a given system have developed over time. The emergence of strategic alliances and networked or virtual organizations, the connectedness imposed by electronic technology, and global awareness of company performance are only a few of the many factors that have enhanced the value of relationships in recent years.

Pollution Prevention Pays at 3M

From 1975 to 2002, 3M's Pollution Prevention Pays (3P) program has prevented 857,282 tons of pollutants and saved $894 million. The 3P program helps prevent pollution at the source—in products and manufacturing processes—rather than removing it after it has been created. The 3P program was updated in 2002 to provide more opportunities for participation by the company's research and development, logistics, transportation, and packaging employees with the addition of new award categories and criteria.

3P is a key element of 3M's environmental strategy and in moving towards sustainability. 3P has achieved that status based on the company's experience that a prevention approach is more environmentally effective, technically sound and economical than conventional pollution controls. Natural resources, energy and money are used to build conventional pollution controls, and more resources are consumed operating them. Conventional control only constrains the problem temporarily; it does not eliminate the problem. 3P seeks to eliminate pollution at the source through:

- Product reformulation
- Product modification
- Equipment redesign
- Recycling and reuse of waste materials

The 3P program depends directly on the voluntary participation of 3M employees. Innovative projects are recognized with 3P Awards. A 3P Coordinating Committee representing 3M's engineering, manufacturing and laboratory organizations—and the Environmental, Health and Safety group—administers the program. 3M employees worldwide have initiated 4,973 3P Projects. Projects must meet these criteria to receive formal recognition:

- Eliminate or reduce a pollutant.
- Benefit the environment through reduced energy use or more efficient use of manufacturing materials and resources.
- Save money—through avoidance or deferral of pollution control equipment costs, reduced operating and materials expenses, or increased sales of an existing or new product.
- A special award also recognizes projects that demonstrate technical innovation.

DISCUSSION QUESTIONS

1. Do you think that the savings from 3M's Pollution Prevention Pays Program are real? Why or why not?
2. If these savings are real, what prevents more companies from undertaking initiatives like 3M's?

Source: 3M Web site, www.3m.com/about3m/ sustainability/policies_ehs_tradition_3p.jhtml (accessed May 4, 2004).

We have argued that integrity is critical to corporate responsibility. Integrity is also essential to building trusting and trustful relationships with stakeholders, with whom companies are increasingly interdependent. It is this interdependence, a characteristic of social capital, that companies are recognizing as critical to their long-term success. Companies that build positive and lasting relationships with their stakeholders, in whatever sphere of activity they operate in, can cope better with the connectedness imposed by globalism and technology. Such companies may also better understand the dynamics and forces operating in the political and civil society spheres of activity than companies with less well developed relationships.

Further, companies that operate with integrity and by developing trusting relationships with all of their stakeholders may also enhance their social and intellectual capital, potentially creating a new source of competitive advantage.[58] An emerging theory of the firm argues, as we have argued here, that a company needs to be understood as a set of complex relationships—a web of relationships—in which the company can be seen as composed largely of relationships with primary stakeholders.[59]

Given this definition of the firm, social capital clearly plays an important role in fostering interaction and efficiency or economizing. Scholars Janine Nahapiet and Sumantra Ghoshal have argued that social capital provides two distinct kinds of benefits to companies. First, social capital increases efficiency, particularly information diffusion, and may also diminish opportunism, thereby decreasing monitoring costs. Second, social capital aids efficiency because it is based on trust and relationship by encouraging cooperation and therefore innovation.[60]

These same scholars make a link between social and intellectual capital, a link that is increasingly important in the knowledge-based economy facing corporate citizens in the 21st century. Defining *intellectual capital* as "the knowledge and knowing capability of a social collectivity," they argue that it is a valuable organizational resource created by the presence of a lot of social capital. The combination of social and intellectual capital contributes to organizational advantage, in part because, based on relationships as it is, social and intellectual capital represents a resource or core competency that is difficult for competitors to imitate.

So we begin to see a system of relationships among the elements we have been addressing as we developed the concept of the stakeholder-relationship-based enterprise. Starting with operational integrity—wholeness and honesty—we see that companies build trusting relationships and therefore social capital both internally and externally by creating constructive and positive operating practices that impact stakeholders. Because they are inextricably embedded in a web of relationships inside and outside the company, corporate citizens will increasingly need to pay attention to the quality of those relationships—to their social capital. They need to do this because building social capital and its associated intellectual capital results in a system that works for all stakeholders.

Even when there are short-term trade-offs, the company that understands the inherent value of its relationships will act respectfully toward its stakeholders, continuing to build social and intellectual capital. As we shall see in the next two chapters, the future is likely to bring more connectedness and greater than ever need for transparency in all actions. Transparency is demanded because of the increased public capacity to know what is happening within and to companies because of the connections made available by the Internet. It is also clear that we live in a world of ever more change and complexity. In such a world, leading corporate citizens will need all of the social and intellectual capital with their stakeholders that they can muster.

Leading Challenges: Making the Value-Added Connection

In a world where the narrow maxim of "maximizing shareholder wealth" is still held in many quarters to be the dominant or only purpose of the corporation, leading corporate citizens with a view toward treating all stakeholders respectfully can be a significant challenge. Yet it is clear that such either/or thinking is more limiting to managerial leadership than would be a both/and approach that valued all stakeholders (and the environment) as ends to be respected and treated with dignity.

Value can be added in many ways that can empower and involve key stakeholders such as employees, customers, and suppliers, making them partners and collaborators in the enterprise of doing business. In this chapter we have explored the business case for corporate responsibility in a number of important stakeholder domains, as well as with respect to the environment.

For leaders of corporate citizens, it is important to be able to explain that doing well and doing good with respect to key stakeholders does not necessitate a trade-off as much as an investment in good relationships. It is in this web of good relationships that the leading corporate citizen will in the future find significant sources of competitive advantage. In the next chapter we will explore some of the specific practices that leading corporate citizens have evolved to develop the web of relationships with their stakeholders on which they depend.

Endnotes

1. Jed Emerson, "The Blended Value Proposition: Integrating Social and Financial Returns," *California Management Review* 45, no. 4 (Summer 2003), pp. 35–38.
2. Ibid.
3. Jim Thomas and John Harris, "Clear Advantage: Building Shareholder Value, Environment: Value to the Investor," Global Environmental Management Initiative (GEMI) report, 2004, www.gemi.org/GEMI%20Clear%20Advantag.pdf (accessed April 15, 2004), p. 20.
4. Ibid., p. 18.
5. William McDonough, and Michael Braungart, *Cradle to Cradle: Remaking the Way We Make Things* (New York: North Point Press, 2002).
6. Clark Eustace, "The Intangible Economy: Impact and Policy Issues," Report of the High Level Expert Group on the Intangible Economy, Enterprise Directorate-General, Brussels: European Commission, October 2002, cited in Thomas and Harris, "Clear Advantage: Building Shareholder Value," p. 2.
7. Quoted in William Blaue, "Moving from the Business Case for SRI and CSR to the Fiduciary Case," sri-adviser.com, www.sri-adviser.com/article.mpl?sfArticleId=1346 (accessed April 14, 2004).
8. Russell L. Ackoff, "On Learning and the Systems That Facilitate It," *Reflections* 1, no. 1 (1999), p. 16: reprinted from the Center for Quality of Management, Cambridge, MA, 1996. Italics added.

9. Dirk Matten and Andrew Crane, "Corporate Citizenship: Towards an Extended Theoretical Conceptualization," *Academy of Management Review* 29 (2004) in press.

10. These two paragraphs are derived from Sandra Waddock and Neil Smith, "Corporate Responsibility Audits: Doing Well by Doing Good," *Sloan Management Review* 105, no. 1 (Spring 2000), pp. 47–63.

11. James C. Collins and Jerry I. Porras, *Built to Last: Successful Habits of Visionary Companies* (New York: HarperBusiness, 1997).

12. Ibid., p. 4.

13. Ibid., p. 4.

14. Ibid., p. 8.

15. See Samuel B. Graves and Sandra A. Waddock, "Beyond Built to Last ... Stakeholder Relations in 'Built-to-Last' Companies," *Business and Society Review*, 2000, 105(3): 323–345.

16. Joshua D. Margolis and James P. Walsh, "Misery Loves Companies: Rethinking Social Initiatives by Business," *Administrative Science Quarterly* 48 (2003), pp. 268–305. The second study cited here is M. Orlitzky, F. I. Schmidt, and S. L. Rynes, "Corporate Social and Financial Performance: A Meta-Analysis," *Organization Studies* 24 (2003), pp. 403–41.

17. See Sandra A. Waddock and Samuel B. Graves, "The Corporate Social Performance–Financial Performance Link," *Strategic Management Journal* 18, no. 4 (1997), pp. 303–19, and "Quality of Management and Quality of Stakeholder Relations: Are They Synonymous?" *Business and Society* 36, no. 3 (September 1997), pp. 250–79, both of which make this argument and provide empirical evidence supporting it.

18. Social Investment Forum, "2003 Report on Socially Responsible Investing Trends in the United States," www.socialinvest.org/areas/research/trends/sri_trends_report_2003.pdf (accessed May 3, 2004).

19. Ibid.

20. Ibid.

21. Stephen Barlas, Alfred King, Peter Leitner, and Curtis Verschoor, "More Evidence of Better Financial Performance," *Strategic Finance* 85, no. 5 (November 2003), pp. 2–3.

22. Go to www.business-ethics.com to for the latest rankings.

23. See www.kld.com for information about KLD's ratings. These ratings will be discussed later in the book in more detail.

24. Barlas et al., "More Evidence of Better Financial Performance."

25. Social Investment Forum, "2003 Report."

26. Barlas et al., "More Evidence of Better Financial Performance."

27. Ibid., p. 3.

28. Jeffrey Pfeffer and John F. Veiga, "Putting People First for Organizational Success," *Academy of Management Executive* 13, no. 2 (May 1999), pp. 37–48. See also Gary Dessler, "How to Earn Your Employees' Commitment," *Academy of Management Executive* 13, no. 2 (May 1999), pp. 58–67, for a similar set of ideas.

29. Pfeffer and Veiga, "Putting People First," pp. 37, 39. The first study cited is B. Gates, "Compete, Don't Delete," *The Economist*, June 13, 1998, pp. 19–21. The second study cited is J. Pfeffer, *Competitive Advantage through People: Unleashing the Power of the Workforce* (Boston: Harvard Business School Press, 1995), p. 9.

30. N. Stein "Winning the War to Keep Top Talent," *Fortune,* May 29, 2000, pp. 132–38.

31. Reported in C. Joinson, "Capturing Turnover Costs," *HR Magazine* 45, no. 7 (2000), pp. 107–19.

32. Stephen Bevan, Nick Isles, Peter Emery, and Tony Hoskins, "Achieving High Performance: CSR at the Heart of Business," The Work Foundation, 2001, www.theworkfoundation.com/pdf/184373017.pdf (accessed May 6, 2004).

33. Jeffrey Pfeffer, *The Human Equation: Building Profits by Putting People First* (Boston: Harvard Business School Press, 1998).

34. Pfeffer and Veiga, "Putting People First," p. 39.

35. See Jerry Watson Wyatt, "Human Capital Index Study," *Drake Business Review,* 1999, cited in Thomas and Harris, "Clear Advantage," p. 21.

36. Jonathan Low and Pamela Cohen Kalfut, *Invisible Advantage* (Cambridge, MA: Perseus Press, 2002), cited in Thomas and Harris, "Clear Advantage," p. 21.

37. Ibid.

38. Jay Barney, *Gaining and Sustaining Competitive Advantage* (Reading, MA: Addison-Wesley, 1997).

39. Kimberly Weisul, *Business Week Online,* January 27, 2004.

40. Charles B. Shrader, Virginia Blackburn, and Paul Iles, "Women in Management and Firm Financial Performance: An Exploratory Study," *Journal of Managerial Issues* 9, no. 3 (Fall 1997), pp. 355–72.

41. Sue Shellenbarger, "Companies Are Finding It Really Pays to Be Nice to Employees," *The Wall Street Journal,* July 22, 1998.

42. Ibid.

43. Examples from ibid.

44. Armand V. Feigenbaum, "Changing Concepts and Management of Quality Worldwide," *Quality Progress* 30, no. 12 (December 1997), p. 46.

45. C. Cone, "2002 Cone Corporate Citizenship Study," http://www.coneinc.com/Pages/pr_13.html (accessed October 6, 2003).

46. Frederick F. Reichheld, "The One Number You Need to Grow," *Harvard Business Review,* December 2003, pp. 46–54.

47. Susan A. Mohrman, Edward E. Lawler III, and Gerald E. Ledford Jr., "Do Employee Involvement and TQM Programs Work?" *Journal for Quality & Participation* 19, no. 1 (January/February 1996), pp. 6–10.

48. Rob Duboff and Carla Heaton, "Employee Loyalty: The Key Link to Value Growth," *Planning Review* 27, no. 1 (January/February 1999), pp. 8–13.

49. Cone, Inc., "'Tis the Season for Cause-Related Shopping," November 17, 2003, www.coneinc.com/Pages/pr_22.html (accessed May 11, 2004).

50. Cone, Inc., "2002 Cone Corporate Citizenship Study," 2002, www.coneinc.com/Pages/pr_13.html (accessed May 11, 2004).

51. See, for example, J. Nahapiet and S. Ghoshal, "Social Capital, Intellectual Capital, and the Organizational Advantage," *Academy of Management Review* 23, no. 2 (April 1998), pp. 242–66.

52. See Waddock and Graves, "Quality of Management and Quality of Stakeholder Relations."

53. Simon Zadek, "Balancing, Performance, Ethics, and Accountability," *Journal of Business Ethics* 17, no. 3 (October 1998), pp. 1421–41.

54. William Blaue and Mark Thomsen, "Innovest's Eco-Enhanced Portfolios Outperform Their Benchmarks," SocialFunds.com, November 12, 2003, www.socialfunds.com/news/print.cgi?sfArticleId=1266 (accessed May 4, 2004).

55. William Blaue, "Morgan Stanley Study Correlates Sustainability with Financial Outperformance," SocialFunds.com, December 5, 2003, www.socialfunds.com/news/print.cgi?sfArticleId=1289 (accessed May 4, 2004).

56. For examples of studies that make this connection, see Richard Florida, "Lean and Green: The Move to Environmentally Conscious Manufacturing," *California Management Review* 39, no. 1 (1996), pp. 80–104; R. D. Klassen and C. P. McLaughlin, "The Impact of Environmental Management on Firm Performance," *Management Science* 42, no. 8 (1996), pp. 1199–1214; and Steve Melnyk, Roger Catalone, Rob Handfield, Lal Tummala, Gyula Vastag, Timothy Hinds, Robert Sroufe, and Frank Montabon, *ISO 14000: Assessing Its Impact on Corporate Performance* (Tempe, AZ: Center for Advanced Purchasing Studies, 1999).

57. Stanley J. Feldman, Peter A. Soyka, and Paul G. Ameer, "Does Improving a Firm's Environmental Management System and Environmental Performance Result in a Higher Stock Price?" *Journal of Investing* 6, no. 4 (Winter 1997), pp. 87–97.

58. See Nahapiet and Ghoshal, "Social Capital, Intellectual Capital, and the Organizational Advantage."

59. Ibid.

60. Ibid.

PART THREE

Leading Corporate Citizens and Their Stakeholders

CHAPTER SIX

Stakeholders: The Relationship Key

Contrary to widespread impressions, Adam Smith, the inventor of economics, celebrated the individual not solely as an end in himself, but as the member of a community, one whose purpose was a better society. He hailed the power of "connections and dependencies" in promoting the greater good. He spoke of the entrepreneur as "a single cell in a larger organism." He said technological progress came from "combining together the powers of the most distant and dissimilar objects." In the very paragraph of *The Wealth of Nations* containing his oft-quoted axiom of self-interest, Smith also makes the following claim: "in civilized societies [the human being] stands at all times in need of the cooperation and assistance of great multitudes." One telling fact: When Smith died, his estate was negligible. He had given it all away.

After a century of hiding, Smith's values are reemerging through the pressures of a complex and interdependent world. Until recently, most business owners saw themselves as lone battlers eking out their claim in a hostile environment; many, perhaps most, still do. But the kind of spectacular success possible in today's economy is accessible not at arm's length but through a full embrace. As the economy splinters into ever-smaller pieces, those very individuals prosper principally through expressions of solidarity. Where business is concerned, the personal and the social are two halves of the identical dynamic, no differently, as it happens, than elsewhere in nature.

Thomas Petzinger Jr., The New Pioneers, *pp. 47–48*

Building Sustainable Stakeholder Links

Business organizations, we have argued, consist of *primary stakeholders*: owners, customers, employees, suppliers (at least in the case of "virtual" or network organizations), and of course partners and allies. Relationships with these primary stakeholders are essential to the long-term health and success of any business enterprise (see Figure 6.1). Depending on their sphere of activity, all business enterprises also have *critical secondary stakeholders* on whom they also depend or who depend on their success. This network of relationships creates a new type of organization, one that researchers James Post, Lee Preston, and Sybille Sachs call the "extended enterprise."[1]

Critical secondary stakeholders include communities in which operations are located and, for most companies, governmental agencies that interact with the enterprise (if the organization is not itself a governmental agency) in setting the relevant rules of societies in which the company operates. Companies depend

FIGURE 6.1   **Primary Stakeholders for Different Organizational Types**

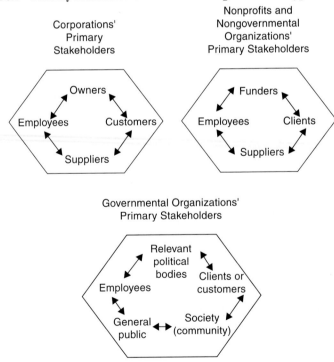

on the infrastructure and supports provided by local communities for their well-being, and they depend on governments for setting the rules of society necessary to make the business system feasible.

Critical secondary stakeholders depend to some extent on the company's success for their own well-being, that is, for taxes and, in the case of communities, for the community outreach and philanthropic activities that help support the development of healthy communities. For highly regulated companies, of course, government might well be a primary stakeholder, and for companies like utilities that are necessarily community-based, community might be a primary stakeholder. Society as a whole might in some cases be considered a critical secondary stakeholder because of companies' long- and short-term impacts.

Further, all business enterprises have an array of *particular secondary stakeholder relationships* that arise because of the specialized interests, business activities, and purposes of the enterprise itself. These relationships can include various activists; the media; relevant citizen groups; nongovernmental organizations (NGOs): intergovernmental organizations (IGOs); partnership enterprises; and relevant trade, industry, and civic associations.

Finally, there are parties in society that fall outside the realm of primary and secondary activities for a company. These parties are nonstakeholders for any firm at a given time. But society is dynamic, as are companies, so one of the important roles of leadership is to scan the external environment constantly and consistently for emerging issues and concerns that may convert nonstakeholders into stakeholders. This scanning process is one of the primary responsibilities of units and managers charged with boundary spanning or boundary scanning, which is what we will be discussing throughout the rest of this chapter. Increasingly, especially in companies where electronic communications and commerce are central to the firm's existence, the responsibility for boundary-spanning activities rests with employees and leaders at all levels of the organization. In many modern companies, it is individuals and groups throughout the company that actually implement the practices that evolve into the stakeholder relationships on which the company depends.

Organizing for Relationship: Boundary-Spanning Functions

To cope with the complexity and dynamism associated with dealing with multiple stakeholders and their associated bottom lines,[2] many companies have established a range of functions that cross organizational boundaries, either internally (as with employee relations) or, more frequently, externally. Such functions are called *boundary-spanning functions*. Boundary-spanning functions in general are those related to developing, maintaining, and assuring the quality of the company's relationship with a particular stakeholder group and aspects of the broader social environment. For the rest of this chapter, we will consider the ways in which companies can organize these boundary-spanning functions so that they can be effective (i.e., do the right thing) as well as efficient (economize) to make the business enterprise a success. Simultaneously, we need to recognize that the responsibility for developing good stakeholder relationships is inherent

FIGURE 6.2 **Boundary-Spanning Functions for Global Corporate Citizenship**

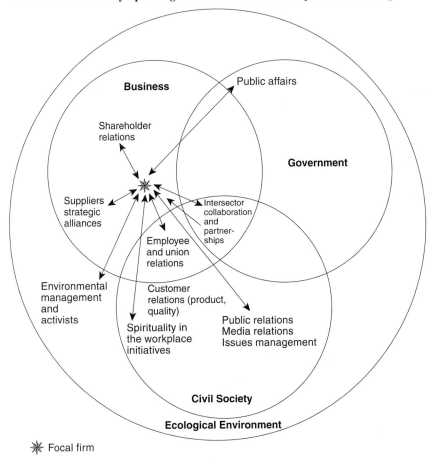

✳ Focal firm

in the job of all managers. Of course, in small companies with few management layers, these responsibilities may be inherent to all of the managerial positions in the firm.

Figure 6.2 illustrates a generic mapping of the critical primary and secondary stakeholder relationships, with their related boundary-spanning functions for a typical firm. The focal organization operates within the business sphere, but, as can readily be seen, has links to entities operating in all of the other spheres. Owners or shareholders, who are represented in the figure by the shareholder relations function, are primary stakeholders. A second group is employees, who are represented by various employee relations and human resource functions, as well as labor and trade unions that protect their rights, designated in the figure by the generic term *employee and union relations.* A third primary stakeholder group includes customers, who are represented through marketing efforts, product quality and service, and designated boundary-spanning functions generically termed *customer relations*. The fourth group of primary stakeholders for many modern companies consists of suppliers, allies, and partners. Companies that have outsourced many functions, creating numerous alliances and partnerships, depend on the knowledge and expertise from outside suppliers. As some companies have discovered to their chagrin, problems within their supply chain can create significant reputation problems for the sourcing company. Ally, partner, and supplier/distributor relations are typically handled through strategic alliances, contracts, and even joint ventures, some of which may well be with organizations that are otherwise considered to be competitors.

Critical secondary stakeholder relationships are also designated in Figure 6.2. In the typical large corporation, community stakeholder relationships are handled by the community relations function. Governmental relationships are managed by the public affairs office, which may also include the firm's lobbying activities and political activity. The public affairs umbrella can also include such particular stakeholder relationships as public relations, media relations, and issues management. Finally, many modern corporations have also established environmental management programs and offices to cope with the need for sustainability and better stewardship of natural resources, and to handle relationships with environmental activists.

Primary Stakeholder Relationships

Coping with boundary-spanning relationships is complex but critical to the success of the modern firm, particularly when we consider that the firm, literally and figuratively, is comprised of its primary stakeholders. The firm's long-term success is intimately related to the way it treats its stakeholders in these essential relationships over time; thus, every manager ultimately is involved in some or most of these relationships. The next sections of this chapter will detail the current state of the art in the particular boundary-spanning functions that deal with specific stakeholder groups.

Owners

According to the neoclassical economic model, which still dominates thinking about the modern corporation, the primary interest of owners in a company is maximizing profits or wealth. The investment made in a company by the owner stakeholder is, of course, financial; hence, the relevant bottom line for stockholders or owners is the traditional financial bottom line. Shareholder relations thus encompass the many ways that companies communicate with and receive feedback from their shareholders, including governance and annual meetings.

Investor Relations

Many companies have investor relations departments whose role involves helping financial analysts correctly determine the company's value so that investors can make the proper decision regarding investment in a given firm. Of course, communicating with existing investors, as well as potential investors, is also a critical element of this unit's job.

The investor relations department is also typically responsible for producing a company's annual report, which provides both financial and strategic information to existing investors or shareholders. Sometimes the investor relations function falls under the broader umbrella of public relations or public affairs, functions also responsible for managing external perceptions of the firm.

Investors are asking whether companies are actually performing well for them, particularly in light of the early 2000s' high-profile corporate scandals (e.g., Enron, WorldCom, and Tyco). The consulting firm McKinsey undertook a study that suggested a new era in corporate governance may be emerging, one that will shift shareholder expectations of boards of directors well beyond the tougher auditing standards and greater executive accountability demanded by the Sarbanes-Oxley Act of 2002. This study indicates that directors themselves expect that investor relations are likely to shift in important ways, including separating the roles of CEO and chair of the board, ensuring that directors are more independent and accountable for their decisions, and reducing excessive levels of CEO compensation, which in 2000 peaked at 531 times the average pay of production workers.[3]

Fiduciary Responsibilities

Appropriate and proper treatment of owners has to do with respecting owners' rights to have input into the governance of the company. Most important, treatment of owners includes the owners' right to a fair return for the financial capital they risk in making their investment in the firm in the first place. The company's directors, who oversee the hiring of top management and the general strategic direction of the firm, thus have a *fiduciary responsibility* to the owners. The top management team is responsible for developing and implementing the company's vision, values, and strategy. Responsibility to owners or stockholders is typically measured in financial terms.[4] The fiduciary responsibility of corporate directors and their agents requires that the management team operate with due care, loyalty, and honesty with respect to the stockholders' financial investment or interest in the firm.[5] When companies don't do this, they can be fraught with fraud, accounting misstatements, and other problems related to their financial performance.

To be profitable, companies need to be productive and economize as much as possible. Profits are a by-product of doing something well for someone—a customer or many customers—rather than an end in and of themselves.[6] Indeed, how companies treat their owners financially is a legitimate concern among investors of all sorts, who have put their financial capital at risk on behalf of the firm with the expectation of good financial returns. Still, the fiduciary responsibility of corporate directors is generally intended by U.S. courts to give corporate directors authority to prevent self-dealing, opportunistic behavior, and too much power-aggrandizing behavior on the part of managers.[7]

The primary relationship between the company and its shareholders is therefore one of safeguarding the investment made by stockholders, and ensuring that the owners as investors receive a fair return for the risk they have taken. The relationship is actually not that of agency, nor is it necessarily a contractual obligation among individual people. Rather, the fiduciary responsibility is intended to "protect legal owners who were not in a position to manage their own affairs from the unscrupulous self-dealing of those administrators the incompetent were forced to rely upon."[8]

Additionally, while shareholders have a right to expect honesty, candor, and care (i.e., integrity) from management, this right is similar to rights that other stakeholders—such as creditors, suppliers and allies, employees, and customers—also expect from companies. Second, courts are now starting to impose fiduciary responsibilities on corporate directors and managers for stakeholders other than owners.[9] Thus, shareholders need to be considered in some respects to be on par with other stakeholders rather than elevated to a unique status as the only important stakeholder.

The key to success is balance. The interests of the primary stakeholders and some critical secondary stakeholders have to be assessed and balanced with each other to achieve the desired outcome: a company that operates with integrity and adds value for owners *and* other stakeholders. To see how this can be done, in the sections that follow we will address how other stakeholders can be treated well.

Employee Relationships

The primary interests of employees are earning a good wage for their efforts and making their personal contributions to the organization's achievement of its vision and values. A firm's major investment in employees used to be for their physical labor; however, modern enterprises, particularly Web-based, e-commerce, and technologically sophisticated companies, tend to invest more in their employees' knowledge, known as intellectual capital. Also, in making a commitment to an enterprise, employees put at risk their work lives, their capacity to contribute, and their earning power. As a result, they have a right, in return, to expect that their work contributes to a meaningful enterprise and that they can know and be valued for the meaning of their own contributions.

Employees and the contributions they make are central to any organization's success. Many companies, recognizing the importance of good relationships with employees, claim to put people first. Despite the rhetoric, the modern corporate landscape is fraught with corporate restructurings, layoffs, outsourcing of work to low-wage countries with low workforce standards, contingent or part-time workforces (to whom benefits do not need to be paid), and other cost-cutting measures that affect employees negatively. Such actions have left many workers feeling devalued and have eroded their loyalty.

People—and their loyalty, commitment, and productive energy—*do* matter to the success and health of the firm. Treating employees well is essential for generating high levels of productivity and performance over time.[10] Treating employees well generates commitment to the organization's purpose, particularly if that purpose is shared with employees and they understand what their role is in accomplishing it. Translating the organization's vision and values into employee policies that actually work is not rocket science. Yet despite their claims to value employees, many companies still operate their employee relationships on failed assumptions; that is, their practice differs greatly from their rhetoric.

Failed Assumptions

Employers' failed assumptions include viewing employees as costs rather than investments, focusing on the short versus the long term, dehumanizing employees (or infantilizing them), and failing to delegate.[11] Leaders tend also to be subject to two perverse norms about what good management is: the idea that good managers are tough or mean, and that the idea that good analysis is the same as good management,[12] a problem sometimes termed the paralysis of analysis.[13] Further, because of embedded cultures and long-term policies that devalue people and their contributions, many companies need to transform their employee policies to bring the rhetoric and the reality of their cultures and operating practices more into line with their vision and values statements.

Successful Employee Practices

Highly successful organizations engage in a number of practices that do provide employees with the sense of meaningfulness that is important to productivity (see Table 6.1). Some of these practices are directly counter to current management practices that result in erosion of employee loyalty and capacity (and, correspondingly, community health as well). All of them are consistent with the work of James Collins and Jerry Porras, as well as that of Jeanne Liedtka, discussed in Chapter 5.

Employees, like other stakeholders, need and want to feel a part of something bigger than they are; that is, they seek meaning in their work and work setting.[14] High-performing companies provide security for employees who are carefully selected to accord with the vision and values of the company. They establish compensation plans that tie rewards not only to individual but also to group and company performance. They value their employees really, not just rhetorically, and demonstrate that valuing by providing extensive training; reducing status differences among levels; and sharing information about the company, its performance, and its policies. Such companies thereby provide a basis on which employees, as stakeholders, know that they are being valued and treated fairly, rather than being subjected to power-aggrandizing management whims or the shifting winds of profitability.

Employee Commitment/Company Commitment

Gaining commitment and loyalty from employee stakeholders requires creating, internally, almost cult-like cultures.[15] Commitment derives from a set of internally developed practices that inspire people to believe in the work of the

TABLE 6.1   **Employment Practices of Successful Organizations**

Source: Summarized from Jeffrey Pfeffer and John F. Veiga, "Putting People First for Organizational Success," *Academy of Management Executive* 13, no. 2 (May 1999), pp. 37–48.

Employment security	Provides job security even when productivity improves; retains knowledgeable, productive workers; builds commitment and retention; and decreases costs associated with layoffs (including training and recruitment).
Selective hiring	Creates cult-like cultures built on common values. Requires large applicant pool, clarity about necessary skills and attributes, clear sense of job requirements, and screening on attributes difficult to change through training.
Self-managed teams and decentralization	Teams substitute peer-based control for hierarchical control; ideas are shared and creative solutions found. Decentralization increases shared responsibility for outcomes, stimulates initiative and effort, and removes levels of management (cost).
Comparatively high compensation	Produces organizational success; retains expertise and experience; rewards and reinforces high performance.
Compensation contingent on organization performance	Rewards the whole as well as individual effort. Requires employee training to understand links between ownership and rewards.
Extensive training	Values knowledge and skills (generalist, not specialist). Relies on frontline employees' skill and initiative for problem solving, innovation, responsibility for quality. Can be source of competitive advantage.
Reduction of status differences	Premised on belief that high performance is achieved when all employees' ideas, skills, efforts are fully tapped. To do this requires reducing differences among levels, both symbolically (language and labels, physical space, dress) and substantively (reduction of wage inequality across levels).
Sharing information	Creates a high-trust organization; helps everyone know where contributions come from and where they stand.

enterprise, generating a clear vision with well-articulated underlying values that clearly demonstrate the contribution that is being made to something bigger than oneself. Commitment also means that the company is willing to commit itself with integrity to the well-being of employees over the long term.

Sustaining employee commitment and building loyalty are not easy in an era, such as we are in now, when loyalty both from and to employees seems a thing of the past. Many of today's employees have essentially been taught by corporate downsizings, restructurings, and rightsizings (or, in plain language, layoffs) that their first objective is to be an individual contributor, almost an entrepreneur within the company, looking out for self rather than others. Others lack loyalty to companies because they are employed as contingent workers, hired temporarily or part-time so that employers can avoid the cost of benefits.

Companies with successful employee practices know that there are significant benefits to be gained by treating employees in the ways that Table 6.1 details. For example, both companies and employees benefit from employment security, as well as from the creation of cult-like cultures built on selective hiring practices that screen out applicants for whom the company's culture is a mismatch. Once hired, employees find value in being in decentralized systems where they can be part of self-managed teams and be well compensated based on their actual contributions and performance. Highly successful companies provide extensive employee training, reduce status differences, and share relevant information with employees so that they can perform their jobs well.[16]

In addition to the practices of successful organizations detailed in Table 6.1, organizations that want to build employee loyalty can stress their clear values throughout the orientation and training programs; implement the values in ways that build an organizational tradition through symbols and culture; and guarantee fairness or justice throughout the system, particularly through comprehensive grievance procedures. They should also provide for extensive two-way communications at all levels, create a sense of community through elaborating the common purpose, and hire people sympathetic with the company's vision and values. Such companies not only distribute rewards equitably and emphasize teamwork but also celebrate achievement and employee development.[17]

Intellectual Capital

In one sense, building positive relationships with employees at its most fundamental is about treating all people with the same dignity and respect with which we would treat family, peers, or organizational superiors. It is not extremely difficult, but it does require sustained effort to overcome the tendency, inherent in business's dominant value of economizing, toward viewing people as means rather than ends. Similarly, the premises of fairness and respect implicit in the practices described in Table 6.1 need to be constantly held up in light of the tendency to value power aggrandizement. In the end, however, the performance results of using a respectful approach toward the critical employee stakeholder make the effort well worthwhile.

The rationale for building respectful relationships with employees, especially for the modern corporation, is that both the intellectual capital housed in the minds of employees and the social capital that can be developed by winning their hearts are great aids to productivity. Intellectual capital is a key, if not the only, source of competitive advantage in many organizations today. Companies that recognize this reality and develop practices that treat their employees with dignity and respect, rather than exploitation, and that develop cultures in which employees can fulfill personal needs and dreams while also working on the corporate vision, will succeed where others fail.

Customer Relationships

Customer relationships have come to the fore in recent years with the emergence of relationship marketing. What marketers and business leaders have recognized is that customers purchase goods and services from one company as opposed to another because they have reason to trust that the company's products will meet expectations. Thus, trust becomes a type of capital. Another type of capital is the loyalty that customers have to the company; some claim that long-term customer commitment is the most critical resource companies can have for growing the top line—revenue.[18]

Relationship marketing theory operates alongside the traditional marketing mix of product, price, place, and promotion. Relationship marketing is especially important in service and knowledge industries, where the relationship itself may be what matters most to customers. Relationships are, however, increasingly important for all types of companies because of technological connectivity, which can turn many products into services delivered electronically.[19] Terms such as *relational contracting, relational marketing, working partnerships, symbiotic marketing, strategic alliances, co-marketing alliances,* and *internal marketing* all have been used to describe aspects of relationship marketing: developing a network of sustained exchange relationships between customers and companies.[20]

Like other forms of relationships among Web-connected companies and stakeholders, customer and supply chain relationships are gaining importance because of the recognition that companies are embedded in networks where cooperative relationships matter at least as much as competitive ones.[21] Equally deeply embedded in this emerging relational perspective on customers is recognition of the need for high-quality products and services, as well as high-quality relationships that will sustain the necessary trust and commitment on which relationship marketing relies.[22] For example, the word *quality* is associated with, among other factors, customer satisfaction; business effectiveness and cost leadership; and cooperative relationships, even partnerships, with customers throughout the company's value chain. Higher quality as assessed by Baldrige Quality Award winners has been found to be linked to better financial performance.[23]

Mutual trust in customer relationships (and other relationships as well) exists when both parties have confidence in each other's reliability and integrity. Commitment exists when both parties value the relationship over time; that is, the relationship is enduring. Among the factors that result in trust and commitment between companies and their customers are shared values, timely communication, and potential costs of ending the relationship. Opportunistic and self-serving behavior on one partner's part will very likely reduce trust and commitment.[24]

Customer Loyalty

The goal of enhancing customer relationships is to build loyalty among customers, who then make a long-term commitment to the company to continue purchasing goods and services and who tell others about the company's products and services.[25] Companies that produce shoddy or harmful products will find it increasingly difficult to maintain customer trust and commitment in an era in which sustained relationships and alliances of all sorts are increasingly central to producing sales and information about problems spreads at the speed of electrons across the World Wide Web. Particularly as information about the nature and quality of products is made readily available electronically, it becomes critical to work with customers collaboratively to ensure that they are actually getting what they need.

There are many benefits of establishing ongoing relationships with customers. First, in a relationship, customers' needs are really met. As customer needs change over time, companies that are in communication with customers can shift accordingly. Costs of maintaining the relationship and selling, distributing, and delivering goods and services (called transaction costs) also decrease as trust and commitment increase. Also long-standing customers can provide excellent feedback that helps improve product and service quality. Customer relationships mean interacting regularly with customers to ensure that value is being added, which can create additional ties through technology, shared knowledge or expertise, or social capital.[26]

Quality and Customers

For most companies today, particularly those competing in the global arena, product and service quality is a given. Along with the quality revolution, which occurred in the United States during the last 20 years of the 20th century and in the prior 30 years in Japan, came customer demands for nearly complete satisfaction with the quality and nature of products and services. Cigarette manufacturers, for example, would have problems justifying their product given all of the research that links tobacco with disease, despite the profitability and presumed quality of their product and despite company protests that the link is not proved.

Quality programs, following the advice of management guru Dr. W. Edwards Deming, typically focus on continual quality improvement through emphasis on statistical process controls and quality management. The quality process, whether for product- or service-oriented companies, ensures that customer expectations are met and that trust is built. Table 6.2 lists the characteristics of service and manufacturing companies considered to be world class and designed to develop excellent relationships with customers (and suppliers), along with employees.[27]

It is interesting to note that many of these characteristics are similar to those needed to generate excellence in employee relationships; both goals require that a company operate with integrity and a sound set of core values, ultimately with principled leadership. In addition, the practices associated with world-class

TABLE 6.2   **Characteristics of World-Class Quality Operations**

Source: Charles C. Poirier and William F. Houser, *Business Partnering for Continuous Improvement* (San Francisco: Berrett-Koehler, 1993).

World-Class Plant	World-Class Service Organization
1. Safety	1. Accessibility and follow-up by employees
2. Involved and committed workforce	2. Competence (required skills and knowledge, proactive)
3. Just-in-time manufacturing and deliveries to customers	3. Attitude (positive, flexible, continuous improvement)
4. Focus on product flow	4. Communication
5. Preventive/predictive maintenance	5. Credibility
6. Bottlenecks managed	6. Features/innovation in services
7. Total quality management program	7. Responsiveness
8. Fast setups	8. Tangible results
9. Extremely low inventories	
10. Supportive policies/procedures	

companies highlight the need for integrity in all of the company's practices, including developing the goods and services that will be delivered to customers with whom the company hopes to establish a long-term relationship for repeat purchases and all-important word-of-mouth marketing.

Some scholars link product and service quality with business effectiveness, making connections among customers, and partnering with suppliers as source of competitive advantage. The quality movement has pushed many companies to benchmark their own operations and product/service quality against those of leading competitors to ensure that they continue to stay abreast of new developments and meet changing customer needs.[28] Companies can enhance actual and perceived quality as well as the relationship with customers by providing technical service and user advice; installing just-in-time logistics systems in customer facilities; adapting invoicing to specific customer needs; and providing technical expertise, information, and social contact with customers, among other services.[29]

Establishing Customer Relationships

An important study exploring the nature of relationship marketing found that trust and commitment emerge when companies focus on relationships by (1) offering resources, opportunities, and benefits superior to those offered by competitors (or alternative partners for the customer); (2) maintaining high integrity, or high standards of conduct and values and associating with partners that have similar standards; (3) communicating important and valuable information that includes expectations, market intelligence, and evaluation of partner performance; and (4) avoiding opportunistic behavior with respect to the partner.[30] The study concluded: "Somewhat paradoxically, to be an effective competitor in today's global marketplace requires one to be an effective cooperator in some network of organizations."[31] Ironically, being competitive sometimes actually means collaborating with companies that might in other circumstances be competitors.

Suppliers, Distributors, Allies, and Partners

Supply chain management has become a hot topic in the current era of anticorporate activism, outsourcing, and network-structured enterprises. Alliances, joint ventures, partnerships, and outsourcing are all ways of reducing nonessential activities and controlling costs, that is, economizing measures. When much of a company is organized through alliances and links to other companies, when major functions are outsourced, and when the companies share information through their computer systems, the company can be called a virtual company. The bottom line of supplier and ally relationships, as with employee relationships, can be found in the intellectual or knowledge capital inherent in the expertise for which the relationship is developed in the first place. Companies increasingly need to manage these relationships proactively to maximize their performance.

Traditional Supplier Relationships

Traditionally and in many cases still today, companies formed relationships with suppliers to gain access to raw materials and services necessary to the company's business. Typical supplier–customer links are based on contracts that spell out the services or products to be delivered, the conditions under which they are to be delivered, and the relevant prices. The contract can stipulate an arm's-length relationship, meaning that the two businesses have little interaction other than that necessary to exchange goods and services and receive payment.

Some companies—particularly in Asian countries where the ideology is communitarian and where long-term relationships are considered essential to doing business with others—develop networks of long-standing intercompany relationships to get access to necessary goods and services. There are families of companies—called *kereitsu* in Japan and *chaebol* in Korea—in similar and sometimes vastly different businesses whose links are sustained over long periods of time. The companies involved establish a form of social capital or a familylike relationship.

Traditional suppliers are interdependent with their customers in that each company in the relationship relies upon the other to deliver what has been promised. But when the relationships are solely contractual rather than based on trust and mutuality of interests, supplier–customer links can be established and dropped as prices or interests change without significant consequences to the purchasing company. Indeed, many companies, using a contractual mindset, attempt to keep multiple suppliers "on the line" so that they are dependent on no single supplier.

Alliances and Supplier–Distributor Relationships

When companies form long-term customer–supplier relationships, joint ventures, or partnerships for receiving supply, they increase their mutual interdependence and therefore their mutual responsibility for the success of their joint endeavors because they view supply and distribution chain management as a critical strategic resource that can enhance performance.[32] Of course, not all joint ventures involve a supplier–customer relationship, but all of them do demand collaboration, integrity of intent, and trust if the relationship is to succeed.[33]

The popularity of strategic alliances over the past two decades arose in part out of recognition of the success of Japanese *kereitsu* during the 1970s and 1980s, when it was noted that cooperative alliances could provide strategic advantages that pure competition could not. Such interlinked networks can, of course, lead to inbreeding and an inability to change, so links need to be balanced with innovation and the capacity to bring in new people and ideas when they are needed. In general, when companies commit to be responsible for their mutual success, they are more willing to invest in necessary equipment, employee development, and market development than they would be if they thought that the relationship could end with the next price increase. Such relationships help companies focus on the long-term rather than the short-term impacts of their decisions and help them through the types of bad times experienced by many Asian networks in the late 1990s. Companies in supplier–customer–distributor or allied relationships rely on each other for business. Because of this interdependence, they frequently make investments that align one company's resources with the other's needs, for example, by developing customer-specific equipment, standards, or products and services based on expectations that the relationship will continue.

Outsourcing

Many companies now outsource formerly internal functions like production, human resource management, or accounting to experts in the particular specialized fields. Thus a company like Nike is actually a marketing company, holding within its structure the marketing and distribution functions, while outsourcing all of its production activity. Many clothing, footwear, sporting goods, and toy companies follow outsourcing strategies for most of what they sell.

As a means of economizing, some large companies outsource their production or even programming operations to smaller suppliers in less developed countries, where wages and working standards are lower. Most companies outsource in the expectation of reducing costs, improving asset efficiency, and increasing profitability, in the hopes that specialists in a function will be able to achieve greater efficiency and quality.[34] The practice of outsourcing supply relationships creates risks. Boundaries between the firm and its suppliers, customers, or competitors tend to blur when the links are tight. Even when the boundaries are quite clear in the eyes of both firms, they may be much less obvious to external observers, who view what happens in the supplying firm as integral to the integrity and responsibility of the supplied firm.

If not managed with great integrity and consideration for the company's vision and values, however, outsourcing relationships can be a source of serious reputational difficulties. Wal-Mart and Nike, among others, have discovered this reality to their dismay, having been targeted by activists for allowing sweatshop conditions to exist in some of their suppliers' operations. The problems can be acute if companies outsource functions or areas of expertise that are sources of competitive advantage or core competencies or if they do not carefully monitor the conditions in their allies' operations.[35]

The Sweatshop Quandary[36]

Companies that have spent the time and energy to work through their vision and values need to ensure that their suppliers are working up to the same set of standards and values. Otherwise, they can find themselves in the midst of controversies, as happened to Wal-Mart when the International Labor Organization (ILO) found dreadful working conditions in Wal-Mart's supplier firms in less developed countries.

In addition to the ILO, watchdog activists like Sweatshop Watch pay close attention to suppliers' working conditions. When the customer firm purchases goods without sufficient attention to the conditions under which workers labor, and when those conditions are significantly worse than would be allowed under domestic law, companies can become the target of the activists.

Conditions and practices that draw attention include child labor, workweeks longer than 60 hours, mandatory overtime, and pay rates lower than the prevailing minimum wage. Treating workers like slaves, allowing them to go to the bathroom only twice a day, forcing female workers to take pregnancy tests and firing those who are pregnant, and dismissing union supporters have also incited activists' attention.

Companies accused of permitting substandard conditions to exist in their suppliers' factories sometimes rightly indicate that it is difficult to monitor these long-distance relationships. Such companies need to recognize that not only does sourcing from companies where such conditions prevail very likely go against the vision and values they have themselves articulated and applied to domestic operations, but they also denigrate the value of human life in other parts of the world. Treating workers as if they were mere cogs in a machine implies a distinct lack of respect for human worth and dignity and for the communities these people come from. Further, negative publicity seriously affects corporate reputations when companies are caught sourcing from substandard suppliers. U.S. firms have been subject to scrutiny by activists for many years, and the scrutiny is now spreading to European firms as well.[37]

Codes of Conduct

To cope with supplier relationships and assure that workers are treated fairly, many companies adopt codes of conduct and apply those codes to their suppliers as well. (The process is complicated, however, as noted in Case 6.1.) Companies also develop codes of conduct internally that detail their relationships with their suppliers and overtly recognize their interdependence. With supply relationships so strategically critical to many companies, it is essential that the conditions of work in those suppliers be carefully monitored if large companies hope to treat all of their stakeholders with the respect and dignity they deserve. Operating with integrity demands nothing less. If integrity alone is insufficient, the growing

A company's ability to enforce its own or global labor and human rights standards is affected by competitive conditions in the industry, which can seem to make living up to higher standards a potential source of competitive disadvantage. According to a report by Elliot Schrage on voluntary initiatives by companies to promote international worker rights, abuses occur even in countries where there are laws on the books that ostensibly prohibit poor labor practices. Details given in this box are drawn from Schrage's report.

China's toy industry serves as a striking example, for although China still does not accept the International Labor Organization (ILO) convention about freedom of association, most Chinese law is consistent with ILO standards. Schrage notes that "Chinese law provides for equal pay for equal work; delegates responsibility to provincial authorities for setting minimum wage standards; guarantees one day off per week; limits hours of work to forty hours per week and overtime to thirty-six hours per month; and prohibits the employment of children under sixteen." Despite the legal mandates, however, China lacks effective enforcement mechanisms, making "violations of worker rights . . . endemic."

Schrage's report presents a striking reality check for anyone interested in the enforcement of labor and human rights standards and concerned about working conditions in China. For example, although China has no national minimum wage, its provinces and cities do have wage standards of around 30 cents per hour and $55 per month. Workers, however, are often paid far less; sometimes money is withheld arbitrarily through fines and other mechanisms. Factory workers in China routinely work more than the maximum number of hours permitted by law. For example, one factory is said to have made workers work

120 days without a day off and paid no overtime.

Chinese law does not recognize the right to free association (i.e., the right to organize and participate in a trade union), which is a fundamental right according to the ILO. When workers attempt to organize or go on strike, they are frequently fired and even arrested. Workers' health and safety are also at risk in many Chinese factories, where workers can be exposed to toxic chemicals and hazardous working conditions. In 1993, a fire in the Zhili toy factory in Shenzhen killed 87 workers because there were no fire alarms, no sprinklers, and no fire escapes. Further, the factory doors were actually locked to keep the workers inside. In many factories, abuse and harassment (sexual and other) are pervasive, with the workers unable to fight back, in part because the vast majority of workers are young women, away from their families, who are attempting to earn enough money to send some home.

In response to allegations of abuse in the toy, apparel, footwear, and sports equipment industries, many big U.S. retailers have adopted codes of conduct for themselves and extended them to suppliers. Of all the large toy companies, only Toys "R" Us has directly addressed the freedom of association issue, which looms large in bringing China into conformity with most of the rest of the world. It did so through its endorsement of the labor standards of SA 8000 (see www.sa-intl.org). Other companies have earned significant negative reputational capital by having but not enforcing their own or international codes.

Toys "R" Us took a leading position in enforcing global standards by adopting the SA 8000 labor standards and agreeing to external certification and verification processes by SAI International. Representatives of industry, labor, and other nongovernmental organizations have agreed to the SA 8000 code, which, though it is not industry-specific, does provide for much stricter requirements than are common in China. For example, as Schrage notes, SA 8000 promotes "parallel means of free association and bargaining" when such rights are legally restricted, allows for only 48 working hours per week and a maximum of 12 hours of overtime, and calls for a living wage that "meets basic needs" and "provide[s] discretionary income."

In signing on to SA 8000, Toys "R" Us explicitly agreed to favor SA 8000–certified factories, which means that the practices within those factories have been independently audited. Unfortunately for Chinese workers, as Schrage points out, only 13 toy factories had been SA 8000 certified as of September 2003. Clearly, even when a company has good intentions, operating as a leading corporate citizen in some circumstances is difficult.

DISCUSSION QUESTIONS

1. What is your assessment of how seriously Toys "R" Us is taking the rights of workers in its supply chain factories?

2. Is there more that a company like Toys "R" Us needs to do with respect to monitoring working conditions in its supply chain?

3. To what extent do you believe that Chinese factory conditions are actually Toys "R" Us's responsibility?

Source: Elliot J. Schrage, *Promoting International Worker Rights through Private Voluntary Initiatives: Public Relations or Public Policy?*, Report to the U.S. Department of State (Iowa City, IA: University of Iowa Center for Human Rights, 2004).

numbers of activists who have access to information and can readily spread that information through worldwide electronic connections will assure that companies pay attention to working conditions.

Critical and Particular Secondary Stakeholders

Governments and communities are critical secondary stakeholders for all companies and sometimes became primary stakeholders, for example, when companies are highly regulated or are community-based, such as utilities are. Governments establish the rules of society by which companies must live, and communities provide essential infrastructure to support company operations. The public affairs function, which is an umbrella for activities coping with numerous particular stakeholders, and the community relations function have evolved to provide venues for ongoing company interactions with these important stakeholder groups.

Public Affairs: Government and "Publics" Relationships

Governments at all levels and in all branches wherever a company operates are critical secondary stakeholders for businesses. Business–government relationships are generally handled through the public affairs function, which can also serve as an umbrella for issues management, media relations, community relations (discussed below), public relations, and other external affairs activities.

The goal of the public affairs office generally is to manage the legitimacy of the organization in its societies[38] and attempt to influence or modify issues, legislation, regulations, and rulings so that they are favorable to corporate interests.[39]

To the extent that public affairs encompasses the other external relations functions noted, its goal is also to present the company in a favorable light to its many publics, or external stakeholders. Thus, the public affairs function is also designed for generally managing external relations, including relationships with respect to public issues and the activists involved, the media, and occasionally agencies in civil society to whom the contributions function is linked. The business–government relations function of the public affairs office is directed toward helping companies understand, anticipate, manage, and ultimately cope with laws, regulations, and rulings generated by various governmental agencies.[40]

Public affairs developed originally as a fairly minor responsibility of the CEO. It was not until the 1950s and 1960s that the function began to become more formalized, with growth in the sophistication of public affairs occurring during the 1980s and 1990s.[41] By 1980 more than 80 percent of large corporations had a public affairs office.[42]

Managing Public Affairs

The underlying goal of the public affairs function is to productively develop and maintain a positive relationship between the company and the various branches and levels of government whose activities influence—or are influenced by—the firm's activities. On one level, the function helps present the company to key public officials and opinion leaders in a positive light. The public affairs office also serves the reverse purpose of helping to explain the political environment to people within the corporation.[43] Public affairs is particularly focused on the political environment and political change as it is likely to affect the firm; its general charge is to establish and maintain relationships with public officials, whose bottom line is political capital and power.

In the global village, these activities take place not only domestically for U.S. corporations but also in other parts of the world when companies need to work cooperatively with local governments. For example, many U.S. companies have divisions operating in the European Union that view themselves as European companies of American parentage (ECAPs) because they want to stress their European roots.[44]

Activities of public affairs officers involve lobbying public officials to ensure that they are well informed about the company's perspective pending legislative or regulatory action. Political strategy for corporations can mean hiring lobbyists, whose job it is to inform the public officials about the company's position on issues and pending legislation and regulation. It might also mean having corporate officers testify on the company's or industry's behalf before the relevant public body. Many companies develop political strategies and support specific candidates for office, frequently through political action committees (PACs).[45]

Political action could mean using corporate resources, often gathered through a PAC, to generate a grassroots letter-writing, phone-call, or e-mail campaign either protesting or supporting a proposed legislative or regulatory action. Lobbying also means providing information to public officials and their staff, who might not otherwise be able to undertake the necessary analysis or find the relevant data. Or it can simply mean hiring lobbyists to represent the company's point of view before public bodies at the local, state/provincial, or national level, whichever is appropriate.

Companies clearly need to develop their political strategies carefully because, as is frequently noted, their resources give them great power. Responsible companies will use this power wisely, not merely to serve the short-term and exclusively financial interests of the firm, but more broadly, to think about the important public responsibilities that leading corporate citizens bear simply because of the resources they command. Recognizing these responsibilities, they will work collaboratively and cooperatively with public officials in the public interest, not purely their private interest. Working collaboratively involves a give-and-take that allows governments and their officials to do their appropriate work of representing the public interest and the common good even, occasionally, when it would be in the short-term interest of the firm to do otherwise.

Issues Management

In efforts to improve their reputation, communicate with stakeholders, and manage business–government or public relations, companies sometimes establish issues management units.[46] These units are sometimes independent of and sometimes within the public affairs function. Issues managers attempt to frame public issues in ways that are helpful to the company. Such framings frequently conflict with those articulated by different activist groups interested in the same issue. Working productively with activists to frame an issue means establishing an ongoing conversation about the nature, scope, and implications of the issue. Research indicates that proactive issues management can improve companies' competitiveness and standing among their peers.[47]

Issues managers must identify emerging issues relevant to corporate concerns, analyze the potential or actual impact of issues on the company, determine what kinds of responses the company should make, and in some cases implement the response or ensure that others implement it.[48] Issues managers are charged with identifying where gaps exist between stakeholder expectations and reality. In the international setting, the scanning process is more complex, in part because so many different cultures and contexts exist in each country, differing levels of development generate different types of issues, and stakeholders may have very different expectations of companies than they do domestically.

Issues can cross national borders or can be located simply in one country. Experience with an issue in one nation, such as dealing with human rights abuses, can help a company cope with it the next time the issue arises. Experience can help companies avoid mistakes in developing relationships with appropriate stakeholders and managing issues locally, but only to the extent that cultural differences and political realities are taken into account in the next country.

Issue Analysis and Management

Issue analysis involves four major steps.[49] The first step is assessing the history of the issue. Second is forecasting how the issue might develop using the issue life cycle model. Third, companies can use forecasting techniques like scenario analysis to think about different possibilities and assign probabilities to each possibility. The fourth step is the actual analysis, in which the company determines what the likely impact of the issue will be on the company. Following these steps allows a company to generate an internal issues agenda that will shape its strategic response to the issue based on the priorities given to the issues.

Following the issues analysis, issues management involves developing and implementing the company's strategy with respect to each of the high-priority issues.[50] Several alternatives are available to the company, including altering its own behavior to reduce or eliminate the issue in the minds and hearts of stakeholders. For example, Johnson & Johnson (J&J) actively led the call for new packaging following the Tylenol crisis of the early 1980s, in which the discovery of cyanide-laced capsules caused the company to withdraw its product temporarily. J&J took a proactive, even interactive, stance with respect to government regulators, who might otherwise have imposed more burdensome regulations on all drug companies.

A company can also try to change stakeholder perceptions or expectations, possibly through educating politicians about the situation (i.e., the lobbying function noted above) or doing a public relations campaign to educate key stakeholders. Advocacy advertising, in which companies state their position on an issue in paid advertisements, is a form of public education, as is the testimony given by company officials in the United States before congressional committees. Because companies have a great deal of power and access to significant financial resources, however, there is considerable controversy about corporate participation in U.S. political life.

Alternatively, a company can attempt to frame an issue in the public policy arena, as the tobacco companies have done to create a debate about smokers' rights and take attention away from the negative health consequences of smoking. Sometimes the education process allows a company to move stakeholders' perceptions closer to the reality of the situation.

When companies operate within numerous different countries or transnationally, they face considerable complications in working with local governments and other stakeholders on relevant issues. Some countries, like the United States, readily permit pluralistic interest groups, including corporations, to contest public issues and provide varying sources of opinion and information to policymakers. In other countries, however, where the ideology, public policy standards, and cultural norms are different, open lobbying on issues may be far less acceptable, particularly for foreign firms. In such circumstances, working through host country trade or industry associations, which represent the general interest of the companies in an industry, may be the only feasible way to try to influence public policy.[51] This attitude may also explain why U.S.-based companies in Europe like to be viewed not as American firms, but as ECAPs, as noted above.[52]

Crisis Management

Organizational crises are highly ambiguous, low-probability situations that have no clear cause or effect but that pose a major threat to the organization's survival and at least some organizational stakeholders. Crises frequently surprise the organization and present a dilemma whose resolution will either help or hurt the enterprise.[53] Although there is controversy about whether crises can be prevented (since they are typically surprises), many organizations, particularly those where crisis is likely, have created crisis management units. A crisis could result when an executive is kidnapped, a plane crash kills members of the top management team, or a major fire or chemical spill happens. For example, a chemical spill at Union Carbide's Bhopal, India, plant in 1984 killed thousands of citizens near the plant. The company was not fully prepared to deal with the consequences this humanly and ecologically disastrous event. Even a single product can create a disaster, as happened in 2000 when the alliance between Ford Motor Company and Bridgestone/Firestone was upset by reports that the Firestone tires were losing their treads and causing numerous deaths.

Companies may not be able to predict that such a crisis will occur, but they need to know what to do—and how to do it quickly—when one does. Although not all contingencies can or should be researched and planned for, actual rehearsal of an implementation plan is a crucial component of good crisis management.[54] That includes public relations and the mobilization of a crisis team or crisis management unit, which is typically organized by existing employees rather than existing as a separate unit. Other types of organizations, such as hospitals, use disaster planning, in which a disaster is simulated to ensure that all parties understand what to do in the event of a real crisis. Crisis management efforts can be considered effective when the organization survives and can resume relatively normal operations, when losses to the organization and its stakeholders are minimized, and when enough is learned that it can be applied to the next crisis.[55] One study of Australian companies found that more than one-fourth of the companies failed following a crisis.[56] Crisis management can also be considered effective when a company's reputation as a good citizen is left undamaged by the actions taken during and following the crisis.

Sociologist Charles Perrow has studied high-risk technologies, such as those found in chemical plants, nuclear facilities, and aircraft. Such technologies have what Perrow terms "interactive complexity," which means they interact in complex ways, and "tight coupling," which means the functioning of each element is closely tied to related parts of the technology. Time may be of the essence should the technology begin to fail; slack may not be available, resulting in the quick escalation of the problem through a cascade of interdependent and generally unexpected effects. Perrow says that systems that are characterized by interactive complexity and tight coupling are prone to "normal accidents," because of the multiple unexpected interactions of failure.[57]

Union Carbide's Bhopal chemical spill, which killed more than 2,000 people and injured many others, was just such a normal accident. It posed a considerable crisis for the company in part because the company was ill-prepared to handle it at the time. Diane Vaughan's comprehensive study of the 1988 space shuttle *Challenger* explosion details a similar perspective, in which NASA and its partners were essentially unprepared for the crisis of a shuttle failure.[58]

Crisis Preparedness

Scanning for potential crises, especially in high-technology companies that risk normal accidents, is critical to preparedness. Companies must break the boundaries of mental models that suggest "it won't happen here." Prepared companies put in place a crisis team, usually comprised of members of the executive team, that is prepared to handle the psychological and sometimes physical trauma that frequently follows a crisis, particularly among employees.

Someone should be appointed to speak to the press and represent the company's perspective on the incident so that multiple messages are avoided. The more quickly the company can release accurate and thorough information, the better off the company will be. Although a crisis necessitates flexibility and improvisation with respect to the roles and responsibilities people assume, prior planning about who will do what, how, and when can reduce the uncertainty associated with the crisis. Planning can also provide a way for stakeholders to come together on behalf of the company facing the crisis and help out rather than getting in the way of efforts to resolve the situation.[59]

Media and Public Relations

The job of the media in a democracy is to report on newsworthy information so that the citizenry can be publicly engaged and politically active, vote knowledgeably, and actively influence policymakers when issues arise on the public policy agenda. The press reports on public issues generally because either the reporter or editor, or an opinion leader, has seen a gap between expectation and reality. At one level, although the media are very influential in shaping and framing public perception about various issues, their real job is to direct public attention to the issues rather than create the issues themselves.[60] In the modern world, this principle may sometimes be violated.

Public relations generally involves efforts by companies to enhance their image in public opinion through positive representation in the media, typically through media reports for which the company does not pay (directly). The founder of the field, Edward Bernays, defined public relations as "'the engineering of consent,' or the ability to get diverse individuals with varying perceptions and values to come to a 'consent to a program or goal.'"[61]

Some public relations practitioners see themselves as advocates for their companies (or, when they are in public relations firms, for their clients). Others see their role as building consensus among stakeholders on various issues of relevance to the firm by creating carefully crafted messages that put the company's point of view in the public's eyes and ears.[62] Thus, modern public relations officers are responsible in part for helping to build local communities and in part for sustaining positive relationships with a company's many stakeholders.[63]

Public relations officers use many means of communicating the public image of the firm, including issuing press releases announcing the company's position on issues or positive developments within the firm (e.g., promotions, new product releases, special events, contributions made by the firm). Press releases can also attempt to get the company's point of view on an issue or situation fairly represented in the print and broadcast press. Thus, the public relations function is another means by which companies attempt to frame issues so that they reflect the company and its perspective positively.

Some companies generate advertisements, called advocacy ads, to state their position on specific issues; oil and tobacco companies are particularly active in advocacy advertising. However, this technique tends to raise issues of credibility for the firm. Companies may sponsor events or particular causes as a means of gaining positive publicity without direct advertising, and they frequently work with community organizations on local causes. Another technique is to establish a speakers' bureau or experts list that can be used by the press when questions about an issue, situation, or area of interest arise.

Many public relations departments are also responsible for employee newsletters and other communications, as well as some of the communications with external audiences. The public relations department may work with the investor relations unit to produce the annual report for investors, as well as environmental reports, social audits, community newsletters, and other reports intended for external consumption.

Increasingly companies use their Web sites to provide information to the computer-using public. The Web site not only offers product information and interactive services but can be a rich source of official information about a company. The company can make available on its Web site everything from its vision, values, and mission statements to its annual report, new product developments and releases, financial information, positive press coverage and information on obtaining its products and services.

Working with the Media

Many companies attempt to work collaboratively with the media in the interest of getting positive stories told. To do so well means developing an ongoing relationship with journalists, who can learn to trust the company as a reliable source. Here integrity matters critically!

Reporters, whether broadcast or print, seek certain things from company representatives. Among them are honesty, respect, and a mutually rewarding relationship built on trust—that is, the integrity expected of a leading corporate citizen. Reporters want to know that they can trust what a spokesperson says about the firm, and that they will have queries responded to quickly, as most reporters are working under tight deadlines. It is also important that company representatives are familiar with editorial policies of the media outlets that might contact the firm so that they can generate a productive and collaborative, rather than an adversarial, relationship.[64]

Community Relationships

Healthy communities are those in which citizens are connected with each other, share a common vision of the community's identity and culture, and are willing to work together for the common good. When they are rooted in and responsible to a community, corporations can play an important role in building and sustaining community health. Companies receive numerous supports from healthy communities, including infrastructure planning and development, an educated workforce, and a working environment that enhances competitiveness. Most companies work directly with their communities, enhancing what is known as social capital (or connections and relatedness) and the ability to attract new employees within the community, through their community relations functions.[65]

Community relations programs in the United States, where they are most common, typically have encompassed a number of areas, including charitable contributions or philanthropy, volunteer programs, and community-based (public–private or social) partnerships. The relationships with communities embodied in these programs are handled through a number of functions that are frequently consolidated into a single office called community relations (CR). Generally speaking, the community relations function deals with community members and groups active in the civil society (and sometimes the political) sphere of influence.

The major investment by the community in a company comes in the forms of social capital generated by strong and healthy communities and the infrastructure generated by communities from taxes paid by individual and corporate citizens. Social capital, as has already been discussed, provides for healthy community-based relationships and positive civic and political action that helps balance both economic and governmental sources of power. The infrastructure provided by communities includes the local educational system, which can provide an educated workforce for a company. Infrastructure also includes roads and highways, communications networks, local community-based services (e.g., garbage removal and sewage systems), and the local regulatory system, without which it would be impossible for firms to operate successfully.

Neighbor of Choice

Best-practice companies in community relations operate on a principle that asks the company to become a "neighbor of choice."[66] Being a neighbor of choice means being a welcome, trusted neighbor with a positive relationship within the communities where the company has operations. Neighbor-of-choice strategies, according to Edmund Burke, who founded the corporate membership organization called Boston College Center for Corporate Community Relations (now the Center for Corporate Citizenship), derive from trusting relationships based on mutual respect and ongoing dialogue with communities and their representatives.[67] The key to becoming a corporate neighbor of choice is, as we have argued earlier for all stakeholders, developing continuing and mutually inter-active, power-balanced relationships. Thus, one important consideration for companies wishing to attain balance between the interests of communities and those of the company is to assure that there is a significant place for community members' voice on corporate activities.

Burke highlights three specific program strategies essential to positive corporate–community relations, recognizing that strong community relations cannot be housed within a single department but are instead the responsibility of everyone in the company. Companies need first to build community relationships, then to identify company-relevant issues and concerns within the community, and finally to design appropriate programs in the community to cope with those concerns.[68] A neighbor-of-choice community relations program begins with an internal assessment of company attitudes and practices toward the community, then moves outward to assess the situation and needs of those communities (in particular) where the company has operations or where it hopes to develop a broad customer base.

To make the community relations programs strategic once needs and opportunities have been identified, companies need to map out the ways in which activities within the community can enhance their strategy. Additionally, companies can attempt to establish and live up to the standards of excellence outlined by the Boston College Center for Corporate Citizenship (see Table 6.3). These standards are supported by a diagnostic tool and emphasize specific practices that companies can develop to establish strong community relationships. One example is the use of strategic philanthropy, for example, a chemical company donating lab facilities and materials that help train technicians to a local high school so that trained workers will later be available. Another is to use volunteer programs to connect employees with local communities so that they can improve not only the community and the company's relationship with the community but also employee morale and connectedness to the values and vision of the firm. Some companies engage in cause-related marketing, in which they donate a percentage of each sale or product use to a cause or charity with which local community members can identify. This technique, which was pioneered by the American Express Corporation, combines philanthropy and marketing.

Community Relations Strategies

Dealing with different communities requires developing specific community relations strategies and programs for each community. This process of relationship building needs to be planned as carefully as any other corporate strategy if the company hopes to be able to work effectively with community constituencies.

There are a number of community relations programs that enable companies to develop ongoing dialogue within the context of a trusting relationship with community stakeholders.[69] Among the programs that companies use to invite community representatives from the different communities of relevance into dialogue and relationship are plant tours and programs that expose people to what is actually going on within the facilities. Some companies also donate the use of their facilities to nongovernmental organizations (NGOs) or nonprofits, including

TABLE 6.3 **Standards of Excellence in Corporate Community Involvement**

Source: Boston College Center for Corporate Citizenship.

Standard I: Leadership	Senior executives demonstrate support, commitment, and participation in community involvement efforts.
Standard II: Issues Management	The company identifies and monitors issues important to its operations and reputation.
Standard III: Relationship Building	Company management recognizes that building and maintaining relationships of trust with the community is a critical component of company strategy and operations.
Standard IV: Strategy	All levels of the organization have specific roles and responsibilities for meeting community involvement objectives.
Standard V: Accountability	All levels of the organization have specific roles and responsibilities for meeting community involvement objectives.
Standard VI: Infrastructure	The company incorporates systems and policies to support, communicate and institutionalize community involvement objectives.
Standard VII: Measurement	The company establishes an ongoing process for evaluating community involvement strategies, activities and programs, and their impact on the company and the community.

allowing access to NGO leaders to corporate training programs when appropriate. Others engage key leaders in mutual problem solving and planning activities related to a community's needs, interests, and quality of life.

Many companies identify key contacts within the company for specific kinds of community questions or needs, thereby creating a degree of needed transparency between the firm and its communities. Working in the reverse direction, some companies also develop their own list of key community contacts so that they will know whom to contact when issues arise and can do so before the issue is framed in ways that go against the corporate interest.

A final way progressive and visionary companies work interactively with community representatives is to create community advisory panels that provide a forum for dialogue about community-based issues of mutual concern. These panels enlist key community members in working with the community on issues that are important to the community. Acting as a liaison between the community and the company, such panels can create a forum for dialogue about what is important to both sides. An advisory panel can provide a common meeting ground and can enhance not only the transparency of the company to the community but also the prospect of developing a shared view of the long-term common good of the community and company alike.

Social Vision and Social Capital[70]

The task of corporate leadership in the 21st century goes well beyond traditional community relations in dealing with the public responsibilities of the firm. As we have argued in earlier chapters, in developing an effective corporate–community relations program it is important to balance the company's interests with those of its communities, many of which are found in the civil society sphere.

Social capital—that is, connectedness among members of the communities of relevance—is the key measure of success in healthy and well-functioning communities. Companies have a choice: They can destroy social capital by economizing at all costs, laying off employees and devastating their communities when lower-cost options arise, or they can develop lasting, trust-filled relationships with local communities and help strengthen those communities; in short, they can become rooted in communities rather than rootless. The result will enable companies to gain access to qualified, well-educated, loyal workers; communities with adequate infrastructure to support company needs; and civil relationships with local leaders who believe that the presence of the company is a benefit to the community (see Case 6.2).

Leading Challenges: Stakeholders and Leadership

Leading corporate citizenship means dealing effectively—and efficiently (i.e., by economizing)—with stakeholders. The double entendre of *leading corporate citizens* becomes clear in this chapter: Companies themselves need to lead others if they hope to gain a competitive advantage. Progressive stakeholder practices that treat stakeholders with respect and dignity, such as those described in this chapter, put companies on a path toward that competitive advantage.

There are many things that leading corporate citizens can do, as Table 6.4 and Table 6.5 summarize, to become respected for their citizenship. Although best practices with respect to any given stakeholder group are always emerging and changing, the tables attempt to summarize from the chapter what the current state of the art is in developing positive and interactive stakeholder relationships with the wide range of constituencies that all companies have. From the company's perspective, there are clearly structures that make sense to stakeholders through which the company can build effective relationships.

But leading corporate citizens is not only a company matter. Leading corporate citizens also applies to the individual leaders and managers within the firm, who are responsible for creating awareness within the firm of its impact on stakeholders and the natural environment. Leadership is particularly important in fostering environmental sensitivity and a positive attitude toward developing sustainable business practices. Only with aware leaders can a company generate a culture that moves it toward constant questioning of its current practices. Such questioning can move the company toward accepting full responsibility for its impacts on the ecological sphere as well as its interactions with stakeholders in the political and civil society spheres. Leadership at this level of awareness demands systems thinking and relatively high levels of cognitive development.

Good Stakeholder Relationships Win Companies Plaudits

In 2004, *Business Ethics* magazine published a list of 29 companies (see Exhibit 1) that had been ranked among the "100 Best Corporate Citizens: Companies That Serve a Variety of Stakeholders Well" for five years running. These companies are rated on their stakeholder relationships and environmental performance using measures from the social investment research firm KLD Research and Analytics in Boston.

These 29 companies exhibit consistent top performance with respect to their stakeholders, the natural environment, governance, and human relations in their supply chains, and are increasingly recognized as doing so by external publics. According to number 6–ranked Deere & Company's Robert W. Lane, chairman and CEO, "No smoke, no mirrors, no tricks: just right down the middle of the field. That's John Deere." In response to Deere's ranking, Lane said, "It's recognition like this that makes you want to get up in the morning."

The St. Paul Companies (an insurance company, now known as St. Paul Travelers companies, Inc.) climbed from number 85 in 2000 to number 4 in 2004 by improving its stakeholder and environmental practices, and Ecolab moved from number 29 in 2000 to number 10 in 2004 because of its creative new product development for unexpected modern hazards. As Al Schuman, Ecolab CEO, noted. "We ramped up quickly in response to the Anthrax scare with our Vortexx products, a fungicide, not to make a buck, but because it was the right thing to do. We also developed antimicrobial disinfectant products to address foot and mouth disease in livestock, and then yet another new product to combat SARS at the Toronto Airport."

EXHIBIT 1 Companies Ranked in the 100 Best Corporate Citizens 2000–2004 (ranks are for 2004 placement)

Rank	Company	Rank	Company
1	Fannie Mae	31	Adolph Coors
2	Procter & Gamble	32	Modine Manufacturing
3	Intel Corporation	33	Clorox
4	St. Paul Companies	43	AT&T
6	Deere & Company	44	Pitney Bowes
7	Avon Products	45	Starbucks Coffee
8	Hewlett-Packard	48	Merck & Company
10	Ecolab Inc.	49	Graco
12	IBM	53	Brady Corporation
14	Herman Miller	47	Medtronic
17	Timberland Company	63	New York Times Co.
19	Cisco Systems	74	Golden West Financial
22	Southwest Airlines	89	Sonoco Products
24	Motorola	98	Whirlpool
27	Cummins, Inc.		

Fannie Mae,* 2004's number 1 company and another all-star, is explicitly focused on achieving the American dream by helping Americans become homeowners—the reason for its unique charter by Congress. The company buys mortgages from local lenders and repackages them for sale as securities. Fannie Mae's dominant presence in the mortgage market enables it to play a critical role in keeping mortgage rates down. Yet its most visible impact is on helping those who traditionally have been underserved obtain homes. Most uniquely, a $10 million Fannie Mae partnership was established with an Islamic financial institution to open up southern California's real estate market to Muslims. It accommodates Islamic law's ban on paying or collecting interest on debt, by negotiating monthly payments based on a property's sale price and fair rental values instead of interest rates. Fannie Mae also tied for second-highest score in service to minorities and women, in part because of the close link of its vision and mission to serving minority groups. As Maria Johnson, Fannie Mae's vice president for diversity, health, and work-life, puts it, "How are we going to accomplish our goal of bringing home ownership to everyone if we don't look like America ourselves?"

Consistency in treating stakeholders and the natural environment respectfully characterizes the 29 companies on the list, another of which is consumer goods giant Procter & Gamble (P&G). P&G excels in service to minorities and women and to the community. The firm has donated help to disadvantaged youth in Vietnam, combated childhood malnutrition in India, and provided earthquake relief in Turkey. P&G also makes deposits in minority-owned banks, has placed substantial insurance with four minority-owned insurance companies, and invests in venture capital funds for minority businesses.

Not all the businesses on the 100 Best Corporate Citizens ranking are perfect by any means—indeed, most if not all have flaws, sometimes significant. For example, Avon Products (number 7) is known for its three-day fund-raising walks for breast cancer and products bearing the pink ribbon associated with the disease. Yet activists cite concerns about how Avon distributes money from the walk and say its products contain cancer-causing ingredients. In 2003, a federal judge ruled that IBM (number 12) had discriminated against older employees in converting to a cash-balance pension program. Washington Mutual (number 29) has been accused of predatory lending, and Eastman Kodak (number 58) was targeted by the Citizens Environmental Coalition for air emissions and on-site hazardous waste incinerators. Both Timberland (number 17) and Sara Lee (number 87) have faced accusations of unhealthy working conditions in overseas factories.

The controversies don't end there. But neither do exemplary practices, which are numerous. In the end, the 100 Best Corporate Citizens list aims to make a simple point: Excellence in business is about more than profits for shareholders—it's about serving a variety of stakeholders well. To put it another way, it's about having your good deeds outweigh your misdeeds.

DISCUSSION QUESTIONS

1. What role, if any, do you think rankings like the 100 Best Corporate Citizens play with respect to companies' stakeholder and environmental performance?

2. How important do you think a company's status on this list is to the companies' executives? Why might it matter? Why might it not matter?

3. Do you think that such rankings achieve the goal of highlighting exemplary practices—and thereby fostering better practice overall? Why or why not?

Source: Excerpted (and slightly adapted) from Peter Asmus, Marjorie Kelly, Sandra Waddock, and Samuel Graves, "2004 100 Best Corporate Citizens: Companies that Serve a Variety of Stakeholders Well," *Business Ethics*, Spring 2004, pp. 8–12.

*To highlight the fragility of reputation, it is important to note that in 2004 Fannie Mae was under federal investigation for accounting issues.

TABLE 6.4   Best Practices in Primary Stakeholder Relationships for Leading Corporate Citizens

Primary Stakeholders	Bottom Line	Relevant Boundary-Spanning Functions	Best Practices of Leading Corporate Citizens
Owners	Financial Intellectual and human capital, commitment and loyalty	Investor relations	Transparency and accountability with respect to fiduciary responsibilities, achieving balance and a fair return for shareholders
Employees		Employee relations	Employment security, selective hiring, self-managed teams and decentralization, comparatively high compensation, extensive training, reduction of status differences, and sharing information
		Human resource management	Create meaningful, inspirational workplaces supported by vision, values, and implementation
		Training and development	Value employees as ends, not means to an end
Customers	Business franchise, trust	Customer relations	Develop trust, commitment, and loyalty
		Relational marketing	Develop loyal customers, build trust through quality products and services that meet real customer needs and are delivered on time as advertised; interact with

continued

concluded

Primary Stakeholders	Bottom Line	Relevant Boundary-Spanning Functions	Best Practices of Leading Corporate Citizens
			customers in an ongoing way Commit to product quality, safety, continual process and product improvements, accessibility, positive attitude, and credibility to develop trust and communication with customers
		Marketing	Build trust and commitment by offering superior resources, opportunities, and benefits, maintaining high integrity and standards, communicating important information, and avoiding opportunism.
Suppliers, allies, and partners	Infrastructure, relationship	Joint ventures Supplier and outsourcing contracts and partnerships, strategic alliances	Monitor suppliers, allies, and partners to assure that quality, employment, safety, and codes of conduct standards are met, and to build a lasting and trusting relationship with allies; assure that the company's vision is communicated to and understood by allies and that they are willing to meet high standards and expectations

TABLE 6.5   Best Practices for Secondary Stakeholder Relationships for Leading Corporate Citizens.

Secondary Stakeholders	Bottom Line	Relevant Boundary-Spanning Functions	Best Practices of Leading Corporate Citizens
Government	Public good, common good	Public affairs	Help public policy makers understand, anticipate, and cope with issues that arise from business practices in a way that serves the public interest/common good; keep policymakers informed about the company's perspectives, interests, and needs without exercising undue power or influence
The general public or society	Trust, development, growth	Issues management	Constantly scan and monitor the external environment for emerging issues; assess history and development of issues, forecast possible futures using issue life cycle analysis, use forecasting techniques to develop scenarios, and determine possible impacts on company, then take necessary steps to contend with these implications
		Crisis management	Try to anticipate and prepare for potential crises, have a crisis management team in place and trained

continued

concluded

Primary Stakeholders	Bottom Line	Relevant Boundary-Spanning Functions	Best Practices of Leading Corporate Citizens
			to deal with physical and emotional trauma that is adaptable to the situation and well prepared to deal with the media and general public, as well as uncertainties of situation
Media	Knowledge	Media relations Public relations	Advocate for the company's perspective and place the company in the best public light by working with community members and building positive relationships with many stakeholders through extensive and interactive communication means; build trust and ongoing relationships with media representatives
Community(ies)	Infrastructure	Community relations Stakeholder relations Corporate citizenship	Become a neighbor of choice by exerting leadership as a corporate citizenship, managing community-related issues effectively, building relationships with community members, developing a community relations strategy and relevant infrastructure that is assessed and measured regularly

As this chapter has demonstrated, both individual and company leadership are critical. Companies need to develop the practices internally that show their true respect for the dignity and worth of each stakeholder rather than trying to dominate or control them. Through this collaborative, interactive, and respectful approach to stakeholders and to the ecological environment on which they depend, companies can prosper and in the long term maintain the legitimacy they need to be accepted in society.

Thus, leaders need to understand the relationships that their companies' activities have with communities, competitors, suppliers, employees, and whole societies in which they are embedded, not to mention the ecological surround on which they ultimately depend. Not only do leading citizens need to be aware of these impacts; they need also to accept responsibility for them and ensure that their companies recognize their own accountability to stakeholders impacted by company activities.

Endnotes

1. James E. Post, Lee E. Preston, and Sybil Sachs, "Managing the Extended Enterprise: The New Stakeholder View," *California Management Review* 45, no. 1 (2002), pp. 6–29.

2. Robert Leaver, president and CEO of New Commons, developed one multiple-bottom-line framework in *The Commonwealth Papers* (Providence, RI: Commonwealth Publications, 1995). I am also grateful to my colleagues in the Leadership for Change Program at Boston College for pushing this line of thinking over many years of collaborative work.

3. Robert F. Felton, Ken Berryman, and Tom Stephenson, "A New Era in Corporate Governance," *McKinsey Quarterly* 2 (2004), pp. 28–44.

4. See Sandra A. Waddock and Samuel B. Graves, "Quality of Management and Quality of Stakeholder Relations: Are They Synonymous?" *Business and Society* 36, no. 3 (September 1997), pp. 250–79.

5. This argument is compellingly made by Richard Marens and Andrew Wicks, "Getting Real: Stakeholder Theory, Managerial Practice, and the General Irrelevance of Fiduciary Duties Owed to Shareholders," *Business Ethics Quarterly* 9, no. 2 (April 1999), pp. 273–93.

6. See James C. Collins and Jerry I. Porras, "Building Your Company's Vision," *Harvard Business Review*, September–October 1996, pp. 65–77.

7. See Marens and Wicks, "Getting Real," and Oliver E. Williamson, *Markets and Hierarchies: Analysis and Antitrust Implications* (New York: Free Press, 1975).

8. Marens and Wicks, "Getting Real," p. 277. The thoughts in this paragraph are derived from this article.

9. These two points are made in ibid.

10. Two studies using *Fortune*'s 100 Best Companies to Work for in America rankings find a positive relationship between company performance and employee satisfaction

and attitudes: Karn C. Chan, Michele V. Gee, and Thomas L. Steiner, "Employee Happiness and Corporate Financial Performance," *Financial Practice and Education* 10, no. 2 (Fall/Winter 2002), pp. 47–52; and Ingrid Smithey Fulmer, Barry Gerhant, and Scott S. Kimberly, "Are the 100 Best Better? An Empirical Investigation of the Relationship between Being a 'Great Place to Work' and Firm Performance," *Personnel Psychology* 56, no. 4 (Winter 2003), pp. 965–94.

11. Jeffrey Pfeffer and John F. Veiga, "Putting People First for Organizational Success," *Academy of Management Executive* 13, no. 2 (May 1999), pp. 37–48. See also Gary Dessler, "How to Earn Your Employees' Commitment," *Academy of Management Executive* 13, no. 2 (May 1999), pp. 58–67, for a similar set of ideas. The framework in this section is developed from these two review articles.

12. Pfeffer and Veiga, "Putting People First," p. 46.

13. R. H. Hayes and W. Abernathy, "Managing Our Way to Economic Decline," *Harvard Business Review*, July–August 1980, pp. 66–77.

14. See Dessler, "How to Earn Your Employees' Commitment," citing Rosabeth Moss Kanter, *World Class: Thriving Locally in the Global Economy* (New York: Simon & Schuster), p. 59. Dessler's ideas are similar to those developed in Chapters 4 and 5 and are congruent with the practices of successful firms identified by Pfeffer and Veiga, "Putting People First."

15. See Collins and Porras, "Building Your Company's Vision."

16. Summarized from Pfeffer and Veiga, "Putting People First."

17. See Dessler, "How to Earn Your Employees' Commitment."

18. Frederick F. Reichheld, "The One Number You Need to Grow," *Harvard Business Review* 81, no. 12 (December 2003), pp. 46–55.

19. See, for example, Christian Gronroos, "From Marketing Mix to Relationship Marketing: Towards a Paradigm Shift in Marketing," *Management Decision* 32, no. 2 (1994), pp. 4–20; and Robert M. Morgan and Shelby D. Hunt, "The Commitment-Trust Theory of Relationship Marketing," *Journal of Marketing* 58, no. 3 (July 1994), pp. 20–38.

20. Gronroos, "From Marketing Mix to Relationship Marketing."

21. Morgan and Hunt, "The Commitment-Trust Theory"; see also M. Rungtusanatham, F. Salvador, C. Forza, and T. Y. Choi, "Supply-Chain Linkages and Operational Performance," *International Journal of Operations & Production Management* 23, no. 9 (2003), pp. 1084–1100.

22. See Kenneth M. York and Cynthia E. Miree, "Causation or Covariation: An Empirical Re-examination of the Link between TQM and Financial Performance," *Journal of Operations Management* 22, no. 3 (June 2004), pp. 291–312; and Kaj Storbacka, Tore Strandvik, and Christian Gronroos, "Managing Customer Relationships for Profit: The Dynamics of Relationship Quality," *International Journal of Service Industry Management* 5, no. 5 (1994), pp. 21–38.

23. Armand V. Feigenbaum, "Changing Concepts and Management of Quality Worldwide," *Quality Progress* 30, no. 12 (December 1997), pp. 45–48.

24. Morgan and Hunt, "The Commitment-Trust Theory." See also Christopher R. Moberg and Thomas W. Speh, "Evaluating the Relationship between Questionable Business Practices and the Strength of Supply Chain Relationships," *Supply Chain Management Review* 24, no. 2 (2003), pp. 1–19.

25. Reichheld, 2004, "The One Number You Need."

26. Gronoos, "From Marketing Mix to Relationship Marketing."

27. Charles C. Poirier and William F. Houser, *Business Partnering for Continuous Improvement* (San Francisco: Berrett-Koehler, 1993).

28. Feigenbaum, "Changing Concepts."

29. Gronroos, "From Marketing Mix to Relationship Marketing."

30. Morgan and Hunt, "The Commitment-Trust Theory," pp. 19–20.

31. Ibid., p. 19.

32. Rungtusanatham et al., "Supply Chain Linkages."

33. Kostas Dervitsiotis, "Beyond Stakeholder Satisfaction: Aiming for a New Forntier of Sustainable Stakeholder Trust," *Total Quality Management & Business Excellence* 14, no. 5 (July 2003), pp. 515–28.

34. Christopher B. Clott, "Perspectives on Global Outsourcing and the Changing Nature of Work," *Business & Society Review* 109, no. 20 (Summer 2004), pp. 153–70.

35. See C. K. Prahalad and Gary Hamel, "The Core Competence of the Corporation," *Harvard Business Review*, May–June 1990, pp. 79–91.

36. For a comprehensive study of the "sweatshop quandary," see Pamela Varley, ed., *The Sweatshop Quandary: Corporate Responsibility on the Global Frontier* (Washington, DC: Investor Responsibility Research Center, 1998).

37. See William Echikson, "It's Europe's Turn to Sweat About Sweatshops," *Business Week*, July 19, 1999, p. 96.

38. Martin Meznar and Douglas Nigh, "Managing Corporate Legitimacy: Public Affairs Activities, Strategies, and Effectiveness," *Business and Society* 32, no. 1 (Spring 1993), pp. 30–43.

39. Peter Hannaford, "What Is Public Affairs?" *Public Relations Quarterly* 33, no. 3 (Fall 1988), pp. 11–14.

40. See, for example, James E. Post, Edwin A. Murray Jr., Robert B. Dickie, and John F. Mahon, "The Public Affairs Function in American Corporations: Development and Relations with Corporate Planning," *Long Range Planning* 15, no. 2 (April 1982), pp. 12–21.

41. The history is given in Charles J. McMillan and Victor V. Murray, "Strategically Managing Public Affairs: Lessons from the Analysis of Business-Government Relations," *Business Quarterly* 48, no. 2 (Summer 1983), pp. 94–100.

42. The current state of the art is detailed in James E. Post and Jennifer J. Griffin, *The State of Corporate Public Affairs: Final Report 1996 Survey* (Boston and Washington, DC: Boston University School of Management and Foundation for Public Affairs, 1996); and Alfred A. Marcus and Allen M. Kaufman, "The Continued Expansion of the Corporate Public-Affairs Function," *Business Horizons* 31, no. 2 (March/April 1988), pp. 58–62.

43. See Keith MacMillan, "Managing Public Affairs in British Industry," *Journal of General Management* 9, no. 2 (1983/1984), pp. 784–90.

44. See D. Jeffrey Lenn, Steven N. Brenner, Lee Burke, Diane Dodd-McCue, Craig S. Fleisher, Lawrence J. Lad, David R. Palmer, Kathryn S. Rogers, Sandra A. Waddock, and Richard E. Wokutch, "Managing Corporate Public Affairs and Government Relations: US Multinational Corporations in Europe," in *Research in Corporate Social*

Performance and Policy, vol. 15, ed. James E. Post (Greenwich, CT: JAI Press, 1993), pp. 103–38.

45. Post and Griffin, *The State of Corporate Public Affairs.*

46. Steven L. Wartick and Pursey Heugens, "Future Directions for Issues Management," *Corporate Reputation Review* 6, no. 1 (Spring 2003), pp. 7–18.

47. Pursey Heugens, "Strategic Issues Management," dissertation abstract, *Business & Society* 41, no. 4 (December 2002), pp. 456–69.

48. See Douglas Nigh and Philip L. Cochran, "Issues Management and the Multinational Enterprise," *Management International Review* 34 (1994, special issue), pp. 51–59.

49. Adapted from ibid.

50. Adapted from ibid.

51. Ibid.

52. Lenn et al., "Managing Corporate Public Affairs."

53. Much of the information on crisis management in this section is derived from Christine M. Pearson and Judith A. Clair, "Reframing Crisis Management, " *Academy of Management Review* 23, no. 1 (January 1998), pp. 59–76. See also Ian I. Mitroff and Robert H. Kilman, *Corporate Tragedies: Product Tampering, Sabotage, and Other Catastrophes* (New York: Praeger, 1984); Ian I. Mitroff, Christine M. Pearson, and L. Kathleen Harrigan, *The Essential Guide to Managing Corporate Crises* (New York: Oxford University Press, 1996); P. Shrivastava, I. Mitroff, D. Miller, and A. Migliani, "Understanding Industrial Crises," *Journal of Management Studies* 25 (1988), pp. 285–303; and Norman R. Augustine, "Managing the Crisis You Tried to Prevent," *Harvard Business Review*, November–December 1995, pp. 147–58.

54. Jonathan Clark and Mark Harman, "On Crisis Management and Rehearsing," *Risk Management* 51, no. 5 (May 2004), pp. 40–43.

55. Pearson and Clair, "Reframing Crisis Management."

56. Les Coleman, "The Frequency and Cost of Corporate Crises," *Journal of Contingencies & Crisis Management* 12, no. 10 (March 2004), pp. 2–13.

57. Charles Perrow, *Normal Accidents: Living with High-Risk Technologies* (New York: Basic Books, 1984).

58. Diane Vaughan, *The Challenger Launch Decision: Risky Technology, Culture, and Deviance at NASA* (Chicago: University of Chicago Press, 1996).

59. Pearson and Clair, "Reframing Crisis Management."

60. Jennifer A. Kitto, "The Evolution of Public Issues Management," *Public Relations Quarterly* 43, no. 4 (Winter 1998/1999), pp. 34–38.

61. Edward L. Bernays, *Public Relations* (Norman, OK: University of Oklahoma Press, 1952), quoted in Burton St. John III, "Public Relations as Community-Building Then and Now," *Public Relations Quarterly* 43, no. 1 (Spring 1998), pp. 34–40.

62. Jodi B. Katzman, "What's the Role of Public Relations?" *Public Relations Journal* 49, no. 4 (April 1993), pp. 11–16.

63. See St. John, "Public Relations as Community-Building," and Augustine S. Ihator, "Effective Public Relations Techniques for the Small Business in a Competitive Market Environment," *Public Relations Quarterly* 43, no. 2 (Summer 1998), pp. 28–32.

64. Ihator, "Effective Public Relations Techniques."

65. Kristin B. Backhaus, Brett A. Stone, and Karl Heiner, "Exploring the Relationship between Corporate Social Performance and Employer Attractiveness," *Business & Society* 41, no. 3 (September 2002), pp. 292–318.

66. The "neighbor of choice" principle is developed at length in Edmund M. Burke, *Corporate Community Relations: The Principle of the Neighbor of Choice* (Greenwich, CT: Praeger, 1999). Discussion of the community relations function within this section is based on Burke's book.

67. Ibid., p. 24

68. Ibid., pp. 47 ff. This section is based on Burke's chapter 4.

69. Ibid., chapter 8.

70. The term is in ibid., chapter 12. The framing of this section is the present author's.

CHAPTER SEVEN

Managing Responsibility and Corporate Citizenship[1]

Learning is not compulsory . . . neither is survival.

If you can't describe what you are doing as a process, you don't know what you're doing.

What we need to do is learn to work in the system, by which I mean that everybody, every team, every platform, every division, every component is there not for individual competitive profit or recognition, but for contribution to the system as a whole on a win–win basis.

It is important that an aim never be defined in terms of activity or methods. It must always relate directly to how life is better for everyone . . . The aim of the system must be clear to everyone in the system. The aim must include plans for the future. The aim is a value judgment.

Quality guru Dr. W. Edwards Deming[2]

Can corporate citizenship or corporate responsibility be managed? What does it mean to practice something like corporate citizenship—or to have one's practices assessed? This chapter argues that corporate citizenship is a managerial responsibility to stakeholders and nature that can be managed exactly as every other activity within a firm is managed—and that it needs to be done so explicitly. Companies' stakeholder and environmental practices form the core of what companies are charged with managing responsibly.

At a very simple level, to *practice*, as in a sport, musical performance, or meditation, is *to repeat something over and over with the intent of improving or developing expertise.* In the sense we are exploring, practicing also involves *careful reflection about what worked and what didn't work so that the practice can continue improving.* The final and most important step is to move toward the betterment implied by having a vision in mind for the practice, that is, *implementing a process of constant learning and improvement.* As must be obvious, practice in the sense we are using it never ends.

Companies attempting to achieve value added through their stakeholder practices and the associated processes (as discussed in Chapter 6) need to be explicit about managing those processes and practices—including quality improvement as well as customer, employee, community, investor, and government relations. There are always improvements that can be made, especially in the turbulence and dynamism of the modern economic and social landscapes. This chapter will focus on establishing processes and practices aimed at continuous improvement in stakeholder and environmental practices—or total responsibility management (TRM) or simply responsibility management (RM). First, however, we will explore the links between quality and responsibility management.

Quality Management: The Link to Responsibility Management

In 1980, most American companies were paying little attention to quality management despite increasing public attentiveness to the quality of products. Yet for 30 years, Japanese firms had been implementing quality improvement processes based on the ideas of W. Edwards Deming and Edward Juran, who had introduced quality control methods to the Japanese after World War II, when U.S. managers had been uninterested.[3] As the public's perception of the quality of Japanese goods shifted from poor to excellent during the 1960s and 1970s, managers in companies that had not yet "discovered" quality began to feel significant competitive heat.

Competition came especially from Japanese companies, which were by the 1970s producing goods of high quality at relatively low cost. A turning point came in 1980 when NBC aired its white-paper documentary on the work of Deming, "If Japan Can . . . Why Can't We?" Shortly afterward, the quality revolution began in earnest in the United States (resulting in, among other things, the Baldrige Award) and in Europe (with the implementation of ISO quality standards and the European Quality Award). As one book on managing quality puts it, "[Deming's] name was soon a household word among corporate executives."[4] Over time, numerous corporations began implementing quality management and improvement systems as a means of regaining global competitiveness in the face of the intense competition posed by the quality of products produced by overseas competitors.

Most large businesses today operate in a fundamentally global competitive environment, both in producing and selling their wares, frequently using long supply chains to actually produce goods. Attention by labor, human rights, and environmental activists to working conditions, use of child labor, hiring and firing policies, and environmental problems, particularly in developing nations, has grown enormously in recent years, particularly as the Internet has fueled global connectivity. For example, significant negative publicity follows on the discovery by labor activists, for example, of sweatshop conditions or child labor in footwear, toy, and apparel industries, causing consumer boycotts and reputational damage that can cost companies customers and revenue. Overall, as Chapter 6 made clear, the attention to working conditions and environmental issues has raised the consciousness not only of activists but also of consumers, investors, and multinational companies themselves to the increasing social expectations that are being placed on companies—and on their suppliers.

Accompanying rising public expectations with respect to human rights, labor, and environmental policies is a proliferation of auditing and reporting methods (see Chapter 10 for an extensive discussion). These approaches include the balanced scorecard; triple-bottom-line accounting; holistic performance assessments; internal and stakeholder-oriented social audits (such as AA 1000 and SA 8000); and the Global Reporting Initiative (GRI), which is attempting to develop standardized reporting practices. Today, competitive pressures on product and service quality and widespread consumer attention to quality mean that companies cannot compete successfully without paying close attention to the quality of their products and services. Although managers' acceptance of quality as a business imperative has not been easy to achieve, failure to pay attention to quality now can quickly contribute to business failure. This chapter posits that a similar evolution is occurring with respect to managing a company's responsibility for its practices regarding labor, human rights, suppliers, customers, and the environment. It argues that companies are responding by developing responsibility management systems comparable in many respects to quality management systems already in place.

Responsibility Management (RM): The Key to Leading Corporate Citizenship

Companies are responding to pressures to manage responsibility with systemic management approaches comparable in many ways to quality management systems. Following the language of total quality management (TQM), Charles Bodwell and I have labeled these approaches total responsibility management (TRM) approaches, in part to highlight the similarity of responsibility management systems to quality management approaches. Here we will simplify the language and avoid the confusion that the word *total* implies by simply calling them responsibility management (RM). RM means that companies undertake systemic efforts to manage a company's relationships with its key stakeholders and the natural environment. These efforts tend to be built on common foundational values and

FIGURE 7.1 The Responsibility Management (RM) Framework

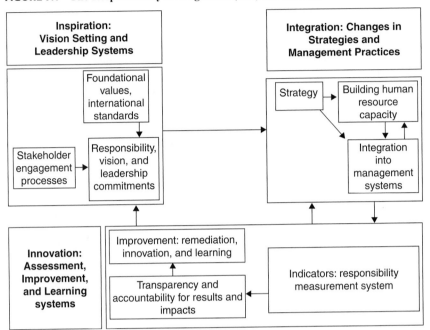

have three main elements: (1) *inspiration*, or the vision setting, commitment, and leadership systems; (2) *integration* of responsibility into employee and other stakeholder relationships and into strategies and practices; and (3) *innovation*, which includes assessment, improvement, and learning systems and their associated indicators (see Figure 7.1).

In much the same way that TQM practices have done for quality, RM approaches represent integrated systems of addressing the full range of companies' responsibilities. They can help companies maximize competitive success by continually monitoring and improving performance through engaged and mutually responsive relationships with employees and other key stakeholders; measuring performance on multiple bottom lines (i.e., the triple bottom line of economic, societal, and ecological criteria); and transparently accepting responsibility and accountability for the impacts of corporate decisions, actions, and results. Figure 7.1 illustrates the interdependent nature of the main components that make up a generic RM approach.

Inspiration: Vision Setting and Leadership Commitment

Inspiration involves the vision setting and leadership commitment processes found in RM approaches, as well as stakeholder engagement and the establishment of foundational values. A key step in developing a RM approach is for the firm to establish and implement its responsibility objectives or the inspirational vision of the sort discussed earlier in this book.[5] The vision needs to be based on the company's unique competitive situation, stakeholders, and corporate history in much the same way that quality management goals are specifically geared to a company's unique situation. Further, RM approaches can be implemented in a single corporate unit or systemically throughout a corporation, for those serving a global market or a single market. The inspiration process, or vision setting and leadership commitment system, creates the organizational context for RM, involving stakeholder engagement processes, recognition of foundational values, and explicit development of the responsibility vision and leadership commitment.

Stakeholder Engagement Processes

TQM is centered on the role of two sets of stakeholders (customers and employees) in the continuous improvement processes on which it is based, while RM approaches focus on multiple stakeholders. TQM emphasizes understanding and meeting customer expectations. In Japanese, the same word—*okyakusama*—is used to mean both "customer" and "honorable guest."[6] The successful TQM-based company seeks to treat the first like the second, maintaining an open dialogue with customers that allows them not only to meet current needs but also to anticipate future needs. TQM also relies on employee involvement, taking advantage of employees' knowledge, creativity, and potential enthusiasm for their job. RM approaches similarly are centered on employees, recognizing that an investment in a workforce is an investment in the capacity of an organization and its suppliers to meet the social objectives it has established. At the same time, such approaches have a broadened focus that includes other stakeholders whose interests and concerns can affect the company, such as suppliers, activists, communities, governments, and of course, customers.

As with TQM, many of the leading firms have worked at establishing processes whereby they receive input from their range of stakeholders. These stakeholder engagement processes, also called multisectoral collaboration or dialogue,[7] have begun to emerge in recent years as mechanisms to gain input from key external and internal stakeholders.[8] Leading firms appear to be dedicated to taking advantage of the potential of employees' capacities to improve the responsibility of their practices. Employee involvement is particularly relevant to labor and human resource practices, because employees are directly affected and most aware of where improvement is needed, and they are responsible for implementing the organization's vision. In the words of one union representative, "Empowered employees are your best source of monitoring; they know where the problems are."

RM approaches provide interaction with external stakeholders as well, including customers, investors, communities, and nongovernmental organizations (NGOs). With increased recognition that companies are accountable not only to owners but also to other stakeholders, leading-edge companies develop engagement processes before they hit trouble spots or make significant changes. Thus, they develop stakeholder engagement processes that include interactive forums, dialogue processes, or online communications.[9] Through dialogue, companies can work with stakeholders to develop trusting relationships where differing points of view can be expressed and input on major issues given in a mutually responsive (but not dictatorial or mandatory) way.

For example, owners, customers, communities, and sometimes even governments can be brought into the stakeholder engagement process. Customers are increasingly aware of the conditions under which products are produced, and they make purchasing decisions on that basis. Customers can readily find out about product quality or any harmful consequences of product use; hence, marketing practices need to be monitored and aboveboard.[10] Similar circumstances exist for other major stakeholders. While RM approaches are inherently more complex than TQM approaches because of the multiple stakeholders involved, they can provide significantly more information to management that can help the business improve its relationships with these key constituents.

Foundational Values

The inspiration process also involves the recognition of foundational values. Foundational values are the baseline set of values below which the company (including members of its supply chain) knows it cannot go and still be accepted as a responsible corporate citizen. Not just any values will do, however. RM approaches rely on employees, which means they need to be built on a foundation of constructive values that support human and worker rights and dignity. Foundational values provide what some scholars term a "moral minimum" of acceptable practice, that is, respect for human dignity, avoidance of child labor, freedom of association, and adequate working conditions.[11] A clearly articulated set of foundational values can be found in numerous international standards developed in recent years, perhaps most prominently in the International Labor Organization's (ILO's) Declaration on Fundamental Principles and Rights at Work (FPRW). (The Declaration on FPRW targets standards to be set at the national legislative level. The corresponding standard applicable at the corporate level, referencing the Declaration on FPRW, is the International Labor Organization's Tripartite Declaration of Principles concerning Multinational Enterprises and Social Policy.) More recently, they are promulgated in the United Nations (UN) secretary-general's Global Compact, which includes the four labor principles present in the Declaration on FPRW as well as three human rights principles, two environmental principles, and one anticorruption principle also derived from other UN documents (see Chapter 10 for a longer discussion).

Many firms have used these fundamental values to set standards for operation within their supply chains and in their own operations, often in the form of codes of conduct. In implementing RM approaches, leading firms go beyond the minimum of foundation values to establish visions that are internalized in the culture of the organization. In doing so they set stretch goals for the organization, in terms of not only profitability or market segment dominance but also social performance.

It is notable that the core values embedded in the quality movement, as exemplified by the Baldrige Quality Award, can readily be matched to value inherent in RM approaches. Table 7.1 illustrates this comparison.

TABLE 7.1 **Core Values and Concepts in TQM/Baldrige Award and RM**

Source: www.quality.nist.gov/2001_Criteriapdf.htm; and Baldridge National Quality Program 2001, Criteria for Performance Excellence.

Baldrige Award Core Values and Concepts	RM Core Values and Concepts
Visionary Leadership	**Visionary and Committed Leadership**
Leaders set direction and create customer focus, clear and visible values, and high expectations.	Leaders set direction of vision, clearly articulated and constructive values, and high expectations about responsible practices with respect to all stakeholders, but particularly employees, and for the consequences of corporate impacts on the natural environment.
Customer-Driven Excellence	**Stakeholder-Driven Excellence and Responsible Practices**
Customers judge quality and performance.	Stakeholders, especially employees, customers, suppliers/allies, and owners, judge responsibility and performance.
Organizational and Personal Learning	**Organizational and Personal Learning through Dialogue and Mutual Engagement with Relevant Stakeholders**
Continuous improvement of existing approaches and adaptation to change lead to new goals and approaches, embedded in daily operations organizationally and individually.	Stakeholder engagement processes provide a forum for continual learning and improvement of corporate practice.
Valuing Employees and Partners	**Valuing Employees, Partners, Other Stakeholders**
Success depends on knowledge, skills, creativity, and motivation of employees and partners.	Success depends on knowledge, skills, creativity, motivation, and engagement of employees, partners, and relevant other stakeholders on issues related to corporate practices and impacts.
Agility	**Agility and Responsiveness**
Success demands a capacity for rapid change and flexibility.	Success demands a capacity for rapid change, flexibility, and responsiveness when stakeholder-related issues or problems arise.
Focus on the Future (Short- and Long-Term)	**Focus on the Future (Short- and Long-Term)**
Pursuit of sustainable growth and market leadership requires a strong future orientation and willingness to make	Pursuit of sustainable growth and market leadership requires a strong future orientation and willingness to

continued

continued

long-term commitments to key stakeholders, customers, employees, suppliers and partners, stockholders, the public, and the community.

respect and make long-term commitments to key stakeholders, customers, employees, suppliers and partners, stockholders, the public, the community, and the natural environment.

Managing for Innovation

Leaders make meaningful change to improve products, services, and processes, and to create new value for stakeholders.

Managing for Responsibility

Leaders make meaningful change to ensure that practices that produce products and services are responsible, respectful, and value creating for key stakeholders.

Management by Fact

Measurement and analysis of performance, derived from business needs and strategy, provide data about key processes, outputs, and results.

Management by Fact, Transparency, Accountability

Measurement, evaluation, and transparency of the responsibility of corporate stakeholder and ecological practices provide data about the responsibility that is integral to corporate practices, outputs, and impacts.

Public Responsibility and Citizenship

Leaders should stress public and citizenship responsibilities, including meeting basic expectations related to ethics and protection of public health, safety, and environment.

Public Responsibility and Citizenship

Leaders should assure that corporate practices related to economic, societal, and ecological bottom lines are responsible, ethical, and transparent to relevant stakeholders and hold themselves accountable for their positive and negative impacts.

Focus on Results and Creating Value

Performance measures should focus on key results, and be used to create and balance value for key stakeholders—customers, employees, stockholders, suppliers and partners, the public, and the community.

Focus on Positive Results, Impacts, and Value Added for Stakeholders with Responsible Ecological Practices

Performance measures should focus on key results and be used to create and balance value for key stakeholders—customers, employees, stockholders, suppliers and partners, the public, the community, and the natural environment.

Systems Perspective

The core values and seven Baldrige criteria provide a systems perspective for managing an enterprise, forming the

Systems Perspective on Responsible Management Practices

RM's core values and criteria provide a framework for developing responsible

continued

concluded

building blocks and integrating mechanism for the system, which, however, requires organization-specific synthesis and alignment.

- *Synthesis* means looking at the organization as a whole and building on key business requirements, strategic objectives, and action plans.

- *Alignment* means using key links among categories to provide key measures and indicators of success.

management practices that can help a company integrate responsibility into all of its stakeholder and ecological practices, in alignment with the goals, objectives, values, and strategy of the organization.

- *Integration* means that responsibility is inherent or integral to corporate practices and cannot be dissociated from them. It also means that management recognizes the responsibility that is inherent to practices and actions that affect stakeholders or nature and works to reduce negative impacts.

- *Alignment* means using key links and indicators to determine how stakeholders and nature are affected by corporate practices and actions.

Responsibility, Vision, and Leadership Commitments

Top management commitment to the company's vision and values with respect to responsibility is needed consistently and repeatedly over time, according to managers interviewed in an ILO supply chain study. Two key questions seem to stand out as needing articulated answers to implement an RM system; these were introduced in Chapter 4. The first question is the traditional strategy question: "What business are we in?" The second, and more critical question for the RM approach, is the enterprise strategy question: "What do we stand for?"[12] As noted earlier in the book, extensive research by James Collins and Jerry Porras demonstrates the importance of corporate vision and underlying values to long-term success.[13]

Top management involvement is critical in the process of establishing and implementing a responsibility vision. Employees typically seek guidance from management, attempting to understand what senior management wants and what management will reward. On the one hand, as many managers interviewed emphasized, if management does not believe in the vision being articulated or sees it as merely a public relations exercise, then there is little hope for its becoming part of operating practices. On the other hand, if top management is involved in the development of a vision and communicates that commitment on a regular basis, if the vision is supported through reward systems, allocations of resources and changes in procedures, then the vision will move forward.

In organizations made up of hierarchical pyramids within pyramids, there are, of course, various levels of top management. Management commitment at each of these levels is crucial; a senior manager in charge of country-level operations, quality control, or purchasing who does not believe in the principles outlined can cause a breakdown of support for corporate responsibility objectives within his or her area of responsibility. Support needs to be generated at all levels in a cascade fashion from the top of the organization all the way down and through supply chain operations to supervisors and workers on the production lines.

Pharmaceutical giant Bristol-Myers Squibb is one company that has developed explicit stakeholder engagement practices to support its corporate citizenship. The information in Case 7.1 is posted on the company's Web site as a means of being transparent about the ways Bristol Myers Squibb engages stakeholders.

Integration: Changes in Strategies and Management Practices

RM approaches *integrate* a company's vision, values, and leadership commitments into its corporate and business level strategies, then operationalize the vision through the operating practices that impact employees, other stakeholders, and the environment. In the companies studied, workers rights, human rights, and working conditions are increasingly becoming part of companies' overall strategies and corporate visions. Interestingly, standards for supplier and distributor operations increasingly mirror those of corporate headquarters and in-house operations. Whether in human resource policies and practices, supplier relationships, or marketing policies, such companies are increasingly paying attention to the impacts that their decisions have on key stakeholders.

Strategy

Once established by the processes of inspiration, the company's responsibility goals and values must be integrated into corporate and functional strategies. In RM approaches, corporate and business strategies reflect the responsibility vision so that it is communicated to all stakeholders. Such visions can help firms deal with crises, as Johnson & Johnson was guided by its Credo during the Tylenol poisonings of the early 1980s, when the Credo guided management's decision to pull Tylenol from the market despite the $100 million cost of doing so. Perhaps more important, a responsibility vision can help a firm in its day-to-day operations, thereby avoiding crises and operating in a consistently responsible manner, as, for example, Timberland Corporation has been guided by its "Pull on your boots and make a difference" motto. Strategies, the broad operationalization of the visions held by the organization, need to clearly reflect the ultimate vision and also be linked to rewards.

In integrating the vision and values into the strategies of the company, a key question must be asked: "How do we do business here?" The next two sections of this chapter focus on how some companies have chosen to answer.

Building Human Resource Capacity

Integration of a company's vision and values takes place first of all in human resource practices as a process of building human resource capacity. There are two interrelated elements. First, human relations issues are typically behind the responsibility visions of organizations, in the best cases becoming part of their strategic

Our stakeholders are similar to those of other major corporations. They encompass interested parties, both internal and external to the company and include:

- Customers and consumers
- Employees and their families
- Retirees
- Shareholders and investor groups
- Suppliers and contractors
- Neighbors and community groups
- Regulators, legislators, and political leaders
- Non-governmental organizations (NGOs)
- Academia

APPROACHES TO CONSULTATION

Bristol-Myers Squibb has a long tradition of open communication and cooperation with our stakeholders on environmental, social, and economic issues. This is a fundamental element of our Pledge. We have an open-door policy with our stakeholders. We encourage more than two-way communications. In addition to inviting questions and comments, we pursue opportunities to partner with each other. Incorporating the wisdom, concerns, and lessons of our stakeholders helps improve our management of the company.

Internally, we foster communications and dialogue with employees through a variety of initiatives, including functional and cross-functional committees, state-of-the-business addresses, Web-based communications on the Internet and intranet, publications, and the Office of Corporate Conduct.

Externally, we actively seek dialogue with stakeholders. For example, we work with external advisors—representing socially responsible investment groups, academia, key customers, and public interest groups—who review and comment on our progress toward sustainable development. We have a

feedback section and a "frequently asked questions" page on our Sustainability Web site, as well as direct e-mail links from the site to management at our corporate office and local operating facilities around the world. We track communications submitted through the Web site and ensure that we respond in a thoughtful and timely manner.

In 2002, we received a total of 246 messages, slightly fewer than the 254 messages we received the year before, from the feedback section on our Web site. Of these, 101 messages related to EHS [employee, health, and safety] information and 145 addressed other topics. The feedback included requests for information on our EHS programs and performance; requests for copies of our sustainability report and material safety data sheets for our products; and comments on animal testing and other company activities.

Bristol-Myers Squibb participates on several multi-stakeholder panels in public meetings. Sitting side-by-side with representatives of government, academia, NGOs, and industry, we discuss emerging issues, including sustainability reporting, EHS metrics, full cost accounting, and product life cycle management. Meetings such as these help to further the understanding of commonly shared challenges.

The company also participates in voluntary initiatives with regulatory authorities. For example, our facility in Lawrenceville, New Jersey, is a charter member in the U.S. Environmental Protection Agency (EPA) National Environmental Achievement Track Program. Our Wallingford, Connecticut, site became a participant in the US EPA and Department of Energy Labs 21 Program for improving laboratory energy and water efficiency, encouraging the use of renewable energy sources, and promoting environmental stewardship.

Our facilities in Hopewell and Lawrenceville, New Jersey, have been accepted into the New Jersey Silver Track Program, which offers incentives—including regulatory flexibility—and public recognition to facilities able to demonstrate and measure improved environmental performance. In addition, we encourage our employees to take an active part in sharing with others our company's expectations and vision for sustainability. These conversations and actions within the community will help support positive change in our society.

INFORMATION GENERATED

The information generated through stakeholder dialogue covers a wide range of topics, including:

- Best practices from other companies
- Expectations of performance from NGOs, governments, and academia
- Feedback from customers on product and company performance
- Opportunities for collaboration with local community organizations and governments
- Community feedback on facility operations and emergency response procedures

USE OF INFORMATION

Information resulting from stakeholder engagements is used to establish the company's Sustainability 2010 Goals, determine the scope and content of information shared with the public, and shape the company's programs and actions.

DISCUSSION QUESTIONS

1. How do you think that Bristol-Myers Squibb's overt approach to dialogue with stakeholders might help the company's corporate citizenship efforts? What benefits derive from this type of interaction?

2. Are there any risks associated with direct stakeholder engagement and transparency like Bristol-Myers Squibb is exhibiting? What are they? What should the company do to mitigate those risks?

Source: Quoted from Bristol Myers Squibb's Web site, www.bms.com/static/ehs/manage/data/stakeh.html (accessed May 12, 2004).

plans for the treatment and development of employees. Second, employees are core to the systems required to make the vision a reality. Reaching a firm's responsibility vision requires the commitment and involvement of managers and the participation of employees throughout supply chains, from the top of hierarchy to the bottom.

The first step is building understanding about the reasons for and benefits of carrying forward the responsibility vision among employees and among managers who allocate resources. This aspect of integration entails the development of supporting materials; training; and regular, consistent communication about the responsibility vision and, if present, the code of conduct. This process also entails modifying reward structures, evaluation procedures, training, and requirement systems so that they support both strategic and responsibility objectives.

Employees are core elements in the implementation of RM approaches. Most codes of conduct incorporate strong elements of responsible treatment of employees, even within extended supply chains. Integrating a corporate vision into human resources practices means assuring that high standards (such as those specified in many codes of conduct and the International Labor Standards) are met. Thus, the codes of conduct that have evolved into RM approaches typically include policies on working conditions; hiring, retention, and dismissal; remuneration (wages and benefits); hours of work; forced and child labor; discrimination; promotion; freedom of association; and collective bargaining.

RM approaches emphasize that these policies need to be upheld within the confines of the firm itself as well as in partners or suppliers. The emphasis on standards within a company's supply chain is particularly critical to RM because the boundaries between a multinational company and its suppliers are increasingly blurred, especially in the eyes of activists, consumers, and other stakeholders.

Integration into Management Systems

RM approaches incorporate the responsibility vision into other operating practices and management systems. Initially, the task of managing the corporate codes of conduct and RM issues rested with compliance departments or other groups specifically dedicated to corporate responsibility. Similarly, prior to the quality revolution, responsibility for quality rested with the quality control officers at the end of the line. Eventually, everyone became responsible for quality—and we might expect that everyone in the system will eventually become responsible for responsibility as well.

Truly carrying out all the elements required by the responsibility vision has broad implications. Moving responsible practices into supplier operations, for example, means that the role of purchasing is crucial. Yet shifting the focus of the purchasing vision from quality, delivery, and cost to include issues of labor practices can be challenging, given the bottom-line financial concerns of the participating firms in a supply chain. Further, a company implementing RM approaches needs to be aware of the implications of its products and process for customers, suppliers, and other stakeholders.

Integration goes further than modifying purchasing procedures, in particular since buyers for firms are only infrequently present in supplier factories. The compliance or responsibility group is typically limited in size, and hence able to visit and monitor suppliers only sporadically. As a result, many managers in firms with heavily disaggregated supply chains highlighted the important role of quality and manufacturing personnel in supporting responsibility objectives. The addition of RM to responsibilities already held by the quality control group, however, can be a point of contention, but the benefits of broader RM can provide a basis on which companies can engage productively with numerous stakeholders. Ultimately, managers throughout the organization need to take responsibility for RM for it to truly take on the total characteristic that quality management does.

Innovation: Assessment, Improvement, and Learning Systems

One of the great benefits of TQM approaches is that they do not expect perfection. Rather, TQM focuses on continually *improving* not just the products or outputs but also the processes associated with developing them. Much the same can be said of RM approaches. No company is—or is ever likely to be—perfect (as the numerous scandals arising from current corporate practices clearly indicate). Companies can, however, put in place processes to determine where problems exist and provide for remediation, innovation, and learning that help to solve those problems. Defining where needs exist is the role of the *innovation and improvement* systems associated with RM approaches, with the help of an RM measurement system that provides relevant *indicators.*

Indicators: The RM Measurement System

As quality management did, RM necessitates new approaches to measurement and information dissemination. RM approaches, as a result, involve measuring operating practices, stakeholder relationships, and results in new ways and on multiple bottom lines rather than strictly in traditional productivity and financial terms. Taking a RM approach involves creating accounting and reporting systems that satisfy the needs of internal stakeholders and managers for information that improves company performance and simultaneously satisfies the demands of external stakeholders, including unions, NGOs, investors, governments, and local communities. Additionally, internal feedback is essential for performance enhancement, while RM implies external accountability and, to make that real, transparency.

RM approaches deal with multiple objectives, frequently the triple bottom line of economics, society, and environment,[14] and measurement and performance systems need to reflect the added complexity of these objectives. Single-bottom-line performance assessment systems are increasingly outdated, with the advent of multiple-bottom-line auditing systems, strategic system audit models,[15] holistic performance assessment models,[16] or balanced scorecard[17] approaches, which will be discussed in more detail in Chapter 8.

Appropriate measures can improve performance, because as the accounting axiom goes, what gets measured and rewarded is what gets done. Thus, RM approaches cover far more than simple productivity and financial performance, because responsible practice is integral to all of a company's operations. Human resource practices need to be assessed to ensure that they are in line with the core values and codes of conduct the company has established. Customer and marketing practices are directly related to product quality, customer satisfaction, and corporate reputation, among other factors. Community relations performance can be assessed, for example, according to the Boston College Center for Corporate Citizenship's standards of excellence. Similarly, quality can be addressed through a wide range of quality standards, such as criteria for the Baldrige Award, the European Quality Award, or the Deming Prize (Japan), which will be demonstrated later in this chapter.[18] Social auditing methods (e.g., internal responsibility audits of employee, community, quality, and environmental processes)[19] or more stakeholder-oriented auditing techniques (e.g., those of AccountAbility in England)[20] can provide useful information, although similar methods can also be developed and applied in-house.

Transparency and Accountability

Indicators found in the responsibility measurement system are a key to providing necessary information for improving the system to organizational decision makers, and doing so cost-effectively, but they are merely a first step. Transparency provides the means for holding the company accountable for its impacts. Access to information and its reporting methods can provide a dynamic tension that moves a company forward, supporting its continuous improvement of practices. Measurement systems stretch up and down throughout the organization. Access to information can help managers determine whether to act to improve practices. Visibility helps ensure that access to information enhances performance, putting pressure on those who can influence the process of achieving responsibility goals to make choices based on responsibility considerations.

Transparency and accountability are also focused externally. Responsible companies know that they are accountable to multiple stakeholders for their operating results, financial performance, and stakeholder and ecological impacts. In many cases, data from the responsibility measurement systems are used to produce responsibility reports addressing internal and external (or boundary-spanning) practices and the impacts of corporate activities. Through transparency (i.e., the issuance of triple-bottom-line reports), companies can develop better relationships with employees and other key stakeholders, such as activists, customers, and communities, not to mention owners. In addition to the supportive pressure to improve that result from transparency and its attendant accountability, triple-bottom-line reporting can lead to the development of trusting relationships with key stakeholders because data are perceived as both valid and reliable.

Innovation, Improvement, and Learning Systems

Implementing a responsibility vision is an ongoing, cyclical process of continual innovation and improvement, remediation for wrongs, and organizational learning. Innovation and learning systems guide managers in encouraging responsible practices and provide an emphasis on continued organizational learning and development, pushing the company toward ever more responsible practice. Remediation links to the foundational values agreed on by the international community and the specific responsibility vision of the corporation by focusing on continually learning and improving practices that may meet basic standards but could be performed better. Further, remediation provides a mechanism for immediately eliminating practices found to be intolerable under the foundational values.

RM approaches to learning and innovation are systemic and multidimensional. The word multidimensional means that information systems provide inputs at the corporate level on success of organization-wide efforts, or on crises that require top-level action. Multidimensional innovations also require inputs at the country level and within factories or operations dispersed around the globe, to flag local issues that need consideration. As with TQM, inspection, measurement, and analysis are expected to take place where the work occurs to provide adequate feedback to improve performance. Such systems can extend responsibility measurement to the lowest levels in the hierarchies of firms, guiding individual managers and employees in problem solving. As with other holistic approaches to organizational learning,[21] RM approaches mean an iterative process of improvement over time rather than a single initiative that is implemented and then ends. See Case 7.2 for a description of one company's mutidimensional RM approach.

CASE 7.2 Sustainable Development and Transparency at Chiquita

Chiquita, which produces one-quarter of the Latin American banana crop, has spent many years working to ensure that all its banana farms in Latin America meet labor and environmental standards that are independently verified by an international nongovernmental organization (NGO). In the often-troubled Latin American banana industry, where labor unions have been seeking change for more than a decade, this company has made a bold and so far lonely move to become a model of best practices on workplace conditions and environmental management.

Chiquita's work allowed it to meet an independently verified social and environmental standard for the 127 banana farms it owns in Latin America. The standard is run by the Rainforest Alliance, an international nonprofit organization responsible for certifying farms under its Better Banana Project (BBP). Chiquita is the only global banana company to have undertaken and met the BBP's standards, which are the centerpiece of a rapidly expanding corporate social responsibility program. Chiquita outlined many of its initiatives in its first corporate responsibility report, published in September 2001. The company has since issued a second corporate responsibility report, which extends the company's assessment to its transportation and logistics operations.

The publication of this report set a high standard for the whole industry. The same can be said for the recent groundbreaking agreement with unions in Latin America that commits Chiquita to respect the core labor conventions of the International Labor Organization and establishes mechanisms for regular consultation and for oversight of compliance. Further, Chiquita joined the United Kingdom–based Ethical Trading Initiative, which brings together companies, NGOs, and unions around bettering human rights, corporate responsibility, and business ethics.

The Rainforest Alliance began the BBP in 1991, around the same time that Chiquita began looking for just such an authoritative environmental standard to improve life for its employees and safeguard the environment.

According to Jeff Zalla, corporate responsibility officer at Chiquita: "Senior management at the company had reached the conclusion through education and increased awareness rather than through any reputational catastrophe that things needed to change. We wanted to improve our social and environmental performance in an authentic way and BBP was the most rigorous standard. We felt we had a particular responsibility as an agricultural producer in developing countries to do something and as a brand to lead our industry." As a result, Chiquita and the Rainforest Alliance began talks that, in 1992, led the company to test out the idea of trying to meet the BBP standards.

The standards, which are detailed in a 19-page document, cover a wide range of topics, from workers' rights to the storage of packaging material on plantations. When two of Chiquita's pilot farms in Costa Rica achieved certification, senior management decided to extend the work. The first batch of Chiquita farms was certified in 1994, and the long haul to 100 percent certification began.

Since then, Chiquita has, among other things, reduced pesticide use, reforested more than 1,000 hectares with native trees, and put 525 hectares of land under protection. On workers' welfare, certification has helped Chiquita employees attain a much higher standard of living than other agricultural workers in the countries where the company operates. Employees in Costa Rica, for instance, now earn more than one and a half times the standard minimum wage. They also have improved training, housing, health benefits, education, and transport. All company workers have the right to associate freely, and Chiquita has almost as many union workers as all other banana companies in Latin America combined.

The Chiquita farms are certified only after frequent visits by trained independent inspectors, who are brought in from a network of conservation organizations affiliated with the Rainforest Alliance. They verify that the changes needed to meet the standards are being made and that farms have introduced measures to improve workers' quality of life, reduce agrochemical use, and increase water quality and wildlife habitat.

All farms owned by Chiquita in Colombia, Costa Rica, Guatemala, Honduras, and Panama—cultivating more than 28,400 hectares—have now been certified. A further 30 percent of independent farms selling bananas to the company have also been certified, and the company is keen to encourage the remaining 70 percent of independent producers to follow suit. Together, according to the Rainforest Alliance, total production from Chiquita's certified owned and independent producer farms amounts to almost 15 percent of banana exports from Latin America.

Complying with the BBP has cost the group more than $20 million in capital expenditure, along with millions of dollars in annual operating costs. However, Tensie Whelan, executive director of the Rainforest Alliance, says the company's "extraordinary efforts to reach compliance are leading the way for the rest of the industry."

George Jaksch, Chiquita's quality director in Europe, also judges that the money has been well spent. "What we have done in our tropical division is hugely important for our European business," Jaksch says. "Many of our retail customers would not be doing business with us unless we had a really thorough and deeply rooted programme like this."

Zalla says the BBP "has helped align the whole organization behind a clear performance standard." He adds: "We see a lot more discipline throughout the company as a result

of what we have done under the BBP. It's hard to put a cost figure on the improvements, but they are very real in terms of workplace conduct and productivity. There have also been real cost savings through measures such as reducing the use of pesticides."

Even without those benefits, Zalla says, Chiquita would have done what it did because "we are committed to doing the right thing." He adds: "In a country such as Colombia there are huge social problems in the areas where we produce bananas. It makes a real difference that the company has a program of this kind. It creates a workplace where people can feel valued and work safely."

In recognition of Chiquita's efforts to manage its responsibilities explicitly and transparently, the UK firm SustainAbility ranked the company's corporate responsibility report as 1st in the food industry, 3rd among all U.S. companies in 2002, and 18th in the world. Despite financial problems that had resulted in the company's declaring— and then emerging from—bankruptcy, Chiquita was selected as the 2004 Corporate Citizen of the Americas by the Trust for the Americas for its work in providing homes to workers through its Neuvo San Juan Home Ownership Project.

DISCUSSION QUESTIONS

1. Chiquita has had serious financial problems that resulted in bankruptcy, yet simultaneously has been pursuing active good corporate citizenship. What, if any, do you see as the advantages of this strategy? Are there disadvantages?

2. Why do you think Chiquita's emphasis is on workers' welfare and ecology? Why has the company been so transparent about both its good works and its problems? (Go to the Chiquita Web site at www.chiquita.com and look at its responsibility reports.)

Source: Jennifer Leigh, based on personal interviews and information from the Chiquita Web site, www.chiquita.com.

Responsibility Management: The Link to Quality

To further highlight the reality that corporate responsibilities to stakeholder and the natural environment can be managed just like any other corporate arena, Table 7.2 compares the Baldrige National Quality Award criteria with those that can be used in a RM system. Note in both approaches the focus on continuous improvement in all stakeholder and ecological categories, the meeting of stakeholder expectations, the need for long-range planning, and employee involvement. Further, there is a decided focus on process management and problem solving through teams that engage relevant stakeholders (customers and employees in the case of quality, and all core stakeholders in RM approaches). Both types of approaches, which can be developed for the unique situation of the particular company, also emphasize development of specific measures so that results can be determined and the commitment of top leaders to the processes involved.

Measurement

One of the most popular techniques used to measure internal performance against a company's responsibility and business goals is the balanced scorecard developed by Robert Kaplan and David Norton of the Harvard Business School, which can be adapted and modified to meet the specific (responsibility) goals identified by a given company.[22] Kaplan and Norton were among the first to recognize that better balance was needed within companies' measurement systems with respect to the dominant financial perspective. The balanced scorecard represents a management approach that provides clear direction for companies to articulate their goals and values, and move them into the strategy with specific stakeholders in mind. Focused on internal business processes and external outcomes, the balanced scorecard approach asks companies to retain traditional financial measures but to supplement them with other critical elements that focus on the ways that they create value for other important stakeholders, including customers, suppliers, and employees, and also pay attention to important process, technological, and innovation issues.

To make the balanced scorecard—or other RM system—concrete, it is necessary to identify specific goals and targets within the areas of stakeholder or ecological interest. Kaplan and Norton suggest four particular areas: the learning and growth perspective for employees, the business process perspective (mission and mission support areas), the customer perspective (satisfaction and focus), and the more traditional financial perspective. Of course, a total RM approach would take into account the goals and practices associated with other stakeholders as well to ensure that not just the vision but also the values of the company are considered.

Like other RM approaches, the balanced scorecard approach has characteristics similar to quality management in its holistic and systems-oriented philosophy and emphasis on continuous improvement through measurement and feedback.

TABLE 7.2 **Baldrige Criteria Extended to Total Responsibility Management (RM)**

Source: www.quality.nist.gov/2001_Criteria.pdf.htm; and Sandra Waddock and Charles Bodwell, *Managing Corporate Responsibility.*

Baldrige National Quality Award Criteria for Performance Excellence	Total Responsibility Management Criteria for Performance Excellence
1. Continuous quality improvement	1. Improvement: remediation, innovation, and learning; continual responsibility improvement for all corporate decisions, actions, processes, practices, and results
2. Meeting customers' requirements	2. Foundational values: lives up to expectations of global business, NGO, and governmental communities regarding responsible relationships with employees, suppliers, customers, and communities through sustainable management practices
3. Long-range planning	3. Long-range planning through vision, values, and management commitments
4. Increased employee involvement	4. Human resource responsibility: meeting employees' expectations about responsible practices through engagement and dialogue, and implementation of employee practices that treat employees and suppliers' workers with dignity and respect, empower workers, and meet international standards on human and labor rights
5. Process management	5. Responsibility integration into management systems: management of stakeholder relationships, practices, and impacts through attention to systems, processes, and outcomes
6. Competitive benchmarking	6. Competitive benchmarking of responsibility systems, including systems/process management for continual responsibility improvement
7. Team-based problem-solving	7. Stakeholder engagement processes: employee, supplier, and customer involvement and empowerment in meeting standards and problem solving

continued

concluded

8. Constant measurement of results	8. Responsibility measurement system: constant assessment of results, externally verified auditing process, communication and reporting out to stakeholders
9. Closer relationships with customers	9. Transparency and accountability for results and impacts: closer, engaged, and mutually respectful stakeholder relationships
10. Management commitment	10. Leadership commitment: top management commitment, management commitment at all levels, employee and supplier commitment; clear articulation of vision, core values, and strategies for continual improvement of stakeholder relations and performance assessment

Responsibility Management: Integrated Approaches to Leading Corporate Citizenship

The RM approaches described in this chapter represent an integrated approach to implementing responsibility objectives, with elements that work together rather than independently or in isolation. The evolution of RM approaches today is about where TQM approaches were in the early 1980s; they are likely to become more established in the future. As with TQM, elements of RM approaches reinforce and are interdependent with other internal management systems to create a context in which all stakeholders involved in the system are aware of the responsibility vision, values, and strategies, and the practices that achieve the vision. RM is a set of processes and goals to be achieved, but not a strict set of guidelines for performance. Thus, the RM approach represents a *framework* within which a company can plan and organize responsibility for its practices and impacts. In this respect, RM is a tool similar to those developed for quality management and can be implemented in unique ways by each company that adopts it.

Self-assessment is a critical component of RM. While external evaluation, monitoring, and certification are important, RM approaches are fundamentally internal and (at this point) voluntary management systems that help companies improve performance with respect to all of their stakeholders rather than just a narrow set of stakeholders. RM is a self-monitoring framework that helps a company and its workers figure out where its problem areas are and make improvements in large part by the active involvement of workers and a well-functioning process of dialogue. By identifying stakeholders and the impacts that company practices have on them, and by engaging in a dialogic process to improve its stakeholder relationships, a company will be better prepared for problems when they do arise—and more likely be able to avert many altogether.

RM approaches can provide a means for integrating external demands and pressures for responsible practice, calls for accountability and transparency, the proliferation of codes of conduct, managing supply chains responsibly and in a sustainable manner, and stakeholder engagement into a single approach for responsibility practices within the firm. Are any companies now implementing complete RM systems? Probably not. But as in the early days of TQM, the pieces are in place in many companies. Recognizing the need for integration as a means of controlling the complexity they would otherwise face, many companies are clearly beginning to move in the direction of total responsibility management.

Endnotes

1. Much of this chapter is coauthored with Charles Bodwell, and is drawn from Sandra Waddock and Charles Bodwell, "From TQM to TRM: Emerging Responsibility Management Approaches," *Journal of Corporate Citizenship* (Autumn 2002), pp. 113–26. Used with permission.

2. Deming quotes taken from www.quotationspage.com/search.php3?Author=W.+Edwards+Deming&file=other (accessed May 12, 2004).

3. J. R. Evans and William M. Lindsay, *The Management and Control of Quality*, 4th ed. (New York: West, 1999).

4. Ibid.

5. Peter Senge, *The Fifth Discipline* (New York: Free Press, 1990).

6. Evans and Lindsay, *The Management and Control of Quality*.

7. Steve Waddell, "Six Societal Learning Concepts in an Era of Engagement," *Reflections: The SoL Journal* 3, no. 4 (Summer 2002).

8. Ann Svendsen, *The Stakeholder Strategy: Profiting from Collaborative Business Relationships* (San Francisco: Berrett-Koehler, 1998); Jerry M. Calton and Steven L. Payne, "Coping with Paradox: Multistakeholder Learning Dialogue as a Pluralist Sensemaking Process for Addressing Messy Problems," *Business & Society*, 42, no. 1 (March 2003), pp. 7–42.

9. Philip H. Mirvis, "Transformation at Shell: Commerce and Citizenship," Business and Society Review 105, no.1 (Spring 2000), pp. 63–85; see also Anne Lawrence, "The Drivers of Stakeholder Engagement: Reflections on the Case of Royal Dutch Shell," In *Unfolding Stakeholder Thinking*, ed. Jörg Andriof, Sandra Waddock, Bryan Husted, and Sandra Rahman (London: Greenleaf, 2002), pp. 201–16.

10. Roland T. Rust, Valerie A. Zeithaml, and Katherine N. Lemon, *Driving Customer Equity: How Customer Lifetime Value Is Reshaping Corporate Strategy* (New York: Free Press, 1999).

11. Thomas Donaldson and Thomas W. Dunfee, *Ties That Bind: A Social Contracts Approach to Business Ethics* (Boston: Harvard Business School Press, 1999).

12. R. Edward Freeman and Daniel R. Gilbert Jr., *Corporate Strategy and the Search for Ethics* (Englewood Cliffs, NJ: Prentice Hall, 1988).

13. James C. Collins and Jerry I. Porras, "Building Your Company's Vision," *Harvard Business Review*, September–October 1996, pp. 65–77; and Jones C. Collins and Jerry I. Porras, *Built to Last: Successful Habits of Visionary Companies* (New York: HarperBusiness, 1996).

14. John Elkington, *Cannibals with Forks: The Triple Bottom Line of Sustainability* (Gabriola Island: New Society Publishers, 1998).

15. Timothy Bell, Frank Marrs, Ira Solomon, and Howard Thomas, *Auditing Organizations Through a Strategic-Systems Lens: The KPMG Business Measurement Process* (KPMG, 1997).

16. Patsy Lewellyn and Maria Sillanpää, "Holistic Performance Model," paper presented at the International Association of Business in Society Annual Meeting, Sedona, AZ, March 2001.

17. Robert S. Kaplan and David P. Norton, "The Balanced Scorecard—Measures That Drive Performance," *Harvard Business Review*, January–February 1992, pp. 71–79.

18. Sime Curkovic, Steven A. Melnyk, Robert B. Handfield, and Roger Calantone, "Investigating the Linkage between Total Quality Management and Environmentally Responsible Mannufacturing," *IEEE Transactions on Engineering Management* 47, no. 4 (November 2000), pp. 444–64, provide a comparison of these different approaches.

19. Sandra Waddock and Neil Smith, "Corporate Responsibility Audits: Doing Well by Doing Good," *Sloan Management Review* 41, no. 2 (Winter 2000), pp. 75–83.

20. Simon Zadek and Richard Evans, *Auditing the Market: A Practical Approach to Social Auditing* (Tyne and Wear, UK: Tradecraft Exchange, 1993).

21. Senge, *The Fifth Discipline*.

22. Kaplan and Norton "The Balanced Scorecard." See also Robert S. Kaplan and David P. Norton, *The Balanced Scorecard: Translating Strategy into Action* (Cambridge, MA: Harvard Business School Press, 1996).

CHAPTER EIGHT

Investment and Assessment for Corporate Citizenship

Measures have great power, almost like genetic code, to shape action and performance. Whether at the equivalent of the cell level, the organ level, or the systems level, measures become the directional device that influence or even dictate the shape of the enterprise. Change the measure, and you change the organism.

Measures have always had the power to shape a corporation's destiny, but the focus on financial figures alone limited their utility. Management accounting of the past forced managers to build world-class organizations with a truncated set of chromosomes. Today, though, with the help of revitalized cost accounting and nonfinancial measurement, managers can develop a full set of instructions—financial, operational, and social—for the enterprise. These instructions give them the capability to create accountability they never had before.

A balanced family of measures can evolve into a powerful system for executing strategy. The measures help to define the strategy, communicate it to the organization, and direct its implementation at every rung of the hierarchy, from the corporate level to the individual. They also keep everyone's efforts aligned, because they link strategy to budgets, to resource-allocation systems, and to pay programs. In the best of cases, they route such high-quality feedback through the organization that executives can make critical, midcourse adjustments in strategy.

Marc J. Epstein and Bill Birchard, Counting What Counts: Turning Corporate Accountability to Competitive Advantage.

Corporate citizens, leading and otherwise, are increasingly being evaluated on social and ecological criteria as well as on financial performance criteria, whether they want to be or not. So much information is available on company practices, in fact, that its very availability in some cases may cause managers to do the right thing because otherwise their decisions are likely to garner unfavorable attention from one external source or another. As activists, nongovernmental organizations (NGOs), and the general public have begun to demand greater accountability, responsibility, and transparency (ART) from companies, new ways of thinking about measurement have begun to evolve.

External assessments were pioneered by the social investment community through measures used to screen out or screen in certain types of practices and products. Other aspects of social investment include direct investment in social projects and ventures with a willingness by investors to take a somewhat reduced rate of return, loans to microenterprises (as pioneered by the Grameen Bank, discussed later in this chapter), social venture capital, and corporate social investment and philanthropy. These aspects of investment and assessment will be discussed throughout this chapter. Additionally, companies are increasingly being evaluated externally through the numerous "best of" ratings and rankings now in existence.

What can be called a responsibility assurance system is beginning to emerge that has the aim of ensuring that companies actually live up to their rhetoric. In addition to the voluntary responsibility management (RM) approaches addressed in Chapter 7, responsibility assurance also has external elements: (1) development and implementation of foundational values, as discussed in Chapter 4 and explored more fully in Chapter 10 in the global context; (2) credible monitoring, verification, and verification systems; and (3) generally accepted reporting procedures. The remainder of this chapter discusses these elements of what I have elsewhere termed a "tipping point" toward corporate responsibility.[1]

Measuring Responsible Practice: External Assessment

Measurement of nonfinancial bottom lines is often thought to be the soft stuff in business. But assessing the quality and impact of company practices on key stakeholders is really about the hard stuff of managing business activities and relationships well and simultaneously doing good for stakeholders and nature because the business is interdependent with them for its success. As Chapter 4 discussed, doing the right thing means meeting certain foundational values based on respect and human dignity, and being mindful of the impact that the company's actions have on stakeholders and nature. Although such responsible practices do have positive productivity and bottom-line impacts (see Chapter 5), companies also need to be responsible simply because it is the right thing to do.

Many observers of corporate citizenship in the business world claim that doing the right thing forms a fundamental basis for societies issuing companies their license to operate. This license to operate is built on the respect, dignity, and constructive values explored in Chapter 4. Ensuring that these values are actually operationalized presents the challenge of assessing performance in domains like treatment of employees, supply chain practices, environmental management and sustainability orientation, and product value and quality, to name just a few. These so-called soft areas of the multiple bottom line are increasingly being addressed through hard-core measurement systems.

As any good accountant knows, determining the numbers for the traditional bottom line—the balance sheet, income statement, and cash flow analyses of financial reporting—requires much judgment. Still, such reporting is a well-established and well-accepted practice in industrialized nations. Because there is a common currency—money—in which to assess the traditional bottom line, accountants and financiers have devised standardized auditing practices and common reporting systems that help accountants and financiers sort out the financial health of a firm. These accounting and finance measures track the traditional bottom line, and all U.S.-based publicly traded companies (and in many other nations, as well) are required to report their financial results annually.

Although a common currency like money is not as readily available for measuring a company's multiple-bottom-line activities, it can be—and is being—done, every day in a variety of ways that are increasingly visible and important. In this chapter we will explore some of the ways that multiple bottom lines are being assessed throughout the world today: assessment of investments from social and ecological perspectives, internal management approaches to assessing multiple bottom lines, and external reporting mechanisms.

External Assessment by Social Investors

External assessment of corporate citizenship in stakeholder and environmental arenas to some extent has developed out of the interests of social investors, that is, individuals or fund managers who develop explicit social and environmental criteria as a part of their investment strategies. Most social investment has some emphasis or purpose related either to (1) improving society or community or (2) putting pressure on companies to change various corporate practices so that specific stakeholders and the natural environment are better treated.

The most prominent type of social investment involves using screening techniques that assess how well companies perform in specific stakeholder, environmental, and issue arenas. Related to the screens is the shareholder activism directed toward certain corporate practices through shareholder resolutions submitted for vote by corporate boards and shareholders. A third approach is actual investment in socially desirable activities such as affordable housing or economic development of disadvantaged areas.[2] The fourth approach is to provide venture capital to small capitalization firms or microenterprises, particularly in disadvantaged areas or to disadvantaged groups, to help them build their own economic base.

Social Screens/Social Investing

In recent years, the movement variously called social, ethical, or values-based investing has begun to come of age. Started long ago by religious investors, by the mid-1980s investor activists had focused attention on companies operating in South Africa under the now-disbanded apartheid system, which subjugated blacks to white dominance.[3] Investor protests caused some companies to disinvest from South Africa and investors interested in this and other important political and social issues called upon large pension funds, universities, and other major institutional investors to pay attention to the ways in which they were investing their money.

By the late 1980s, social screening was being done on companies' investment or presence in South Africa (and later Burma and other countries with authoritarian regimes in which human rights abuses are rampant) using "issue screens." Issue screens now include numerous issues of concern to certain investors. For example, negative screens focus on corporate involvement with certain products or services, such as tobacco, alcohol, gaming, pornography, and military contracting, as well as involvement in nuclear power, child labor practices, and animal testing. Negative or exclusionary screens, which are generally issues-based, tend to focus on issues that certain investors actively wish to avoid because they pose what those investors perceive to be unacceptable and incalculable risks to certain stakeholder groups or to society in general.[4]

By the early 1990s, as investor interest in a range of corporate practices had grown, so had social screening for investment purposes. Several investment houses, led by Franklin Research and Development (now Trillium), Calvert Funds, and the Domini Fund, developed and expanded rating systems to encompass specific stakeholder arenas in addition to the issue screens. In the United States, KLD Research and Analytics was formed for the explicit purpose of rating all of the Standard & Poor's (S&P) 500 largest companies (now the Russell 3000) annually, initially along 8 dimensions of social performance and now 10 dimensions. KLD sells social and ecological information to interested investors and Wall Street financial houses. KLD also constructed an index, called the Domini Index, consisting of equities that have passed KLD's screens, (adding some smaller capitalization firms beyond the S&P 500 to balance the portfolio (see www.kld.com). The Domini Index can be tracked in the same way that other indexes, such as the Dow Jones Industrial average, are tracked.[5]

According to the nonprofit Social Investment Forum (SIF), by 2003 more than $2.16 trillion was invested in equities in the United States that were in managed portfolios that use socially screened portfolios, shareholder advocacy, or community investing strategies.[6] These forms of social investing account for more than

11 percent of total investments under professional management in the United States. From 1995 to 2003, social investing has grown 40 percent faster than other types of managed investment assets in the United States.[7] Social investments are made by individuals and by funds concerned not only about financial performance but also about the ways in which companies treat various stakeholders.

Social investment, like other forms of assessing leading corporate citizenship, puts companies' stakeholder and environmental practices under considerable scrutiny by investors as well as outsiders. Today activists, customers, and NGOs can readily communicate dissatisfaction with company practices globally through the World Wide Web. Anticorporate and antiglobalization demonstrations around the world by labor, human rights, and environmental activists, which first erupted notably at the 1999 World Trade Organization meeting in Seattle (which journalists dubbed "the battle of Seattle") to protest continuing globalization, highlight the speed with which information now travels around the world and the power of unsatisfied stakeholders to take concerted action.

Spurred in part by pressures from social investors and the 1986 publication of the Council on Economic Priorities' *Rating America's Conscience*, which later became the *Shopping for a Better World* list of companies for consumers,[8] systematic rating of corporate performance along these softer stakeholder lines evolved quickly in the late 1980s. Stakeholder screens that are both positive and negative in their assessment of corporate practices (rather than only negative, as the exclusionary screens are) tend to focus on the types of risks associated with stakeholders. The screens evolve with the interests of investors and as new issues arise in the social and environmental arenas. Table 8.1 lists KLD's rating criteria in use as of 2004, along with sample strengths and concerns.

Just as the negative screens do, stakeholder screens permit companies to be assessed for negative or problematic behaviors that pose concerns for investors. Stakeholder screens also provide for companies to be rewarded for proactive and progressive behaviors that can be viewed as strengths. Other screens, used by managers of social choice funds, which tend to be for the sole use of investors in those funds, are built around similar ideas (see, for example, Trillum Asset Management, at www.trilliuminvest.com, or Calvert Group Mutual Funds, at www.calvertgroup. com).

The Screening Process

Different raters approach social ratings differently in terms of which specific things are measured; however, most attempt to assess company performance systematically from year to year. The first task is to select the categories that will be rated. Typical categories are those used by KLD, which performs negative ratings on issues that include involvement in alcohol, tobacco, gambling, military contracting, and nuclear power production. Positive and negative ratings or stakeholder screens are performed on a range of stakeholder categories. These categories include environment, community relations (philanthropy and volunteerism), diversity (women and minority groups), employee relations, product, human rights, and governance. KLD researches nearly 3,000 companies annually.

TABLE 8.1 **KLD Rating Criteria and Sample Strengths and Concerns**

Source: KLD Research and Analytics, www.kld.com/research/ratings.html (accessed June 8, 2004).

Rating Criterion	Sample Strength	Sample Concern
Community	Generous giving	Investment controversies
Corporate Governance	Limited top management compensation	High compensation
Diversity	Women, minorities, and/or the disabled hold 4+ seats on the board	Substantial fines related to controversies related to affirmative action
Employee Relations	History of strong union relations	Safety controversies
Environment	Beneficial products and services	Hazardous waste
Human Rights	Indigenous peoples relations strength	Labor rights concern or major controversies
Product	Long-term well-developed, companywide quality program	Substantial fines or civil penalties on product safety

Controversial Business Issues

KLD notes when companies are involved in controversial issues, such as abortion, adult entertainment, alcohol, contraceptives, firearms, gambling, military, nuclear power, and tobacco because some social investors are interested in these issues.

KLD is joined in this type of activity by numerous U.S.-based investment houses that keep their data proprietary for their own investors. In addition, a global network of social rating firms from 11 countries, the Sustainable Investment Research International (SIRI) Group, attempts to develop social research data that are comparable across many nations and different types of markets and industries. Members of the SIRI Group as of 2004 are listed in Table 8.2.

Obviously, gathering all of this information annually, which is done from a range of publicly available data sources, as well as company information, is a massive task. It is clear, however, that once researchers have gathered and made available to interested parties such information, it can readily be used by investors—and other interested groups. Interested parties use such data to assess company practices in ways that go far beyond the traditional bottom line. In fact, data like these begin to provide consistent means of evaluating and comparing companies on a range of practices and policies. Notably, such multiple bottom line evaluation is taking place on many large companies annually, whether or not the companies themselves are undertaking internal social audits or explicit responsibility management approaches.

Numerous corporate watchdogs also regularly assess corporate performance across multiple measures related to corporate responsibility and citizenship. Among these watchdogs or activist organizations are Ethical Investment Research

TABLE 8.2   **2004 Members of the Sustainable Investment Research International (SIRI) Group**

Source: Copyright 1999, Perseus Books Group. Reprinted with permission.

- Avanzi SRI Research s.r.l., Italy (www.avanzi-sri.org)
- Centre Info SA, Switzerland (www.centreinfo.ch)
- Dutch Sustainability Research BV, Netherlands (www.dsresearch.nl)
- Fundación Ecologia y Desarollo, Spain (www.ecodes.org)
- GES Investment Services AB, Sweden (www.ges-invest.com)
- KLD Research & Analytics, Inc., USA (www.kld.com)
- Michael Jantzi Research Associates Inc., Canada (www.mjra-jsi.com)
- Pensions & Investment Research Consultants Ltd., UK (www.pirc.co.uk)
- Scoris GmbH, Germany (www.scoris.de)
- Sustainable Investment Research Institute P/L, Australia (www.siris.com.au)
- Stock at Stake NV, Belgium (www.stockatstake.com)

Service (www.eiris.org), which provides information on social investing; the Interfaith Center on Corporate Responsibility (www.iccr.org), which is an association of faith-based investors attempting to drive more responsible corporate behaviors; and the Investor Responsibility Research Center (www.irrc.org), which provides independent research on corporate governance and responsibility. Such watchdogs pay close attention to how companies treat stakeholders and the natural environment, and their assessments influence interested investors.

In the United States many socially responsible investment (SRI) activities are reported by the Social Investment Forum (www.socialinvest.org), whose mission is to promote the concept, practice, and growth of SRI. In the United Kingdom, there is a similar organization promoting SRI called the UK Social Investment Forum (www.uksif.org), and the European Social Investment Forum (www.eurosif. org) addresses broad SRI issues across the European Union (EU), where the EU Commission has taken a highly proactive stance on social investment.

One measure of the movement of social investment in the early 2000s has been the emergence of numerous indexes responsive to socially concerned investors and geared toward comparing the stock market performance of companies rated as being more socially responsible to traditional indices. In the United States, for example, the KLD ratings are used for several indexes, the earliest of which was the Domini Social Index, established in 1990 to benchmark against traditional nonscreened indexes like the Dow Jones Industrial Average. KLD now has several indexes, including the KLD Broad Market Social Index and the KLD Nasdaq Social Index, focused on smaller capitalization firms.

In 1999, the Dow Jones Sustainability Index was launched in the United States as the first global index of leading companies focused on sustainability. In England, the FTSE4good index (www.ftse.com/ftse4good/index.jsp), launched in 2001, tracks companies that meet globally recognized corporate responsibility standards. The Morningstar rating firm launched the first Japanese SRI index in 2003, and in 2003 Kempen Capital Management and SNS Asset Management launched

Europe's first SRI index for smaller companies. In 2004, the Johannesburg Stock Exchange launched the first South African SRI index, containing 51 companies that met specific social criteria. Also in 2004 a nonprofit organization, an accounting firm, and two newspapers introduced the Corporate Responsibility Index (CRI) in Australia, which targets the 150 largest capitalization Australian companies.

The indexes mentioned above are only a few of the ever-growing array of indexes that track corporate responsibility practices and go well beyond the philanthropic and community relations programs that many associate with corporate citizenship. They go right to the heart of issues of stakeholder relationships and ecological sustainability. Although it is clear that even companies on these indexes are far from perfect, the pressure of external scrutiny by a growing number of investors around the world pushes companies to be more aware of their impacts than ever before (see Case 8.1).

Social Investing in Projects and Ventures

Another form of social investing occurs when investors are desirous of investing their assets in projects explicitly aimed at benefiting society or some disadvantaged groups in society. There are several emerging types of social investment projects: investments in projects to economically, academically, or socially develop otherwise disadvantaged communities or groups; using philanthropy strategically given to nonprofit and public agencies to meet the dual bottom line of social benefit and business gain; and using venture capital affirmatively to fund small businesses or even microbusinesses operated in disadvantaged areas or by disadvantaged groups and individuals.

Social Investment Projects

Sometimes social investors wish to invest their assets in socially beneficial projects, such as hotels or businesses that can help rebuild an economic base in disadvantaged communities. Some investors expect market returns from these investments, while others are more concerned with making a difference in society and are therefore willing to accept less than market rates of return. The Calvert Social Investment Foundation (www.calvert foundation.org) focuses on issues such as affordable housing, microenterprise (see below), and community development. Calvert has developed funds with the explicit goal of making such investments. In these funds, investors can sometimes choose the rate of return (less than market) that they desire. Their investment is then used to fund, for example, economic development activities in inner cities, such as a new hotel complex that has been constructed in Harlem in New York City.

Additionally, lending institutions, particularly banks, in the United States are subject to the requirements of the Community Reinvestment Act (CRA) of 1977.[9] The CRA requires banks that benefit from and are subject to the regulatory oversight of the Federal Deposit Insurance Corporation (FDIC) to prove that they are acting to meet the credit needs of the entire community within their service areas.

A bank's entire service area includes low- and moderate-income neighborhoods, particularly those in the inner city and rural areas that have been historically

The business case for socially responsible investing and corporate social responsibility may not drive individual investors, but the fiduciary case engages institutional investors. Ever wonder why people feel the need to make the "business case" for socially responsible investing (SRI) and corporate social responsibility (CSR) (corporate citizenship)? Implicitly, the business case defends against the charge that a practice or policy is not worth employing unless its profitability can be proven.

"Why on earth should one need to make a 'business case' for doing the right thing?" asks Matthew Kiernan, CEO of Innovest Strategic Value Advisors, a global rating firm that links sustainability performance to financial performance.

The question arises: is the business case for SRI and CSR a tool for attracting investment, or is it more of a defense against critics of SRI and CSR?

"I am constantly asked to make 'the business case for SRI,' which translated means, 'prove to us that companies that do good do well and that therefore we'll do very well,'" said Peter Kinder, president and co-founder of Boston-based KLD Research & Analytics. KLD provides research on corporate social and environmental performance to investors. "The 'business case' test for SRI and CSR is a means of dismissing and denigrating both, and we should not entertain the question," Mr. Kinder told SocialFunds.com. "By validating the question by responding to it, we admit the validity of the business case for precisely the behavior we want to change: prioritizing profit over all else."

To some, financial performance may not be as important a consideration for implementing SRI and CSR as promoting social and environmental sustainability. Others may feel that they cannot hold that view. "Many stakeholders have an interest in sustainability for other reasons than performance—and

rightfully so," said Alex Barkawi, managing director of Zurich-based Sustainability Asset Management (SAM), which manages the Dow Jones Sustainability Indexes (DJSI). "At the same time, performance is a prime concern of most investors—this is especially true for institutional investors who often even have a legal obligation to maximize returns. In this context, it is crucial to demonstrate the positive links between sustainability and performance."

In other words, institutional investors' fiduciary duty may require them to consider the business case for SRI and CSR. Interestingly, instead of compromising SRI and CSR, the "fiduciary case" may in fact invigorate SRI and CSR uptake by requiring so-called mainstream investors to evaluate the effects of social and environmental issues on financial performance.

"The 'prudent fiduciary' equation is slowly but surely being turned on its head; increasingly, fiduciaries are being seen as derelict in their responsibilities if they do not ensure that environmental and social risks are addressed," states Dr. Kiernan. "Baker & McKenzie, a prestigious U.S.-headquartered law firm which also happens to be the world's largest, has gone so far as to publish a report opining that U.S. fiduciaries may be obligated to address CSR issues and risks."

The fiduciary case requires institutional investors to examine the effects of corporate social and environmental performance on financial performance. While the majority of empirical studies correlate strong social and environmental performance to neutral or positive financial performance, these studies have not established causation. Thus SRI and CSR cannot be said to guarantee positive financial performance.

"There is nothing automatic about success—the pulling of the social responsibility lever does not automatically result in cash appearing on the bottom line," said Mallen Baker, development director for London-based CSR advocate Business in the Community (BITC). Mr. Baker notes that financial performance and social and environmental performance cannot be isolated from one another, but rather are interdependent. "The smart CEO knows that being profitable is a key precondition of CSR—a failed company with thousands of lost jobs cannot deliver a positive impact on society," Mr. Baker told SocialFunds.com. "CSR is about doing business successfully and achieving a positive impact on society as a result."

DISCUSSION QUESTIONS

1. Should investors and managers have to make a business case for being responsible? Why or why not?

2. The fiduciary case for SRI and corporate citizenship/responsibility suggests that there are risks that investors might avoid by being more selective in their investments. What might some of these risks be? Do you think this fiduciary case is a real one?

Source: William Baue, *CSR Wire,* February 19, 2004, www.csrwire.com/sfprint.cgi?sfArticleId=1346.

---

underserved by financial institutions. Many of these areas have been subject to redlining by banks in the past, a practice involving drawing (figurative or literal) red lines on municipal maps to indicate where loans are discouraged or not made. The CRA was intended to stop this practice, opening up those neighborhoods to loans, credit, and other banking services that are readily accessible in more advantaged areas.

To ensure that banks meet their CRA obligations and invest in their communities appropriately, the FDIC rates banks' CRA performance on a scale from outstanding to substantial noncompliance. As with other data assessing corporate performance on significant stakeholder dimensions, CRA ratings are published by the government.[10] This information, then, is part of the information that becomes available to activists, community members, and other parties interested in institutional performance.

To deal with the CRA, many U.S. banks have created community development banks to work locally with communities. Perhaps the best-known community development bank is ShoreBank of Chicago, which states that is mission is to "invest in people and their communities to create economic equity and a healthy environment."[11] ShoreBank is known for its investment in housing and real estate in Chicago's South, Mid-South, and West Side neighborhoods, particularly focusing on acquisition and renovation of multifamily housing by local residents. Many community development banks were initially established to meet CRA requirements, but they have proved useful mechanisms for building community and establishing new connections—new social capital—among different types of people and organizations within urban areas.[12]

Advantages of Disadvantaged Areas

Some people have come to believe in recent years that there can be great competitive advantage to investments in disadvantaged areas when an asset- and resource-based approach, rather than a deficit-based approach, is used. One creative initiative (among many) is that undertaken by Harvard professor Michael Porter through the Initiative for a Competitive Inner City (ICIC; www.icic.org), established in 1994. Taking an asset-based perspective on economic development of disadvantaged areas, ICIC is based on Porter's ideas about how cities can gain competitive advantage, which were published in the *Harvard Business Review*.[13] Porter recognized that a systemic approach to rebuilding deteriorated inner cities was necessary and that social and community health depends on access to jobs that pay a living wage, that is, a solid economic strategy. Using an asset-based approach to understanding the inner city, Porter developed a framework to determine what the competitive advantages of the inner city might be.

In his article "The Competitive Advantage of the Inner City," Porter displaced the mistaken idea that the only advantages of the inner city are low-cost real estate and lower labor costs, and he identified four main competitive advantages: (1) strategic location in the downtown area (and, as it turns out, access to highways); (2) local market demand; (3) integration with regional clusters within and surrounding the city; and (4) human resources. Competitive clusters, according to Porter, create advantages in terms of new business formation, particularly for business-to-business opportunities, and access to downstream products and services in local markets.

Projects like the ICIC are particularly focused on inner cities within the United States; however, the asset-based perspective is applicable to any disadvantaged or less developed area, as Porter's framework suggests. These and similar projects illustrate the "both/and" logic of operating with an asset-based approach to community and economic development. They also suggest interesting new approaches that businesses and investors interested in making a positive difference in their communities can take. One approach is to recognize excellence in economic development of inner cities through a ranking of the 100 best growth companies in inner cities published annually by ICIC, Merrill Lynch, and *Inc.* magazine. (A similar organization has been spawned in London.)

Research by the ICIC suggests that inner cities have many relatively untapped assets, including approximately 8 million households, which represent about $85 billion in retail spending (or 7 percent of total retail spending) annually. Porter's work also finds that there is significant unmet demand in inner cities, or about 25 percent of retail demand that either goes unfilled or is fulfilled elsewhere. Further, there is a large pool of talent available in inner cities to meet the increasing—and structural—need for employees that many businesses face. Interestingly, there is some evidence to suggest that inner-city residents spend more in absolute dollars on apparel than does the average American household.

Couple these findings with the fact that businesses that have already made investments in the inner city have succeeded beyond their dreams. Again, the ICIC finds that the average inner-city grocery store in New York outperforms the regional average by 39 percent and that business-to-business services are outpacing their regional counterparts in San Francisco. Additionally, the workforce in the inner city of Kansas City is reported to have lower than average turnover, with 80 percent rated good to excellent.[14] Through this research, Porter and his colleagues have demonstrated that there is indeed a competitive advantage—business opportunities—in troubled inner cities and that making social investments can simply be good business.

Social Venturing through Microenterprise

Globally, about 3 billion people live on less than $2 per day. Some remarkable new efforts to invest in disadvantaged areas in the United States are now being applied in less developed countries and rural areas for economic development. Done well, this form of development and investment does not strip countries of their autonomy, nor does it strip people of their traditional sources of livelihood, but instead allows them to improve their own chances in life by using resources readily at their disposal: their own talents and energies, and local needs and interests.

Attempts to improve the lives of people living in dire poverty historically have come through grants, technical assistance, and other forms of philanthropy. Poor people were typically viewed as having deficits that needed to be overcome through the help and assets that could be provided by wealthier people. Traditional approaches to poverty, including much corporate philanthropy and foundation giving, assumed that poor people needed money because they could not help themselves. The problem with this approach is that only a tiny fraction of people who need help can be reached through charitable donations.

In recent years, both in the United States and around the world, a different model—an asset-based model—has begun to take shape. This perspective assumes not that poor people have deficits and are in need of fixing, but rather that they have many assets; possess many strengths; and, given the right opportunities, will find a way to become more advantaged through their own resources. A philosophy similar to that now being used by social venture capitalists investing in U.S. inner cities, such as the ICIC, has emerged—the concept of positive deviancy.

Positive deviancy was developed through the Save the Children Foundation.[15] Positive deviants are those individuals (or groups) who use intentional behaviors to depart from social norms in honorable or positive ways[16] and thereby help improve the situation. By tapping into local resources and ideas, social entrepreneurs can help local residents find acceptable ways of improving their living conditions, health, and other aspects of their lives. In one Vietnamese village, for example, Save the Children's Jerry Sternin and his-wife, Monique, found that some families in a very poor community had well-nourished children. By determining which culturally acceptable, but not widely used, ways of feeding children were being used by a few families—positive deviants—and allowing villagers to spread the word themselves, the Sternins were able to greatly improve the well-being of the children.[17]

Such asset-based views of poor people say that, given some resources, many poor people will be able to start, manage, and grow small businesses that will enable them to build better lives for themselves and their children. One key to making this perspective work is the growing field of microenterprise development, which is a form of social investment that has proved to pay enormous social dividends through organizations like the Grameen Bank, founded in Bangladesh in 1976 by Mohammad Yunas and formalized as a bank in 1983.[18] Recognizing that individuals, particularly women, living in dire poverty found it difficult to get even the minimal amount of capital needed to begin small businesses that could support them and their families, Yunas created a system in which small loans (usually well under $1,000) could be granted to entrepreneurs. Each person then becomes accountable for paying back the loan to a peer group of other (about five or six) microentrepreneurs living in the same village. A bank employee meets with each group once a week to ensure that the loans are on track to being repaid and that things are going well for the entrepreneurs, who still struggle with daily existence.

Grameen Bank's system (like other microenterprise systems) uses peer pressure and the social capital generated through weekly meetings of people who interact with each other regularly to create a system in which not repaying the loan breaks trust with others. By creating a trust-based system, Grameen reverses traditional banking practices—and costs. By tapping the individual energies of borrowers and their strengths, this grassroots initiative taps an emergent form of creative energy to generate both social and financial capital within very poor villages. Most borrowers have little or no collateral, except that they are known and respected by others within their village, who form with them into a lending unit.

Today, Grameen Bank has more than 3.12 million borrowers, of whom 95 percent are women, because Yunas believes that women will use the fruits of their entrepreneurship to feed, clothe, and shelter their families more directly than men will. The bank's services covered some more than 43,000 villages in Bangladesh by 2004, and the loan recovery rate was 99.06 percent, which would be the envy of any traditional bank, with the bank profitable in all but three years of its history. By the end of 2003, Grameen had loaned more than $4.1 billion in total and had become a model for microlending, a concept central to the United Nations' strategy for economic development around the world.[19]

To complement its microlending, Grameen has also started numerous other types of businesses as a means of building not only healthy communities but also bigger enterprises that can at some point begin to operate in the world economy. For example, Grameen Uddog/Handloom represents an effort to revive the weaving industry in Bangladesh, while Grameen Krishi/Agriculture Foundation has a goal of building tubewells that provide safe drinking water. Other large-scale initiatives involve fisheries, communications, and energy production.[20]

In the United States and Latin America, an organization called Accion International also has done pioneering work in providing microloans to entrepreneurs.[21] With some loans as small as $500 in the United States and $100 in Latin America, Accion International helps entrepreneurs get off of welfare, rebuild their communities through business activities, and create new jobs in places that large corporations have abandoned. Like Grameen, Accion uses a peer-network system that draws on local social capital to ensure repayments and site visits to replace traditional bank paperwork (and reduce costs to make the loans feasible). By 2003, Accion was serving as an umbrella organization for lending activities in more than 30 U.S. cities and 19 Latin American, Caribbean, and sub-Saharan African countries. Accion, which has loaned money to more than 3.2 million people, has had similar success with its loan repayment rate as Grameen's, achieving a 97 percent repayment rate.

Microlenders' goal is to eradicate poverty by creating sustainable business enterprises at the micro and eventually macro levels. Accion's loans are intended to cover the organization's own costs and return enough money through interest paid on the loans to help finance the cost of lending to the next borrower. Accion's average loan in the United States in 2002 was about $5,400, while in Latin America, where the cost of living is significantly less, loans averaged about $566. Accion made nearly 3,800 loans in the United States, contrasted with about 750,000 in Latin America, and nearly 60,000 (averaging just over $300) in its relatively new African program, with about 45 percent of its clients being women.

The payback rates associated with both Grameen's and Accion's microloans, and the general history of microloans using similar techniques, create revolving funds that can be used for additional loans once they are repaid, thereby fostering additional entrepreneurship among disadvantaged people. Both Grameen and Accion, along with numerous other microenterprise lenders that have sprung up to attempt to cope with global poverty, assume their clients have numerous assets on which they will build their enterprises. For example, Grameen bases its loans on three Cs of credit: character (integrity and past history of the borrower); capacity (debt capacity, income stream, and repayment history); and capital (current assets of the borrower as a form of collateral). Microenterprise activities have been so successful globally that in 1997 the United Nations issued a resolution promoting the use of microlending on a global scale. Indeed, the activities of both Grameen and Accion have helped to spawn an industry of microlenders who believe that helping people to help themselves is a far better way for countries and individuals to pursue economic development than simply giving handouts. And it can be a profitable way to socially invest as well.

Social Venture Capital

Another type of social investment is providing venture capital to firms or individuals working to improve the lot of the disadvantaged through community and economic development enterprises. Businesses that can use social venture capital are significantly larger than those that need microlending, requiring amounts, for example, over (sometimes significantly over) $100,000. Sometimes social venture capital takes the form of loans for working capital, equipment purchases, debt refinancing, business acquisition, expansion, or credit lines. One of the pioneers of this type of lending is Chicago's ShoreBank. In other situations, social venture capital is supplied in return for an ownership interest in the firm, just as traditional venture capitalists expect.

Social venture capitalists tend to focus on underserved populations, otherwise unmet social needs, and ventures that attempt to improve the natural environment. They use the same criteria of due diligence regarding management strength, product or service concept, market opportunity, and expected financial return as traditional venture capitalists (though some are willing to accept less than market rates of return). In addition, however, they tend, as the Calvert Social Investment Foundation does, to ask additional questions of the entrepreneur. Such questions might focus on whether the project meets an unmet social or ecological need, what the impact of the project on future generations is likely to be, and whether the project's results are likely to have a positive impact on society. Recent Calvert social venture investments have involved investments in H2Gen (a company manufacturing low-cost hydrogen generators for industrial applications) and Cyclex (a bioscience company focused on developing products that help physicians better manage cancer patients' care).[22]

Corporate Social Investment and Strategic Philanthropy

Another type of social project investing occurs in *corporate social investing*, which is when corporate philanthropic donations are dedicated to helping nonprofit and public institutions improve as a result of the investments made.[23] Companies using this approach seek at least dual-bottom-line benefits from their investments. Business benefits can accrue, for example, from having better-educated workers when a company devotes significant charitable resources to local schools.

Corporate social investing is related to *strategic philanthropy*, in which managers take a strategic approach to corporate contributions programs, hoping to see some benefit to their businesses over time. Corporate social investing allows companies to take credit for contributions that go beyond donations—for example, volunteer programs, memberships and sponsorships for which no specific benefits are received, and cause-related marketing. Because many companies are under considerable financial pressure to produce results, strategic use of philanthropic monies can benefit the company with respect to its community stakeholders, while also showing its owner stakeholders what types of benefits are sought in making the contributions. Companies undertaking this type of social investment program are encouraged to report out on all of their social investments, rather than just financial contributions alone.

Shareholder Activism and Corporate Governance

Many people in the social investment community view shareholder activism as another form of social investment; hence, it will be discussed here, in part because leading corporate citizens need to be aware that such activism can affect their decisions—and that activists are watching their citizenship practices. Managers can hardly make decisions in a vacuum when shareholders are affected—or when they wish to exert influence. In the past 20 years, shareholders have found new ways of having their voices heard.

Shareholders—owners—are supposed to be the stakeholders to whom corporate managers pay the most attention, according to the logic of the neoclassical economic model, which dominates the financial community in the United States and is gaining attention in Europe and Asia. Yet the many scandals in the early 2000s, although in part pushed by managers' efforts to maximize shareholder wealth, in reality ended up hurting shareholders when the companies collapsed and ended up in bankruptcy (think of Enron or WorldCom). In at least some of the scandals, managers put self-interest well ahead of shareholders' interest. Thus, even within the logic of putting shareholders first, some shareholders have found it difficult to have a voice in corporate affairs. Most large companies have millions of shares held by numerous investors, for whom corporate practice is distantly removed from day-to-day events. As a result, management dominates corporate decision making, leaving some shareholders wanting more influence. The issue of corporate governance—how well companies' boards of directors represent stockholder and other stakeholder interests, especially around financial performance—is therefore a major concern of activist shareholders.

Shareholder activists tend to operate through the votes accorded to them via their ownership interest in the firm, typically by submitting shareholder resolutions to a vote during the annual meeting. Shareholder resolutions might draw attention to concerns about possible corporate abuse of power, weak governance structures, and poor managerial decision making. In some cases, the resolutions attempt to counter corporate tendencies to economize (e.g., through excessive layoffs) or to improve efficiency (e.g., by paying top managers inflated salaries and benefits). In other cases, activist shareholders work on a company's tendency to power-aggrandize by making acquisitions simply for the sake of growth when there is little strategic reason to do so. To cope with such tendencies, some investors have attempted to influence corporate practice directly through calling for discussion on shareholder resolutions at their companies' annual meetings. In this process, they also gather publicity for the issue of concern to them. Case 8.2 describes an example of shareholder activism.

Obstacles to Good Governance

Shareholder activists have identified multiple obstacles to good corporate governance.[24] Among these are issues of whether directors' interests are properly aligned with long-term shareholder value. Obstacles here include structural issues, such as the way directors are compensated and whether board members have conflicts of interest. Cultural issues also pose barriers to good governance within the board—for instance, whether directors are overly in alignment with the CEO, whether they are active in corporate decision making and sufficiently informed to make good decisions, and whether they sufficiently recognize their shareholder and fiduciary responsibilities.

A second set of obstacles to good governance has to do with the way boards are structured. Structural issues include board member appointments, member status as insiders versus outsiders, the ways in which board committees are structured and operate, the performance criteria for evaluating the board and the CEO, and the degree of independence from management that board members have and actually exercise. Generally, independent outside board members, who can view

Occidental Petroleum is one company that bowed to pressure from shareholder activists in 2004 when it agreed to adopt a formal human rights policy before shareholders actually voted on the resolution. In an initiative led by the Jesuits (Society of Jesus) and other religious investors through the Interfaith Center on Corporate Responsibility (ICCR), social activists submitted a shareholder resolution demanding that the company's code of conduct be amended to include a human rights provision (see Exhibit 1).

ICCR's global corporate accountability program director, David Schilling, called the move a "significant step," important because Occidental agreed to base its policy on the United Nations' Universal Declaration of Human Rights, the International Labor Organization's Declaration on Fundamental Principles and Rights at Work, the Voluntary Principles on Security and Human Rights, and other international humanitarian law.

The withdrawal reflects the companies' willingness to engage with the activists on the issue of human rights and cede that their position has merit. More than 60 of the 860-plus resolutions submitted through ICCR's offices during the 2003–2004 shareholder resolution season were withdrawn, mostly because the company chose to engage with the activists rather than face a proxy vote on specific issues, such as human rights. The list of issues on which shareholder resolutions are submitted is extensive, and includes demands for HIV reporting, reporting political contributions, sexual orientation discrimination, pay disparity, health risks from products (e.g., cigarettes), global warming impacts, reporting on genetically modified foods, annual elections of board of directors, and ethical criteria for military contracting. ICCR reports complete listings of current and past resolutions on its Web site as well as the ways in which they were resolved.

According to Dr. Ray Irani, CEO of Occidental, "Occidental believes that a policy formalizing our longstanding commitment to support human rights has value for the corporation and its stakeholders. To this end, Occidental is committed to consulting with the proponents of the proposal and others as it works toward the adoption of a formal human rights policy."

Activists view the move as particularly important because Occidental has been the subject of litigation on human rights abuses. For example, in 2003, the International Labor Rights Fund sued the company for its alleged "complicity in the 1998 killing of citizens in Santo Domingo, Colombia. The suit alleges that the Colombian Air Force, which Occidental funded to protect its Cano Limon pipeline, bombed Santo Domingo and killed 19 villagers with logistical support from Occidental's private security firm, AirScan." Occidental denied the allegations. However, it did commit to "work and collaborate on this until we get a policy," according to corporate legal counsel.

EXHIBIT 1 Shareholder Resolution: Adopt Human Rights Policies 2004—Occidental Petroleum Corporation.

Source: www.iccr.org/shareholder/proxy_book04/HUMAN%20RIGHTS/HR_OXY.HTM.

Sponsors:

Lead: Society of Jesus—California Province, Doris Gormley SRI Consultant;
Catholic Equity Fund; Christian Brothers Investment Services; Christus Health; Congregation of the Srs. of Charity, Incarnate Word, Houston; Sinsinawa Dominicans; Society of Jesus—New Orleans Province

continued

Exhibit 1 *concluded*

Whereas:

We believe transnational corporations operating in countries with repressive governments, ethnic conflict, weak rule of law, endemic corruption, or poor labor and environmental standards face serious risks to their reputation and share value if they are seen as responsible for, or complicit in, human rights violations;

We commend our company for developing and implementing a Code of Business Conduct and for endorsing the Global Sullivan Principles;

We remain concerned that among the various nations where our company operates, Colombia has consistently been noted as violating basic human rights;

Since the inception of its operations in Arauca, one of the regions in Colombia most affected by human rights abuses, our company has provided material aid to and worked closely with the Armed Forces of Colombia in return for the protection of its pipeline operations. Among the troubling outcomes of our company's alleged collaboration with and support of the Colombian military is the 1998 Santo Domingo massacre, killing 18 civilians, including 7 children. (*Los Angeles Times*, 3/17/02) This incident is the subject of an ongoing lawsuit against our company in the U.S. District Court for the Central District of California. (*Los Angeles Times*, 4/25/03)

Several of our company's competitors have already adopted a human rights policy based upon the Universal Declaration of Human Rights (1948) and;

In August 2003 the United Nations Sub-Commission on the Promotion and Protection of Human Rights took historic action by adopting "Norms on the Responsibilities of Transnational Corporations and Other Business Enterprises with Regard to Human Rights" (www1.umn.edu/humanrts/links/NormsApril2003.html) specifically applying to transnational corporations therefore;

We believe significant commercial advantages may accrue to our company by adopting a comprehensive human rights policy based on the above mentioned UN Human Rights Norms which would serve to enhance corporate reputation, improve employee recruitment and retention, improve community and stakeholder relations, and reduce risk of adverse publicity, consumer boycotts, divestment campaigns and law suits and;

"Activist U.S. courts are accepting more and more claims against multinational companies for their business practices in developing countries. The courts are increasingly willing to apply international human rights standards to corporate conduct." ("Emerging Threat: Human Rights Claims," *Harvard Business Review*, August, 2003)

"In the post-Enron environment, every global company's board of directors needs to oversee its assessment and management of these risks. Given the magnitude of potential claims, liability may even extend to individual directors if they are not seen as exercising proper oversight." (*Harvard Business Review*, August 2003)

Resolved:

Shareholders request the Board to review and amend the Code of Business Conduct to include a comprehensive human rights policy. We request the Board to prepare a report to shareholders, prepared at reasonable expense and omitting proprietary information, on the above policy and its implementation by November 1, 2004.

Supporting Statement:

We believe our company's human rights policy should be comprehensive, transparent, verifiable and based on the provisions contained in the "Responsibilities of Transnational Corporations and other Business Enterprises with Regard to Human Rights."

DISCUSSION QUESTIONS

1. How effective do you believe that shareholder resolutions are in bringing about real change in companies?

2. Do or should shareholders hold a special position?

3. Are there other mechanisms that might work better? What are they?

Sources: William Blau, "Occidental to Adopt Formal Human Rights Policy, Shareowners Withdraw Resolution," *CSRwire*, March 18, 2004, www.csrwire.com/sfpring.cgi?sfArticleId=1371 (accessed June 10, 2004); and Investor Responsibility Research Center and Interfaith Center on Corporate Responsibility, "2003 Shareholder Proxy Overview: Social and Corporate Governance Resolution Trends," www.shareholderaction.org/files/proxy_season_overview_2003.PDF (accessed June 10, 2004).

corporate activities more objectively than individuals closely tied to management interests, are considered to offer better governance. Cultural issues include the adequacy of information provided to board members, their degree of involvement in strategic decisions, and directors' capacity to ask good questions of management without micromanaging the company.

The third set of barriers to good governance has to do with the extent to which shareholders are, and are readily permitted to be, interested in corporate activities—or conversely, the extent to which they are disenfranchised. Concerns arise when managers institute self-protective measures, such as golden parachutes (overly generous severance pay) or greenmail (reselling stock in the company at prices above market value), to further entrench themselves and consolidate their own power without due consideration to the good of the corporation. Other structural issues have to do with the voting procedures instituted for shareholders and the extent to which these procedures are fair and equitable. Cultural issues have to do with communication between the company and its shareholders, which fosters the level of involvement by owners in corporate affairs.

Principles of Good Corporate Governance

Overcoming the obstacles to good corporate governance means adhering to principles of good governance, which are well recognized by leading corporate citizens. Although institutional investors, the large money managers that control equity funds, have basic fiduciary or financial obligations to meet, some have also become active in pressuring managers to change their practices to conform to shareholder expectations and to govern themselves according to certain principles. Among these activist institutional investors is the California Public Employees' Retirement System (CalPERS), which recently issued a set of corporate governance core principles and guidelines that it believes well-governed companies should follow.[25]

CalPERS's principles are based on six global principles that this influential pension fund believes are important to better overall corporate governance and, in the end, company management:

1. *Accountability*: Companies need to assume responsibility for the impacts of their practices, policies, and processes and the decisions that stand behind those practices.

2. *Transparency*: Corporate actions and decisions must be visible to interested stakeholders.

3. *Equity*: Company resources must be allocated and distributed fairly to relevant stakeholders.

4. *Voting methods*: Voting must be open and accessible to all stakeholders.

5. *Codes of best practices*: Companies must adopt and implement ethical and values-based codes.

6. *Long-term vision.*

To make boards of directors more accountable to shareholders, CalPERS makes the following recommendations:

- Independent directors should comprise a substantial majority of seats on a board.
- Unless the board is led by an independent chairperson, an independent lead director should be designated.
- No director may also serve as a consultant or service provider to the company; competing time commitments of directors should be specifically addressed by each company.
- A mix of director characteristics, experience, and diverse perspectives should be reflected on each board.
- The board should consider director tenure and take steps to maintain an openness to new ideas and a willingness to critically re-examine the status quo.[26]

Many large institutional investors as well as business associations have become involved in the effort to make boards of directors and their corporations more accountable for performance, as well as for social impacts. In addition to CalPERS, other groups include the investor associations like Council of Institutional Investors and the National Association of Corporate Directors in the United States. Major business associations, such as the Business Roundtable, and other large institutional investors like the Teachers Insurance and Annuity Association/College Retirement Equities Fund (TIAA-CREF), as well as religious activists, including the Interfaith Center on Corporate Responsibility, all have efforts to build in guiding principles for corporate governance.

Similar policies about good governance have been developed by the Council of Institutional Investors and TIAA-CREF, one of the world's largest pension fund managers.[27] Internationally, a great deal of work has been done to develop similar codes and principles for governing multinational corporations and making them accountable to their important stakeholders. Countries as far ranging as Australia, Belgium, Canada, Germany, Hong Kong, India, Italy, Japan, the Netherlands, South Africa, Span, Sweden, the United Kingdom, and the United States have experienced various efforts to reform or improve governance practices within corporations. In 2004, for example, the 30 countries of the Organization for Economic Cooperation and Development (OECD) approved a revision of the OECD's Principles of Corporate Governance.[28]

A study of directors concludes that "independent, intrepid, informed, diverse (in background and expertise) directors willing to speak up when concerned or in doubt and to challenge management and each other are crucial to healthy and constructive boardroom dynamics and to effective corporate governance."[29] Meeting growing obligations to govern corporations properly means living up to the types of standards found in the principles discussed above. As must be clear, the principles tend to revolve around clear and fair election rules for directors, director independence from management, disclosure of sufficient information that shareholders and directors can make effective strategic decisions (transparency), and board committee structures that are independent of undue management influence.

The reason for focusing shareholder activism on issues of governance is, perhaps, best stated by the great Supreme Court Justice Louis Brandeis:

> There is no such thing to my mind . . . as an innocent stockholder. He may be innocent in fact, but socially he cannot be held innocent. He accepts the benefits of the system. It is his business and his obligation to see that those who represent him carry out a policy which is consistent with the public welfare.[30]

Corporate Rankings and Reputation

Having a good reputation is essential to leading corporate citizenship and is another of the many visible factors that are constantly under public scrutiny today. Regular rankings identify the best corporations for a whole range of behaviors, including one by *Business Ethics* magazine that identifies the top 100 corporate citizens, using the KLD ratings discussed above.[31] Bradley K. Googins, director of the Boston College Center for Corporate Citizenship, claims that a corporation's citizenship reputation will be a determining factor in gaining competitive advantage in the future. Rankings that measure one or another aspect of that citizenship are increasingly common.

The business—and interest groups—press regularly investigates corporate practices and behaviors with respect to particular stakeholders. Following the lead of *Fortune*, which has issued a "most admired corporations" list since 1983, numerous other publications now develop lists of companies that are the best or worst in various categories. These best-companies lists rank or name companies that are, for example, the "best to work for," "best for Blacks and Hispanics," "most family friendly," "best and worst governed," "best corporate citizens," "best companies for gay men and lesbians," and "best for working women," to name only a few.

Reputation is essentially the external assessment of a company or any other organization held by external stakeholders. Reputation includes several dimensions, including an organization's perceived capacity to meet those stakeholders' expectations, the rational attachments that a stakeholder forms with an organization, and the overall net image that stakeholders have of the organization.

FIGURE 8.1 Corporate Reputation Chain

Source: Gary Davis, www.mbs.ac.uk/corporate/cri/reputation_chain.htm (accessed June 11, 2004).

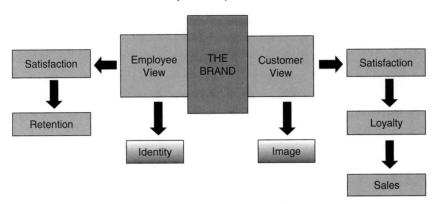

Corporate reputation tends to be associated with a company's brand identity and image, according to Gary Davies of the University of Manchester in England (see Figure 8.1). A company's identity has to do with how it views itself, while its image is what is projected out to stakeholders. As Figure 8.1 suggests, employee satisfaction and retention are linked to corporate identity, and customer loyalty and satisfaction are linked to image.[32]

Fortune magazine annually issues a corporate reputation index and list that many companies aspire to be on because of the prestige associated with being listed. One interesting analysis of Fortune 500 companies undertaken by New York University researcher Charles Fombrun highlights the number of times various companies appeared on the reputation list. Fombrun found that of the 16 years in which *Fortune* issued its rankings, one company, the pharmaceutical giant Merck, was ranked 14 times, while Coca-Cola was ranked 12 times, and two companies, 3M and Rubbermaid, made the rankings a total of 11 times.[33] Other most frequently cited companies include Boeing (7 times), Dow Jones (5), Hewlett-Packard (6), IBM (5), J. P. Morgan (5), Johnson & Johnson (8), Liz Claiborne (6), Procter & Gamble (10), and Wal-Mart Stores (6).

In addition to *Fortune*, annual company ratings are beginning to appear in other countries, including *Asian Business*'s "Asia's Most Admired Companies," the *Far Eastern Economic Review*'s "Review 200," *Management Today*'s "Britain's Most Admired Companies," and the *Financial Times*' "Europe's Most Respected Companies." Obviously, as more and more such rating systems emerge, companies will have to pay increased attention to their stakeholder-related practices because they will be coming under intense external scrutiny.

Other work on corporate reputation by Fombrun[34] and the New Economics Foundation in England[35] assesses corporate reputation and performance from the perspective of stakeholders themselves. Using this methodology, Fombrun has actually been able to attach a dollar amount to the value of reputation in relationship to a company's stock price. Such measures, it is likely, will gain increasing public attention in the future, further enhancing the critical importance of reputation to companies not only for sustaining customer goodwill and continued purchases but also for being granted a license to operate by communities and governments. Fombrun also suggests that a growing body of research links corporate reputation to financial performance, making the link between reputation and corporate citizenship increasingly clear.

External Monitoring, Verification, and Certification

Antiglobalization and anticorporate rhetoric combined with corruption, accounting restatements, outright frauds, and ecological scandals have created a context in which public trust in companies in the early 2000s is perhaps at an all-time low. Outsourcing of many manufacturing activities from companies in industrialized nations to smaller companies in countries where labor is inexpensive and standards are not rigorously enforced has resulted in numerous charges of sweatshop working conditions, child labor, abuse of workers, environmental problems, and complicity in violence and human rights abuses by transnational corporations.

As the public has become aware of these problems, it has come to demand accountability from corporations and to demand that companies prove they are actually living up to their rhetoric of corporate citizenship and good ethics. As a result, new systems for monitoring, verifying, and certifying company performance, both in extended supply chains and within established companies themselves, are emerging as means of establishing credibility. We will discuss two of the most notable of these systems: the AA 1000 stakeholder engagement framework and the SA 8000 labor standards. As we will discuss in Chapter 10, credible verification, monitoring, and certification processes are an important element of an emerging global responsibility assurance system that attempts to hold companies accountable for their impacts.

AA 1000: Stakeholder Engagement

The AA 1000 framework was launched in 1999 by the UK firm AccountAbility to provide a way for companies to systematize their stakeholder engagement practices and to provide some assurance about the quality of those engagements. Using an inclusive approach that encompasses stakeholders of different persuasion, the AA 1000 provides a series of indicators, targets, and reporting systems, complementing the Global Reporting Initiative (GRI). Critical to AA 1000 is stakeholder engagement (the outside circle in Figure 8.2) that assures overall corporate accountability, which is embedded in a cycle (the middle circle Figure 8.2) of continuous learning, innovation, improvement, and ultimately performance similar to that in the responsibility management approach discussed in Chapter 7.

FIGURE 8.2 AA 1000 Process Model

Source: AccountAbility, www.accountability.org.uk/aa1000/default.asp# (accessed June 11, 2004).

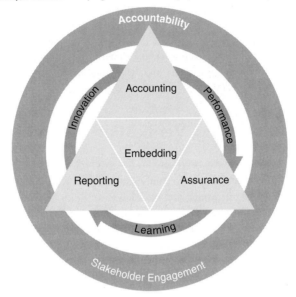

There are four key aspects of the stakeholder engagement processes of AA 1000. First is planning, which means ensuring that there is adequate commitment and governance of the process. Stakeholders then need to be identified and values reviewed. Figure 8.2 shows the process used by AA 1000. In the accounting stage, issues are identified so that the extent of the AA 1000 process can be determined, the process scope is outlined, indicators are identified, and information is collected and analyzed with the idea of developing an improvement plan. Reporting means that reports need to be prepared and published to relevant stakeholder communities. Embedding means establishing ongoing internal management systems that ensure that changes actually take in the organization, aligning the company's vision, values, and ways of adding value.

AccountAbility defines *accountability* to include transparency, responsiveness, and compliance (i.e., with existing norms and laws). AA 1000 is based on a series of principles, such as inclusivity, defining the scope and nature of the project, the meaningfulness of the information, and the ongoing management of the project. The AA 1000 process asks companies to embed accountability and engagement into the companies' practices.[36]

SA 8000: Labor Standards

The SA 8000 labor standards are specifically geared to providing accountability for companies with extended supply chains operating in global networks. Promulgated by the human rights organization SAI International, (founded in 1996), SA 8000 aims at improving workplaces and communities globally through assuring that responsible labor practices are in place.[37] The SA 8000 standards are particularly focused on labor standards, ensuring that internationally accepted labor rights, in particular those of the International Labor Organization, are upheld. SA 8000 monitors and certifies company practices related to child labor, forced labor, worker health and safety, free association and the right to collective bargaining, nondiscrimination, discipline (no corporal punishment, coercion, or abuse), working hours, compensation, and management systems.

Behind the SA 8000 standard are criticisms of companies' operating practices within extended supply chains. These standards attempt to provide a credible means for the contracting transnational corporations to ensure that there are no lingering problems in factories. SAI International believes that workers, trade unions, and NGOs will benefit from implementing an SA 8000 process because of increased capacity to organize unions, educate workers about labor rights, and work directly with businesses on labor issues, as well as increasing public awareness about working conditions. Businesses can benefit because they are directly putting their values into action while simultaneously ensuring the viability and credibility of their brand and reputation, improving their ability to recruit and retain employees, and developing overall better supply chain management. Customers and investors will benefit from the credibility deriving from the assurance process itself, and knowing that products are made ethically.

Transparency: Reporting

Internal monitoring using approaches like AA 1000, SA 8000, or the ISO family of quality approaches, including the ISO 14,000 environmental management approaches, are important ways that companies can demonstrate their corporate citizenship. Because these approaches are voluntary, each company can make its own determination about what to monitor and how or even whether to report the results publicly. Many corporate critics are unsatisfied with unstandardized and voluntary assurance programs, particularly since there is currently little comparability across the different reports being issued by companies. In 1997, the Global Reporting Initiative (GRI) emerged as a means of providing a common set of reporting guidelines for social, environmental, and ecological reporting—the so-called triple bottom line.[38] Designed through a multistakeholder collaborative process involving representatives of businesses; accounting and investment firms; and environmental, human rights, labor, and research organizations, the GRI is still voluntary but seeks to provide common standards around a sustainability framework (see Note 8.1 for the vision and mission statement). GRI, as with AA 1000 and SA 8000, is linked to the UN's Global Compact initiative, which will be discussed in more detail in Chapter 10.

GRI follows certain principles so that reports will (in its own words):

- present a balanced and reasonable account of economic, environmental, and social performance, and the resulting contribution of the organisation to sustainable development;

VISION STATEMENT

To support global progress towards sustainable development, the Global Reporting Initiative (GRI) Sustainability Reporting Guidelines will become the generally accepted, broadly adopted worldwide framework for preparing, communicating and requesting information about corporate performance.

MISSION STATEMENT

The Global Reporting Initiative (GRI) promotes international harmonization in the reporting of relevant and credible corporate environmental, social and economic performance information to enhance responsible decision-making. The GRI pursues this mission through a multi-stakeholder process of open dialogue and collaboration in the design and implementation of widely applicable sustainability reporting guidelines.

Source: GRI Web site, www.globalreporting.org/about/mission.asp (accessed June 14, 2004).

- facilitate comparison over time;

- facilitate comparisons across organisations; and

- credibly address issues of concern to stakeholders.[39]

The core principles of GRI (see Figure 8.3) attempt to create a common set of reporting guidelines similar to generally accepted accounting principles (GAAP) in the financial realm, but expanded to encompass social, ecological, and economic impacts and outcomes. The principles of transparency, auditability, and inclusiveness provide an overall framework for the report. The principles of completeness, relevance, and sustainability/context are meant to help companies determine what they should be reporting on. The principles of accuracy, neutrality, and comparability define ways to ensure that what is reported is truthful and that data can be compared from company to company. Finally, the principles of clarity and timeliness attempt to ensure that what is reported is understandable and reported on a reasonably regularly scheduled basis.

As of mid-2004, some 455 companies had used the GRI's guidelines to issue multiple-bottom-line or sustainability reports. These companies operated in a wide array of industries, including automobiles, utilities, consumer products, pharmaceuticals, financial, telecommunications, energy, and chemicals. Some NGOs, governmental agencies, and nonprofits had also used the guidelines in their reporting. GRI's organizers believe that there are numerous benefits deriving from using these common standards, including helping with internal management processes, providing for comparability across units and companies, enhanced reputation, and possible strategic differentiation, among others.

FIGURE 8.3 GRI Core Principles

Source: GRI Web site, www.globalreporting.org/guidelines/2002/b23.asp#fig3 (accessed June 14, 2004).

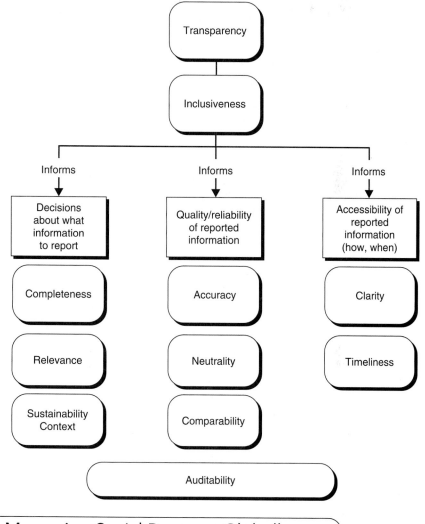

Measuring Social Progress Globally

Many groups around the world are concerned that current measures of economic progress are inadequate. In part, this concern arises because typical assessments of gross domestic product (GDP) include extraction of resources from the environment as economic gains rather than the losses that they actually represent, and because many indicators of progress actually make people or societies worse off rather than better off. For example, GDP does not take into account increases in inequality among the rich and poor or damages to the environment, while it does count problematic social developments, such as higher divorce rates, as productivity gains because of increased legal fees, while ignoring their social costs.[40]

GDP as currently constructed, following the dictates of the Bretton Woods Conference after World War II, is a sum of products and services sold, developed purely on economic grounds. It makes few distinctions between activities that add to social health and well-being and those that detract from it. Thus, installing pollution equipment is considered an economic gain, while the destruction of the environment that necessitated that equipment is not accounted for.

Even the creator of the GDP admitted in 1934 that its coverage is limited, stating, "The welfare of a nation can scarcely be inferred from a measurement of national income."[41] Furthering the conversation about what is meant by progress, the United Nations Development Programme (UNDP) states that all countries need to pay more attention to the quality of growth, not just the quantity as assessed by GDP. Indeed, the UNDP identifies five forms of growth that it actually considers damaging: (1) *jobless growth*, or growth that does not translate into jobs; (2) *voiceless growth*, or growth unmatched by the spread of democracy; (3) *rootless growth*, or growth that snuffs out separate cultural identify of nations, regions, and other locales; (4) *futureless growth*, or growth that despoils the environment; and (5) *ruthless growth*, or growth in which most of the benefits are seized by the rich.[42]

Unfortunately, despite the problems of growth identified by the UNDP, most business and governmental leaders are still locked into thinking that GDP is the best assessment of progress. Some of the criticisms of measuring social progress more broadly are that it is difficult to obtain adequate measures of real social progress. As with assessment of corporate stakeholder and issues-related practices, however, companies today are paying significant attention to measuring progress more broadly and in ways that can be applied consistently over time to all types of situations. The next section of this chapter will explain one of the more important of these efforts.

Indicators of Development Progress[43]

In a unique and important collaboration among global intergovernmental organizations (IGOs) and nongovernmental orgranizations (NGOs), substantial progress is being made on defining and beginning to implement core indicators of social and development progress. Among the entities that have come together for this purpose are the World Bank; the United Nations (including the Statistics Division, UNDP, UNESCO, UNICEF, UNFPA, WHO, Commission on Sustainable Development); and developing-country statisticians, policymakers, and donors to the Development Assistance Committee. This Index of Sustainable Economic Welfare (ISEW) has received considerable attention in recent years.[44]

The ISEW has focused on economic goals like reducing extreme poverty by half and social goals like providing universal primary education, eliminating gender disparity in education, reducing infant and child mortality by three-quarters, and providing universal access to reproductive health services. Further, its members have specified environmental sustainability and regeneration goals that include implementation of a national strategy for sustainable development in all countries by 2005 to be able to reverse trends in the loss of environmental resources by 2015. They have also identified important qualitative factors that these numerous groups believe will result in a better world: participatory development, democratization, good governance of organizations, and implementation of human rights broadly.

To demonstrate that social progress is measurable, this group has developed a working set of core indicators that measure development progress (see Table 8.3). The set of indicators is not inclusive of all possible indicators and is generally still under development, but it shows that it is quite feasible to measure progress not only in economic but also in human terms.

Another set of measures that attempts to look at national health through a broader lens than GDP is the Calvert-Henderson Quality of Life Indicators. Based on the work of futurist Hazel Henderson in conjunction with the social investment firm Calvert, these indicators use systems thinking to explore the shifts and changes in the world by creating a constellation of measures on education, employment, energy, environment, health, human rights, income, infrastructure, national security, public safety, recreation and shelter.[45] Indicators are updated regularly at Henderson's Web site (www.hazelhenderson.com).

The indexes cited are just a few among many emerging sets of measures and indicators that attempt to reframe and broaden our understanding of what it means to live well in human society. Life, obviously, goes well beyond economics, yet until these pioneering developments, we have confined much of our thinking about progress to the realm of economics. The developments in measuring stakeholder and ecological progress noted above, and the many others that had to be omitted for space reasons, show that it is quite feasible to think broadly about what we actually mean by progress and the quality of life we are living.

Measures such as these, which account for benefits and drawbacks of various activities to society, can only help businesses desiring to operate responsibly with respect to the many stakeholders with whom they are interdependent. Such measures are especially important when we begin to look, as we shall in Chapter 9, at the ways in which value is added to stakeholders' lives by corporate activities.

Leading Challenges: The Measurement of Responsible Practice

You get what you measure. That slogan is the core of accounting practice, and it is also at the heart of leading corporate citizenship. Leaders of companies that hope to meet the highest standards of corporate citizenship need to take the time to identify what those standards are and the best ways to assess the extent to which they are actually meeting them. Having a clear corporate vision with its attendant values is only the first step in what is actually an iterative process that involves next

TABLE 8.3 Working Set of Core Indicators for Measuring Development Progress

Source: Organization for Economic Cooperation and Development, www.oecd.org/dac/Indicators/index.htm (2002).

Goals	Indicators
Economic Well-Being	**Economic Well-Being**
The proportion of people living in extreme poverty in developing countries should be reduced by at least one-half by 2015.	1. Incidence of extreme poverty: population below $1 per day. 2. Poverty gap ratio: Incidence times depth of poverty. 3. Inequality: Poorest fifth's share of national consumption. 4. Child malnutrition: Prevalence of underweight children under five years old.
Social Development	**Social Development**
There should be universal primary education in all countries by 2015.	5. Net enrollment in primary education. 6. Completion of fourth grade of primary education. 7. Literacy rate of 14–24-year-olds.
Progress toward gender equality and the empowerment of women should be demonstrated by eliminating gender disparity in primary and secondary education by 2005.	8. Ratio of girls to boys in primary and secondary education. 9. Ratio of literate females to males (15–24-year-olds).
The death rates for infants and children under the age of five years should be reduced in each developing country by two-thirds the 1990 level by 2015.	10. Infant mortality rate. 11. Under five mortality rate.
The rate of maternal mortality should be reduced by three-fourths between 1990 and 2015.	12. Maternal morality ratio. 13. Births attended by skilled health personnel.
Access should be available through the primary health care system to reproductive health services for all individuals of appropriate ages, no later than the year 2015.	14. Contraceptive prevalence rate. 15. HIV prevalence in 15–24-year-old pregnant women.
Environmental Sustainability and Regeneration	**Environmental Sustainability and Regeneration**
There should be a current national strategy for sustainable development, in the process of implementation, in every country by 2005, so as to	16. Countries with national sustainable development strategies. 17. Population with access to safe water. 18. Intensity of freshwater use.

continued

concluded

ensure that current trends in the loss of environmental resources are effectively reversed at both global and national levels.	19. Biodiversity: land area protected. 20. Energy efficiency: GDP per unit of energy use. 21. Carbon dioxide emissions.
General Indicators	**General Indicators**
Population Gross national product	GNP per capita Adult literacy rate Total fertility rate Life expectancy at birth Aid as % of GNP External debt as % of GNP Investment as % of GNP Trade as % of GNP

determining what kinds of measures are appropriate internally, as well as the ways in which the company will be—and is already being—evaluated externally.

What this chapter makes clear is that assessment of corporate citizenship is an ongoing proposition—and it goes on whether the company itself is involved or not. Social as well as traditional investors and, increasingly, customers seek information about companies from research services and from socially conscious investment firms. Others, including major business magazines as well as academics, produce reputational and other types of ratings that compare the performance of one company to another, publishing their results in highly visible places and gaining significant publicity from these rankings. Some observers, including the U.S. government as well as customers, are concerned about whether banks invest their business resources appropriately in local communities in various forms of social investing. Others want to assure that corporate philanthropy is used to advance society's interests in a whole range of ways.

Companies that are truly on the leading edge of corporate citizenship take these demands for accountability, responsibility, and transparency very seriously. Further, their leaders know that the best defense is a good offense and take the initiative to understand how their external stakeholder view them, to engage in dialogue with stakeholders, and to assess their own internal practices long before they become visible to outsiders. Increasingly, these leaders of corporate citizens do such responsibility auditing long before the company has problems. Ideally, they also make the results of their evaluations accessible to stakeholders. In addition, they try to learn from their evaluations how to improve their stakeholder-related performance, knowing that, in the end, it is their corporate practices that implement their visions and values—and that lead to both corporate effectiveness in carrying out their visions and to satisfying financial performance.

While the recognition of the importance of learning from such intensive self-assessments is only beginning to dawn on some corporate leaders, many already know that their company's performance on a whole range of dimensions related to primary and critical secondary stakeholders is visible to the investing community. If what gets measured is what you get, then what companies that pay attention to measuring stakeholder performance will get is better relationships with those who matter.

Endnotes

1. Sandra Waddock, "What Will It Take to Create a Tipping Point for Corporate Responsibility?" in *The Accountable Corporation*, ed. Marc Epstein and Kirk O. Hanson (Greenfield, CT: Praeger, in press).

2. See the Social Investment Forum (SIF) Web site, www.socialinvest.org.

3. See, for example, Eric M. Weigand, Kenneth R. Brown, and Eileen M. Wilhem, "Socially Principled Investing: Caring about Ethics and Profitability," *Trusts & Estates* 135, no. 9 (August 1996), pp. 36–42.

4. This view of incalculable risks was put forward by Steven R. Lydenberg and Karen Paul in "Stakeholder Theory and Socially Responsible Investing: Toward a Convergence of Theory and Practice," *Proceedings of the International Association for Business and Society*, ed. Jim Weber and Kathleen Rehbein (March 1997), pp. 208–13.

5. There is, additionally, a passive fund, called the Domini Social Fund (DSF), consisting of the companies in the Domini Index. The DSF is separately managed and should not be confused with the index.

6. See Social Investment Forum Web site, www.socialinvest.org, for general information and www.socialinvest.org/areas/research/trends/sri_trends_report_2003.pdf for the 2003 Trends Report.

7. SIF Web site, www.socialinvest.org.

8. Steven Lydenberg, Alice Tepper Marlin, and Sean Strub, *Rating America's Corporate Conscience* (Reading, MA: Addison-Wesley, 1986).

9. For more information, see www.ffiec.gov/cra/about.htm (accessed June 10, 2004).

10. See www.ffiec.gov/cracf/crarating/main.cfm (accessed June 10, 2004).

11. See ShoreBank's Web site, www.sbk.com/livesite/main (accessed June 10, 2004).

12. For a dissertation on this topic that emphasizes the ways social capital has been built between banks and community-based organizations, see Steven J. Waddell, "The Rise of a New Form of Enterprise: Social Capital Enterprise ... A Study of the Relationships Between American Bank-Community-Based Organizations," unpublished dissertation, Boston College Sociology Department, 1997.

13. Michael E. Porter, "The Competitive Advantage of the Inner City," *Harvard Business Review*, May–June 1995, reprint number 95310. Ideas in this and the following paragraphs are derived from Porter's article.

14. From Initiative for a Competitive Inner City Web site, www.icic.org/factoids.htm.

15. Jerry Sternin and Robert Choo, "The Power of Positive Deviancy," *Harvard Business Review*, January–February 2000, pp. 14–15.

16. Gretchen M. Spreijtzer and Scott Sonenshein, "Toward the Construct Definition of Positive Deviance," *American Behavioral Scientist* 47, no. 6 (February 2004), pp. 828–47.

17. Sternin and Choo, "The Power of Positive Deviancy."

18. For the story of the history, development, and achievements of Grameen Bank see David Bornstein, *The Price of a Dream: The Story of the Grameen Bank* (Chicago: University of Chicago Press, 1996).

19. Data in this paragraph are from the Grameen Bank's Web site, www.grameen-info.org/bank/GBGlance.htm (accessed June 10, 2004).

20. See Bornstein, *The Price of a Dream*, and see www.grameen-info.org for current data and information.

21. See Accion's Web site, www.accion.org (accessed June 10, 2004). Data in this and the following paragraphs are from this Web site.

22. See www.calvert.com/sri_654.html for details (accessed June 10, 2004).

23. This type of social investment is described at length in Curt Weeden, *Corporate Social Investing* (San Francisco: Berrett-Koehler, 1998), from which material in this section is derived. See also the associated Web site, www.bnsinc.com/csi/intro.html.

24. See the California Public Employees' Retirement System (CalPERS), "Obstacles to Good Corporate Governance," www.calpers-governance.org/principles/other/barriers/page01.asp (accessed June 10, 2004), for more details of the study reported in this section.

25. See the CalPERS Web site, www.calpers-governance.org (accessed June 10, 2004). See also the principles of corporate governance established by the Organization for Economic Cooperation and Development (OECD), a division of the United Nations, at www.oecd.org/topic/0,2686,en_2649_37439_1_1_1_1_37439,00.html (accessed June 10, 2004).

26. CalPERS, www.calpers-governance.org/forumhome.asp (accessed June 10, 2004). Complete copies of the principles for both U.S.-based and global companies can be found at www.calpers-governance.org/principles/default.asp (accessed June 10, 2004).

27. See the CII's at www.cii.org/dcwascii/web.nsf/doc/policies_index.cm and TIAA-CREF's at www.tiaa-cref.org/pubs/html/governance_policy (both accessed June 10, 2004).

28. The OECD's principles can be found at www.oecd.org/dataoecd/32/18/31557724.pdf (accessed June 10, 2004).

29. Lorin Letendre, "The Dynamics of the Boardroom," *Academy of Management Executive*, 18, no. 1 (2004), pp. 101–4.

30. Quoted in Robert A. G. Monks and Nell Minnow, *Power and Accountability*, www.ragm.com/library/books/poweracc/contents.html (accessed June 29, 2004), chapter 1.

31. See *Business Ethics* magazine's Web site for the 100 Best Corporate Citizens, www.business-ethics.com/100best.htm (accessed June 11, 2004).

32. Gary Davis, Reputation Institute, University of Manchester, www.mbs.ac.uk/corporate/cri/reputation_chain.htm (accessed June 11, 2004).

33. See Charles J. Fombrun, "Indices of Corporate Reputation: An Analysis of Rankings and Ratings by Social Monitors," *Corporate Reputation Review* 1, no. 4 (1998).

34. See www.reputationinstitute.com/sections/research/rsch.html (accessed June 11, 2004) for some background on Fombrun's work on reputation, as well as that of other scholars.

35. See the New Economics Foundation's Web site, www.neweconomics.org/gen (accessed June 14, 2004).

36. Details of the AA 1000 process can be found on the AccountAbility Web site, www.accountability.org.uk/uploadstore/cms/docs/AA1000%20Overview.pdf (accessed June 11, 2004).

37. Information on SAI International and the SA 8000 standards can be found at www.cepaa.org/Overview.doc (accessed June 11, 2004).

38. The term comes from the New Economics Foundation, www.neweconomics.org/gen (accessed June 29, 2004), and was written about in John Elkington, *Cannibals with Forks: The Triple Bottom Line of Sustainability* (Gabriola Island: New Society Publishers, 1999).

39. Posted at GRI Web site; www.globalreporting.org/guidelines/2002/b22.asp (accessed June 14, 2004).

40. There are a number of useful sources for exploring this issue of redefining what is meant by progress, including: www.flora.org/sustain (accessed June 29, 2004); www.foe.co.uk/campaigns/sustainable_development/progress (accessed June 29, 2004); and www.oecd.org/home/0,2605,en_2649_201185_1_1_1_1_1,00.html (accessed June 14, 2004).

41. Quoted in www.foe.co.uk/campaigns/sustainable_development/progress/annex1.html (accessed June 14, 2004).

42. From ibid.

43. See the Friends of the Earth Web site, www.foe.co.uk/campaigns/sustainable_development/progress, for more information on this specific set of progress indicators. Much of this section is derived from this site.

44. You can see what the specific measures are and how they compare with traditional measures of GDP at the Friends of the Earth Web site, www.foe.co.uk/campaigns/sustainable_development/progress/ServletStoryISEW.html (accessed June 14, 2004).

45. Hazel Henderson, Jon Lickerman, Patrice Flynn, eds., *Calvert-Henderson Quality of Life Indicators* (Calvert Group, 2000).

CHAPTER NINE

Sustainability and the Global Village

Partnership is an essential characteristic of sustainable communities. The cyclical exchanges of energy and resources in an ecosystem are sustained by pervasive cooperation . . . Partnership—the tendency to associate, establish links, live inside one another, and cooperate—is one of the hallmarks of life.

In human communities partnership means democracy and personal empowerment, because each member of the community plays an important role. Combining the principle of partnership with the dynamic of change and development, we may also use the term "coevolution" metaphorically in human communities. As a partnership proceeds, each partner better understands the needs of the other. In a true, committed partnership both partners learn and change—they coevolve. Here again we notice the basic tension between the challenge of ecological sustainability and the way in which our present societies are structured, between economics and ecology. Economics emphasizes competition, expansion, and domination; ecology emphasizes cooperation, conservation, and partnership.

The principles of ecology mentioned so far—interdependence, the cyclical flow of resources, cooperation, and partnership—are all different aspects of the same pattern of organization. This is how ecosystems organize themselves to maximize sustainability.

Fritjof Capra, The Web of Life[1]

Sustaining a Healthy Natural Ecology

During the last third of the 20th century it became clear that the health of the natural environment that surrounds and underpins societies and the economies they produce is increasingly in peril. Environmental problems assumed a global rather than a local scope, necessitating that companies and communities alike develop significantly new approaches to the use and disposal of natural resources. Corporate programs of environmental management, especially those aimed at sustainability of both the natural and community environments, have assumed a great deal of importance in bringing more responsible practice to the use of environmental resources.

Environmental problems facing the planet include global warming and ozone depletion, water and air pollution, pesticide use, toxic waste disposal, and waste disposal in general. Add in the burning of tropical rain forests to clear land for short-term farming, other processes leading to deforestation and even desertification, the resulting decimation of wildlife species (some of which have yet to be discovered), and coastal and wetlands erosion resulting from development; further consider the scarcity fresh water in some regions of the world, acid rain, and severe climate patterns that some attribute to changes in the ecology; then recognize the continuing pressures that population growth places on ecological resources, especially water—and it quickly becomes clear that human civilization faces ecological crises the likes of which have never before been seen.

Many ecological problems are boundaryless in that they cannot be contained readily, or at all, within community, regional, or even national borders. The impacts of many of these problems affect communities far beyond their sources and require wholly new approaches to sustainable development.

Pressures on the Ecology

One interesting study showed that people in the developed world make significantly larger ecological footprints than do people in the less developed world. This innovative study, pioneered by Mathis Wackernagel and his colleagues, estimated the available amount of biologically productive land per capita and deducted the roughly 12 percent of biological capacity that is considered politically feasible to allocate for the biodiversity that is essential according to the World Commission on Environment.[2] The researchers came to the conclusion that the earth can sustain human civilization at a rate of 1.7 hectare[3] per capita.[4] In 2004, humanity's total ecological footprint was 13.2 billion hectares and the world average was 2.18 hectares per capita (see Table 9.1).

Table 9.1 indicates that the United States is the biggest consumer of environmental resources per capita, with an average ecological footprint of 9.57 hectares compared to those of less developed countries like Indonesia and Bangladesh, which are well under the 1.7 hectares per capita defined as the

TABLE 9.1 **Ecological Footprints of Selected Nations**

Source: Jason Venetoulis, Dahlia Chazan, and Christopher Gaudet, "Ecological Footprint of Nations, 2004," www.redefiningprogress.org/publications/footprintnations2004.pdf (June 16, 2004).

Country	Footprint (global hectares per capita)
United States	9.57
Canada	8.56
New Zealand	8.13
Australia	7.09
France	5.74
Germany	4.26
Japan	3.91
The Netherlands	3.81
Ukraine	3.53
Italy	3.26
Argentina	3.18
Chile	3.04
Malaysia	2.09
Botswana	2.70
Mexico	2.59
The World	2.18
Iran	1.85
Bosnia-Herzegovina	1.49
Uganda	1.29
Ghana	1.23
Philippines	1.11
Kenya	1.08
Zimbabwe	1.05
Myanmar (Burma)	0.76
Nepal	0.57
Bangladesh	0.50

sustainable rate. Figure 9.1 shows that, by these calculations, the earth reached its carrying capacity in the mid-1970s. Though there is a tremendous burgeoning of population in less developed countries, individuals' ecological footprints are much smaller, in part because poor people consume far fewer environmental resources to maintain their lifestyles. Given lack of industrialization, developing nations do not consume or waste nearly as much as do developed nations, where lifestyles are much more encompassing of material goods.

Wackernagel and his colleagues conclude: "Humanity lives too heavily on the Earth."[5] Indeed, they note that "if everyone on earth lived like the average North American, it would require at least four more earths to provide all the material and energy to sustain that level of consumption."[6] What this means is that current approaches to economic and societal development are draining the

FIGURE 9.1 **Global Footprints and Biocapacity**

Source: Jason Venetoulis, "Sustainable Consumption and the Ecological Footprint,"
www.sustainablebusiness.com/features/feature_template.cfm?ID=1092 (accessed June 14, 2004).

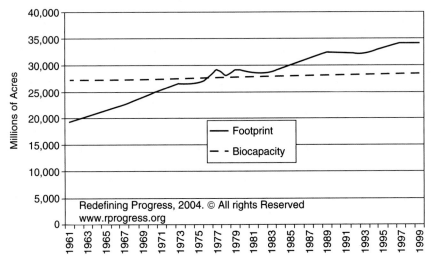

earth's resources faster than nature can replace them even without the explosive growth in population that is expected over the next several decades. Clearly, the current approach to development and lifestyles is unsustainable in the long term.

Organizing Environmental Management

Sustainability of ecological resources and the so-called greening of business are fast becoming norms in leading corporate citizens with visions supported by values that respect both nature and human civilization, particularly when companies openly recognize their ecological impact. Leading corporate citizens recognize that their own survival and well-being—as well as those of their customers, employees, and other stakeholders—depend on a shift of perspective related to business's impacts on the natural environment and the necessary changes in corporate practices to move toward sustainability. They know we all need a healthy ecological system to survive, as the four system constraints of The Natural Step, outlined in Chapter 1, highlight.

To cope with the increased need to operate in long-term sustainable ways that respect both the natural environment and local communities, not to mention sustaining themselves as companies, many companies are adopting environmental management practices and better stewardship of environmental resources. The following sections of this chapter focus on ways in which companies manage their relationship with the earth.

Change of Perspective

Truly greening a company involves generating a new awareness of the importance of the natural environment among its leaders. This shift of consciousness moves thinking away the dualism, fragmentation, and mechanistic view of nature found in traditional Western ways of viewing the world toward the more holistic, organic, and integrated perspective, what Peter Senge called a *metanoi*, or shift of consciousness.[7] The shift of consciousness and awareness depends in part on the cognitive, emotional, and moral development processes discussed in Chapter 3. Making this shift, however, can help better align the interests of all three spheres of activity with those of the ecological sphere that underpins human civilization. Where this shift of perspective takes hold, it becomes clear to observers that balance among all the spheres is essential to long-term sustainability and that corporate citizens, which are responsible for much of the consumption of earth's resources, have a significant role to play in the movement toward sustainability.[8]

Throughout the United States, European Union, and Asia, corporations are adopting environmental management practices because they are under significant pressures from stakeholders to create more sustainable products and a more sustainable world.[9] Some researchers believe that this shift and the accompanying changes in awareness may even represent a new industrial revolution, although that revolution is clearly in its early stages.[10] To manage this change of perspective, many companies are adopting proactive practices of environmental management, focused on waste reduction and cost cutting that have the by-product of satisfying customer demands for greener businesses and social investors' interest in environmental sustainability. Additionally, many companies are finding to their surprise, that there is a "both/and" of enhanced profits and greening.[11] Indeed, a recent study found that multinational corporations, rather than suffering from environmental regulations, are actually rewarded with higher stock market performance when they adopt strict global environmental standards.[12]

Companies that have been certified as being in compliance with ISO 9000 quality standards are now beginning to adopt voluntary environmental quality management standards called ISO 14000 and ISO 14001 (see Chapter 10 for a more complete exposition), which bring their environmental policies in the direction of sustainability. These standards, however, are largely oriented toward internal efficiency or economizing rather than full sustainability over the long term. Imposition of voluntary standards, which can become a source of competitive advantage through waste reduction, quality improvements, and improved customer relations, comes after years of corporate resistance to such standards and efforts to avoid command-and-control regulation by governments.[13] And the ISO standards are only one among many new environmental management practices that have emerged within the last two decades.

Stages of Environmental Awareness

Ecologist and management theorist Stuart Hart has proposed a developmental framework along which firms and their leaders progress as they begin to shift their thinking toward environmentally sustainable strategies.[14] More recently, he and Mark Milstein have created a "sustainable value framework" that highlights how companies move from an internal-today-oriented mind-set focused on pollution prevention to an external-today-oriented strategy aimed at product stewardship.[15] Hart points out that pollution prevention strategies resemble the quality movement, in that they emphasize continual improvement in reducing energy use and waste. Built on a logic resembling 3M's Pollution Prevention Pays program (see Chapter 5, Box 5.2), pollution prevention is also aligned with the emerging global environmental standards embodied in ISO 14000 and 14001. Importantly, Hart notes that "the emerging economies [and the environment itself] cannot afford to repeat all the mistakes of Western development."[16]

Companies operating in a product stewardship mode attempt to minimize not only pollution related to manufacturing processes but also all other sources of environmental impacts. Full-cost or life-cycle accounting for products can be used to reduce materials usage and really begin a process of fundamental change in product and process design, which is necessary in the shift toward sustainability. Fully costing production of both goods and services enhances leaders' awareness about the all of the company's ecological impacts.

For developing nations, it makes sense to emulate not the plunder-and-pillage environmental strategies of earlier stages of development, but rather the best modern practices associated with sustainable development. Of course, this way of thinking represents a long-term view in which costs are internalized; thus, the focus shifts to tomorrow rather than today, and costs are internalized rather than externalized.[17] Some developing nations find it difficult to think about ecological sustainability when they need to help their citizens put food on the table and shelter overhead. Hart's point, however, is that this long-term thinking is critical for world health, as well as for the ultimate health of developing nations.[18]

The third stage in Hart's framework is called clean technology. In this stage, companies shift production and products toward altogether new technologies that use many fewer resources and that last a long time. This shift, which is still rare, happens when leaders recognize that no matter how much they reduce waste or conserve resources, many of today's technologies are simply not sustainable. The payoff for companies engaging in clean technology comes in repositioning the company in an attempt to reduce the company's ecological footprint.[19]

A final stage, driven by population growth, poverty, and inequity in the world, is called the sustainability vision. In Hart and Milstein's view, this vision taps into the huge unmet need in the world, providing a growth trajectory for companies, while simultaneously focusing on the long-term vision of sustainability oriented toward meeting external demands and needs.[20] According to Hart and Clayton Christensen, of the Harvard Business School, companies can both generate internal growth and satisfy the social and ecological needs of stakeholders through "a 'great leap' to the base of the economic pyramid, where 4 billion people aspire to join the market economy for the first time."[21] To do so effectively, however, companies have to develop technologies, manufacturing processes, and resource uses that are sustainable for the entire population over the long term. Although few companies have yet reached this stage of development, many ecologists, such as Hart, believe this is the necessary next step for the planet's ecological health.

Environmental Management Practices

In recent years, significant gains have been made in environmental sensitivity and performance in developed nations, mostly resulting from the so-called greening of business, tough environmental regulations, and outsourcing practices that have removed heavily polluting industries to less industrialized nations.[22] Of course, outsourcing pollution creates potential problems in that, as developing countries industrialize, they generate additional pollution and extract more natural resources, shifting the ecological balance in a negative direction. Hart claims that a different and more enlightened path must be followed today by developing nations. Already, there are quite a number of management practices that can help move companies toward ecological sustainability.

According to researchers Michael Berry and Dennis Rondinelli, comprehensive environmental management systems include five major elements: "waste minimization and prevention, demand-side management, design for environment, product stewardship, and full-cost accounting."[23] Each of the elements of this comprehensive system is explained in Table 9.2. Berry and Rondinelli note that demand-side management can actually improve profitability. For example, International Truck and Engine Corporation, which manufactures buses, trucks, and parts, reduced its lead component by 98 percent, saving, time, money, and energy.[24]

Demand-side management allows better relationships with customers because customers are being sold only and exactly what they need, rather than having salespeople simply filling their quotas. Stewardship involves taking care of the resources and products that are developed by paying close attention to all aspects of their development and use, that is, by assuming full responsibility for the products/services and their impacts, whether those impacts are direct or indirect. Full-cost accounting (or life-cycle accounting) is necessary to take into account all of the costs of production, sales, distribution, and use, rather than externalizing them to society.

Environmental Cost Accounting

One managerial tool being used increasingly frequently to assess the overall ecological costs of producing goods and services is called environmental cost accounting. Traditional cost accounting is a tool used by managers to assess the full costs of producing something within the firm (i.e., including indirect as well as direct costs of production). Similarly, environmental cost accounting attempts to take into account all of the ecological costs of production, such as energy consumed, waste produced, cleanup costs, and possible liabilities associated with production.[25]

TABLE 9.2 Elements of Comprehensive Environmental Management Systems

Source: Adapted from Michael A. Berry and Dennis A. Rondinelli, "Proactive Corporate Environment Management: A New Industrial Revolution," *Academy of Management Executive* 12, no. 2 (May 1998), pp. 38–50.

Element	Explanation
Waste minimization and prevention	Prevent rather than control pollution by reducing, minimizing, or eliminating pollutants and wastes at their source. Includes materials substitution, process modification, materials reuse, recycling, and reuse within different processes.
Demand-side management	Understand customers' needs and preferences so (1) product is not wasted: (2) what is sold is exactly what is needed; (3) the customer becomes more efficient in using the product.
Design for environment	Produce for disassembly, modular upgradeability, and recyclability initially, rather than facing product disposal, thereby reducing reprocessing costs and returning products to the market more quickly.
Product stewardship	Stewardship implies taking care in design, manufacturing, distribution, use, and disposal of products to reduce environmental risks and problems. Life-cycle analysis determines waste reduction at all stages. Seek less polluting or wasteful alternatives; reduce conformance and liability costs.
Full-cost accounting	Identify, quantify, and allocate direct and indirect environmental costs of operations. Four levels of costs: (1) direct costs, like labor, capital, and raw materials; (2) hidden costs, such as monitoring and reporting; (3) contingent liability costs, such as fines and remedial action; and (4) less tangible costs, such as public relations and goodwill.

In a sense, environmental cost accounting is similar to life-cycle accounting because it takes into account all of the costs of production, including dealing with any by-products and long-term societal impacts of production. Three categories of costs need to be considered in an environmental cost system: failure costs, prevention costs, and appraisal costs.[26] These costs need to be assigned to specific product/service lines so that each is fully costed out, both in terms of all direct costs as well as for the environmental costs incurred, some of which may be hidden from traditional costing methods. Environmental cost accounting helps leading corporate citizens be aware of their impacts on society, both retrospectively and prospectively.[27]

Life-Cycle Accounting

Taking environmental cost accounting even further, some companies are using life-cycle accounting, which attempts to holistically assess the impacts of a product or service throughout its entire life cycle.[28] Based on the principle of

TABLE 9.3 **Components of a Complete Life-Cycle Assessment**

Source: Society of Environmental Toxicology and Chemistry, cited in William G. Russell, Steven L. Skalak, and Gail Miller, "Environmental Cost Accounting: The Bottom Line for Environmental Quality Management," *Total Quality Management* 3, no. 3 (Spring 1994), pp. 255–68.

Life-cycle inventory	An objective, databased process of quantifying energy and raw material requirements, air and water emissions, solid waste, and other environmental releases incurred throughout the life cycle of a product, process, or activity.
Life-cycle impact analysis	A technical, quantitative, and/or qualitative process to characterize and assess the environmental effects of energy, materials, and emissions identified in the life-cycle inventory. The assessment should include both environmental and human health considerations.
Life-cycle improvement analysis	A systematic evaluation of opportunities to reduce the environmental impact associated with energy and raw materials use and emissions throughout the entire life of a product, process or activity.

ecological stewardship—or care taking—life-cycle accounting encompasses multiple disciplines in a holistic assessment of the planning for a product, its management during its useful life, industrial design associated with it (including engineering and design specification), and costs associated with environmental and health protection.[29]

The Society of Environmental Toxicology and Chemistry has defined a complete life-cycle assessment as having three interrelated parts, which are listed in Table 9.3. These three elements—life-cycle inventory, impact analysis, and improvement analysis—combine to create a system through which costs can be calculated for all of the impacts of designing, developing, producing, delivering, and finally disposing of a product or service.

Environmental Audits

Because leading corporate citizens take responsibility for their ecological impacts, they frequently undertake and publish environmental audits, along with audits associated with other stakeholder impacts. Environmental audits focus on ecological areas of concern to relevant stakeholders, including compliance officers who work with regulatory agencies and employees, whose training should include environmental stewardship issues. An environmental audit uses life-cycle, full-cost, or environmental-cost accounting techniques, as noted above, to assess the real and fully internalized costs of company production and distribution practices to the company and the customer (and, as a by-product, to society). As with other audits, environmental audits are published for interested stakeholders' use, frequently as part of triple-bottom-line reports.

The audit, once completed, highlights where potential problems exist and where opportunities for waste or pollution reduction exist—and potential cost savings as well. The audit can also be used to help the company establish a cost basis for operations and set priorities for future initiatives.[30] Indeed, one scholar argues that investments in environmental sustainability make sense simply because they help companies gain a competitive advantage, achieve positive financial returns, reduce risks, and outpace competitors, who may be using less progressive practices.[31]

Current Sustainability Practice

In recent years environmental regulatory agencies have begun to move away from their original command-and-control stance toward more market-based and less adversarial tactics intended to encourage sustainability. While the command-and-control legal frameworks still exist and indeed dominate most countries, there are instances of market incentives, such as the selling of pollution rights, and numerous public–private partnerships that foster a more collaborative approach to the environment between business and government.

In the Netherlands, for instance, there has been a decided movement toward problem-solving techniques involving the establishment of covenants or voluntary agreements. Throughout Europe, such agreements focus on specific environmental problems like waste management or energy efficiency, but in the Netherlands, they have assumed a new character. Newer covenants emphasize reducing emissions from whole industry sectors over a long time and involve "institutionalized cooperation between industry and government."[32] Although these agreements have had numerous obstacles and stumbling blocks and have not reached their full potential, they do represent an important alternative to adversarial relationships on important environmental matters, particularly during certain phases of environmental policy development.[33]

In the United States, efforts to move corporate thinking toward sustainable practice have tended to focus on ways in which companies can build new businesses, save money, or gain a competitive advantage through more environmentally responsible practices. One approach, as articulated by Forest Reinhardt, is to try to use the problems of the environment strategically to gain advantage.[34] Reinhardt identifies five approaches that companies can use to integrate an environmental perspective into business operations. According to Reinhardt, businesses can:

- *Differentiate* by using products or processes with great environmental benefits or that use fewer natural resources in their production, for which ecologically sensitive consumers will pay higher prices (e.g., as Wal-Mart has done in identifying its green products for consumers).
- *Manage competitors* by working with industry groups to change society's rules or the rules of competition so that competitors need to incur higher costs to respond to environmental regulation maintaining a first-mover advantage because the company has been able to anticipate what will be needed (e.g., as the chemical industry has done in establishing its Responsible Care initiative).

- *Save costs* by improving environmental performance internally (e.g., as hotels have done in asking customers to reuse towels and linens).

- *Manage environmental risk* by avoiding costs associated with accidents, spills, consumer boycotts, and environmentally related lawsuits.

- *Redefine markets* by using several of these approaches simultaneously and convincing customers of their benefits ecologically and competitively (e.g., as BMW has done with cars that can be disassembled for recycling and are now in compliance with strict German "take-back" laws).[35]

Management systems are also keys to responsible environmental practice. Companies using proactive environmental management and cost accounting systems also emphasize pollution prevention and recycling, responsible purchasing policies, and new manufacturing strategies that reduce waste. Additionally, because communities are frequently impacted by environmental problems, community involvement is a critical aspect of a good environmental management system.[36] It is likely that in the future traditional and environmentally oriented accounting methods will be integrated as more and more companies are expected to account for all of their costs rather than externalizing them to society.

Future Sustainability Practices

Simply using the environment as a source of competitive advantage, as many companies are currently doing, overlooks the fundamental problem of sustainability. Ultimately, balance demands a far broader perspective from leading corporate citizens. This broader perspective takes into account not only economic but also societal and political considerations in determining what the public good is, as well as ecological long-term sustainability. This shift of perspective is the basis of much of the triple-bottom-line thinking, which emphasizes performance on economic, social, and ecological criteria and requires the postconventional levels of cognitive and moral development.

A number of emerging corporate practices can help move a company along the path toward sustainability. One is product accountability, which applies the stewardship principle to all of the negative impacts of a product or service, as does life-cycle accounting. Another is life-cycle management, discussed above with reference to life-cycle accounting, but here applied to the managerial practices along the entire value chain associated with developing, selling, using, and ultimately disposing of a product. A third practice involves spreading the costs among all emitting parties, thereby eliminating both free ridership and prisoner's dilemma situations. Some companies concerned with carbon dioxide emissions are also using benchmarking to compare their own performance with that of best-practice firms in a fourth practice likely to become more popular as ecology continues to gain corporate citizens' interest and attention.[37] Other leading corporate citizens are signing on to principles like those developed by the Coalition for Environmentally Responsible Economies (CERES)—see Case 9.1.

The CERES Principles and Environmental Reporting

The Coalition for Environmentally Responsible Economies (CERES) has emerged as the worldwide leader in standardized corporate environmental reporting and promoting the transformation of environmental management within firms. Formed out of a unique coalition of some of America's largest institutional investors and environmental and advocacy groups, CERES has pioneered an innovative, practical approach toward encouraging greater corporate responsibility on environmental issues.

Formed in 1989, the CERES coalition originally brought fifteen major U.S. environmental groups together with an array of socially responsible investors and public pension funds. By 2004, more than 70 companies had become signatories to the CERES Principles (see Exhibit 1), which evolved out of the Valdez Principles, developed after the Exxon *Valdez* spilled millions of gallons of oil in Alaska in the late 1980s.

ENDORSING COMPANY STATEMENT FOR CERES PRINCIPLES

CERES endorsing companies, at minimum, are expected to complete the CERES Report each year, remit annual fees, and maintain an open and forthright relationship with CERES.

Endorsing the CERES Principles commits a company to integrating the aims of the Principles into its policies, programs, practices and processes, working toward improving environmental performance to the point of both economic and ecological sustainability.

The success of a CERES endorsing company relationship depends greatly upon trust, openness and collaboration. CERES expects that participating companies intend to improve their environmental performance meaningfully and consistently over time. CERES seeks to enter into a partnership with member firms whereby information and opinions move freely and beneficially between Coalition members and participating businesses.

ENVIRONMENTAL REPORTING IS PART OF CERES

According to CERES, corporate environmental reporting serves many different purposes for different stakeholders: It empowers people with the information they need to hold corporations accountable, and invites stakeholders more fully into the process of corporate goal setting. It permits investors to harness the power of the capital markets to promote and ensure environmentally superior business practices. It allows companies and their stakeholders to measure companies' adherence to the standards set forth in their statements of environmental principle, and their various goals and objectives. As an internal driver of change, it helps illuminate weaknesses and opportunities and set new goals. It will allow society better to understand the full implications of corporate activity thereby to design more sustainable local and global systems.

A growing number of companies are now voluntarily disclosing environmental information, both as stand-alone corporate reports and as special environmental or sustainability sections within corporate annual reports. However, if each firm utilizes its own format, indicators and metrics, comparisons between these reports become impossible. Report users—investors, environmentalists, consumers, employees, other stakeholders, and other firms—have great difficulty in using reports to inform investment decisions, guide consumer product choices, and benchmark performance against comparable firms. The result is that the substantial resources firms spend on data development and analysis, report production, and report dissemination yield far less value than they could and should.

EXHIBIT 1   The CERES Principles

Source: www.ceres.org/our_work/principles.htm (accessed June 16, 2004).

Protection of the Biosphere
We will reduce and make continual progress toward eliminating the release of any substance that may cause environmental damage to the air, water, or the earth or its inhabitants. We will safeguard all habitats affected by our operations and will protect open spaces and wilderness, while preserving biodiversity.

Sustainable Use of Natural Resources
We will make sustainable use of renewable natural resources, such as water, soils and forests. We will conserve non-renewable natural resources through efficient use and careful planning.

Reduction and Disposal of Wastes
We will reduce and where possible eliminate waste through source reduction and recycling. All waste will be handled and disposed of through safe and responsible methods.

Energy Conservation
We will conserve energy and improve the energy efficiency of our internal operations and of the goods and services we sell. We will make every effort to use environmentally safe and sustainable energy sources.

Risk Reduction
We will strive to minimize the environmental, health and safety risks to our employees and the communities in which we operate through safe technologies, facilities and operating procedures, and by being prepared for emergencies.

Safe Products and Services
We will reduce and where possible eliminate the use, manufacture or sale of products and services that cause environmental damage or health or safety hazards. We will inform our customers of the environmental impacts of our products or services and try to correct unsafe use.

Environmental Restoration
We will promptly and responsibly correct conditions we have caused that endanger health, safety, or the environment. To the extent feasible, we will redress injuries we have caused to persons or damage we have caused to the environment and will restore the environment.

Informing the Public
We will inform in a timely manner everyone who may be affected by conditions caused by our company that might endanger health, safety or the environment. We will regularly seek advice and counsel through dialogue with persons in communities near our facilities. We will not take any action against employees for reporting dangerous incidents or conditions to management or to appropriate authorities.

Management Commitment
We will implement these Principles and sustain a process that ensures that the Board of Directors and Chief Executive Officer are fully informed about pertinent environmental issues and are fully responsible for environmental policy. In selecting our Board of Directors, we will consider demonstrated environmental commitment as a factor.

Audits and Reports
We will conduct an annual self-evaluation of our progress in implementing these Principles. We will support the timely creation of generally accepted environmental audit procedures. We will annually complete the CERES Report, which will be made available to the public.

Among the companies that now issue reports based on the CERES principles are:

- American Airlines
- Anderson Lithograph
- Bank of America
- Baxter International
- Coca-Cola, North America
- Ford Motor Company
- Interface, Inc.
- Seventh Generation
- Sunoco
- The Timberland Company
- Wainwright Bank

DISCUSSION QUESTIONS

1. Do you think it important or useful for companies to sign on to principles like the CERES principles? Why or why not? Will signing on help the environment? Is it enough?

2. What rationale would you give your boss for becoming a signatory?

3. Might there be competitive advantage or disadvantage gained by signing? What would be the sources of either?

Source: Excerpted from the CERES Web pages, www.ceres.org/about/questions.htm#1, www.ceres.org/about/endorsing_companies.htm (accessed June 16, 2004), and earlier Web pages.

Ecology and Development

Developed nations, which leave a much larger ecological footprint than do less developed nations, account for about 1 billion of the world's 6 billion people. This 7 percent, of the global population accounts for about 60 percent of the world's private consumption[38] and creates most of the industrial, toxic, and consumer waste that is generated.[39] Between 1980 and 2000, according to the World Bank, the world's population grew from 4.4 billion to 6 billion people, with most of that growth in developing nations. The World Bank expects that another billion will be added by 2015, with the expectation that by 2015 possibly six of every seven people will live in developing nations.[40] Combined with governmental policies, economic development, distribution of technological and land resources, and consumption patterns, this growth puts significant strains on ecological resources. Population growth, which some believe is at the level of crisis, illuminates the need for bringing balance among the three spheres of human activity and the natural environment as an imperative no human being or enterprise can any longer afford to ignore.

Surveys undertaken by organizations like the Worldwatch Institute showed in 2004 that private consumption expenditures of over $20 trillion in 2000 were highly dominated by the United States (with 5.2 percent of the population and 31.5 percent of the spending) and Western Europe (with 6.4 percent of the population and 28.7 percent of the spending—see Table 9.4. This same report identified other interesting tidbits, such as that three-fourths of the world's population has at least one television set and that consumers now spend $35 billion annually on bottled water. Still, Worldwatch estimated that 2.8 billion people still live on less than $2 per day and that as many as one-fifth of the world's population does not have adequate access to safe drinking water. Worldwatch claims that providing adequate food, clean water, and basic education for the world's poorest could all be achieved for less than people spend annually on unnecessary consumer goods. For example, consumers spend $18 billion on makeup annually versus the $12 billion

TABLE 9.4 Consumer Spending and Population by Region, 2000

Source: Worldwatch Institute, "State of the World 2004: Consumption by the Numbers," www.worldwatch.org/press/news/2004/01/07 (accessed June 11, 2004).

Region	Share of World Private Consumption Expenditures	Share of World Population
United States and Canada	31.5%	5.2%
Western Europe	28.7	6.4
East Asia and Pacific	21.4	32.9
Latin America and the Caribbean	6.7	8.5
Eastern Europe and Central Asia	3.3	7.9
South Asia	2.0	22.4
Australia and New Zealand	1.5	0.4
Middle East and North Africa	1.4	4.1
Sub-Saharan Africa	1.2	10.9

estimated for reproductive health care for all women, $11 billion on ice cream in Europe versus $1.3 billion for immunizing every child, and $14 billion on ocean cruises versus $10 billion estimated for clean drinking water for all.[41]

Worldwatch also finds that the United States, with 5.2 percent of the global population, uses a quarter of the world's fossil fuel resources (26 percent of the coal, 26 percent of the oil, and 27 percent of the natural gas). In 2003, gas-guzzling sports utility vehicles were the most popular vehicles in America—and houses had become McMansions, at 38 percent bigger in 2002 than 1975, despite the fact that families were smaller.[42]

Economic development in the current economizing mode, where externalities are shifted to society, clearly has many deleterious impacts on the natural environment, in part because as nations develop economically, people tend to make larger ecological footprints, consuming more resources in their daily lives and generating more waste and pollution. Factors that appear to result in this greater ecological impact include increasing urbanization and associated patterns of migration from more rural to more urban (as well as resource-rich coastal) areas.[43] Consumption of goods and services, as well as energy, tends to be higher on a per capita basis in urban than rural areas.

According to futurist Hazel Henderson, population growth poses two critical issues for balancing the ecological impacts of human civilization. The first is that industrialized societies' levels of consumption and ecological footprints are significantly greater than those of less development nations, which as we have seen above is inherently unsustainable. Second, there is a growing global consensus that one way to stabilize population growth is to educate and empower poor women, who serve as family educators, food producers, and family providers. Such empowerment of women is ideologically problematic for certain fundamentalists in patriarchal societies and religious traditions.

Water wars may be the next big global ecological concern, as scarcity of water is predicted for many nations in the not-too-distant future. A study undertaken in 2002 by the World Resource Institute, a non profit environmental think tank, suggests that it is becoming harder to ensure adequate supplies of water for both human consumption and nature. This study shows that humans now withdraw as much as 20 percent of the flow of the world's rivers annually and that about 41 percent of the world's population (or about 2.3 billion people) now live in conditions of "water stress" and are subject to frequent water shortages. Estimates are that 3.5 billion people, or about 48 percent of the projected population, will live in "highly stressed" conditions by 2025.[44]

Energy consumption increased by 100 times in the years between 1850 and 2000, with consequent increases in carbon dioxide emissions, creating the so-called greenhouse effect and possible global warming. Between 1950 and 1995, fossil fuel use and emissions accelerated by some 3.6 times, with the Unites States as the largest producer (or consumer, depending on your point of view).[45] Only about 1 percent of the world's fresh water supply is readily available for human use—and demand is growing. Further, freshwater fish species are experiencing serious decline globally; it is estimated that some 20 percent of species have already gone extinct.[46]

The list of environmentally degraded and endangered resources could go on virtually endlessly.[47] The real point, however, is that ecological sustainability must be married with societal and community-based sustainability that balances political, civil societal, and economic interests in a healthy whole. Accomplishing this goal requires true shift of mind—or *metanoia.*

For example, as the world's leading beverage company, Coca-Cola relies on adequate water resources—and also recognizes that these resources are growing more limited. Because of this recognition, the company has taken a proactive stance toward its own water usage policies and actively posts information about water resources on its Web site. Case 9.2 draws on the company's Web site to highlight Coke's approach to the use of increasingly scarce water resources.

The proactive stance that Coca-Cola has taken toward its water use and the relative transparency of the company's admissions about water have not prevented controversies from arising. For example, in March 2004, Reuters issued a press release announcing that Coke's premier water product, Dansani, is, like many other bottled waters, nothing more than purified tap water.[48] Mere weeks later, the company was forced to recall all of its British Dasani because of contamination by potentially cancer-causing bromates.[49] The company has also been charged with "swallowing up" local clean water in villages in India[50] and elsewhere, adding to the complexity of attempting to manage its resources appropriately—and in the context of its attempts to be a leading corporate citizen.

Integrating Sustainability and Social Capital into Economic, Political, and Civil Society

Sustainability, increasingly, is being used as a term that applies not only to the natural environment but also to communities and, indeed, whole societies. The rest of this chapter will discuss society as an ecological system and attempt to

The Coca-Cola Company exists to benefit and refresh everyone it touches. Founded in 1886, our Company is the world's leading manufacturer, marketer, and distributor of nonalcoholic beverage concentrates and syrups, used to produce nearly 400 beverage brands. Our corporate headquarters are in Atlanta, with local operations in over 200 countries around the world.

The basic proposition of our business is simple, solid and timeless. When we bring refreshment, value, joy and fun to our stakeholders, then we successfully nurture and protect our brands, particularly Coca-Cola. That is the key to fulfilling our ultimate obligation to provide consistently attractive returns to the owners of our business.

CORE BELIEFS AND VALUES

There is much in our world to celebrate, refresh, strengthen and protect. The Coca-Cola Company is a vibrant network of people, in over 200 countries, putting citizenship into action. Through our actions as local citizens, we strive every day to refresh the marketplace, enrich the workplace, protect the environment and strengthen our communities.

We are a local employer, with responsibility to enable our people to tap into their full potential; working at their innovative best and representing the diversity of the world we serve.

We are an investor in local economies and a driver of marketplace innovation, with a responsibility to act as a good steward of our natural environment.

And we are a local citizen, understanding our responsibility to contribute to an improved quality of life in our communities.

COCA COLA'S APPROACH TO WATER USAGE

Water is one of the world's most precious resources. Although many people may assume that water is limitless and will always be available, its future is in fact quite uncertain. In many places in the world, freshwater resources are facing unprecedented challenges from over-exploitation, increasing pollution, and poor management.

Without access to clean and safe water, natural systems are threatened, economies sputter, and communities wither. For companies like ours, continuing success depends on ensuring adequate water for both ourselves and for the communities where we operate. We are committed to benefiting and refreshing consumers and their communities, and being an active partner in addressing water challenges is a crucial part of that commitment.

CORE TO THE BUSINESS

Water is fundamental to our business—in fact, without water, we have no business.

We use it in our products as well as in our manufacturing processes. Aside from being our largest ingredient, packaged drinking water is now a fast-growing product category. In our manufacturing processes, water is used for washing and rinsing bottles and packages, cleaning mixing tanks and pipes, producing steam, and cooling. Water also has many uses in our office buildings, truck washes and for landscape irrigation.

Because water is so integral to our business, our ability to prosper as a business depends on how well we use and manage this resource. Therefore, we have implemented various initiatives to address water quality, scarcity and efficiency.

For instance, we closely monitor the quality of the water used in our products, we carry out rainwater harvesting programs in arid parts of the world, we provide wastewater treatment in regions that lack such municipal services; and we use desalination at plants that have access only to salt water.

Working with our bottlers and supply chain partners, we strive to continuously improve our environmental performance while increasing our efficiencies. We have found that most environmentally beneficial practices actually improve our business efficiency.

And in addition to the business benefits, preserving and protecting the environment also furthers our promise to benefit and refresh everyone we touch and our commitment to enhance the local communities we serve.

PACKAGED WATER BUSINESS

In addition to considering water as a crucial ingredient in products such as carbonated soft drinks, we also serve large markets for packaged drinking water in communities around the world. The actual products available vary considerably, from purified bottled waters to packaged spring waters to bulk water distribution to flavoured and fortified water products. The consumer demand for packaged water products has grown dramatically over the last decade, and shows no sign of slowing down.

In the packaged water business, people pay for a product because they know it is safe, high quality, available, and convenient. When The Coca-Cola Company sells drinking water in its various forms, it is not charging for the water per se, but rather for the value we add to the water to make it a branded beverage. For instance, we treat water to high safety and quality standards, put it into convenient packages to suit different needs, distribute the product to places where people want to consume it, and cool it for immediate consumption.

CASE EXAMPLE OF COKE'S CONSERVATION EFFORTS

The Coca-Cola Company's Southern & East Africa Division has partnered with Roundabout Outdoor, a company that The World Bank recognized in 2000 for its innovative Playpump

concept. The Playpump operates like an inverted windmill. Children play on the round-about—turning it and riding it like a merry-go-round—to create the pressure needed to pump fresh, safe drinking water out of the ground and into storage tanks for future use.

Last year, the Company sponsored nine Playpumps in the Eastern Cape, a region of critical water needs, and has committed to sponsor a total of 50 pumps. Roundabout Outdoor estimates that nearly 200,000 individuals will benefit from the Company's contribution.

"Water is essential to life, and as a company we are committed to finding solutions to help alleviate the scarcity of water in some of our neediest communities," said Dave Govender, the Company's Division Manager for Environmental Affairs. "Coca-Cola also recognizes the value of access to this precious resource for its business operations, and we believe that the Playpump concept offers communities and schools an excellent way to access fresh water for their needs."

DISCUSSION QUESTIONS

1. How serious do you think Coca-Cola is about conserving water resources? Should other companies be similarly engaged in this process?

2. What other details of Coke's water strategy can you find on the company's Web Site?

3. Given the problems with water product quality and increasing scarcity, what recommendations would you make to Coca-Cola regarding its water usage?

Sources: Coca-Cola Web site at www2.coca-cola.com/index.html and subcategories related to environment and water (accessed June 30, 2004).

form an integrated perspective on the links needed to build effective societies, communities, and businesses that sustain themselves ecologically and are filled with meaningful relationships among their members. Business has an essential role to play in this mix, a role in which its power needs to be balanced with that of actors in the political and civil society spheres.

One of the agents that brings balance is the presence of social capital. Social capital seems to be important in all three spheres of human activity that we have been discussing throughout this book. It forms a kind of social glue that can be used to generate decision-making policies aimed at long-term sustainability. The World Bank concurs with this definition, arguing,

> Social capital refers to the institutions, relationships, and norms that shape the quality and quantity of a society's social interactions. Increasing evidence shows that social cohesion is critical for societies to prosper economically and for development to be sustainable. Social capital is not just the sum of the institutions which underpin a society—it is the glue that holds them together.[51]

Political and Civil Society Spheres

Social capital, according to political scientist Robert Putnam, also "refers to features of social organization such as networks, norms, and social trust that facilitate coordination and cooperation for mutual benefit.[52] High levels of social capital are, as we shall see in reviewing Putnam's research, associated not only with healthy communities that seek and share a common good but also with enhanced democratic government.

Putnam's research suggests that benefits of high levels of social capital include the development of norms of reciprocity among individuals and groups, as well as trusting relationships. When trust exists, it is easier to coordinate, collaborate, and communicate within the network, especially as reputations are gained that establish others' trustworthiness. Also, it is harder in such systems to engage in deceitful or opportunistic behavior, because others have developed expectations based on one's reputation. Finally, as Putnam notes, "dense networks of interaction probably broaden the participants' sense of self, developing the 'I' into the 'we.'"[53]

Putnam found that, depending on their level of social capital, people seem to be either more or less involved in the democratic institutions of society and governments appear to be more or less successful as a result of that involvement. More social capital results in higher levels of civic participation and better government. In his study of Italy's regional governments, Putnam attributes their success to trust that other citizens will act fairly and obey laws, and to values of honesty and equality. Additionally, social networks in the more successful regions appear to be, as they are in more successful companies today, horizontally, not hierarchically, organized.[54]

The concept of social capital is widely in use today because institutions like the World Bank and the Inter-American Development Bank believe that developing it in societies has the potential to improve them economically, socially and politically. The reasons for improvement are numerous, including enhanced trust, which reduces transaction costs and increases accountability among people and organizations, and creation of greater faith in the future, which provides a basis for investments of all sorts. Social capital also helps secure property rights, as well as providing access to economic opportunities for those in poverty and increased participation in democratic processes.[55]

Civil Society, Ideology, and Corporate Power

One of the issues associated with corporate power in the modern world has to do with the impact of economic development—and multinational corporations in particular—on national and local communities, that is, on civil society or the set of relationships in which people's and communities' lives develop meaning. Local cultures are affected by forces that political scientist Benjamin Barber, in somewhat radical terminology, calls McWorld (see Chapter 2). McWorld's forces are those of globalization, represented by the homogenization of the world through look- and feel- and taste-alike McDonald's throughout the world to a set of simultaneous and countervailing forces he terms Jihad. The forces of Jihad, in contrast to those of McWorld, are the countervailing forces of extreme localism, sectarianism, and, by implication, a zealous adherence to a local identity of some sort that excludes all who are not inside the particular system.[56]

Both of these contesting forces, according to Barber, represent threats to democracy or the political sphere, largely because they are indifferent to their impact on the state or community. In part, Jihad arises from attempts to sustain cultural identity and, when not bound up in an extremism that excludes all who are nonbelievers or different, cultural identity is a significant and important aspect of the global village that most people agree should be preserved. McWorld represents a threat because of its homogenizing influences and because many global companies act as if they were without roots in any specific communities, hence abrogating their connectedness and sense of responsibility for impacts. Lack of rootedness also lends itself to lack of consideration for the types of ecological concerns we have focused on earlier.

The Countervailing Power of Rootedness

Cultural identity and national ideology, as we have seen earlier in this book, are core elements of civil society. As billionaire financier George Soros has pointed out in a controversial article, "The Capitalist Threat," "Societies derive their cohesion from shared values. These values are rooted in culture, religion, history, and tradition."[57] Values and beliefs, Soros argues, are fundamental in shaping community life, conduct, and ultimately civil society, as well as democratic participation. Others have argued that treating corporations like persons and simultaneously providing limited liability for directors and top managers creates problems of power and lack of rootedness that need to be overcome by more democratic processes.[58]

Healthy civil societies, as Putnam and others show, have multiple layers of connectedness and a sense of community that is shared by members. This sense of community and connectedness develops out of shared beliefs that typically go beyond purely economic beliefs and that rest on shared assumptions about the nature of humanity, community, and society; about what is important and meaningful; and about how community members should live and work together.

Corporate citizens, and their leaders, need to understand and respect these values as they attempt to do business in the diverse communities that constitute the world. To do this well, corporations need to understand the communities in which they operate very well, respect the local traditions and culture, and enter into a partnership that enhances, rather than detracts from, community life. Doing these things well ultimately requires that companies acknowledge localness as well as globalness and make some effort to become locally rooted to complement their globalism.

Rootedness represents acknowledgment of a sense of place, a home, and the sense of connectedness and community that develops from that sense of place. It respects local as well as global in the "both/and" logic we have argued is increasingly necessary for corporate success. Rootedness is also located within the natural ecology, since leading corporate citizens that acknowledge their rootedness know that they cannot exist when the earth itself is being unsustainably abused.

Economic Sphere

Ironically, despite the forces of globalization and the intense competition that characterizes much of the modern economic sphere, local connections and a sense of the ecology of the whole of society connected with nature still appear to be vitally important to long-term economic (never mind societal) success. Innovative work by economist Michael Porter has highlighted this ecological perspective.[59] In studying successful firms all over the world, Porter discovered that businesses are most successful when they operate in clusters representing critical masses of related businesses not when they attempt to operate independently of such networks.[60] In what he terms the "paradox of location in a global economy," Porter finds that long-term competitive advantage lies in creating localized advantages that rivals find hard to duplicate. The sources of these advantages, far from being low-cost outsourcing that has the potential of mistreating employees, turns out to be the soft stuff of knowledge, relationships, and motivation.

Porter defines *clusters* as "geographic concentrations of interconnected companies and institutions in a particular field."[61] Clusters include an array of stakeholders: suppliers of inputs specialized to the industry or creators of industry-specific infrastructure, customers (particularly for business-to-business relationships and purchases), and manufacturers of complementary products and services.

Further, as Porter notes, clusters can also include key educational institutions (such as Harvard and MIT in the Boston/Cambridge/Route 128 area, which provide talent for the local high-technology cluster), as well as governmental bodies and trade associations. All of these institutions can work collectively when they are in a cluster to support the industry cluster in ways that a company acting alone would find impossible. Note that these enterprises are found in all three spheres of activity that we have been discussing.

Clusters have interesting characteristics. They represent, at one level, an ecological system comprised of interdependent, symbiotic, collaborative and simultaneously competitive organizations that take diverse forms. These are the very same characteristics of a healthy ecosystem, as discussed above. The boundaries of a cluster can be determined by assessing the "linkages and complementarities across boundaries that are most important to competition."[62] Clusters are not necessarily bounded by standard industry classification schemes because so many types of institutions are included, just as the effects of burning down large sections of rain forest go well beyond the boundaries of the forest itself and, indeed, may affect the global climate.

Interestingly, Porter views clusters as a new way of creating a value chain and a new form of organizing without as much dependence on the hierarchical values associated with power aggrandizing. Clusters, in their ecological formation, are more emergent in that they are self-organizing to a very large extent, with new businesses and other institutions springing from entrepreneurial roots as the need for them is recognized.

Healthy Clusters

Healthy clusters affect competitiveness in three ways, according to Porter. Clusters enhance productivity, they drive innovation, and they stimulate the formation of new businesses to serve cluster needs.

Productivity is enhanced because there is better access to employees and suppliers locally, as well as to other inputs, and because companies can source what they need without resorting to complex formal arrangements like alliances and joint ventures. They also offer access to specialized information that grows up within the network of organizations operating within a specific cluster and provide for complementarities across organizations because each picks up its own piece of the business and serves others by doing so. They create pressures on local governments and communities to create access to public institutions and to public goods, such as infrastructure, that make doing business easier. And, because local rivalry tends to be high within clusters, they enhance motivation and measurement of results.

Innovation is enhanced by clusters for some of the same reasons that productivity is improved and also because clusters tend to generate sophisticated and demanding buyers. Companies within clusters also tend to be more flexible than those outside of clusters; they are able to move quickly when necessary, and they can operate at lower costs because of their interrelatedness and constant mutual reinforcement of what is needed to compete successfully.

New business stimulation is enhanced in clusters because they have concentrated customer bases, which lowers risks and makes spotting opportunities relatively easier. As Porter points out, gaps in products or services are readily noted, while barriers to entry within a cluster tend to be lower for players already in the cluster (and even some from without). Additionally, local financial institutions know what to ask and seek in making loans and credit available. Overall, the perceived risk of investment is reduced within a cluster.

"Glocal" Companies and the Multiple Bottom Lines

Clusters create "glocal" companies, that is, companies that are simultaneously able to compete globally but that are strongly rooted in local communities.[63] Because they are local as well as global, glocal companies operating within clusters— arguably all companies—need to be actively aware of their multiple-bottom-line responsibilities to the different primary and critical secondary stakeholders on whom they depend and who depend on them. In part, this interdependence arises because glocal companies are deeply rooted in the local culture, community, and cluster. Such rootedness, based on the social capital that emerges out of economic clusters, seems to be an important indicator of the potential for economic sustainability and even competitive advantage.

Long-Term Competitive Success and Social Capital

Porter's work on clusters highlights an important though frequently overlooked reality: one of the most important factors in successful economic development derives from the existence of trusting relationships and long-term connectedness among the entities that comprise his economically successful clusters. Ironically, it is this form of social capital, a cooperative and collaborative posture of interdependence, that arises as a key factor in success rather than individual action and cutthroat competition. Research on the relationship between economic and political development substantiates the notion that dense links among economic institutions provide a basis of success, as Putnam's work discussed above highlights. Examples include Asia's "network capitalism," and the industrial districts that develop when there is collaboration among workers and small entrepreneurs.[64]

Other research supports the link between plentiful social capital and economic success. As reported in *Business Week*, researchers at the American University found that high levels of trust were associated with strong economic performance.[65] The reasons given for these findings are that businesses operating where there are many positive social ties and a lot of trust have incentives for innovation and capital accumulation, because they are confident about the future.

Further, work in fields as diverse as education, urban poverty, unemployment, crime and drug abuse, and health care has shown that communities—civil society—too are more successful when there are strong social bonds.[66] Finally, as we have noted, Putnam's research on Italy's political districts suggests that governments are also more successful when there are rich norms of connectedness and civic engagement.[67] World Bank research corroborates these findings, suggesting that whole villages are better off if social capital is plentiful.[68] Economic prosperity appears to be complementary to a sense of community and place. Community and place need to be sustained as an ecology themselves and in balance with the natural environment on which we all depend.

Promoting Healthy Glocalities

Companies that want to be leading corporate citizens need to be world class in terms of productive capacity to meet the challenges of the modern economy. The natural environment demands ecological sustainability to preserve human civilization and leading corporate citizens are beginning to meet that challenge. Civil society requires healthy and positive relationships among all citizens in societies. "Glocality" means that companies may need to be located within healthy clusters as well as globally competitive and working toward sustainable development. Healthy clusters depend on healthy civil societies supported by strong enough and democratically based governments to meet the public interests identified by the people. Acting in the public interest to produce a balance among the three spheres suggests significant and important roles that government must play not as adversary to economic interests but as ally or partner.

Porter identifies some of the important roles that governments, local and national, need to play to foster healthy glocalities that generate active world-class business clusters.[69] Through their educational institutions, governments need to ensure that citizens are well educated and able to take active roles in a knowledge-based economy. They must also develop local infrastructures—including transportation, phone, and electronic access, as well as other supports such as sewage systems—that businesses need to survive and compete.

As all governments do, modern governments hoping to support and enhance cluster development and social capital need to set appropriate rules of competition, particularly enforcing intellectual property and antitrust laws, to foster innovation and productivity. Creating what some observers call global action networks, which integrate the perspectives of stakeholders form multiple sectors, is yet another way to create connections among multiple actors in society.[70] Finally, governments can, by working creatively and interactively in partnership with other institutions such as businesses, reinforce and build on emerging clusters through providing needed public goods. Building a balance among the spheres of activity in human civilization, in effect, demands a sufficiently powerful and creative set of governmental organizations to establish and maintain rules of the game that balance resources, interests, and distribution of goods and services equitably.

Leading Challenges: Integrity—Gaining a Sense of the Whole

Integrity, as was we have noted, involves honesty, wholeness, and adherence to a code or standard. It is the sense of the whole, the systems perspective, and building an ecological balance among individual, business, government, and community interests that creates a healthy and sustainable world. Thus, it is not just civil society but also economic productivity and the success of political or governing bodies that are enhanced when social capital is high—and that form a cornerstone of leading corporate citizenship. Because of the importance of social capital in all three spheres of human civilization and because a balance of human beings' interests with those of nature is essential to humankind's long-term survival, corporate citizens must think carefully about their roles, relationships, and impacts on the sustainability of societies and nature.

Integrity in leading corporate citizens also means integration, that is, integrating ecologically sustainable practices into corporate life on a day-to-day basis. Leaders of companies today need to be aware of the pressures all companies are facing for both transparency and accountability with respect to their impacts, on communities as well as on the natural environment. It is not enough to operate as if in an economic vacuum. Blinders no longer work in a world where the demands and pressures can change at the flick of a mouse and where unacceptable practices can be instantaneously broadcast around the world.

Rather, leaders need to take a systemic perspective on how companies' practices affect the communities in which they invest and the natural environment that they draw resources from. Operating with integrity means operating in the interests of the whole, as well as with honesty and forthrightness, and it means integrating principles into practices. Doing so frequently requires adhering to increasingly important and widely accepted principles and standards, on which we will focus in Chapter 10.

Endnotes

1. Fritjof Capra, *The Web of Life* (New York: Anchor Doubleday, 1995), p. 301.
2. Reported in Mathis Wackernagel and William Rees, *Our Ecological Footprint: Reducing Human Impact on the Earth* (Philadelphia: New Society Publishers, 1995); and Mathis Wackernagel et al., "Ecological Footprints of Nations: How Much Nature Do They Use? How Much Nature Do They Have?" www.ecouncil.ac.cr/rio/focus/report/english/footprint (1999; accessed June 14, 2004).
3. A hectare is a metric unit of measurement, equivalent to 2.471 acres or 10,000 square meters.
4. You can calculate your own ecological footprint at www.lead.org/leadnet/footprint/intro.htm (accessed June 14, 2004).
5. Wackernagel et al., "Ecological Footprints of Nations."
6. Cited in (accessed June 14, 2004).
7. Peter Senge, *The Fifth Discipline* (New York: Free Press, 1990).
8. One view of this transition is presented in Rogene A. Buchholz, *Principles of Environmental Management: The Greening of Business*, 2nd ed. (Englewood Cliffs, NJ: Prentice Hall, 1998).
9. D. Maxwell and R. van der Vorst, "Developing Sustainable Products and Services," *Journal of Cleaner Production* 11, no. 8 (December 2003), pp. 883–95.
10. Michael A. Berry and Dennis A. Rondinelli lay out this argument in "Proactive Corporate Environment Management: A New Industrial Revolution," *Academy of Management Executive* 12, no. 2 (May 1998), pp. 38–50.
11. See, for example, Stuart L. Hart, "Beyond Greening: Strategies for a Sustainable World," *Harvard Business Review*, January–February 1997, pp. 66–76.
12. Glen Dowell, Stuart Hart, and Bernard Yeung, "Do Corporate Global Environmental Standards Create or Destroy Market Value?" *Management Science* 46, no. 8 (August 2000), pp. 1059–74.
13. Berry and Rondinelli, "Proactive Corporate Environment Management."
14. Hart, "Beyond Greening," and Stuart L. Hart and Mark B. Milstein, "Creating Sustainable Value," *Academy of Management Executive* 17, no. 2 (2003), pp. 56–69.
15. Hart and Milstein, "Creating Sustainable Value."
16. Hart, "Beyond Greening," p. 71.

17. Hart and Milstein, "Creating Sustainable Value."

18. Hart, "Beyond Greening."

19. Hart and Milstein, "Creating Sustainable Value."

20. Ibid.

21. Stuart L. Hart and Clayton M. Christensen, "The Great Leap: Driving Innovation from the Base of the Pyramid," *Sloan Management Review*, Fall 2002, pp. 51–56.

22. Hart, "Beyond Greening."

23. Berry and Rondinelli, "Proactive Corporate Environment Management," p. 5.

24. See the Environmental Protection Agency's Web site, www.epa.gov/epaoswer/hazwaste/minimize/intl_trk.htm (accessed June 16, 2004).

25. Amy Persapane Lally, "ISO 14000 and Environmental Cost Accounting: The Gateway to the Global Market," *Law & Policy in International Business* 29, no. 4 (Summer 1998), pp. 401–538.

26. William G. Russell, Steven L. Skalak, and Gail Miller, "Environmental Cost Accounting: The Bottom Line for Environmental Quality Management," *Total Quality Management* 3, no. 3 (Spring 1994), pp. 255–68.

27. Lally, "ISO 14000 and Environmental Cost Accounting."

28. Russell, Skalak, and Miller, "Environmental Cost Accounting."

29. Ibid.

30. Berry and Rondinelli, "Proactive Corporate Environment Management."

31. Forest L. Reinhardt, "Bringing the Environment Down to Earth," *Harvard Business Review*, July–August 1999, pp. 149–57.

32. Pieter Glasbergen, "Modern Environmental Agreements: A Policy Instrument Becomes a Management Strategy," *Journal of Environmental Planning and Management* 41, no. 6 (November 1998), pp. 693–709.

33. Ibid.

34. Reinhardt, "Bringing the Environment Down to Earth," exemplifies this way of thinking, which comes from within the current set of management assumptions. The ideas in this and the next paragraph are derived from Reinhardt's article. His ideas are more fully developed in *Down to Earth: Applying Business Principles to Environmental Management* (Cambridge, MA: Harvard Business School Press, 2000).

35. Reinhardt, "Bringing the Environment Down to Earth."

36. Russell, Skalak, and Miller, "Environmental Cost Accounting."

37. Glasbergen, "Modern Environmental Agreements."

38. Worldwatch Institute, www.worldwatch.org/features/consumption/sow/trendsfacts/2004/02/04 (accessed June 17, 2004).

39. Hart, "Beyond Greening."

40. World Bank Web site, www.worldbank.org/depweb/english/modules/social/pgr (accessed June 28, 2004).

41. Worldwatch Institute, "State of the World 2004: Consumption by the Numbers," www.worldwatch.org/press/news/2004/01/07 (accessed June 17, 2004).

42. Worldwatch Institute, www.worldwatch.org/features/consumption/sow/trendsfacts/2004/02/04 (accessed June 17, 2004).

43. Hazel Henderson, *Building a Win-Win World: Life Beyond Global Economic Warfare* (San Francisco: Berrett-Koehler, 1996).

44. Carmen Ravenga (edited by Greg Mock), "Will There Be Enough Water? Pilot Analysis of Global Ecosystems: Freshwater Systems," World Resource Institute, Earth Trends Web site, October 2000, http://earthtrends.wri.org/pdf_library/features/wat_fea_scarcity.pdf (accessed July 1, 2004).

45. Henderson, *Building a Win-Win World*.

46. Ravenga, "Will There Be Enough Water?"

47. For some current statistics and information, see the World Resource Institute's Earth Trends Web site, http://earthtrends.wri.org/index.cfm (accessed July 1, 2004).

48. Trever Datson, "Coca-Cola Admits that Dasani Is Nothing but Tap Water," Common Dreams Newscenter, March 4, 2004, www.commondreams.org/cgi-bin/print.cgi?file=/headlines04/0304-04.htm (accessed June 30, 2004).

49. Anthony France, "Coca-Cola Recalls Water," *Sydney Morning Herald On Line*, March 22, 2004, www.smh.com.au/articles/2004/03/21/1079823239704.html?from =storyrhs& oneclick=true (accessed June 30, 2004).

50. Ratheesh Kaliyadan, "India: Coca-Cola Swallows Villagers' Fresh Water," *GreenLeft*, May 22, 2002, www.greenleft.org.au/back/2002/493/493p20.htm (accessed June 30, 2004).

51. World Bank, www.worldbank.org/poverty/scapital/whatsc.htm (accessed June 29, 2004).

52. Robert D. Putnam, "Bowling Alone: America's Declining Social Capital," *Journal of Democracy* 6, no. 1 (January 1995), p. 67. Benefits of social capitalism described in this paragraph are also derived from this article.

53. Ibid., p. 67.

54. Robert D. Putnam, *Making Democracy Work: Civic Traditions in Modern Italy* (Princeton, NJ: Princeton University Press, 1993).

55. Andrew Holm, "A (Social) Capital Idea: Making Development Work," *Harvard International Review*, Winter 2004, pp. 24–27.

56. Benjamin Barber, *Jihad vs. McWorld* (New York: Times Books; Random House, 1995).

57. George Soros, "The Capitalist Threat," *Atlantic Monthly* 279, no. 2 (February 1997), www.mtholyoke.edu/acad/intrel/soros.htm, p. 7 (accessed July 6, 2004).

58. Charles Derber, *Regime Change Begins at Home: Freeing America from Corporate Rule* (San Francisco: Berrett-Koehler, 2004); see also Charles Derber, *People Before Profit: The New Globalization in an Age of Terror, Big Money and Economic Crisis* (New York: St. Martin's Press, 2002).

59. See Michael E. Porter, "Clusters and the New Economics of Competition," *Harvard Business Review*, November–December 1998, pp. 77–90.

60. Ibid. See also Michael E. Porter, *The Competitive Advantage of Nations* (New York: Free Press, 1990), and Michael E. Porter, "The Competitive Advantage of Nations," *Harvard Business Review*, March–April 1990, pp. 73–93.

61. Porter, "Clusters," p. 78.

62. Ibid., p. 79.

63. Thomas L. Friedman, *The Lexus and the Olive Tree* (New York: Anchor Books, 2000).

64. Putnam, "Bowling Alone," p. 65.

65. This work by Stephen Knanck of American University and Philip Keefer of the World Bank is cited in Karen Pennar, "The Ties That Lead to Prosperity," *Business Week,* December 15, 1997, pp. 154–55.

66. Putnam, "Bowling Alone," p. 65.

67. Putnam, *Making Democracy Work*.

68. Noted in Pennar, "The Ties That Lead to Prosperity."

69. The following discussion is taken from Porter, "Clusters."

70. See the Global Action Network Web site, http://gan-net.net (accessed June 29, 2004).

PART FOUR

Leading Corporate Citizens into the Future

CHAPTER TEN

Global Standards/ Global Village[1]

Our experience with the Global Compact over the past four years has shown conclusively that voluntary initiatives can and do work. But we have also learned that they have to be made to work. Governments have to do the right thing: to govern well, in the interests of all their people. Business must restrain itself from taking away, by its lobbying activities, what it offers through corporate responsibility and philanthropy. And civil society actors need to accept that the business community is not a monolithic bloc; that it has leaders and laggards; and that leaders should be encouraged when they take positive steps, even though they may occasionally stumble, and not to be frightened off from trying in the first place . . .

The Compact's core comparative advantages are the universality of its principles, the international legitimacy that only the United Nations embodies, and the Compact's potential to be a truly global platform with great appeal not only in the industrialized countries, but also in the developing world. The Compact's new strategic concept must therefore give special emphasis to the potential for links, synergies and mutual support between the global and local levels of our activities.

Kofi Annan, Secretary General, United Nations, June 23, 2004

Global and Local Standards

Many companies will want to—and should—develop their own codes of conduct, ethical principles, operating standards, and core values to reflect their unique purpose, customer groups, and internal values. In developing these internal principles, companies can define what they stand for and what their standards of integrity are. Yet it is clear that internally developed standards will have to satisfy the external scrutiny of increasingly sophisticated stakeholders and meet the foundation standards articulated in documents like the United Nations' Global Compact, the Global Sullivan Principles, the CERES environmental principles, and the United Nations' Code of Conduct for Multinationals. To cope effectively with all these principles, companies need to ensure that their own standards are at least meeting the minimum standards set by various industry, governmental, nongovernmental (NGO), and coalition groups.

The processes of globalization and the explosion of connectivity engendered by the World Wide Web have made obvious that some standards and principles of action need to be global. Further, implementation of these standards can help corporate citizens avoid free ridership, externalities, and prisoners' dilemma problems that place some companies and countries at a disadvantage to others. Emerging standards and principles are therefore based on end values that attempt to ensure balance among the spheres of human activity and with nature, and to provide for respect for basic human dignity.

Global standards and principles are typically established through consensus-building processes set up by international bodies, sometimes industry organizations, and frequently coalitions of various interested stakeholders. Despite the vast diversity and pluralism of societies in the world, the emergence of these statements of principles and codes of conduct is testimony to the fact that, after all is said and done, we live one world.

To cope with the recent proliferation of standards and accountability measures, this chapter will explore the emergence of standards in all three of the spheres of human civilization as well as those that have emerged with respect to the natural environment. In this exploration, we will see that although global accountability measures are still in the early stages of development, more and more agreement is being generated about the standards to which global companies will have to adhere.

As public attention shifts from topic to topic, global brands are often targets of exposés and activist pressures.[2] Among other incidents, religious groups spearheaded a consumer boycott of the Nestlé Corporation for its sales of infant formula in developing nations in the late 1970s; the boycott culminated in Nestlé's appointment of an internal infant formula audit commission. Combined with a global boycott of products from companies operating in South Africa, these and similar forms of consumer activism vividly demonstrate the usefulness of consumer movements to attempt to change corporate behavior and hold companies accountable.

Another source of increasing pressure for corporate accountability is the social or ethical investing movement, which is now estimated by the Social Investment Forum to include some $2 trillion in equities screened on social criteria in the United States alone. Although social investing is yet to become fully mainstream, there is enough investor interest, with about one of every eight dollars invested in screened equities,[3] that even major investment houses like Smith Barney and large pension funds like TIAA-CREF have begun to create social funds. By the late 1990s, corporate governance activists had also become sophisticated in their use of shareholder resolutions targeted at specific corporate practices.[4]

Outsourcing, strategic and other alliances, and just-in-time inventory management systems began to blur the boundaries between companies and their suppliers and customers during the 1980s and 1990s. Outsourcing created new global supply chains, often in developing nations, and human rights, labor, and environmental activists became concerned about corporate practices in the increasingly long supply chains of consumer goods, clothing, and toy companies.[5] Boundaries between multinational companies and their suppliers, clear perhaps in the eyes of managers, have been much less clear to activists wanting to create corporate accountability.

The Gap between the Ideal and the Real

Demands for greater corporate transparency and accountability, as well as anticorruption measures, are fostering significant new accountability, reporting, and transparency initiatives among coalitions of business, labor, human rights, investor, and governmental bodies. Indeed, a database created by the International Labor Organization and available over the Internet lists nearly 450 Web sites of industry and business associations; corporate, NGO, and activist groups; and consulting organizations that have developed and are promulgating a wide range of relevant policy initiatives. These initiatives include a mix of transparency and reporting initiatives, codes of conduct, principles, and fair trade agreements.[6] Responses to these demands are varied. Many companies, particularly those under NGO and social activist pressures to reform labor and human rights abuses in their supply chains, have formulated their own codes of conduct. Notable among these companies are Levi Strauss, Nike, and Reebok, all significant targets of activism.

The array of emerging standards suggests that there is a gap between growing public expectations from a variety of stakeholders and actual company performance. Pressures from a wide range of stakeholders appear to be pushing companies toward a common set of guidelines of what *ought* to be and away from the stark and not always pleasant realities of global competition.[7]

Foundation Principles

Corporate critics might ask whether a company that employed 180 forced laborers yesterday and only 160 today could really be considered to be a leading corporate citizen. The company has shown improvement, but its basic practice of forced labor—slavery—is reprehensible. It violates a fundamental value inherent in responsible practice. Such baseline-level behaviors, practices, and values are foundation principles. *Foundation principles are generally agreed-on standards that provide a floor of acceptable practice below which it is ethically and managerially problematic to go.* Business ethicists Thomas Donaldson and Thomas Dunfee term such general principles or values "hypernorms" and suggest that a relatively universal consensus must be reached for them to exist at all. They define hypernorms as "principles so fundamental to human existence that they serve as a guide in evaluating lower level moral norms."[8]

General agreement by businesses on a common set of foundation principles—a baseline or a moral minimum for operating practice—is important to providing a level playing field for companies. One author argues that a set of universal moral standards would include trustworthiness, respect, responsibility, fairness, caring, and citizenship; such standards could underpin the development of codes and principles themselves.[9] Agreement on foundation principles could help companies avoid the information overload and code mania that some are currently experiencing as the number and types of initiatives grow, as well as disparities between developed and developing nations.[10]

Donaldson and Dunfee provide a framework for core values, built on the need for system integrity that builds trust and the mutual respect that emerges from the philosopher Immanuel Kant's categorical imperative.[11] Donaldson argues that these basic principles of respect are useful aids for searching out foundation values:

- Respect for core human values, which determine the absolute moral threshold for all business activities.
- Respect for local traditions.
- Respect for the belief that context matters when deciding what is right and wrong.[12]

From these guiding principles, Donaldson articulates three core values, all involving the critical element of respect. Core or foundational principles seemingly need to emphasize what leadership theorists James McGregor Burns terms end values,[13] which ultimately respect:

- Human dignity.
- Basic rights.
- Good citizenship (which involves working together to support and improve the institutions on which the community depends).[14]

These guiding principles negotiate the tension that exists in treating people as ends, not means, and treating each individual as unique and deserving of respect and dignity, while simultaneously holding valuable the context of community or common good that makes societies work.

Spheres and Related Values

The three spheres of human civilization and the ecological surround discussed in earlier chapters provide a useful framework for considering the range of possible foundation principles. As discussed earlier, core purposes within each of these spheres differ; hence, there are likely to be foundation principles associated with each sphere, though these will clearly merge into other spheres as well. To the extent that foundation principles exist, chances are they exist within broad-based consensus documents, generated not from theory but from agreements by the nations of the world, such as those promulgated by the United Nations (UN), perhaps the longest-existing multilateral global enterprise. Although a few nations may not agree with principles articulated in these broad-based consensus documents (e.g., China on human rights), they nonetheless represent the world's best efforts to date to find agreed-on values.

Indeed, the recent development of the UN's Global Compact, launched in 1999 by Secretary-General Kofi Annan, provides significant insight into the relatively few values that may have achieved the status of global agreement that may serve as candidate for actual hypernorms. Four principles deal with labor rights and can be said to fall within the economic sphere. Two principles deal with human rights, which fall within the civil society sphere, and three are ecological principles within the environmental sphere that underpins human civilization. A tenth anti-corruption principle, which falls most dominantly within the governmental sphere, was added in 2004 at a summit of leaders engaged in Global Compact activities. In the following sections we will explore foundation principles associated with each of the spheres before moving to a discussion of accountability.

The Global Compact

At the World Economic Forum, held in Davos, Switzerland, in January 1999, UN Secretary-General Kofi Annan challenged world business leaders to "embrace and enact" a Global Compact, both in their individual corporate practices and by supporting appropriate public policies. The principles articulated by Annan include human rights, labor standards, the natural environment, and corruption (see Table 10.1). The Global Compact initially involved establishing a coalition of businesses, business associations, workers' or labor organizations, national governments, and other types of organizations that are attempting to establish standards for business and industry. It is an effort by Annan to establish a standard for corporate citizenship by developing global companies into model corporate citizens who voluntarily agree to operate in accordance with a core set of principles that establish standards with respect to labor, human rights, and environmental practices.

Not everyone greeted Annan's attempt with cheers. Indeed, many NGO leaders believe that the Global Compact puts the UN's credibility at risk because it too closely aligns the UN with corporate forces.[15] In part, the critiques arise

TABLE 10.1   **Principles of the Global Compact**

Source: The Global Compact, www.unglobalcompact.org/Portal/Default.asp (accessed July 2, 2004).

The Global Compact's ten principles in the areas of human rights, labor, the environment, and anti-corruption enjoy universal consensus and are derived from:

- The universal Declaration of Human Rights
- The International Labour Organization's Declaration
- The Rio Declaration on Environment and Development

The Global Compact asks companies to embrace, support and enact, within their sphere of influence, a set of core values in the areas of human rights, labor standards, and the environment. The principles are as follows.

Human Rights

Principle 1: Businesses should support and respect the protection of internationally proclaimed human rights, and
Principle 2: make sure that they are not complicit in human rights abuses.

Labor Standards

Principle 3: Businesses should uphold the freedom of association and the effective recognition of the right to collective bargaining,
Principle 4: the elimination of all forms of forced and compulsory labor,
Principle 5: the effective abolition of child labor, and
Principle 6: the elimination of discrimination in respect of employment and occupation.

Environment

Principle 7: Businesses should support a precautionary approach to environmental challenges,
Principle 8: undertake initiatives to promote greater environmental responsibility, and
Principle 9: encourage the development and diffusion of environmentally friendly technologies.

Anti-Corruption

Principle 10: Businesses should work agains all forms of corruption, including extortion and bribery.

because the 50 or so companies that had signed on with the Global Compact by the end of 2000 had done so voluntarily. Additionally, there is little or no external monitoring of their activities on the three main areas covered by the principles and little enforcement power of the standards. Clearly, corporations hoping to live up to the principles embedded in the Global Compact, as well as some of the other standards noted below, have a long way to go before their activities are fully transparent to NGOs and activists and before they can be held fully accountable.

Beyond Economizing: Economic Sphere Foundation Principles

Businesses operate within the economic sphere with the dominant goal of economizing. Since it is employees who produce the work of organizations, labor standards are certainly one important arena in which foundation principles are needed. Economizing means using resources, including human resources, in the most efficient way. In the economic sphere, principles derived from International Labor Organization (ILO) standards and the UN Declaration on Human Rights are particularly relevant.[16] The International Labor Standards of the ILO were developed with government policy in mind, targeting the development of national labor laws. Companies, of course, are subject to labor laws in countries where they have a presence, but the International Labor Standards do not generally specifically target companies. Such standards involve the fundamental principles of respect for humans as ends, not means, and, fundamentally, for human dignity at work.[17]

The International Labor Standards cover a broad range of areas and lack universal acceptance in their entirety; thus, they lack key traits necessary to serve as a foundation for economic sphere principles. Specifically with respect to labor standards, one analysis of existing global labor standards (building on the concept of human dignity and rights identified as fundamental by Donaldson and Dunfee) has demonstrated that there *are* certain basic labor rights that are relatively universally acknowledged.[18] These minimal labor rights are derived from the UN Declaration on Human Rights; the UN International Convention on Economic, Social and Cultural Rights; the Caux Round Table Principles; and the International Labor Organization labor standards. They are operationalized by the SA 8000 labor standards, as well as being found in many corporate and business association codes of conduct. The following foundation principles may represent the minimal set of conditions and standards to which all companies' labor standards should adhere:

- Just and favorable working conditions, including a limit to the number of hours a human should have to work each day and a healthy working environment.
- Minimum age and working conditions for child labor.
- Nondiscrimination requirements regarding the relative amount that a worker should be paid and the right to equal pay for equal work.
- Freedom from forced labor.
- Free association, including the right to organization and to bargain collectively in contract negotiations.[19]

Beyond Power Aggrandizing: Governmental Sphere Foundation Principles

Sustaining the integrity of the business and economic system demands *trust* in the system, particularly at the intersection between government (with its power to regulate and create the rules by which businesses operate) and business.

Trust, as noted in the discussion of social capital in Chapter 9, is the key to sustainable nations and a sustainable economic system. Governments have the capacity to use coercive power (or power-aggrandizing tendencies) to create the system under which other types of entities exist. System integrity is fundamentally undermined by corruption and bribery, which have the tendency to make both the economic and political systems untrustworthy. Accountability in corrupt systems is nonexistent, and companies that participate in corruption work against system integrity and the necessary foundation of trust. Transparency International (TI) and the World Bank, two global organizations working at the country level on the issue of corruption, have highlighted the need for foundational principles built on the concept of system integrity, and the UN Global Compact added a tenth anticorruption principle in 2004 to deal with this important issue.

As stated on the TI Web site (www.transparency.org), there are several reasons for fostering system integrity, integrity that structures business-government relationships and ultimately fosters democracy. The reasons are:

- Humanitarian, as corruption undermines and distorts development and leads to increasing levels of human rights abuse.
- Democratic, as corruption undermines democracies and in particular the achievements of many developing countries and countries in transition.
- Ethical, as corruption undermines a society's integrity.
- Practical, as corruption distorts the operations of markets and deprives ordinary people of the benefits which should flow from them.[20]

TI's core principles form the foundation of possible baseline principles with respect to the interactions of business and government, as well as providing some guidance for business transactions and reporting. Interestingly, TI's core principles are similar to the ethical principles of the numerous business initiatives aimed at improving management practice analyzed by Jeanne Liedtka (see Chapter 4), suggesting their broad applicability. TI's mission statement articulates its foundation principles as:

- Participation.
- Decentralization.
- Diversity.
- Accountability.
- Transparency.[21]

The UN Global Compact's tenth principle states the core value very simply: Business should work against corruption in all its forms, including extortion and bribery.[22]

Making Civilizing Real: Civil Society Sphere Foundation Principles

Basic human rights are possible candidates for fundamental principles associated with the civil society sphere, which is the realm of social organizations: family, church, schools, NGOs, and so on. Foundation principles related to human rights are most well known from their promulgation in the UN Declaration on Human Rights, first written in 1948 and more recently updated to include basic environmental concerns as well as human rights. Based on this declaration and other sources, Donaldson and Dunfee suggest that there is significant cross-cultural agreement on the following principles, all of which respect the dignity and humanity of individuals:

- The right to freedom of physical movement.
- The right to ownership of property.
- The right to freedom from torture.
- The right to a fair trial.
- The right to nondiscriminatory treatment.
- The right to physical security.
- The right to freedom of speech and association.
- The right to minimal education.
- The right to political participation.
- The right to subsistence.[23]

Some of these foundation principles are highly congruent with the labor rights identified in the preceding section of this chapter. As with the governmental foundation principles, the foundational human rights also foster democratic values (i.e., the right to political participation and the freedoms of speech and association) rather than more authoritarian values. Simultaneously, these rights allow for individual, national, and cultural differences (i.e., nondiscriminatory treatment and the freedom of speech and association), in what Donaldson and Dunfee term the "moral free space" in which individual differences of opinions about right and wrong exist.

Sustainability: Ecological Sphere Foundation Principles

If nature can be said to have a goal, it is likely to be ecologizing. The economizing that is inherent in industrialization when combined with the basic ecologizing processes of nature points in the direction of a possible foundation value for the nature environment of:

- Sustainability or ecologizing.

Nature, that is, wastes nothing. What is waste for one process becomes food for others, creating a cycle that sustains itself in creating the conditions for life on earth as we know it, or what some have called the Gaia hypothesis, the hypothesis that the earth itself is a living system.[24]

TABLE 10.2 Foundation Values in the Spheres of Human Civilization and Natural Environment

Source: Sandra Waddock, "Foundation Principles for Making Corporate Citizenship Real," *Journal of Business Ethics* 50 (2004), pp. 313–27.

Economic Sphere	Governmental Sphere	Civil Society Sphere	Ecological Sphere
• Just and favorable working conditions • Minimum age and working conditions for child labor • Nondiscrimination • Freedom from forced labor • Free association	• Participation • Decentralization • Diversity • Accountability • Transparency	• Freedom of physical movement • Ownership of property • Freedom from torture • Right to a fair trial • Nondiscriminatory treatment • Physical security • Freedom of speech and association • Right to at least a minimal education • Right to political participation • Right to subsistence	• Sustainability • Precautionary (preventative) approach to environmental challenges • Responsible and ethical management products and processes • Development and diffusion of environmentally sound technologies

The UN Global Compact, building on the consensus fostered through the UN's Agenda 21 and the Declaration on Human Rights and Environment, reinforces the need for sustainability by emphasizing the following core environmental principles as its foundation principles:

- Taking a precautionary (preventative) approach to environmental challenges.
- Responsible and ethical management products and processes from the point of view of health, safety, and environmental aspects.
- Development and diffusion of environmentally sound technologies.[25]

This extended discussion of values as they apply to the spheres is summarized in Table 10.2. An example of one company's attempts to respond to a moral and strategic challenge is given in Case 10.1.

Emerging Trends in Standards, Principles, Codes of Conduct

During the late 1990s and early 2000s, an enormous wave of scandals brought attention to the need to provide coherent, consistent guidelines to ensure accountability, responsibility, and transparency with respect to how businesses

Pfizer's Multisector Engagement: AIDS Drugs in the Developing World

The world's largest pharmaceutical maker, Pfizer Inc., faced a moral and strategic challenge: How could it respond to the HIV/AIDS epidemic, the most devastating disease of the third world, in a way that was commensurate with the company's leading position in its field? Pfizer's own portfolio of marketable therapies had little to offer in combating the disease, yet it nonetheless faced internal and external pressures to expand access to health care for the world's most needy. In response, in 2003 Pfizer began mobilizing the technical skills and expertise of its own employees in the fight. Under the personal oversight of the company's chairman and CEO, Henry A. McKinnell, the Pfizer Global Health Fellows volunteer program, dubbed "Hank's Peace Corps," sends skilled personnel to developing countries to help nongovernmental organizations (NGOs) build the health and social infrastructure of communities ravaged by HIV/AIDS. McKinnell's vision, extending beyond traditional industry responses of cash and drug donations and ordinary volunteerism, is a novel experiment in large-scale international development: Pfizer intends to eventually scale up the program to include volunteers from many companies, and in so doing has the rare opportunity to establish a new model of cross-sector engagement at the deepest level of organizations to confront AIDS and potentially other global crises.

As many sectors of society evolve to the conclusion that medical care is a human right, the Fellows program advances the moral and practical discussion about the role and means of various institutions—especially the critical pharmaceutical industry—to ensure those rights. In its intended scale, leverage, and social value, the program demonstrates Pfizer's support for the first UN Global Compact principle that seeks the protection of human rights, by attempting to safeguard the most basic one—to life itself. As HIV/AIDS increasingly leads to inequities in the society and workplaces of developing countries, the program also addresses the goal of the sixth principle, "to eliminate discrimination in employment and occupation," by reducing the stigma of the disease through education and prevention.

In its approach to these goals, Pfizer has partnered with nonprofit aid organizations ("NGO partners") already in the target regions and steeped in a common mission. In turn, the NGOs engage their own field staffs or local organizations, such as community clinics and research and training institutions ("field organization beneficiaries") in the developing world to identify solutions to their most pressing needs. Under this arrangement, the NGO partners expect to gain a number of benefits from Pfizer personnel—generally in capacity-building analysis, planning, and training that they couldn't otherwise afford. Because each volunteer's assignment is different, these benefits take many forms, among which are improved epidemiological skills to better identify health trends and plan interventions; increased efficiency in NGO program management, learning, reporting, and fund-raising; improved drug-trial competence that in turn attracts more first-world resources; AIDS education, prevention, and economic-support tools for workplaces and care centers; and training in state-of-the-art medical skills.

Pfizer fully anticipates many advantages from the Fellows program as well. As a personnel development tool, it encourages volunteers to come home with new operational and business insights, as well as better understanding of the company's many stakeholders (patients, communities, NGOs). These insights should inform future social policies, business processes and decisions—not the least of which include bringing future AIDS therapies to market. For many employees impassioned by public-health issues, the program is also expected to be a valuable recruitment and retention tool. And, significantly, it is intended to help build relations with both critical activist organizations and powerful legislative and regulatory authorities—many of whom believe the pharmaceutical industry must make more effort to address the developing world's health crises.

A number of lessons from the early phases of implementation are valuable for the light they shed on the nuances of building cross-sector partnerships around the contributions of corporate volunteers. Some of these lessons include:

- The labor-intensive planning to accommodate the needs of all stakeholders—the corporation, the NGO, its field staff, beneficiaries, and the individual volunteer—cannot be overestimated.

- Field assignments are most productive when they're driven by beneficiary needs and not simply to accommodate the desires of available volunteers.

- The personal traits of successful corporate employees are not always suited to the rigors of the third world; thorough screening and preparation are vital.

- NGO adjustment to the culture and disciplines of for-profit corporations is nearly as significant.

- Corporate executives' enthusiasm can help but also hinder the program development process.

- First-world corporate expertise does not always transfer easily to third-world conditions, and work-arounds are difficult to find.

- Midmanagers' willingness to allow volunteers time off is critical to such a program's success, and the burden felt by colleagues back home can jeopardize that approval.

- Expectations by all parties of the others must be firmly set—and then constantly adjusted.

Clearly the challenges Pfizer has addressed with the Fellows program are profoundly significant; there is perhaps none more so than the politically charged and intractable dilemma of AIDS, especially for a pharmaceutical developer today. The volunteer approach is an innovative attempt to bring the company's core medical and managerial competencies to bear on difficult infrastructure challenges, which inhibit the efficacy of drug and cash donations and hinder the successful treatment and prevention of AIDS. While the Fellows program is admittedly a modest beginning, Pfizer ambitiously seeks to scale it to meaningful impact. This approach has been appreciably more challenging than Pfizer, the NGOs, and field organizations first imagined. Sharing the knowledge of Pfizer's own specialists shows deeper organizational commitment than other avenues it could have chosen, such as donating more cash or drugs, and is far more difficult than it probably needed to pursue if its motivation were purely image building.

The Fellows response, however, stops short of tackling knotty business strategy changes called for by critics of the pharmaceutical industry in recent years. For example, a tiered and transparent global pricing system would allow health authorities in poor countries to purchase critical drugs at lower and more predictable prices and could lead the industry to even more profound benefits for the disadvantaged. Pfizer does not pose the Fellows program as a substitute or ultimate solution to such issues. However, one can imagine that its most significant contribution ultimately may be the influence of its returning volunteers on management's future thinking about such policies. In this way, the program has the potential to create change within the company's processes, of the sort the Global Compact intends.

DISCUSSION QUESTIONS

1. How would you evaluate Pfizer's efforts to deal with the AIDS crisis?

2. Do you think Pfizer's efforts go far enough? Why or why not?

3. Does Pfizer's commitment to working with NGOs adequately show the company's commitment to the Global Compact's first principle? Why or why not?

4. What advice would you give to Pfizer to sustain its initiatives over time?

Source: Jonathan Levine, for the Center for Corporate Citizenship at Boston College, 2004.

behave in the world and the impacts that they have. In the following sections we briefly explore some of the major initiatives attempting to evolve principles, standards, and codes of conduct to which businesses can (and should) adhere.

Protecting the Ecological Surround

The United Nations has recognized the importance of environmental sustainability through development of its Agenda 21 initiative, which was adopted at the global environmental conference held in Rio de Janeiro, on June 14, 1992.[26] Agenda 21 is based in part on the principles of environment and development adopted at the Rio conference, which was the first-ever global conference on the environment.[27] Among the most important principles for leading corporate citizens to be aware of are the sovereign right of nations to use their own natural resources to meet the needs of future and present generations. The principles emphasize the need for sustainable development and its link to environmental protection, through focusing on eradicating poverty, meeting the needs of developing countries as a priority, and paying particular attention to ensuring that the voices of vulnerable groups—such as women, youth, indigenous, and oppressed peoples—are heard.

The Rio Principles also emphasize the need for global partnership in conserving and protecting the earth's ecosystem, through an open and global economic system, with fair trade policies, discouragement of transfer of environmentally harmful activities to more vulnerable or weaker nations, and internalization of costs. Nation-states are encouraged to promote countrywide initiatives to improve sustainability, scientifically and technologically, through citizen participation, and effective environmental legislation along with active citizen participation in the setting of national laws and regulations. The principles also encourage global intercountry cooperation in the interest of the environment and a spirit of collaboration and partnership.

Agenda 21 is a comprehensive document that sets forth an ambitious series of agenda items and goals linking economic and social development with ecological sustainability. Specific goals of Agenda 21 are: (1) promoting sustainable development through trade liberalization; (2) making trade and environment mutually supportive; (3) providing adequate financial resources to developing countries and dealing with international; and (4) encouraging macroeconomic policies conducive to environment and development.[28]

Agenda 21 focuses on combating poverty, changing consumption patterns, encouraging sustainability, and responding to population or demographic shifts. It also focuses on protecting and promoting human health, while simultaneously promoting the integration of environment and development in decision-making processes. Arenas of environmental concern include the atmosphere, the forests, and fragile ecosystems (including focusing on the increasing desertification of some areas of the world resulting from overpopulation and overuse of the land and creating sustainable mountain, agricultural, and rural areas). Companies and nations need to learn to manage and protect biological diversity, and to manage biotechnology safely. Pollution and waste management systems are aimed at improving the oceans and other bodies of water and the atmosphere, and reducing hazardous wastes and toxic chemicals, solid wastes and sewage, and radioactive wastes.

Responses from Businesses

Businesses today are coming under increasing pressure from environmental activists, regulatory agencies, governments, and NGOs to move toward sustainable development. Some business groups are responding to these pressures by creating self-regulatory initiatives that focus their internal practices on more sustainable practices.

One of the foremost business-oriented organizations in fostering collaborative relationships among the many parties interested in sustainable ecology has been the Coalition for Environmentally Responsible Economies (CERES). Composed of more than 50 investor, environmental, religious, labor, and social justice organizations, CERES has drafted a set of principles that nearly 50 companies and organizations had endorsed by the end of the 20th century. Another business-oriented organization acting to promote sustainable ecology is the World Business Council for Sustainable Development (WBCSD). A third is the chemical industry's Responsible Care initiative.

CERES Principles

The CERES Principles, presented in Chapter 9, came into existence following the Exxon *Valdez* oil spill in Alaska. The spill brought renewed activist and indeed global public attention to the need for ecologically sustainable business practices. Initiated in 1989, the CERES Principles were first called the Valdez Principles and were then broadened in scope and tactics toward influencing corporate strategies with respect to the environment through using shareholder resolutions to initiate conversations with corporate directors about company practices.[29]

The CERES coalition views itself as successfully modeling cooperation and dialogue among investors, environmentalists, and companies; as a leader in standardizing corporate reporting on the environment; and as a catalyst for measurable improvements in companies' environmental practices. CERES has accomplished much of this through its 10 principles, detailed in Chapter 9. These principles point to specific ways that companies can change their behaviors and practices to achieve the ecological sustainability demanded by the four core principles of The Natural Step process discussed in Chapter 2. Among the current signatories are Sun Oil, Arizona Public Service Company, Bethlehem Steel, General Motors, H. B. Fuller, and Polaroid Corporation. By signing the CERES Principles, companies agree to meet although clearly the signatories do not yet actually operate in sustainable ways.

World Business Council for Sustainable Development

The World Business Council for Sustainable Development (WBCSD) is a coalition of 170 transnational companies from 35 countries and 20 industry sectors that have the shared goal of a commitment to sustainable development through a triple-bottom-line orientation—economic, ecological, and social. The WBCSD aims to establish business leadership in the area of sustainability, innovation, and corporate social responsibility. The coalition has four main goals: business leadership in sustainability, policy development that will help businesses create a framework for sustainability, best-practice dissemination, and global outreach.[30]

WBCSD came about as a way to get businesses involved in the UN's Earth Summit in Rio in 1992, where Agenda 21 was developed. Since that time, in addition to providing information and bringing together the nearly 1,000 business leaders involved around issues of environment, the WBCSD has undertaken a number of projects, involving accountability, advocacy, capacity building, energy and climate, the role of the financial sector, sustainable livelihoods, and water.[31]

Responsible Care

Another example of an industry-led environmental effort is the Responsible Care initiative of the Chemical Manufacturers Association, which has received considerable public attention for its leadership. The chemical industry is, for obvious reasons, under significant pressure to improve its environmental performance. Like the CERES Principles, Responsible Care is a voluntary effort by chemical companies to commit to continual environmental, health, and safety improvements in a manner that is responsive to the public interest.[32] Significant aspects of Responsible Care are that companies signing on commit themselves to continually improving performance, collaboration to help improve each others' environmental performance, measuring progress, and gaining regular public input on their efforts. The effort operates through a set of guiding principles and detailed guidelines for management practice in six operating arenas important to chemical companies.

ISO 14000

Another set of emerging environmental standards to which many companies, particularly those operating in the European Union, are paying attention are the ISO 14000 standards. Modeled in part on the International Organization for Standardization (ISO) 9000 quality standards, ISO 14000 focuses companies' attention on environmental management, that is, on avoiding or minimizing the harmful effects of corporate activities on the environment. ISO 14000 and the related ISO 14001 auditing standards are largely industry driven and, unlike the CERES Principles, generally represent internally developed standards, rather than a more globally defined set of absolute standards and principles to which a company agrees to adhere.[33]

Like the CERES Principles, ISO 14000 emphasizes the operating policies and practices within the company, rather than the nature or use of products or services generated.[34] The goal of the ISO standards is to reduce harmful environmental effects of the production process itself that occur from pollution and waste or from depletion of natural resources. ISO 14000 is actually a family of related standards that attempts to align businesses, industries, governments, and consumers around common ecological interests. Generally, ISO expects that companies will develop their own standards and environmental management systems, in compliance with relevant legislation and regulations, and then audit their practices to assure conformance to internal standards. Companies operating under the ISO 14000 standards are also expected to focus on continual improvements in their environmental practices.

ISO 14000 standards emphasize several different aspects of environmental management, including life-cycle assessment, which describes the environmental performance of products, the integration of environment into design and development to improve environmental performance, and communication about environmental performance (e.g., through labels, declarations, and general corporate communications). Other aspects of this process, which is similar to the quality management process of plan, do, check, act, are ongoing monitoring of environmental performance and auditing performance.[35] Many companies now must use the ISO 9000 quality standards to compete successfully, simply because their allies demand it. A similar developmental cycle is likely for the ISO 14000 family of environmental standards and/or the CERES Principles. Hence, it makes sense for companies that wish to be leading corporate citizens to begin moving toward meeting such standards.

Global Accountability and Sustainability

Natural Capitalism

In their *Harvard Business Review* article "A Road Map for Natural Capitalism," Amory Lovins, L. Hunter Lovins, and Paul Hawken argue that simple changes in corporate practices can provide significant benefits that will not only protect the natural environment but also potentially be very profitable.[36] If the idea of natural capitalism—sustainability—truly takes hold (and earlier chapters of this book have provided a good deal of evidence that it well might), then becoming sustainable will require four dramatic shifts in business practices:

- Dramatically increase the productivity of natural resources by reducing wasteful practices, changing production design and technology, and stretching ecological resources significantly further than they are being stretched today.
- Shift to biologically inspired closed-loop production models, in which all the by-products of one process become an input for another process so that nothing is wasted.

- Move to a solutions-based business model, in which value is delivered as a flow of services rather than products and well-being is measure by satisfying expectations for quality, utility, and performance of products and services.

- Reinvest in natural capital by restoring, sustaining, and expanding the planet's ecosystem.[37]

In part, natural capitalism is based not on the law of diminishing returns, which informs much current economic thinking, but rather on a radically different perspective: the concept of expanding returns. This concept, which underpins approaches like lean manufacturing and whole system design, implies that saving a lot of resources can be less costly than saving a smaller amount.[38]

The authors of this radical approach to capitalism argue that by thinking about the whole system–the closed loop—leaders can find numerous small changes that result in big savings, a point that Peter Senge calls finding leverage in his important book *The Fifth Discipline.*[39]

Kodak Corporation, for example, eliminated 700,000 pounds of landfill waste and produced savings of $600,000 yearly by developing a new material that wraps photographic paper.[40] By changing from a foil wrapping that could not be recycled to a more environmentally friendly wrapping for its paper, the company found that it would actually save money, eliminate the landfill problem, and address ergonomic safety issues that were the original incentive for thinking about the change. Lovins and his coauthors argue that companies can go further and rethink manufacturing processes entirely, creating new products and processes that actually prevent waste in the first place. This technique, which requires shifting one's perspective away from looking just at production to looking at the whole system, is biologically based in the concept of "waste equals food."[41]

Respect for Human Dignity

Respect for human dignity and worth is at the core of all stakeholder relationships and certainly fundamental to the global principles businesses are expected to employ regarding basic human rights. In the following sections we will briefly explore some of the most important principles, and their promulgating organizations, to help provide a framework for leading corporate citizens. Basic human rights can be found within the sphere of civil society, where we begin this exploration. In addition to the UN Global Compact, there are a number of other important initiatives worthy of discussion.

Working Conditions: The Sweatshop Controversy

Companies that outsource production to suppliers in developing nations must establish pay standards. Forced in part by pressures from activist groups like United Students Against Sweatshops, Sweatshop Watch, Corporate Watch, UNITE, and the International Labor Organization (among many others), many companies now are paying much more attention to working conditions in supplier firms than they have had to do in the past.

Nike, Reebok, Liz Claiborne, Phillips–Van Heusen, and many other companies that have faced considerable controversy about their sourcing practices have banded together to form a self-regulatory association called the Fair Labor Association (FLA). The American Apparel Manufacturers Association (AAMA), which is an industry trade group, has also created a less stringent set of standards for monitoring factories.[42]

The Union of Needletrades, Industrial and Textile Employees (UNITE), the Retail, Wholesale and Department Store Union, and the Interfaith Center on Corporate Responsibility are among the activist groups that believe that corporate-based regulation of suppliers' working conditions is mainly a public relations, rather than a substantive, move. Sweatshop Watch, which combines labor and community (civil society) interests, argues that the real solutions to sweatshop conditions will come not from industry self-regulation but from implementation of enforceable labor standards and protection in international trade agreements and relatively standardized and enforced national and international laws.[43]

The companies forming the FLA hope that by regulating themselves, they will be able to avoid some of the negative publicity and associated diminishment of, their reputational capital and customer loyalty associated with activists uncovering human rights and worker abuses in supplier companies. Companies in industrialized nations sourcing from developing nations naturally argue that if they were to pay prevailing domestic wage rates to workers in developing nations, they would lose the very competitive advantage and economizing benefits they had sought to gain in outsourcing production in the first place.

Human rights and labor activists, on the other hand, argue that working conditions and pay scales need to be monitored not just by industry groups like the FLA and the AAMA, which are likely to be biased in favor of the companies, but by external and more objective monitors. In fact, activist groups have strongly criticized the formation of industry-based monitoring organizations. One activist group, Corporate Watch, converted its 1998 Greenwash Award into a "Sweatwash Award," given to the FLA because it was concerned that the creation of FLA would mean that only cosmetic, rather than real, improvements in working conditions would be made.[44] Governments of developing nations, of course, argue that transnational companies bring much-needed jobs and economic development to their nations; they are therefore sometimes willing to overlook transgressions of basic human rights and dignity in the interest of economic development.

Sweatshop Watch defines a sweatshop as "a workplace where workers are subject to extreme exploitation, including the absence of a living wage or benefits, poor working conditions and arbitrary discipline."[45] The following is an excerpt from the Sweatshop Watch's homepage, describing conditions in sweatshops both in the United States and in developing nations:

> The overwhelming majority of garment workers in the U.S. are immigrant women. They typically toil 60 hours a week in front of their machines, often without minimum wage or overtime pay. In fact, the Department of Labor estimates that more than half of the country's 22,000 sewing shops violate minimum wage and overtime laws. Many of these workers labor in dangerous conditions including blocked fire exits, unsanitary bathrooms, and poor ventilation. Government surveys reveal that 75% of U.S. garment shops violate safety and health laws. In addition, workers commonly face verbal and physical abuse and are intimidated from speaking out, fearing job loss or deportation.
>
> Overseas, garment workers routinely make less than a living wage, working under extremely oppressive conditions. Workers in Vietnam average $0.12 per hour, and workers in Honduras average $0.60 per hour. Sweatshops can be viewed as a product of the global economy. Fueled by an abundant supply of labor in the global market, capital mobility, and free trade, garment industry giants move from country to country seeking the lowest labor costs and the highest profit, exploiting workers the world over.[46]

Sweatshop conditions clearly fail to respect the basic human dignity of the workers who labor there. Companies that operate with integrity and hope to implement their vision and values through their stakeholder relationships, particularly with suppliers, need to be well aware of the conditions of work in those suppliers' operations. Integrity demands closely monitoring working conditions and assuring that employees are treated with respect and dignity, including providing a living wage even when economizing pressures push a company toward exploitive practices in the interest of a better financial bottom line. The values-driven company also pays attention to the social and ecological costs of its activities in, at minimum, a triple-bottom-line framework. (See Case 10.2 for a discussion of Nike, in particular.)

The Living Wage Debate

The criterion for wage payment that is rapidly evolving in the international community is the "living wage," which pegs the wage scale in any nation relative to the standard of living in that nation. Exactly how to calculate this living wage is yet undetermined; there are, however, various approaches, all of which attempt to ensure that basic human needs for shelter, food, and clothing are met. For example, one coalition of activists, academics, and representatives of developing countries defined living wages in the global garment and shoe industries. The living wage is defined as a take-home wage earned by working within the country's legal maximum hours per week (but not more that 48 hours) that provides nutrition, water, housing, energy, transportation, clothing, health care, child care, and education for the average family, plus some savings or discretionary income.[47]

The Sweatshop Watch has also attempted to define what is meant by a living wage in a way that accommodates the different standards for meeting basic needs in different nations. The method is presented in Note 10.1.

Business Week made the initial proclamation: "After years of pressure to stop abusive practices in Nike's overseas plants, CEO Philip Knight has decided to revamp labor policies. In doing so, he becomes the one applying pressure—on other US companies to match his new standards." In a program the company calls Transparency 101, Nike is working with external auditors from Pricewaterhouse-Coopers and Nike's internal compliance office to ensure that the company's foreign suppliers, which employ more than half a million workers, are in compliance with the company's standards.

To cope with the plethora of criticisms directed against it, Nike instituted labor standards that included external monitoring, hiring PricewaterhouseCoopers to do its audits, providing financial assistance to factories, and improving environmental standards and working conditions in its supplier factories. Among the benefits Nike hopes to supply are increased overtime pay, new counseling programs, better safety procedures, new recognition programs, better ventilation, cleaner working environments, and enhanced training programs in its supplier factories.

Of course, it's not always that easy to ensure that standards are being met. But for years Nike experienced firsthand what it is like to be targeted by human and labor rights activists unhappy with its practices—and the bad press that followed. Activist groups still keep a close watch on the company's activities in developing nations because, even with the standards in place, compliance is not always ensured. For example, after Nike instituted the new standards, activists found that the auditors overlooked major problems and therefore continued questioning both the company's motives and its performance.

Not only does Nike have to deal with the aftermath of all the bad press it received about its labor practices, but it also has to cope with competitive realities of shifting fads and fashions that have caused its sneaker sales to drop. The decline in sales occurred almost simultaneously with CEO Phil Knight's demand that the company "just do it" by meeting significantly higher labor standards while rebuilding the company competitively from top to bottom.

Despite years of efforts to improve its factories, Nike still faces criticisms from activists. The global activist nonprofit organization Oxfam has a NikeWatch Web site that tracks activities. The following is an excerpt from that site:

> Ever wondered, as you slipped on your sneakers or pulled on a pair of jogging shorts, what life might be like for the person who made them?
>
> Nike promotes sport and healthy living, but the lives of workers who make Nike's shoes and clothes in Asia and Latin America are anything but healthy. They live in severe poverty and suffer stress and exhaustion from overwork. Oxfam Community Aid Abroad is part of an international campaign to persuade Nike and other transnational corporations to respect workers' basic rights.

DISCUSSION QUESTIONS

1. Investigate Nike's current labor standards and practices.

2. Why has the company moved so aggressively to implement factory monitoring and ensure transparency?

3. What are the implications of the problems that Nike faced in the 1990s for its reputation as a leading corporate citizen?

4. Should Nike have put all of these resources into these monitoring and accountability systems? Why or why not?

Sources: Kelley Holland and Aaron Bernstein, "Nike Finally Does It," *Business Week*, May 25, 1998, pp. 46 ff; Louise Lee, "Can Nike Still Do It?" *Business Week*, February 21, 2000, pp. 12–128; www.nikebiz.com/labor/index.shtml; "Opening Comments before the Global Compact," Philip H. Knight, New York, July 26, 2000, www.nikebiz.com/media/n_compact.shtml; and Oxfam, "NikeWatch," www.oxfam.org.au/campaigns/nike/index.html (accessed July 2, 2004).

In 1998, a coalition of organizations hosted a Living Wage Summit, at which the following consensus about how to calculate a living wage was reached, and ultimately published by the activist organization Sweatshop Watch:

4. The cost of housing and energy is divided by the average number of adult wage earners. Housing and energy needs are considered to expand in proportion to the number of wage earners in the household.

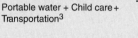

$$\text{Take home wage}^1 = \frac{\text{Average family size}^2}{\text{Average \# of adult wage earners}} \times \frac{\text{Cost of nutrition} + \text{Clothing} + \text{Health care} + \text{Education} + \text{Portable water} + \text{Child care} + \text{Transportation}^3}{\text{Average \# of adult wage earners}} + \frac{\text{Housing} + \text{Energy}^4}{} + \text{Savings}(10\% \text{ of income})^5$$

1. The take home wage is based on the number of hours worked in a legal working week (not exceeding 48 hours in one week). The take home wage is the worker's weekly net wage (subtracting out union dues, taxes, etc.).

2. The average family size is divided by the average number of adult wage earners in a family. As noted below, it has not yet been determined what data would be used to quantify this analysis.

3. This list of "basic needs" was derived from a larger list that also included: entertainment, vacation, paid family leave, retirement, life insurance and personal liability insurance. This list is not definitive and may vary depending on regional factors.

5. A random factor of 10 percent has been included for savings in order to permit workers to have some discretionary income and to allow workers to send money home to their families.

DISCUSSION QUESTIONS

1. What is the living wage for your area? (You will have to gather data to make the calculation.)

2. Does the minimum wage in your area enable families to earn a living wage?

3. If not, what policy recommendations would you make to local business leaders? To government officials?

Source: Sweatshop Watch, www.sweatshopwatch.org/swatch/wages/formula.html (accessed July 2, 2004).

Economic Sphere: Respect for the Economic System

By establishing high standards and operating principles and adhering to them, and, further, by engaging in dialogue about important issues with other stakeholders, business leaders can carve out a satisfactory economic agenda. If that agenda is to succeed long-term, however, it must be aligned with the agendas of stakeholders in the civil society and political spheres, who now have access to communications technology that enables them to transmit information, ideas, and plans globally virtually instantaneously. Thus, respect for all stakeholders' points of view is gaining in importance, and corporate citizens increasingly need to carry out their responsibilities with integrity, transparency, and accountability to satisfy their many constituencies.

Emerging Business Standards

Among the most notable of the groups that are developing voluntary standards for business practices with respect to labor, human rights, environment, and ethics is the Global Reporting Initiative (GRI), discussed in Chapter 8. The standards include the Caux Round Table Principles, the Global Sullivan Principles, and Organization for Economic Cooperation and Development's Guidelines for Multinational Enterprises. Additionally, in 2004, the International Organization for Standardization (ISO) which promulgates quality and environmental standards, announced that it would be broadening its scope to multiple stakeholders and developing guiding standards for corporate social responsibility.[48] ISO expects that its standards, which will not, at least in the short term, be used for certification purposes, will supplement existing standards and principles. The reputation of the ISO will lend great credibility to procedures that attempt to assure that companies are being responsible.

OECD Guidelines for Multinational Enterprises

Thirty-eight nations have agreed to a nonbinding set of guidelines for the behavior of multinational corporations through the Organization for Economic Cooperation and Development (OECD), to which 30 member nations and eight affiliates belong. These guidelines, called the OECD Guidelines for Multinational Enterprises, provide guidance on all aspects of firm behavior in the global arena, including employment and industrial relations, human rights, environment, information disclosure, competition, taxation, and science and technology.[49] By following these guidelines, companies can live up to societal and government expectations. Because they are issued by the OECD, the guidelines have a considerable credibility and are rapidly becoming one of the world's best sources of guidance for companies about their corporate responsibilities.[50]

Caux Principles for Business

The Caux Round Table, working in collaboration with the Minnesota Center for Corporate Responsibility, bases its principles for business on two basic ethical ideals. One ethical ideal is the Japanese concept of *kyosei*, which means living and working together for the common good, to enable cooperation and mutual prosperity to coexist with health and fair competition. The second ethical ideal is that of human dignity, which in Caux's usage simply refers to the sacredness or intrinsic value of each person as an end, not as a means to the fulfillment of others' purposes.[51] The Caux Round Table was founded in 1986 by Frederick Philips, former president of Philips

Electronics, and Olivier Giscard d'Estaing, vice chairman of INSEAD. Its purpose is to reduce trade tensions by enhancing economic and social relationships among participants' countries and focus generally on building a better world. The Caux principles build on an earlier effort by the Minnesota Center for Corporate Responsibility.[52] These principles attempt to move businesses and their leaders toward a perspective that says they should look first to their own actions and behaviors when they are determining what is the right thing to do.

Global Sullivan Principles

Similar in their intent to the UN Global Compact's 10 principles, the Global Sullivan principles were developed in 1977 by the Reverend Leon Sullivan, who was concerned about businesses participating in the then-apartheid regime in South Africa. Topics covered by the Global Sullivan Principles include universal human rights, equal opportunities, respect for freedom of association, levels of employee compensation, training, health and safety, sustainable development, fair compensation, and working partnership to improve quality of life. As of 2004, about 100 companies had become signatories.

Equator Principles

Demonstrating that the financial community increasingly recognizes the importance of principles, the Equator Principles were first adopted by 10 banks in 2003 and had accumulated 25 signatories in 14 countries within a year.[53] The principles are aimed at helping financial institutions adequately manage the social and environmental risks in financing projects around the world, particularly in emerging markets.

The Equator Principles Web site quotes Herman Mulder, a banking executive who helped bring about the principles, as saying: "It is our fundamental belief that the Equator Principles are appropriately becoming the reference standard for financial institutions to ensure that the principles of responsible environmental stewardship and socially responsible development are embedded within our project finance activities. Moreover, the Equator Principles are an excellent example how our financial sector is able to self-regulate on high value issues."[54]

Political Sphere

Companies operating in the global arena know that they need to understand how local governments operate in all of the countries where they locate facilities, market products and services, or source materials. They need to be aware of local rules and regulations, as well as the ways companies are expected to operate in different cultures and with respect to governments. Different ideologies make for very different contexts, each of which must be analyzed individually and discussed by corporate leaders to ensure that integrity is maintained.

One of the serious issues facing companies when they operate outside their homelands is the apparently differing standard of integrity in different cultures. In some countries, it seems, business leaders face corrupt officials (and businesspeople) when they attempt to operate locally. What companies have discovered, however, is that, difficult as it may be, sticking to their own internally developed values and standard of integrity is, in the long run, the best practice. In this section we will focus on dealing with corruption when operating in the global arena, particularly as it applies to the political sphere of activity.

Pervasive Corruption

"Corruption is found, to some degree, in every society. As a sign that something has gone wrong in the relationship between society and the state, corruption is becoming a pervasive phenomenon."[55] So begins Transparency International's source book on national integrity systems.

Transparency International (TI) is a Berlin-based international nongovernmental organization (INGO) that has as its mission increasing government accountability and curbing national and international corruption. Founded in 1993 by Peter Eigen, TI works by creating coalitions of people with integrity from all three spheres of activity.

Because corruption undermines the integrity of not only the business system but also the political and civil society systems, Transparency International has multiple concerns:

- humanitarian, as corruption undermines and distorts development and leads to increasing levels of human rights abuse;
- democratic, as corruption undermines democracies and in particular the achievements of many developing countries and countries in transition;
- ethical, as corruption undermines a society's integrity; and
- practical, as corruption distorts the operations of markets and deprives ordinary people of the benefits which should flow from them.[56]

Using a systems perspective on each country in which it operates, TI attempts to understand the causes, loopholes, and incentives feeding corrupt practices locally. It then attempts to determine the main types of corruption within the public domain and the leverage points for change within that system. According to TI, "Policy response to combating corruption has several elements common to every society: the reform of substantive programs; changes in the structure of government and its methods of assuring accountability; changes in moral and ethical attitudes; and, perhaps most importantly, the involvement and support of government, the private business sector, and civil society."[57] Some of these areas for change can be addressed quickly, while others require longer periods of time.

According to TI, reform efforts need to be both serious and concerted in order to be effective. TI has identified eight characteristics of successful corruption reform initiatives:

1. A clear commitment by political leaders to combat corruption wherever it occurs and to submit themselves to scrutiny.
2. Primary emphasis on prevention of future corruption and on changing systems (rather than indulging in witch hunts).
3. The adoption of comprehensive anticorruption legislation implemented by agencies of manifest integrity (including investigators, prosecutors, and adjudicators).
4. The identification of those government activities most prone to corruption and a review of both substantive law and administrative procedures.
5. A program to ensure that salaries of civil servants and political leaders adequately reflect the responsibilities of their posts and are as comparable as possible with those in the private sector.
6. A study of legal and administrative remedies to be sure that they provide adequate deterrence.
7. The creation of a partnership between government and civil society (including the private sector, professions, religious organizations).
8. Making corruption a "high-risk" and "low-profit" undertaking.

According to TI, five areas of reform are particularly helpful in reducing corrupt governmental practices: public programs, government reorganization, law enforcement, public awareness, and the creation of institutions to prevent corruption. Each country's situation must be analyzed to determine what specifically can be done, in part because action in any one of these areas will have ripple effects to the others, that is, they are part of a whole system where change needs to be leveraged to have the greatest effect.

TI also annually produces a Corruption Perceptions Index that ranks countries on a scale from 10 (highly clean) to 0 (highly corrupt). To create the index, TI consolidates the results of 16 different surveys, requiring a minimum of three surveys for each country included, so as to assure validity of the results.

Bribery Is Now Outlawed Globally

To cope with corruption globally requires enforceable and consistent laws on an international scale. There are positive signs that corruption is increasingly becoming less well accepted globally. For example, not only has TI made tremendous inroads into dealing openly with corrupt systems, but also in 1998 some 34 nations signed a new international treaty designed to outlaw bribery on a global scale.[58] Of these, 29 nations are members of the OECD; that is, they are among the largest economies in the world. Prior to this treaty, only the U.S. government had outlawed bribery, through the Foreign Corrupt Practices Act, which business leaders sometimes felt put their companies at a competitive disadvantage. With passage of this treaty, bribery became a criminal act in virtually every important economy in the world.

TI points out that company directors and leaders need to understand and accept their responsibility for staying within both the letter and the spirit of the law in countries where they operate. Voluntary codes of conduct, accompanied by internal enforcement procedures, can help companies sustain their integrity in the face of potential lost business when a bribe is not paid. And, as TI points out, "grand corruption is the enemy of high standards and efficiency,"[59] and thus goes against business's core value of economizing in the long run.

Accountability: Public Policy Mandate

Although responsibility management and assurance represent improvements in leading corporate citizenship, they are in many respects incomplete without a system of accountability. The principles described in this chapter and the initiatives discussed in Chapter 8 are still voluntary and have been adopted by but a small fraction of the estimated 70,000 transnational corporations in the world, and probably by an even smaller proportion of the many millions of small and medium-sized enterprises. Indeed, it appears that the largest, most visible brand-name companies are the ones adopting these standards of performance, while business-to-business companies and those without a certain degree of visibility go largely under the radar screen of accountability.

In the current U.S. legal system and increasingly those in other parts of the world, corporations are accountable only to their shareholders and only for profit maximization, without regard to the impacts that they might have on other stakeholders. While numerous U.S. states now permit companies to take other stakeholders' interest into consideration, the main thrust of current law is to embed a narrow shareholder orientation into corporate goals. Indeed, one legal expert and outspoken critic argues that corporate executives cannot legitimately pursue goals other than financial wealth. Further, he suggests that companies addressing any social goals at all, or even reducing profits to implement costly responsibility measures, is effectively illegitimate behavior.[60]

There is increasing recognition among critical observers of corporations that voluntary responsibility management approaches may not be enough to curb corporate power or forestall future abuses. Corporate critics argue for some significant countervailing power to the increasingly global power commanded by corporations.[61] This power could come from political nation-states or from the types of civil society and NGO interests expressed at protests against organizations like the World Trade Organization around the world during the late 1990s and early 2000s. It could involve political action by citizens to dismantle some of the privileges that have allowed corporations to gain the power they currently have.

Emerging Regulations and Laws

Despite the seemingly entrenched power of corporations and the unwillingness of many to pursue corporate citizenship in good faith, there are signs emerging in the early 2000s that accountability will be enforced through an array of new laws and regulations (see Table 10.3). In the wake of the many scandals, accounting irregularities, and evidence of financial misdealings and executive

TABLE 10.3 Social Disclosure Regulations in Existence as of 2004

Sources: European regulations are listed in the Reputation Institute's *In-Sights*, January–February 2004; information Japan is from Masahiko Kawamura, "Japanese Companies Launch New Era of CSR Management in 2003," Social Development Research Group, www.nli-research.co.jp/eng/resea/life/li030806.pdf (accessed April 22, 2004); and www.calpers.com/index.jsp?bc=/investments/riskmanagesystem.xml (accessed April 21, 2004).

Europe

United Kingdom	Socially Responsible Investment Regulation (2000) requires pension fund managers to disclose their policies on socially responsible investment, including shareholder activism.
Belgium	Social Label Law (2003) requires annual reporting indicating how CSR is assessed in pension funds.
France	Annual reports require social and environmental impact assessment of company activities (2001) if listed on the French stock exchange. Retirement funds should rely on financial and social criteria in investment selection.
Germany	Companies need to indicate how social and environmental policies are being integrated (2001), and companies must declare whether codes are being followed or not.
The Netherlands	Mandatory compliance with OECD guidelines for multinationals to obtain export credits (2002).
Norway	All enterprises need to include environmental reports in yearly balances (1999).
Sweden	All enterprises need to include environmental reports in yearly balances (1999).
European Commission	In a communication to the Parliament required that corporate. social responsibility criteria be introduced in legislation of member states.

Other Nations

Japan	As of 2003, audits of listed companies are required to disclose material information on risk related to corporate viability, including financial and business risks, but extending to reputation and "conspicuous deterioration of brand image."
Australia	As of 2003, a law passed in 2002 requires all investment firms to disclose how they take socially responsible investment into account.

United States

Sarbanes-Oxley Act (2002)	Establishes independence of audit committees on corporate boards, corporate responsibility for financial reports (CEOs and CFOs are required to certify the appropriateness of financial statements and disclosures), makes it unlawful for officers and directors to fraudulently influence, coerce, manipulate, or mislead auditors, forces repayment or forfeiture of bonuses and profits in the case of accounting restatements, allows the SEC to bar people who have violated SEC regulations from holding officer and

continued

concluded	
	director positions, prohibits insider trades during pension fund blackout periods, establishes rules of professional responsibility for attorneys, and authorizes the SEC to establish funds for the relief of victims.
Voluntary Pressure Tactics	CalPERS recently stated: "CalPERS has embarked on a large-scale project to develop and deploy a comprehensive framework for measuring, monitoring, and managing risk . . . Over the next several years, risk management will become a driving force in the decision-making process used for our portfolio management."
	A coalition of SRI firms, including Calvert, Citizens Funds, Domini Social Investments, Green Century, Capital Management, Parnassus, Trillium, and Walden Asset Management submitted a letter to the SEC in 2002 seeking disclosure of financially significant environmental risk.

greed in the United States, the Sarbanes-Oxley Act establishes at least some baseline requirements for boards of directors, chief corporate officers, and those who serve them.

Other interesting nonregulatory developments that will force corporate attention to social and environmental matters, in addition to financial ones, include the California Public Employees Retirement System's emphasis on good corporate governance and more recent attention to measuring, monitoring, and managing risk, including the types of risk that come with environmental and social problems (see Chapter 8). Further, a coalition of socially responsible investment (SRI) firms petitioned the U.S. Securities and Exchange Commission (SEC) in 2002 to require that companies disclose financially significant environmental risk. While not mandated into law at this point, such moves put new pressures on companies for transparency about their impacts and seek to hold them accountable.

Around the world, more proactive governments are beginning to establish new expectations of corporations and fund managers regarding triple-bottom-line issues. In the United Kingdom, for example, the 2000 Socially Responsible Investment Regulation requires pension fund managers to disclose policies on SRI, including shareholder activism. While pension fund managers do not actually have to *do* anything differently—or even take triple-bottom-line issues into account—the regulation creates significant peer pressure on pension fund managers to think about such matters and, by implication, companies as well. In 2001 France became the first nation in the world to require social and environmental impact assessment in corporate reports for all companies listed on the French stock exchange. In the wake of this law, French retirement funds need to rely on both financial and social criteria in making investment decisions. While implementation is not yet fully achieved, some progress is being made.

Germany, since 2001, has required companies to indicate how social and environmental policies are being integrated, and to declare whether or not codes of conduct are being followed. The Netherlands has required mandatory compliance with the OECD's Guidelines for Multinational Enterprises if companies are to obtain export credits since 2002. Sweden and Norway have required environmental reports since 1999. The European Commission has signaled its support of corporate responsibility and SRI generally through a white paper issued in 2002 and has communicated to the European Union's Parliament that corporate social responsibility criteria be introduced in legislation of member states.

As of 2003, audits of listed companies in Japan are required to disclose material information on risk related to corporate viability. Included risks go beyond financial and business risks to encompass reputational and brand-image-related risks. Finally, as of this writing at least, since 2003, Australia requires investment firms to disclose how they take SRI into account.

Such laws are only the very early steps of a framework capable of holding companies and investment managers accountable for social and ecological performance as well as financial performance. They do, however, signal a future that could conceivably be different than the present with respect to the art of corporate citizenship. In some ways, regulations like these play an important role in leveling the playing field for all companies, by establishing the same—and presumably fair—rules of the game to which all must adhere, rather than allowing some companies to forgo disclosure or operate without consideration for long-term social and ecological impacts. Accountability, responsibility, and transparency are the fundamental demands that companies are facing today to sustain their legitimacy in society—or maintain their so-called license to operate.

Leading Challenge Ahead: Responsibility Assurance

This chapter has identified a set of foundational principles for the issues of labor, human rights, system integrity, and environmental practices, based on what is contained in globally agreed-on (mostly UN-based) documents and the new regulations that are beginning to evolve around corporate accountability. These initiatives promulgate basic standards that *ought* to be followed by brands, retailers, and their suppliers around the globe. Of course, as evidenced by a continuing stream of exposés put forward by the BBC, the *New York Times*, *Sixty Minutes*, and a host of other outlets, frequently such standards are not met. After years of hard-won progress in the major industrialized countries on the range of issues covered by these foundation principles, the globalization of production and the disaggregation of supply chains appears to have brought us back full circle to some of the more egregious business practices of the past, including sweatshops, abusive working standards, and growing ecological deterioration.

Given this unsatisfactory state, it is not surprising to find a wide variety of initiatives emerging to better regulate companies, ensure compliance with standards, and establish some system of accountability and comparability. To avoid external regulation, many companies are engaged in the types of voluntary initiatives to monitor their own practices through codes of conduct or by joining initiatives that attest to their adherence to foundation principles.

Combined with internal responsibility management systems, these initiatives constitute the beginnings of a responsibility assurance system. We can see the outlines of a voluntary global system that establishes standards and enforces standards beginning to emerge, in part the result of civil society and NGO anticorporate activism, but at this point the system is still voluntary and many critics of globalization and of the power of the modern transnational firm believe that voluntary standards will need to be complemented by mandate. For example, the Global Compact, Global Reporting Initiative (GRI), SA 8000, and AA 1000 contain three core elements of responsibility assurance: standards of conduct or the foundational principles discussed above (e.g., the Global Compact), monitoring, verification, and certification processes to ensure that what companies say they are doing is what they are actually doing (e.g., AA 1000 and SA 8000), and reporting guidelines for reasonably standardized external communication of what is being done that is relatively comparable across companies and nations (e.g., GRI). Elements of the emerging responsibility system are:

- *Generally accepted foundation principles, values, and guidelines* that provide minimal standards that all companies are expected to meet with respect to core stakeholders and the natural environment.
- *Globally recognized systemic approaches to responsibility management* that can be applied uniquely to each company but provide for comparable levels of responsibility and stakeholder-related outcomes.
- *Globally accepted multiple-bottom-line audit and reporting guidelines* and principles that detail the content, scope, and credibility of what is reported, comparable to generally accepted accounting principles (GAAP).
- *Credible external verification, monitoring, and certification systems* built around overall responsibility management practices or related to specific issues (e.g., child labor, sweatshop working conditions, labor rights, living wage, environment, corruption).

Such voluntary initiatives may never satisfy corporate critics, particularly in light of the reality that, for example, of the nearly 70,000 transnational corporations, only about 1,500 had signed the Global Compact by late 2004, whose reach hardly extends to the millions of small and medium-sized enterprises in the world today. Peer pressure from companies within the same industry does have the capacity to shift corporate attention to the reporting of social and ecological as well as economic/financial performance—and what gets measured is what mangers tend to pay attention to.

Here we can make an analogy to the quality movement. Quality became a business imperative during the 1980s in part because of customer demands for better quality, in part because the Japanese had already set a high standard of quality that forced others to focus on quality, and in part because European Union companies began requiring that suppliers meet ISO quality standards.[62] Perhaps it will take a similar sequence of events around corporate responsibility, underlying corporate responsibility for all companies, branded or not, to begin taking foundation principles seriously. For instance, what might be the impact of current European Union companies requiring their suppliers to meet SA 8000 labor standards, to join the Global Compact, and to uphold the principles, reporting out using GRI standards?

Alternatively, what if several major transnational corporations that have long or extensive supply chains (e.g., Wal-Mart) or employ people on a global basis (e.g., McDonald's) determined that they and all of their suppliers had to be certified as meeting foundational standards? The chain reaction of such a move would create a cascade effect, as in the quality movement, that would make the meeting of foundation principles a way of doing business. Resultant attention from the general public, the press, and competitors could conceivably create an entirely new context in which foundation principles are met as part of the company's basic license to operate—its fundamental social contract.

The world today is far from either voluntary or mandated assurance that foundation principles—basic human and labor rights, ecological principles, or the transparency that provides trust in the integrity of the system—are in fact being implemented. Yet forces are pushing companies to make corporate citizenship real, not just rhetoric. Only time, competitive conditions, political will, and underlying social movements will determine whether the ultimate outcome is in the best interests of humanity—meeting the basic needs of people for respect and dignity, of human civilization for a sustainable global ecology, of democracy for systemic integrity.

For leaders of corporate citizens, the emergence of standards, and continued demands for transparency and accountability pose significant new challenges—and new ways of doing business in the global context. Standards around labor practices, human rights, the use of environmental resources, and government regulations have gained great public awareness over the past two decades. This attention to making corporations accountable for their impacts is unlikely to diminish in an age where members of civil society who care about the ways in which people are treated and about the health of the natural environment are now globally connected. Corporations, it is likely, will be held accountable for their actions and held to very high standards indeed if they hope to continue their global march.

For leading corporate citizens, the message is clear. Being out in front of the wave of potential global regulation is one way to achieve competitive advantage. Companies that attempt to hide behind veils of secrecy will only become subject to activism, protests, and negative publicity that damage their reputations and their credibility. Leaders of corporate citizens who recognize the significant advantages to be gained in being forthcoming with and respectful of external stakeholders by adhering to high standards will truly put their companies into the lead. We all depend on a healthy ecological system for our very breath and sustenance. The economic system needs to be free, but it also needs to operate within the rules that societies establish in order to balance the interests of consumption and materialism with other values in society. The political sphere needs to operate with integrity, free of corruption and abuse if people are to live freely themselves and if democratic values are truly to spread throughout the world, as many people believe desirable. And enterprises in civil society need to be active participants in the economic and political systems, carrying a strong voice for the socializing effects of relationships, meaning, and values that bring civility to the world.

The principles and standards discussed in this chapter, and others that had to be omitted in the interests of time and space, are among the most important features of the modern economic and societal systems in which we live. We all need to learn to operate with integrity, individually and organizationally, and these standards provide a positive and proactive set of guideposts to help us along the way.

Endnotes

1. Portions of this chapter are drawn from two of my papers. The discussion on principles, and some of the conclusions, are from Sandra Waddock, "Creating Corporate Accountability: Foundational Principles to Make Corporate Citizenship Real," *Journal of Business Ethics* 50 (2004), pp. 313–27. The discussion on emerging regulations is drawn from Sandra Waddock, "Unfolding Corporate Citizenship: New Demands for a New Era," in *Corporate Social Responsibility*, ed. José Allouce (New York: Palgrave-McMillan, in press).

2. See, for example, Naomi Klein *No Logo: No Space, No Choice, No Jobs* (New York: Picador, 2000); or Eric Schlosser, *Fast Food Nation: The Dark Side of the All-American Meal* (Boston: Houghton Mifflin, 2001).

3. See, www.investorhome.com/sri.htm (accessed July 6, 2004). This screen is notably broad, including shareholder resolutions as well as direct investments in screened companies and mutual funds.

4. See, for example, Pietra Rivoli, "Labor Standards in the Global Economy: Issues for Investors," *Journal of Business Ethics* 43, no. 30 (March 2003), pp. 223–32; see also Samuel B. Graves, Kathleen Rehbein, and Sandra Waddock, "Fad and Fashion in Shareholder Activism: The Landscape of Social Policy Resolutions, 1988–1998," *Business and Society Review* 106, no. 4 (Winter 2001), pp. 293–314.

5. See Rivoli, "Labor Standards in the Global Economy."

6. See ILO, "Business and Social Initiatives," http://oracle02.ilo.org:6060/vpi/VpiSearch.First?p_lang=en.

7. See, for example, D. O'Rourke, "Monitoring the Monitors: A Critique of PricewaterhouseCooper's Labor Monitoring," white paper, released September 28, 2000; and Stephen J. Frenkel, "Globalization, Athletic Footwear Commodity Chains and Employment Relations in China," *Organization Studies* 22, no. 4 (2001), pp. 531–62.

8. Thomas Donaldson and Thomas W. Dunfee, "Toward a Unified Conception of Social Contracts Theory," *Academy of Management* 19, no. 2 (1994), pp. 252–84; and Thomas Donaldson and Thomas W. Dunfee, *Ties That Bind: A Social Contracts Approach to Business Ethics* (Boston: Harvard Business School Press, 1999), p. 265. See also, Thomas Donaldson, "Values in Tension: Ethics Away from Home," *Harvard Business Review*, September–October 1996, Reprint # 96402, pp. 1–12.

9. M. S. Schwartz, "A Code of Ethics for Corporate Codes of Ethics," *Journal of Business Ethics* 41, no. 1/2 (November–December 2002), pp. 27–42.

10. J. N. Behrman, "Adequacy of International Codes of Behavior," *Journal of Business Ethics* 31, no. 1 (May 2001), pp. 51–63.

11. Donaldson and Dunfee, *Ties That Bind.*

12. Donaldson, "Values in Tension," p. 6.

13. James McGregor Burns, *Leadership* (New York: Harper Torchbooks, 1978).

14. Donaldson, "Values in Tension," pp. 7–8.

15. UNWire, "Globalization: NGOs Assail UN Ties to Corporate-Led Trend," September 7, 2000, www.unfoundation.org/unwirebw/archives/show_article.cfm?article=1173 (accessed July 6, 2004).

16. Laura P. Hartman, Bill Shaw, and Rodney Stevenson, "Exploring the Ethics and Economics of Global Labor Standards: A Challenge to Integrated Social Contract Theory," *Business Ethics Quarterly* 13, no. 2 (April 2003), pp. 193–225.

17. Donaldson and Dunfee, *Ties That Bind.*

18. Hartman, Shaw, and Stevenson, "Exploring the Ethics and Economics of Global Labor Standards."

19. Ibid.

20. Transparency International Web site, www.transparency.org/welcome.html.

21. Ibid.

22. UN Global Compact Web site, www.unglobalcompact.org/Portal/?NavigationTarget=/ roles/portal_user/dialogue/Dialogue/nf/nf/transparency (accessed July 2, 2004).

23. Donaldson and Dunfee, *Ties That Bind*, p. 68.

24. James Lovelock, *Gaia: A New Look at Life on Earth* (New York: Oxford University Press, 2000).

25. UN Global Compact Web site, www.unglobalcompact.org/Portal/?NavigationTarget=/ roles/portal_user/aboutTheGC/nf/nf/theNinePrinciples (accessed July 2, 2004).

26. The full text of Agenda 21 can be found at www.unep.org/Documents/Default.asp? DocumentID=52unep/neworg.htm (accessed July 6, 2004).

27. The Rio Declaration can be found at www.unep.org/unep/rio.htm (accessed July 6, 2004).

28. From Agenda 21, gopher://unephq.unep.org:70/00/un/unced/agenda21/a21c02.txt.

29. Additional information about CERES and the CERES Principles can be found at www.ceres.org (accessed July 6, 2004).

30. World Business Council for Sustainable Development Web site, www.wbcsd.ch/ templates/TemplateWBCSD1/layout.asp?type=p&MenuId=NjA&doOpen= 1&ClickMenu=LeftMenu (accessed July 2, 2004).

31. Ibid.

32. Information and the complete set of principles for Responsible Care can be found at www.dowethics.com/r/environment/care_info.html (accessed July 6, 2004).

33. For an extended discussion of ISO 14000 and 14001, see Amy Pesapane Lally, "ISO 14000 and Environmental Cost Accounting: The Gateway to the Global Market," *Law & Policy in International Business* 29, no. 4 (Summer 1998), pp. 401–538.

34. Additional information on ISO and the various sets of standards can be found at www.iso.ch.

35. Information about the ISO 14000 family of standards can be found at www.iso.ch/iso/en/prods-services/otherpubs/iso14000/index.html (accessed June 15, 2004).

36. Amory B. Lovins, L. Hunter Lovins, and Paul Hawken, "A Road Map for Natural Capitalism," *Harvard Business Review*, May–June 1999, pp. 145–58.

37. Ibid., pp.146–48.

38. Ibid., p.148.

39. Peter M. Senge, *The Fifth Discipline* (New York: Free Press, 1990).

40. See www.kodak.com/US/en/corp/environment/1998/kodakPark/savingsRecycling.shtml.

41. Lovins et al., "A Road Map for Natural Capitalism," p. 152.

42. See, for example, Aaron Bernstein, "Sweatshop Reform: How to Solve the Standoff," *Business Week*, May 3, 1999, pp. 186–90.

43. See www.sweatshopwatch.org/swatch/about (accessed July 6, 2004).

44. See www.corpwatch.org/trac/greenwash/sweatwash.html (accessed July 6, 2004).

45. From www.sweatshopwatch.org/swatch/industry (accessed July 6, 2004).

46. Ibid.

47. From Sweatshop Watch Web site, www.sweatshopwatch.org/swatch/newsletter/4_2.html#living_wage (accessed July 6, 2004).

48. International Organization for Standardization (ISO) Web site, www.iso. org/iso/en/commcentre/pressreleases/2004/Ref924.html (accessed July 12, 2004).

49. For more information, see the OECD Web site, www.oecd.org (accessed July 2, 2004).

50. OECD Guidelines, "Report by the Chair, 2003." www.oecd.org/dataoecd/3/47/15941397. pdf (accessed July 2, 2004).

51. Details about the Caux Round Table and this framing of the two ethical ideals can be found at www.cauxroundtable.org/default.htm.

52. The Caux Roundtable principles can be found at http://astro.temple.edu/~dialogue/Codes/caux./htm (accessed July 2, 2004).

53. Information on the Equator Principles can be found at www.equator-principles.com (accessed July 2, 2004).

54. Quoted in ibid.

55. Jeremy Pope, *TI Source Book 2000: Confronting Corruption: The Elements of a National Integrity System*, www.transparency.org/source-book/index.html (accessed July 6, 2004).

56. Transparency International Web site, www.transparency.com

57. Pope, *TI Source Book*, Executive Summary, p. 2.

58. Information in this paragraph is from Skip Kaltenheuser, "Bribery Is Being Outlawed Virtually Worldwide," *Business Ethics*, May–June 1998, p. 11.

59. Pope, *TI Source Book*, Part B, p. 3.

60. Joel Bakan, *The Corporation: The Pathological Pursuit of Profit and Power* (New York: Free Press, 2004).

61. Ibid. See also John Cavanagh and colleagues, *Alternatives to Economic Globalization* (San Francisco: Berrett-Koehler, 2002); Charles Derber, *Regime Change Begins at Home: Freeing America From Corporate Rule* (San Francisco: Berrett-Koehler, 2004).

62. J. R. Evans and W. M. Lindsay, *The Management and Control of Quality*, 4th ed. (New York: West, 1999).

CHAPTER ELEVEN

Values Added: Global Futures

Mister! He said with a sawdusty sneeze,
I am the Lorax. I speak for the trees.
I speak for the trees, for the trees have no tongues.
And I'm asking you, sir, at the top of my lungs—
He was very upset as he shouted and puffed—
What's that THING you've made out of my Truffula tuft?

. . . So I quickly invented my Super-Axe-Hacker
which whacked off four Truffula Trees at one smacker.
We were making Thneeds
four times as fast as before!
And that Lorax? . . . He didn't show up any more.

But the very next week
he knocked
on my new office door.
He snapped. I'm the Lorax who speaks for the trees
which you seem to be chopping as fast as you please . . .

I meant no harm. I most truly did not. But I had to grow bigger.
   So bigger I got.
I biggered my factory. I biggered my roads.
I biggered my wagons. I biggered the loads
of the Thneeds I shipped out. I was shipping them forth

to the South! To the East! To the West! To the North!
I went right on biggering . . . selling more Thneeds
And I biggered my money, which everyone needs . . .

I yelled at the Lorax, Now listen here, Dad!
All you do is yap-yap and say, Bad! Bad! Bad! Bad!
Well, I have my rights, sir, and I'm telling *you*
I intend to go on doing just what I do!
And, for your information, you Lorax, I'm figgering
on biggering
and biggering
and BIGGERING
and BIGGERING,
turning MORE Truffula Trees into Thneeds
which everyone, EVERYONE, *EVERYONE* needs!

And at that very moment, we heard a loud whack!
From outside in the fields came a sickening smack
of an axe on a tree. Then we heard the tree fall.
The very last Truffula Tree of them all!
No more trees. No more Thneeds. No more work to be done.

Dr. Seuss, The Lorax[1]

Scanning the Future: Finding Pattern in Chaos

Leading corporate citizens know that they need to think through the consequences of their decisions and actions carefully, lest we end up with "No more trees . . . No more work to be done." They also need to understand very clearly the forces at play not only in the competitive/economic sphere but also in the political and civil society spheres. Corporate leaders are learning that they need to operate in sustainable ways with respect to the natural environment because of the limitations of the ecological system in supporting life as we know it on earth. To further this learning, we need to enhance awareness of what is likely to happen in the future.

We cannot predict the future, but we can understand patterns and potentials. Like many of the dynamics and relationships we have explored in this book, future trends are embedded in chaotic processes, the immediate outcomes of which cannot be known. Chaos and complexity theories tell us that *we can seek patterns that provide significant insights.* These patterns become evident when we look carefully at dynamics and think creatively about what is happening now, what might happen, and what the implications are.

Using all of our leadership insights and our expanded awareness so that we can hold multiple perspectives (remember the higher stages of development discussed in Chapter 3), we can explore what might initially seem to be a chaos of information, trends, and interrelationships. The future actually exhibits large-scale patterns that can help us think through appropriate actions that provide significant expertise in coping with a changing world. To do this effectively, we need to know how to study the future, what data to look at, and how to think more creatively about possibilities.

To do futures pattern seeking, leading corporate citizens carefully monitor the shifting dynamics and concerns of their multiple stakeholders, as well as the broader (and, importantly, more subtle) technological, competitive, and social shifts that take place throughout the various societies in which they operate. They do this monitoring not only because these forces and dynamics may pose problems but also because they represent interesting and potentially profitable new opportunities for business development. If one company overlooks opportunities or challenges, other companies that pay closer attention can gain competitive advantage.

Once a company uncovers current trends, data, and patterns, it can use a range of techniques to project these patterns out into the future and think about their potential implications for the enterprise. One such technique, called scenario analysis, has been used successfully by Royal Dutch/Shell, among other prominent companies. Scenario analysis was particularly helpful to Shell in preparing for falling oil prices (which some observers had considered unrealistic) in the 1980s. Other techniques are future search conferences and open space meetings; we will explore these at the end of the chapter.

For any corporate citizen, having a futures monitoring role is a critical element of the boundary-spanning functions discussed in Chapter 6. The company can use information gathered within functions to develop future scenarios to help prepare for any of multiple possible outcomes. It is important that leaders of corporate citizens heed the advice of baseball great Yogi Berra, who once said, "If you don't know where you're going, you wind up somewhere else."[2]

This chapter will explore some of the current dynamics and trends that will shape the future. It will provide a basic framework for thinking about the ways in which leading corporate citizens can cope with the inevitable patterns of change and complexity they will face in creating and sustaining positive relationships with their stakeholders. The values are added, as the chapter title suggests, because we need to think not only about sustainability but also about what is meaningful to people, to stakeholders, and ultimately to ourselves as citizens of organizations, of particular societies, and of the world.

The Shape of the Future

What is it that shapes our future? Although we as human beings have little control over nature, we do in many senses control our own destiny. We make decisions that impact our future on a daily basis, whether in our leadership capacities or within the companies we manage. For example, to the extent that we take stewardship responsibility for our own impacts on the ecological environment, nature will reward us bountifully. To the extent that we provide for appropriate balance among the three spheres of activity in human civilization, not only with respect to the natural environment but also with respect to each other, societies will be productive and meaningful places in which to live, work, and play. And it is developing meaningful relationships within society and respecting all stakeholders that are keys to long-term effectiveness (and efficiency, or economizing) of leading corporate citizens.

The world of tomorrow will continue to change rapidly, even chaotically. But, as we have learned from thinking about life processes organically and applying that thinking to our ideas of management, even chaotic systems have patterns that are, to a large extent, comprehensible and understandable. Understanding patterns and developing new ways of thinking about the implications of even potential patterns can help raise awareness of the implications of corporate decisions on stakeholders and nature. Ultimately, it can also help us lead better lives as individuals in society and as corporate citizens.

Clearly, understanding future patterns demands relatively high levels of cognitive, emotional, and moral development. As developmental psychologist Robert Kegan puts it, without this development, we will really be *In Over Our Heads*[3] amid the "mental demands of modern life." Tomorrow's leaders will need to work productively to develop a sense of what is meaningful to others and to think through the systems implications of their decisions to move themselves toward understanding the future. Such systems thinking—built as it is on understanding where the points of leverage are and what the interactions among different variables, issues, and relationships mean—also requires shifting perspectives to encompass data that might ordinarily be ignored or overlooked. Small shifts, as chaotic systems illustrate, can result in large changes down the road. As leaders of corporate citizens, we need to be intensely aware not only of the larger patterns of society but also of the small shifts that can provide meaningful opportunities—or challenges—in the future.

This chapter presents some current data on the state of the world, then looks at some of the predictions that futurists—people who study the future—are making that are likely to affect leaders and leading corporate citizens. Let us begin this exploration with some information about the current state of the world's social, political, economic, and ecological spheres. Then we will look at predictions of challenges and opportunities made by futurists that will inevitably (even if we don't know exactly how) shape global futures.

The State of the World

The United Nations Development Program (UNDP) established a set of Millennium Goals in 2000 that it hoped to achieve by 2015. (Table 11.1 lists the goals and summarizes progress made toward them as of 2004.) These goals deal with the world's major problems of poverty, lack of education, and inequity. Businesses have important roles to play in achieving these goals.

Huge social problems exist in the world beyond the ecological problems discussed in Chapter 8. For example, although there are reports that the AIDS epidemic may be slowing down, the U.S. National Institute of Allergy and Infectious Diseases reported in January 2004 that some 40 million people globally—37 million adults and 2.5 million children—were living with HIV/AIDS. Nearly two-thirds of these people live in sub-Saharan Africa, and another 18 percent are in Asia and the Pacific. These numbers translate to a global epidemic affecting about 11 of every 1,000 adults, with as much as 8 percent of the population in sub-Saharan Africa affected.[4] Further, the UNDP reports that 28 million people had already died of HIV/AIDS by 2001 and that without a massive intervention as many as 100 million people were expected to be affected; seven countries already have more than 20 percent of their populations affected, and two countries, Botswana and Zimbabwe, have rates as high as 39 percent and 34 percent, respectively.[5]

Other problems are highlighted by the following statistics. For example, although the percentage of people in the world living on less than a dollar a day dropped from 40 percent to 21 percent between 1981 and 2001, progress is unevenly distributed, with countries in Asia and Southeast Asia benefiting the most from economic development, and countries in Africa, Latin America, Eastern Europe, and Central America the least.[6] A group called World Centric has gathered some startling statistics that are included in Table 11.2. The challenge for leading corporate citizens is to find ways of doing business in a world that increasingly demands attention to issues of not only ecology but also social sustainability—and to do so in a way that fosters social justice rather than injustice.

The statistics in Table 11.2 are startling enough, but evidence of the gap between the haves and the have-nots in the world continues to mount. This shift in the distribution of wealth brings significant implications for the potential growth and prosperity of nations as well as of companies. Thinking about the differences between wealthy and less wealthy nations and people suggests that there may be new business opportunities in serving less developed nations with ecologically sustainable products that still meet their needs, while attempting to close the growing gap between rich and poor.

We have already recognized that economic development cannot continue apace without consideration of what is ecologically and socially sustainable. Sustainability in this case also includes the sustainability of democratic institutions, free-market economies, and healthy local communities in the face of enormous inequities in the distribution and use of resources. The wide availability of information will create significant disturbances among peoples with less if some

TABLE 11.1 The UNDP's Millennium Goals and Progress Made toward Them

Source: UNDP Web site, www.undp.org/mdg/abcs.html#Indicators (accessed July 7, 2004).

1. Eradicate Extreme Poverty and Hunger

Target for 2015: Halve the proportion of people living on less than a dollar a day and those who suffer from hunger.

More than a billion people still live on less than a dollar a day; sub-Saharan Africa, Latin America and the Caribbean, and parts of Europe and Central Asia are falling short of the poverty target.

2. Achieve Universal Primary Education

Target for 2015: Ensure that all boys and girls complete primary school.

As many as 113 million children worldwide do not attend school, but the target is within reach. India, for example, should have 95 percent of its children in school by 2005.

3. Promote Gender Equality and Empower Women

Targets for 2005 and 2015: Eliminate gender disparities in primary and secondary education preferably by 2005, and at all levels by 2015.

Two-thirds of illiterates are women, and the rate of employment among women is two-thirds that of men. The proportion of seats in parliaments held by women is increasing, reaching about one-third in Argentina, Mozambique, and South Africa.

4. Reduce Child Mortality

Target for 2015: Reduce by two-thirds the mortality rate among children under five.

Every year nearly 11 million young children die before their fifth birthday, mainly from preventable illnesses, but that number is down from 15 million in 1980.

5. Improve Maternal Health

Target for 2015: Reduce by three-quarters the ratio of women dying in childbirth.

In the developing world, the risk of dying in childbirth is 1 in 48, but virtually all countries now have safe motherhood programs.

6. Combat HIV/AIDS, Malaria and Other Diseases

Target for 2015: Halt and begin to reverse the spread of HIV/AIDS and the incidence of malaria and other major diseases.

Forty million people are living with HIV, including 5 million newly infected in 2001. Countries like Brazil, Senegal, Thailand, and Uganda have shown that the spread of HIV can be stemmed.

7. Ensure Environmental Sustainability

Targets:

- *Integrate the principles of sustainable development into country policies and programs and reverse the loss of environmental resources.*

continued

concluded

- *By 2015, reduce by half the proportion of people without access to safe drinking water.*
- *By 2020 achieve significant improvement in the lives of at least 100 million slum dwellers.*

More than 1 billion people lack access to safe drinking water, and more than 2 billion lack sanitation. During the 1990s, however, nearly 1 billion people gained access to safe water and the same number to sanitation.

8. Develop a Global Partnership for Development

Targets:

- *Develop further an open trading and financial system that includes a commitment to good governance, development and poverty reduction—nationally and internationally.*
- *Address the least developed countries' special needs, and the special needs of land-locked and small island developing states.*
- *Deal comprehensively with developing countries' debt problems.*
- *Develop decent and productive work for youth.*
- *In cooperation with pharmaceutical companies, provide access to affordable essential drugs in developing countries.*
- *In cooperation with the private sector, make available the benefits of new technologies—especially information and communications technologies.*

Indicators

Many developing countries spend more on debt service than on social services. New aid commitments made in the first half of 2002 could mean an additional $12 billion per year by 2006.

UNDP, in collaboration with national governments, is coordinating reporting by countries on progress toward the UN Millennium Development Goals. The framework for reporting includes eight goals—based on the UN Millennium Declaration. For each goal there is one or more specific target, along with specific social, economic, and environmental indicators used to track progress toward the goals.

The eight goals represent a partnership between the developed countries and the developing countries determined, as the Millennium Declaration states, "to create an environment—at the national and global levels alike—which is conducive to development and the elimination of poverty."

Support for reporting at the country level includes close consultation by UNDP with partners in the UN Development Group, other UN partners, the World Bank, IMF and OECD and regional groupings and experts, The UN Department of Economic and Social Affairs is coordinating reporting on progress toward the goals at the global level.

Monitoring progress is easier for some targets than for others and good quality data for some indicators are not yet available for many countries. This underscores the need to assist countries in building national capacity in compiling vital data.

TABLE 11.2 **Some Facts about Our World**

Source: World Centric, www.worldcentric.org/state/#rich (accessed July 7, 2004).

Rich and Poor World

- The amount of money that the richest 1 percent of the world's people make each year equals what the poorest 57 percent make.
- The world's 358 billionaires have assets exceeding the combined annual incomes of countries with 45 percent of the world's people.
- The richest 5 percent of the world's people have incomes 114 times that of the poorest 5 percent.
- The combined wealth of the world's 200 richest people hit $1 trillion in 1999; the combined incomes of the 582 million people living in the 43 least developed countries is $146 billion.
- The GDP (Gross Domestic Product) of the poorest 48 nations (i.e., a quarter of the world's countries) is less than the wealth of the world's three richest people combined.
- A few hundred millionaires now own as much wealth as the world's poorest 2.5 billion people.
- An analysis of long-term trends shows the distance between the richest and poorest countries was about: 5 to 1 in 1820; 11 to 1 in 1913; 35 to 1 in 195-; 44 to 1 in 1973; 72 to 1 in 1992.

Consumption/Waste

- 20% of the population in the developed nations consume 86% of the world's goods.
- A mere 12% of the world's population uses 85% of its water, and these I2% do not live in the Third World.
- Globally, the 20% of the world's people in the highest-income countries account for 86% of total private consumption expenditures—the poorest 20% a minuscule 1.3%. More specifically, the richest fifth:
  1. Consume 45% of all meat and fish, the poorest fifth 5%.
  2. Consume 58% of total energy, the poorest fifth less than 4%.
  3. Have 74% of all telephone lines, the poorest fifth 1.5%.
  4. Consume 84% of all paper, the poorest fifth 1.1%.
  5. Own 87% of the world's vehicle fleet, the poorest fifth less than 1%.
- U.S. per capita consumption of paper is 681 pounds per year—7 trees a year.
- 91% of paper comes at the expense of 4 billion trees per year.
- The human race as a whole generates over 350 million metric tons of hazardous waste each year; the United States generates 180 million tons, or 4 pounds a day per person.
- 5 percent of the world's population lives in the U.S., but Americans produce 50 percent of the world's waste.
- Mobile phones will be discarded at a rate of 130 million per year by 2005, resulting in 65,000 tons of waste.
- 75% of all carbon dioxide emissions are caused by the industrialized world.
- The cost of providing basic health care and nutrition for all would be less than is spent in Europe and the U.S. on pet food.

moves are not made to close the growing gap, sometimes called the digital divide. The gap exists between rich and poor in most if not all nations, as well as, generally speaking, between northern and southern countries or, alternatively, developed and developing nations.

New, more ecologically sensitive and responsible practices are needed to serve the needs of the billions of people in the world who now live in poverty. Businesses, obviously, have an essential role to play in developing the goods and services needed to close these gaps. What is true, however, is that facing up to these global realities means that some significant shifts in lifestyle and production processes may be needed, particularly for wealthier and more powerful citizens. For aware and innovative leading corporate citizens, significant opportunities may exist.

Global Trends, Issues and Opportunities

Certain significant trends, issues, and opportunities—some technological, some economic, others social and political—make understanding the complexities of global dynamics an imperative for those leading corporate citizens today. Some trends may also provide significant business opportunities for creative entrepreneurs. Futurists can help provide understanding by identifying significant shifts in the world around us. The next two sections of this chapter will briefly explore some of the major shifts likely to affect corporate citizens in the 21st century.

Trends

The Center for Strategic and International Studies (CSIS) in Washington, D.C., has developed a project called the Millennium Project, which has attempted to identify the major trends in the world today.[7] Michael J. Mazarr, author of a report titled *Global Trends 2005*, says of the current era:

> The basic transition . . . is from the industrial era of human society, around since the late 18th century, to a new age that goes by a variety of names—the information age, the postmodern era, and others. We call it the "knowledge era," because one way (though only one) of understanding it is as a time when the acquisition, diffusion, use, storage, and transmission of knowledge becomes the basic activity of human societies. This one fundamental shift will refashion all the institutions of our lives.

If Mazarr and the panel of experts that CSIS has put together are correct, leaders of corporate citizens have a lot to think about in figuring out how to responsibly manage their relationships in all spheres of human society and the environment. *Global Trends 2005* focuses on six major trends, which can be presented here only in simplified terms, hardly in all of their complexity. Citizens in all spheres of society, and particularly corporate citizens, clearly need to be aware of and know how to cope with these trends effectively if they hope to sustain competitive advantage—and, simultaneously, build collaborative relationships with stakeholders essential to productive engagement in their worlds.

Mazzar and the other futurists identify several foundations as part of the first trend: demography, natural resources, and the environment and culture.

Demography, Ecology, Culture

Although the world's population *growth rate* is slowing (see Case 11.1), population itself continues to grow and will do so until it levels off somewhere between 8 and 12 billion people globally. Trends of modernization, education, and expansion of women's rights reduce fertility and have tended to slow the rate of population growth. But because 95 percent of that growth will occur in less developed countries, the gap between rich and poor can be expected to widen and processes of urbanization, already under way, will likely continue.

Although sustainable development is gaining momentum, population growth and many current organizational practices will place significant strains on the natural environment. Although knowledge businesses are less dependent on the ecology than industrial businesses are, significant ecological problems can be expected with respect to agricultural yields, demand for crop lands, the intensity of modern farming methods, with resulting soil erosion, desertification, and overfarming, and a crisis in fisheries. Some 80 countries already face significant water shortages, and this problem is only likely to be exacerbated by continued population growth.

As we discussed in Chapter 2, culture and ideology are essential aspects of human life and one of the foundational elements of the Millennium Project's projections. As Mazarr points out, culture plays an essential role in determining a nation's economic prospects, as well as its international relationships.[8]

Science, Technology, Modernization

An important factor in the dynamics facing corporate citizens, according to the Millennium Project, has to do with the push supplied by science and technology, which in turn contribute to the process of modernization. Among the technological and scientific shifts that can be expected are processes of miniaturization, biogenetic engineering, and continued revolution in information and communications technology (including the information thereby made available). The gap between rich and poor will intensify the gap between the information/technology rich and poor as well, as access to technological advances becomes essential to taking a role in the modern world.

Mazarr observes, "Richer countries tend to look the same—freer, more individualistic and less hierarchical, more concerned with the environment."[9] Not only does this "looking alike" tend toward greater homogeneity, but it also places considerable pressures for constructive—toward democratic—reform on repressive regimes. And, Mazarr notes, this process may well result in more peace and less war!

Human Resources and Complexity

The third trend identified by the Millennium Project involves the move toward a knowledge-based economic system and the resulting expected increased attention

Population Explosion Ends in a Whimper

If asked to make a list of the top 5 or 10 problems facing the world, most people educated in developed countries would include overpopulation. We have grown up with the threat of the population bomb, and with great hoopla and concern the global population crossed the 6 billion mark in the year 2000.

What if population growth were no longer a problem? Sometime within the next 10 years a global conference will convene on the question, "What are we to do about the declining population in the world?"

This still surprises most people, though we are beginning to wake up in the past year or so. What is actually happening? The rate of global population growth is slowing steadily. In the year 2000 it is expected that 78 million persons will be added to the global population, compared to 86 million at the peak of population growth a few years ago. More than 60 nations in the world, including Russia, Canada, Australia, Japan, all of Europe, and elsewhere have fertility rates which have fallen below the rate needed to maintain a steady state population. This rate is 2.1 children per woman. Only four nations in the world have seen their fertility rate increase since 1980—Denmark, Norway, Sweden, and Ethiopia—and among these only Ethiopia has a fertility rate greater than 2.1.

The United Nations has been revising its population forecasts downward, and while it still assumes nearly a century of growth and a peak near 9.5 billion, it seems more likely that further downward revisions are likely. In fact, the best bet is that the world population will peak by 2025, at something around 7.8 billion, and decline after that.

Don't believe this? Russia, Germany, and Japan have all officially raised alarms this year about declining population in their countries, and more countries will soon follow. Among the implications:

- The need to open immigration laws to allow for greater movement of the global work force.

- The likelihood of intense values-based political debate about whether to encourage larger families in developed nations, eventually in all nations.

- Whether advances in longevity will offset the decline in birth rates such that population growth will be sustained longer into the 21st century.

- A declining number of young people compared to a growing number of old people.

- How we will maintain a growing global economy if there are fewer customers each year (and debate whether we should grow).

DISCUSSION QUESTIONS

1. What are the business implications of global population decline?

2. Is holding the world's population steady a good or bad thing? Why?

3. How should leading corporate citizens begin to think about issues related to population?

4. Are there inherent business opportunities in this situation? What are some of them?

Source: © 2000 Glen Hiemstra, Futurist.com, www.futurist.com/portal/science/science_population_explosion.htm (accessed July 7, 2004).

to and value on human resources—employee stakeholders. Mazarr identifies four features of the "new economy" to which leading corporate citizens will need to pay attention:[10]

- Human capital—because knowledge resides in human beings.
- Freedom and empowerment—because empowered people create and innovate.
- Disorganization—because companies using complexity and chaos theories as a base for organizing will outpace companies organized more hierarchically and traditionally.
- Networks and alliances—because partnerships will become critical to organizational effectiveness and efficiency.

Mazarr identifies the principles of the knowledge era as being speed, flexibility, decentralization, and empowerment. Using these principles implies that organizations trust their stakeholders, in particular their employees, and give them responsibilities that go far beyond traditional responsibilities. Ultimately, what these principles mean is that companies will have to design themselves in the ways we have been discussing throughout this book so that integrity and responsibility are values embedded within all of their operations.

Global Tribalism

Although processes of globalism proceed apace on a global basis, much trading occurs *within*, not among, the three major trading blocs of Europe, the Americas, and East Asia.[11] Mazarr points out that this globalization process will demand increased global awareness, resulting from enhanced communications and the rise of the multinational corporation as a powerful social institution. But, when threatened, such ideological forces tend to erupt in the forms of tribalism that political scientist Benjamin Barber calls Jihads. Thus, we can expect continued attempts by various ethnic, religious, political, and cultural groups to sustain their identities in the face of global pluralism.[12]

Transforming Authority

According to the Millennium Project, traditional institutions will face increased challenges to their authority in the knowledge era, in which communications are instantaneous and information is widely shared. This trend is most related to the political sphere of activity, because it foresees a trend toward greater levels of democratization throughout the world, as information becomes more readily available and widely shared.

Among the factors that will influence authorities are tendencies to decentralize their organizations, creating virtual structures (as many companies already are doing), influencing through knowledge and allegiance rather than coercion, and acquisition of power from competence and effectiveness rather than tradition.[13]

Cognitive, Emotional, Moral Demands on Humans

As Robert Kegan, whose ideas we discussed in Chapter 3, notes, the many demands on human beings today place considerable strain on our capacity to understand and step into the perspectives of others, as well as to hold multiple perspectives in our heads simultaneously.[14] Mazarr, writing for the Millennium Project, also believes that the knowledge era will stretch the limits of human understanding. These demands will push the need for many more people to develop higher level skills of cognitive, moral, and emotional development. The pace of change, the multiplicity of stakeholders and their numerous demands, and the complexity of coping simultaneously with technology all create the potential, Mazarr says, for anxiety and alienation.

Lessons from the Global Trends

Mazarr concludes *Global Trends 2005* with three major lessons that strike to the core of what this book is all about:

> The three most important lessons suggested by this transition are these: the decisive role of education, as the activity that equips people for success in the knowledge era; the primacy of moral values and social responsibility at a time when both are urgently needed; and the need for a "New Capitalism," a reform of some elements of capitalist theory to ensure that markets capture the true costs and implications of economic activities.[15]

Issues and Opportunities

The coming of the new millennium has challenged many thinkers and leaders to work together to try to predict the major issues and opportunities the planet will face. Another initiative, also called the Millennium Project, has brought together more than 200 futurists and scholars from over 50 countries to analyze what issues, opportunities, and strategies are arising globally. This project is organized by the American Council for the United Nations University, in cooperation with the Smithsonian Institution, the Futures Group, and the United Nations University. Funded by the U.S. Environmental Protection Agency, the United Nations Development Program (UNDP), and UNESCO, the project's goal is to develop capacity to think about the future globally.[16]

The Millennium Project's "2004 State of the Future" report identified 15 global issues, 15 challenges, and 15 opportunities to which leading corporate citizens—as well as members of society generally and political leaders generally— need to pay attention in the next century. These issues and opportunities, which remain current, create potential new economic opportunities, as well as significant problems to be solved. The issues are reproduced in Table 11.3.

The Millennium Project's report discusses each issue in greater detail. Coping with these issues demands collaboration among organizations from all sectors of society, including corporations that will have to meet the economic demands of the future and do so responsibly, with vision and values guiding the way. Significant creativity and capacity to understand the fundamental problems, while

TABLE 11.3 **The Millennium Project's 15 Global Issues**

Source: www.acunu.org/millennium/isandop.html.

1. World population is growing; food, water, education, housing, medical care must grow apace.
2. Fresh water is becoming scarce in localized areas of the world.
3. The gap in living standards between rich and poor promises to become more extreme and divisive.
4. The threat of new and re-emerging diseases and immune microorganisms is growing.
5. Diminishing capacity to decide (as issues become more global and complex under conditions of increasing uncertainty and risk).
6. Terrorism is increasingly destructive, proliferating, and difficult to prevent.
7. Adverse interactions between the growth of population and economic growth with environmental quality and natural resources.
8. The status of women is changing.
9. Increasing severity of religious, ethnic, and racial conflicts.
10. Information technology's promise and perils.
11. Organized crime groups becoming sophisticated global enterprises.
12. Economic growth brings both promising and threatening consequences.
13. Nuclear power plants around the world are aging.
14. The HIV epidemic will continue to spread.
15. Work, unemployment, leisure, and underemployment are changing.

simultaneously maintaining respect for others' needs and differences, especially when they are in deprived economic circumstances or from very different cultures, will be necessary to find effective and efficient—or economizing—solutions to some of these issues.

Where there are issues, there are also opportunities, some for economic development and others for collaboration among the three spheres of human society, as the Millennium Project's list of 15 global opportunities indicates (see Table 11.4).

There are significant business opportunities embedded in the opportunities noted in Table 11.4 for leaders who can understand how to tap into them. Of course, the future is much more chaotic and emergent than these neat lists of possibilities suggest. What techniques such as scenario analysis can do is help those who must cope with the future figure out both the messy aspects and ways to cope, as well as creative approaches for handling the inherent uncertainty of the future.

Because messy problems frequently cross sector and sphere boundaries, however, individual companies acting alone may be less successful in tapping into them than companies that know how to collaborate with enterprises from the other spheres. What this blurring of boundaries means is that advantage will go to those companies, countries, and alliances that can generate new ideas for dealing with

TABLE 11.4 The Millennium Project's 15 Opportunities

Source: www.acunu.org/millennium/isandop.html.

1. Achieving sustainable development.
2. Increasing acceptance of long-term perspectives in policy making.
3. Expanding potential for scientific and technological breakthroughs.
4. Transforming authoritarian regimes to democracies.
5. Encouraging diversity and shared ethical values.
6. Reducing the rate of population growth.
7. Emerging strategies for world peace and security.
8. Developing alternative sources of energy.
9. Globalizing the convergence of information and communications technology.
10. Increasing advances in biotechnology.
11. Encouraging economic development through ethical market economy.
12. Increasing economic autonomy of women and other groups.
13. Promoting the inquiry into new and sometimes counterintuitive ideas.
14. Pursuing promising space projects.
15. Improving institutions.

the emerging issues and opportunities. The next section will briefly explore new research on such trisector collaborations.

Intersector Partnership and Collaboration

The interactions among enterprises in the civil society sphere,[17] the political sphere, and the business/economic sphere have typically been given scant attention in management thought. To their credit, many global business leaders have recognized the need to create strategic alliances and more cooperative strategies not only with each other but also with governmental and nongovernmental organizations, as the burgeoning in social and trisector partnerships around the world attests.[18] Clearly this aspect of the pluralistic global economic and societal situation demands new skills of collaboration and mutual understanding of differences in perspective, culture, and ideology, among other factors, some of which shape the economic and political worlds as well as the relational world of civil society.

The kinds of problems identified above suggest that old-fashioned single-sector solutions will no longer work. These problems by their nature cross boundaries and are what scholar Russell Ackoff has termed "messes," that is, intractable and difficult problems that various organizations, groups, and individuals must work together to resolve. Such unstructured problems require innovation and creativity, placing significant demands on any one organization's knowledge, skills, and resource base, and thus elicit multisector approaches for their solutions.

When problems cross organizational and sector (sphere) boundaries, when stakeholders are interdependent in dealing with problems, and when there is a rich network of ties—or social capital—among the stakeholders, then multisector collaboration becomes a useful vehicle for effecting social change. Businesses have found this out in the United States, where for years they have been working with schools to help schools reform themselves. Increasingly it has become clear that not only do businesses and schools need to be involved in these improvement efforts, but because education is at its root a social problem, all the relevant stakeholders, from all three spheres of activity, need to be involved in such efforts.[19]

Although establishing multisector collaborations is not easy, there is increasing information on some of factors that make such collaboration successful. First, there has to be some overriding reason why the actors should work together—a compelling shared vision, a common problem, a crisis to overcome, or a leader everyone wants to work with. Then there need to be ways in which the relevant actors and organizations can be brought together, through networks and alliances, through a "brokering" or mediating enterprise of some sort (e.g., a grant or an organization that plays a mediating role). Finally, there needs to be sufficient mutual education about other stakeholders and their interests, and sufficient benefits to be gained by all to keep these parties, which typically may never interact, working together over time.[20]

In recent research on trisector collaborations, involving organizations from the civil society, economic, and political/governmental spheres, Steve Waddell shows how these factors interact to make partnership feasible. For example, he studied a road maintenance project in Madagascar, a country that has a weak governmental infrastructure but that needed improved roads. So poorly maintained were the roads that anarchy and banditry were serious problems. To solve the problem, villagers formed nongovernmental "road users associations," and the government delegated its authority to those associations. By financing much of the improvement work with tolls, working with road contractors to improve their road-building techniques, and working on a peer basis with government officials, the associations brought villagers, government, and private contractors into a collaboration that has been largely successful in improving the roads.[21]

Such collaborative efforts will become more and more necessary in dealing with global futures issues. As perhaps the most powerful among institutions in societies today, corporate citizens will be increasingly looked on as resources for helping to resolve societies' significant problems, challenges, and opportunities.

Only if they operate with integrity, transparency, sustainability, and respect for stakeholders in all spheres of society will corporate citizens be in a position to be effective (and efficient) in their emerging leadership roles, topics discussed at length in Chapters 8 and 10. Further, leading corporate citizens anticipate rather than react to future trends, issues, and problems and work interactively with the appropriate stakeholders in different spheres of activity to find solutions. They can do so best if they are engaged in continuing activities with their stakeholders to scan the future. Just how future scanning by leading corporate citizens in conjunction with stakeholders from other spheres can be done will be briefly explored in the next sections.

Scenarios and Future Searches

Having scanned the current situation and sought out important trends, as well as the weak signals that might become levers of dramatic change, how do companies cope with all of this information? A technique called open space technology, developed by Harrison Owen, can be helpful in determining what is going on and what needs to be changed in highly complex, emergent, and generally messy situations.

Two other techniques specifically aim at helping decision makers plan for the future: scenario analysis, which has been extensively used by Shell Oil, and future search conferences, which have been used by communities and others to assess what issues are likely to arise. To conclude our look at the future, we will briefly explore some key aspects of each of these important techniques.

Open Space Technology

Open space technology is a technique, developed and written about by Harrison Owen (with, as he admits, input from many others).[22] Open space technology enables multiple stakeholders with widely divergent perspectives to come together around a problem of mutual interest to develop workable solutions.[23] Typically, an open space meeting brings together many interested parties to work together in a circle on the problem at hand. Open spaces can be used to devise corporate citizenship and competitive strategies, or to bring multiple resources to bear on a strategic, community-based, or technological problem. Or they can be used effectively to deal with large-scale social problems.

An open space can be created anywhere a circle large enough to contain as many participants—stakeholders—as are relevant to the problem can be formed. Owen believes that setting stakeholders into a circular format enables the type of interaction that will be necessary to create the type of third-way thinking or boundary-less thinking that is needed to deal with complex problems. One of the first rules of open space, then, is to invite to the meeting "Whoever cares," and a second important rule is that once the relevant stakeholders have been invited, "Whoever comes is the right group." Open space has been used successfully with groups as small as 5 and as large as 1,000.

The time frame for an open space meeting also needs consideration. While they can be held for periods of less than a day, most successful open space meetings last between two and three days (at the outside) to give participants sufficient time to deal with the complexity of the issues at hand. While space prohibits a complete description of the open space technology, Owen emphasizes that there are four principles and one law to any open space meeting (see Table 11.5).

TABLE 11.5 Open Space Technology

Source: Harrison Owen, *Open Space Technology: A User's Guide*, 2nd ed. (San Francisco: Berrett-Koehler, 1997).

The Four Principles of Open Space

- Whoever comes is the right people.
- Whatever happens is the only thing that could have.
- Whenever it starts is the right time.
- When it's over, it's over.

The One Law of Open Space

- The law of two feet: if during the course of the gathering, any person finds him- or herself in a situation where they are neither learning nor contributing, they must use their two feet and go to some more productive place.

Basically, the open space technique involves everyone present placing his or her ideas onto a board (typically using stickies or other ways to attach notes of some kind). Those present then organize the stickies into activities on which those present will work, assuming that someone is willing to lead a session and ultimately (within the time frame of the meeting) produce a report on that topic, and then allowing those present to self-organize into a working group.

The basic idea is that if the key stakeholders have been invited to the open space, then the important issues related to the topic at hand will be raised and organized by those present. Anyone interested in a particular aspect of the issue will then either post a meeting on that issue and run it or attend a meeting that someone else has organized. Interested parties will contribute to the way in which that issue is framed and possible resolutions and action steps developed. Small groups meet on particular aspects of the issue to consolidate their ideas and develop strategies and creative new approaches for dealing with that aspect. After each group meeting, those in attendance are expected to produce a report that can be combined, at the end of the entire meeting, into a book of action plans and projects that have come out of the open space meeting.

Although open space technology is not explicitly designed to deal with the future, it can provide a platform for understanding the complexities of the present and lead interested parties into designing a way forward into the future. In that sense, open space technology can be considered a useful futures planning tool.[24]

Future Search

A related technique, but more explicitly futures-focused, is the future search conference. Developed by Marvin Weisbord and others, the future search conference involves bringing a diverse group of stakeholders interested in an issue, industry, community, or problem together to share their views and wisdom about it.[25] The outcome of a future search conference is an action plan that stakeholders, who participate actively in identifying and analyzing the issues as well as developing the action steps, are expected to implement. The general idea is to get the relevant stakeholders together so that they can devise workable solutions together. As with open space meetings, future search conferences use emerging knowledge of how groups work to design the meeting so that everyone's input is taken seriously in the process of devising solutions and action steps.

The future search conference focuses on five tasks: reviewing the past, exploring the present, creating ideal future scenarios, identifying common ground among participants, and making action plans. A future search conference brings together groups of stakeholders that may not interact or join in conversations under normal circumstances (i.e., groups from different spheres of activity). A future search conference—or similar open space technology event—can thus get people working together in new and exciting ways. Examples of the use of future search conferences include gaining citywide consensus on future city plans, bringing a union and management together for joint planning, and doing regional economic development.[26]

Future search conferences, like open space meetings, need to bring together all of the relevant stakeholders into a common location to do the planning together. Future searches, like open space meetings, also use techniques to get the group to self-manage and tend to be organized in three-day blocs. The general idea is to get the gathered participants to think about the current reality and explore—together—possible common futures.[27]

Several ground rules apply to future search conferences. First, as with brainstorming techniques, all ideas are valid. Second, participants should record everything on flip charts (this creates a record that can be used later on). Third, listen to each other (remember the techniques of dialogue discussed earlier in the book?). Fourth, observe established time frames, which respects everyone's time. Finally and importantly, seek common ground and action rather than problems and conflicts.

The approach for a future search conference is to get the whole system into the room. Then the group explores, also using flip charts and stickies, what each participant's view of the situation, problem, or issue is, by getting everything onto large spaces, where lines can be drawn and the system can basically be described according to everyone present's input. Using techniques of dialogue in which active listening, respect, and sharing are important, conversations can be held even about highly conflictual situations or issues.

The focus of a future search is on finding *common ground*, rather than on differences, and is *future-oriented*, rather than oriented to the past or present. In other words, the idea is that participants will not dwell on current conflicts and problems, but will focus rather on ways of thinking creatively about what values and goals they share, so as to be able to come up with creative new ways of dealing with the problems at hand.

The design for a future search conference involves getting stakeholders to sit together in mixed groups. For example, in an economic development conference, the stakeholders from the economic sphere should be mixed with those from civil society and government. The first step is to review the past by creating a timeline to the present about the relevant topic, a step Weisborg terms "recalling the past." The next step is to focus on the present: external trends affecting the relevant topic, a step termed "appreciating the present." It is in this step that a complex diagram of the situation, called a "mind map," is generally created on large boards or walls using the inputs of everyone present. The mind map serves as an essential vehicle for creating a picture of the future: what is needed, what links exist between what is already present and what is needed, and where new ideas can be generated.

Four rules are essential to creating the mind map: (1) all ideas are valid, (2) the person who names the issue says where it goes, (3) opposing trends are OK, and (4) examples must be concrete.

The critically important next step is to be "living the future," that is, creating a desirable future based on input from all and creative ideas about what might emerge—in terms of common goals and ideas—from what is already present now. Then the groups, if there are multiple groups at work, consolidate their ideas into the common themes and ideas, and move into an action planning stage.

Scenario Analysis

One other technique that has been widely used specifically to help companies plan strategically to cope with otherwise unforeseen events is scenario analysis. It also has broad applicability for coping with multiple stakeholder interests. Groups interested in using scenarios undertake significant research on the topic of interest, seeking out all the available information, and also being sure that relevant stakeholders are participating in the process since all points of view need to be represented. The group gets together to construct alternative scenarios, that is, different descriptions of the future. Typically, several scenarios are constructed: a best case, worst case, and at least one radically different alternative where the unexpected happens.[28]

By developing the scenarios as stories, planners can make them compelling and begin to think through the implications for a specific company and its vision, or for a group of stakeholders to a key issue or concern. One company that has had a great deal of success using scenarios is Shell Oil, which was able to prepare itself for the October 1973 oil shock and subsequent energy crisis using scenarios.[29]

Scenario analysis is helpful because it provides for multiple different alternative futures and helps break leaders out of the notion that simply extrapolating from the present is the only likely outcome of present trends. By asking for best and worst case scenarios as well as radically different alternatives, scenario analysis allows for possible discontinuities that make current projections meaningless—and helps prepare organizations for those potentialities.[30]

Scenario Analysis Process

Scenario planning is simple in its concept, although doing it well requires considerable research into current trends, gathering of extensive data, and synthesizing it into meaningful stories. First, a team of scenario analysts (anyone interested in a particular problem, issue, or strategy) is gathered and discusses its perceptions of the key uncertainties around whatever the focal issue or topic is. The topic might be future strategy of a company, new competitive threats, or how to proceed with economic development for a region, just as examples. The group should outline and define the relevant environment or issue, then determine key uncertainties, whether they are inside or outside of that group's control. The group should also consider the major constraints facing the planning group or company, because these define available strategic responses to the issue and determine what the major decisions or decision points might be with respect to the issue. The key issue is to determine how the future environment will be defined and constrained.

Next the group establishes a priority ranking with respect to the uncertainties identified, focusing on those with the greatest potential impact and those that are most poorly understood. The group then selects two or three critical uncertainties as the "driving uncertainties" and combines them for developing future scenarios.

Scenario development involves exploring the selected driving uncertainties and their implications in great detail. Typically, groups will create stories, or narratives based on the driving uncertainties with an internal logic. Stories are compelling ways for leaders to begin to understand the implications of the uncertainties on the relevant organizations and stakeholders, especially if widely differing points of view have been incorporated into the different scenarios. As each story is written, different possible advantages and disadvantages, or implications, for the relevant organizations and stakeholders emerge, and possible strategic, development, or stakeholder-relationship responses begin to emerge.

The scenarios then are used to explore possible futures and to test out how different strategies for coping with the scenario will work. A critical test of a strategy, for example, is to see how it would work under vastly different scenarios. Doing such testing can help determine the robustness of a particular response. If a response to one scenario seems as though it will dramatically falter under another scenario, planners may wish to evolve a different strategy that would have a better chance of working under both scenarios. Key questions that should be asked—and answered—by scenario analysts are summarized in Table 11.6, as a way of guiding decision making and future strategies by the group of stakeholders that has been gathered to address an issue of relevance to all.

Common Ground on Planning the Future

Obviously, there are many more details that go into planning a successful future search conference, open space meeting, or scenario analysis. It is clear, however, that all of these techniques use inputs from *all* relevant stakeholders, provide for sharing of concerns and ideas, use dialogical and brainstorming techniques, and demand that participants let go of preconceived ideas and agendas. Only in these ways can stakeholders to an issue work toward common ground—*and* analyze possibilities without being biased by any one point of view. The general idea is

TABLE 11.6 **Guidelines for Future Responses by Scenario Analysts**

Source: Eric K. Clemons, "Using Scenario Analysis to Manage the Strategic Risks of Reengineering," *Sloan Management Review*, Summer 1995, pp. 61–71.

Determine the applicability of potential decisions and action steps by asking:

- What are the "no brainers," the actions common to all scenarios, that will be required in all foreseeable futures? These actions should be undertaken.
- What are the "no regrets," the actions that may be valuable in some scenarios, less valuable in others, but not damaging in any way? These actions might be undertaken, but might be stopped if they become damaging in any way.
- What are the "contingent possibilities," the actions that may be valuable in only selected scenarios?
- What are the "no ways!" the scenarios that are deemed unacceptable? How should such actions be avoided?

to bring participants onto common ground, where fruitful generative new ways of working collaboratively can be developed, where there is open sharing of multiple points of view, and where reaching common ground—and shared solutions—is the goal.

Such techniques can be an important basis for generating not only innovative ideas (as Fetzer Vineyards does, see Case 11.2) but also actual commitments to carrying them out, especially when the issues and opportunities to be addressed are open-ended and ambiguous, and when decision makers are present.[31] At some level these types of techniques also can help companies that want to be leading corporate citizens do far more than respond to the future: They can help companies work together with groups from the political and economic spheres, as well as those representing the interests of the natural environment, to create a common world that we can all live in. Futures assessments can also be helpful to companies and other organizations in avoiding significant problems that might otherwise arise because they are completely unexpected.

Leading Challenges: We Cannot Predict the Future, but We *Can* Create Relationships

Leading corporate citizens cannot predict the future, as it is an inherently chaotic process in which small changes can make large and fundamental differences. They *can*, however, prepare themselves and their organizations to cope with whatever happens by being aware of the changes that impact both internal and external stakeholders. They *can* implement dialogue and conversation with primary and critical secondary stakeholders who are capable of providing important input into the company's future plans, and they *can* continually scan the horizon for significant developments, whether technological, ecological, social, or political. By

Fetzer Vineyards' CEO, Paul Dolan, long ago saw the future—and made the move to becoming totally organic for his vineyard. Not only are all 2000 acres of Fetzer-owned vineyards certified organic, but Dolan has plans to convert all 200 of the growers who supply Fetzer to organic growing by 2010. Dolan knows what he is talking about, since he converted Fetzer to organic ways as long ago as 1986, when he was still head winemaker at the company. An organic gardener hired to grow delicious foods to be served with the Fetzer wines challenged Dolan and his boss, Jim Fetzer, about why they were using poisons in growing the grapes. When they tried an experimental patch using organic methods, the improved taste led the team toward the eventual outcome—full organic production on Fetzer-owned land and a commitment to convert suppliers by 2010.

An article in *Fast Company* magazine in 2003 highlighted the dramatic shift that has taken place within the company since those early trials and some of the thinking that lies behind the progressive, profitable, and highly productive methods in use at Fetzer, which have resulted in the company's being the best-selling brand in the $7–$10 category in 2002 and awards for the quality of its wines too numerous to mention. According to *Fast Company*:

> The results of the experiment convinced Dolan that years of applying chemical pesticides and fertilizers had stripped the soil of its richness and that the resulting dull grapes were affecting the quality of Fetzer's wine. In 1991, Fetzer launched a label called Bonterra (meaning "good earth"), made of 100% organically grown grapes. It was the first mass-marketed organic wine in the United States. The philosophy extends even to the packaging: To spare trees, Bonterra labels are made from a plant fiber known as kenaf and are printed with soy-based inks; the corks aren't sanitized with chlorine; and the cases are made from recycled cardboard.

A year later, Louisville, Kentucky-based Brown-Forman purchased Fetzer (adding the winery to its existing brands including Jack Daniel's, Southern Comfort, and Finlandia Vodka), and named Dolan president of Fetzer. One of his first decisions was to commit to going 100% organic by 2010. All the grapes on Fetzer-owned land—about 20% of the total—are already organic. Without chemicals to fertilize the grape crop and keep insects and fungi away, growers had to learn different ways to address these same problems. They undertook what was then a fairly unusual practice of growing "cover crops," which have since become standard at wineries around the world. In the aisles between the vines as well as in fallow fields, growers plant different crops to crowd out weeds, repel bugs, and provide soil nutrients. If diseases persist, growers have other remedies, such as sprinkling sulphur dust and copper sulfates (which are approved for organic use) on the roots of vines and spraying assorted oils on the grapes to keep away pests and fungi.

Dolan is a fourth-generation wine maker who grew up steeped in the wine country's culture. His organic conversion led him to believe that protecting the environment meant more than simply growing grapes without chemicals. It meant improving the environment for workers and investing in their skills and futures. It meant reducing emissions from farm vehicles and figuring out how to eliminate solid waste at the winery. And it meant making enough money so that Fetzer could serve as an industry example of how to do things differently. Fetzer employees named this vision E3, which stands for economics, environment, and equity, or the triple bottom line. Every decision at the company is put to the E3 test: Does it support fair and safe standards for employees? Does it protect or improve the environment? Does it make economic sense?

The commitment to organic production, employee development, and the triple bottom line extends to all aspects of the business at Fetzer, including seeking input from employees—and improving pay scales as a result, running farming equipment on a fuel composed of soy and used cooking oils from local fast food restaurants, teaching English to laborers (and thereby avoiding translation problems), to name just a few.

In his 2003 book *True to Your Roots*, Dolan argues that all businesses should commit to the triple bottom line of economic, social, and ecological impacts and performance, and provides some insights into the visionary and farsighted business principles his company lives by:

- Your company's culture is determined by the context you create for it.
- Your business is part of a much larger system.
- True power is living what you know.
- The soul of your company is found in the hearts of its people.
- You can't predict the future, but you can create it.
- There is a way to make an idea's time come.

Clearly Dolan and Fetzer have seen the future—and are, in fact, leading the wine industry in California toward more sustainable growing practices. In 2003, inspired by Fetzer's successes not just with organic growing but also in producing better wines, California's wine industry introduced a Code of Sustainable Winegrowing Practices, a harbinger of a drive toward more ecological sustainability in a state with a fast-growing population and an industry that has frequently been criticized for lack of attention to environmental matters. Developed partially as a survival plan for the $33 billion industry, the code aimed to have at least 10 percent of the state's 600,000 acres of vineyards environmentally assessed during the first year. The voluntary initiative exceeded all expectations when during the first year 29 percent of the vineyards and 53 percent of the production facilities completed the assessment. In a model of responsibility management, the goal of the effort is to measure the current status then by adhering to the code's standards, emphasizing constant improvement in their practices.

DISCUSSION QUESTIONS

1. Do you believe that Fetzer might have a competitive edge because of its approaches to the environment and successes in producing high-quality wine using organic methods?

2. How do you think customers are likely to respond to organic wines? Why?

3. Assume you are a winemaker using traditional methods. What kinds of future-scanning methods would help you figure out how to successfully compete with Fetzer?

Sources: Paul Dolan, *True to Our Roots: Fermenting a Business Revolution* (Bloomberg Press, 2003); Alison Overholt, "The Good Earth," *Fast Company* 77 (December 2003), p. 85, www.fastcompany.com/magazine/77/goodearth.html (accessed July 8, 2004); and Tim Tesconi, "California Wine Growers Moving Toward Sustainability," *Organic Consumers Association*, October 15, 2003, www.organicconsumers.org/organic/wine102303.cfm (accessed July 8, 2004).

establishing these *relationships* with key stakeholders, companies can prepare themselves—in an ongoing way—for what the future is likely to bring.

Leading corporate citizens need not be surprised by technological advances, activism, or social changes that put their businesses at risk. As the sections on future search conferences, open space meetings, and scenario analysis indicate, there are numerous techniques available that companies can use on a continual basis to establish communication links with potential critics, key stakeholders, and social activists. Getting the kind of information that can only be gained when people with *different* points of view are brought together can not only enhance a company's capacity to be a respected corporate citizens but also provide the basis for revealing new trends, competitive threats, and possible new opportunities. Many of these possibilities could never be discovered through traditional channels of market research and new product/service development.

By putting in place the types of dialogic processes with stakeholders that have been described above, by focusing on continually learning and incorporating that learning into constructive new stakeholder practices, leading corporate citizens can, in fact, operate with integrity and be successful. They can also provide the means to achieve a better balance among the spheres in society and with the natural environment because the different points of view represented in these spheres will be better understood.

Is using these dialogic techniques easy? Of course not. They require a commitment to internal learning and change—and a commitment to real and recognized input from outsiders. They imply a willingness to listen to those who may be less powerful or have fewer resources than the company itself. But using such dialogue-based techniques to raise up the emerging issues, concerns, technologies, and problems, may be, in fact, a better way of operating with integrity than to assume that economizing is all important. Business, after all, was created to serve society's interests, not vice versa. All of this, of course, suggests the need for a shift of paradigm in organizing and leading corporate citizens, the subject of the next and final chapter.

Endnotes

1. From The Lorax by Dr. Seuss, copyright® and copyright © by Dr. Seuss Enterprises, L.P. 1971, renewed 1999. Used by permission of Random House Children's Books, a division of Random House Inc.

2. Robert Spiegel, "Yogi Berra's Business Wisdom, Growth and Leadership," *Business Know-How*, www.businessknowhow.com/growth/yogi.htm (accessed July 6, 2004).

3. Robert Kegan, *In Over Our Heads: The Mental Demands of Modern Life* (Cambridge, MA: Harvard University Press, 1994).

4. National Institute of Allergy and Infectious Diseases, "HIV/AIDS Statistics," January 2004, www.niaid.nih.gov/factsheets/aidsstat.htm (accessed July 7, 2004).

5. Hákan Björkman, "HIV/AIDS and Poverty Reduction Strategies," UNDP Policy Note, 2002, www.undp.org/hiv/docs/hivprsEng25oct02.pdf (accessed July 7, 2004).

6. World Bank, www.worldbank.org/WBSITE/EXTERNAL/NEWS/0..contentMDK: 20194973~menuPK:34463~pagePK:64003015~piPK:64003012~theSitePK:4607.00. html (accessed July 7, 2004).

7. See, for instance, the Center for Strategic and International Studies website, www.csis.org. Trends identified in this section are from Michael J. Mazarr, *Global*

Trends 2005: The Challenge of a New Millennium (Washington, DC: Center for Strategic and International Studies, 1997) See www.csis.org/gt2005.

8. See Mazarr, *Global Trends 2005.*

9. Ibid., p. 13.

10. Ibid., pp. 16–24.

11. Ibid., p. 25.

12. Benjamin Barber, *Jihad vs. McWorld* (New York: Times Books; Random House, 1995).

13. Mazarr, *Global Trends 2005*, p. 31.

14. Kegan, *In Over Our Heads.*

15. Mazarr, *Global Trends 2005*, p. 37.

16. See www.geocities.com/CapitolHill/Senate/4787/millennium/new.html.

17. This topic is discussed at length by Robert D. Putnam in *Making Democracy Work: Civic Traditions in Modern Italy* (Princeton, NJ: Princeton University Press, 1993); also see his articles "Bowling Alone: America's Declining Social Capital," *Journal of Democracy* 6, no. 1 (January 1995), pp. 65–78, and "The Strange Disappearance of Civic America," *American Prospect* 24 (Winter 1996), http://epn.org/prospect/24/24putn.html.

18. See Sandra Waddock, "Public-Private Partnership as Product and Process" in *Research in Corporate Social Performance and Policy*, Vol. VII, James E. Rest, ed. (Greenwich, CT: JAI Press, 1986) and "Building Successful Social Partnerships," *Sloan* Management Review 29, no. 4 (Summer 1988), pp. 17–23; also Steve Waddell, "Market–Civil Society Partnership Formation: A Status Report on Activity, Strategies, and Tools," *IDR Reports* 13, no. 5 (1998).

19. See, for example, Sandra Waddock, *Not by Schools Alone: Sharing Responsibility for America's Education Reform* (Greenwich, CT: Praeger, 1995).

20. See, for example, Sandra Waddock, "Understanding Social Partnerships: An Evolutionary Model of Partnership Organizations," *Administration and Society* 21, no. 1 (May 1989), pp. 78–100.

21. Steve Waddell, "Business-Government-Nonprofit Collaborations as Agents for Social Innovation and Learning," paper presented at the 1999 Academy of Management Annual Meeting, Chicago, IL, 1999.

22. Information about Harrison Owen's development of open space technology can be found at www.openspaceworld.com/index.htm (accessed July 4, 2004).

23. See Harrison Owen, *Open Space Technology: A User's Guide*, 2nd ed. (San Francisco: Berrett-Koehler, 1997); and *Expanding Our Now: The Story of Open Space Technology* (San Francisco: Berrett-Koehler, 1997).

24. More details about open space technology can be found at www.change-management-toolbook.com/OpenSpace.htm (accessed July 7, 2004). By clicking on Home, you can link to other change management tools and techniques as well.

25. Marvin R. Weisbord and Sandra Janoff, *Future Search: An Action Guide to Finding Common Ground in Organizations & Communities* (San Francisco: Berrett-Koehler, 1995).

26. Information on future searches can be found at www.futuresearch.net (accessed July 7, 2004).

27. More information about future searches can be found at www.change-management-toolbook.com/FS.html (accessed July 7, 2004).

28. The steps are outlined online at www.du.edu/~bhughes/WebHelpIFs/ifshelp/scenario_analysis.htm (accessed July 7, 2004).

29. For a good overview of how to do scenario analysis see Peter Schwartz, *The Art of the Long View: Planning for the Future in an Uncertain World* (New York: Doubleday Currency, 1996).

30. Ibid. See also Eric K. Clemons, "Using Scenario Analysis to Manage the Strategic Risks of Reengineering," *Sloan Management Review*, Summer 1995, pp. 61–71.

31. To learn about future search conferences, see Marvin R. Weisbord and Sandra Janoff, *Future Search: An Action Guide to Finding Common Ground in Organizations & Communities* (San Francisco: Berrett-Koehler, 1995). For information on open space technology, see Harrison Owen's two books *Open Space Technology: A User's Guide*, 2nd ed. (San Francisco: Berrett-Koehler, 1997), and *Expanding Our Now: The Story of Open Space Technology* (San Francisco: Berrett-Koehler, 1997).

CHAPTER TWELVE

Leading Global Futures: The Emerging Paradigm of Leading Corporate Citizenship

Imagine a global economy that is healthy and self-governing. Imagine markets that are organized to empower people. Imagine an economy that is free, humane, competitive, profitable, decentralized, nonbureaucratic, and socially accountable. Imagine a global economy that operates for the common good, a market that develops local-to-global structures to build sustainable community.

This sort of economy is what we are talking about in civil development. It requires a new order of thinking about global markets characterized by freedom and accountability.

Severyn Bruyn, *A Civil Economy: Transforming the Market in the Twenty-First Century*. Published by the University of Michigan Press, 2000.

Severyn Bruyn's remarkable statement synthesizes much of what this book is about: creating corporate citizens that have respect for human dignity, and the natural ecology that supports it, through a balanced approach to the three spheres of human activity that constitute civilization—economic, political, and civil society. All along we have been talking about developing managers into leaders who take their responsibilities seriously and proceed with their decisions and their impacts wisely by consistently implementing a value- and values-added approach.

Past chapters have demonstrated that economic success is the result when companies treat stakeholders with dignity and respect, and when their practices match their rhetoric about vision and values. We have seen the need for balance among economic, political, and civilizing interests, all three of which are necessary to create successful and ecologically sustainable societies. We have seen the need for higher levels of awareness and development, both individually and organizationally, to cope with today's, and particularly tomorrow's, complexities and challenges. We have seen, in short, the need for and the beginnings of a shift of perspective on what it means to be a leading corporate citizen, both individually and organizationally.

Shifting Perspectives

This book has presented what I hope is a realistic but fairly radical perspective on how companies as citizens in the global village can be successful not alongside or separate from but rather with, in, and of societies. The systems perspective presented through the three-spheres framework, combined with the links among vision, values, and value added integrates responsibility, meaningfulness, and the energy and capacity of whole persons directly into organizational life.

By understanding that responsibility is integrated into all of the organizational practices that impact stakeholders and the ecological environment, organizations are discovering the power of vision to create meaning and purpose for the organization and its stakeholders, as well as the power of treating others with respect and dignity. Such a stance not only balances power among the three spheres of human activity but also tends to bring more equity and power balance into relationships within organizations as well. When companies tap the full resources of individuals and treat them as human beings, the tendency to treat people as mere cogs in the great machine of business diminishes. Respect and dignity are enhanced.

Transformation Based on Nature

Fully incorporating the emerging paradigm of corporate citizenship into the dominant management paradigm will require radical shifts in the current business model, in power dynamics, and in balance among the three spheres of human activity, which themselves must be put into sustainable *relationships* with stakeholders and the natural environment. Part of the needed wisdom can derive from principles embedded in nature itself, using what author David Korten terms a "life-centered approach" that taps the wisdom of nature and ecological systems. Certainly, if we hope to sustain productivity and use ecological resources wisely, a shift of balance in the powers among the spheres is needed.

Balancing power means that corporate activities can be undertaken on a scale accessible to human beings and with the best interests of all stakeholders kept

TABLE 12.1   Korten's Lessons of Life's Wisdom and Progressive Design Elements

Source: Adapted from David Korten, *The Post-Corporate World* (San Francisco: Berett-Koechler, 1999).

Lessons of Life's Wisdom	Progressive Corporate Design Elements
1. Life favors self-organization.	Human-scale self-organization.
2. Life is frugal and sharing.	Renewable energy self-reliance. Closed-cycle materials use. Regional environmental balance.
3. Life depends on inclusive, place-based communities.	Village and neighborhood clusters. Towns and regional centers.
4. Life rewards cooperation.	Mindful livelihoods.
5. Life depends on boundaries.	Interregional electronic communication.
6. Life banks on diversity, creative individuality, and shared learning.	Wild spaces in nature and within organizations.

firmly in mind and well balanced. Duly elected democratic governments can resume their rightful powers to determine the public interest and the common good. And the relationships fostered and sustained in civil society can nourish the spirit and the bodies of productive members of societies and productive corporate stakeholders.

Korten offers six lessens drawn from what is now known about self-organizing ecological systems that potentially help in rethinking the way that corporate life is currently scaled and operates (see Table 12.1).[1] We can relate these, to some extent, to some of the design elements that Korten develops for his visionary postcorporate world. And many of them are similar to ideas that we have been discussing throughout this book. Perhaps it is time to begin imagining different types of futures that provide inspiration for human life in the midst of nature, where resources are equitably distributed among all of the peoples of the world.

First, Korten says, life favors self-organization, and companies would be wise to do so as well. Self-organization is the process of organizing that tends to emerge when (in this case) people are together for a purpose. But self-organization is best suited to reasonably small-scale endeavors that are rooted locally, thus favoring human-scale enterprises that not just rhetorically but truly empower people to self-organize. Human-scaled enterprises allow people to engage in a positive vision that enables them to achieve *meaningful* personal *and* company purposes. Second, Korten notes, life is frugal and sharing, values that are certainly found in the economizing that underpins corporate efficiency. But from an ecological perspective, this also means thinking about operating in a sustainable manner for the long term, hence ecologizing, which effectively means wasting nothing.

Third, life depends on inclusive, place-based communities, what we earlier termed rootedness. Corporations that are accountable to the communities that depend on them and their numerous stakeholders within those communities will respect the boundaries that communities attempt to erect. Communities develop on a human scale, not globally, though clearly technology permits some global communities to exist electronically. It is not protectionism, in the negative sense, that exists when a community attempts to sustain its uniqueness and sense of place, but rather an attempt to free the human spirit with the sustenance of relationships, personal knowledge, and a shared sense of the common good found in community.

Fourth, as noted early on in this book, life rewards cooperation. Symbiosis (i.e., interdependency) strengthens the bonded organism, whether individual or community, in its attempts to compete for necessary life resources. Rather than fostering a dog-eat-dog hypercompetitive environment based on the accumulation of material goods, the whole human being is rewarded by helping others, and doing his or her bit to make the world a better place for self and others. This is not altruism but rather a belief in the goodness of the human spirit. Such a spirit is fostered by what Korten calls "mindful livelihoods," which entails finding meaning in work no matter where one works or what one does.

Finally, life banks on diversity, creative individuality, and shared learning, as do successful companies in the global environment. Only by tapping what Korten calls "wild spaces" can this diversity of enterprise be maintained. But these wild spaces need to be more than based in the natural environment (though these are certainly important). Wild spaces are those that allow for innovation and personal meaning-making to develop within leaders throughout an enterprise. Organizational wild spaces turn everyone into leaders because they tap the richness of potentialities that are inherent in every human being and allow for that richness in the context of shared vision and values.

Wild spaces can be created through the types of dialogic practices discussed as part of the exploration of the future in Chapter 11 and also can be created by engaging regularly with stakeholders who have different perspectives than leaders of a company. Creating wild spaces in leading corporate citizens ultimately means hiring many different types of people with many different backgrounds, and tapping their insights and knowledge extensively. It means having the self-confidence—as a leader and as a company—to bring in diverse points of view, and incorporate them into corporate values and operating practices. Doing so successfully may necessitate a significant shift of perspective.

Metanoia: A Shift of Perspective

Leading corporate citizens create meaningful visions and underpin those visions with operating practices that result in integrity in all senses of the word. Powerful and meaningful visions create a sense of higher purpose for the enterprise that brings everyone involved into a common vision and helps create a strong internal community and sense of belonging, where all know what they individually have to contribute and how that contribution helps move the vision along. Such visions are underscored by constructive values that help stakeholders, employees in particular, know their place in the organization's efforts to make significant contributions to building a better world and a sustainable future. The combination of vision and stakeholder-meaningful values results in the development of responsible day-to-day practices that allow the organization to add value in the by-product of profits and wealth generation. Combined, all of this means operating with integrity.

We have argued that it is leading corporate citizens with these characteristics that will succeed in the complexities, dynamism, and connectedness likely to continue to evolve in the future. They will do so in conversation with their stakeholders. Such corporate citizens also incorporate not only objective data and information—that which can be observed—but also the subjective and intersubjective or more interpretive elements of life, such as aesthetics, emotions, and meaningfulness, into their everyday activities. They understand the need for ecological and community sustainability and are prepared to operate with issues of sustainability fully in mind. Developing corporate citizens that have these attributes calls for nothing less than a shift of mind. Peter Senge calls this shift *metanoia*, which literally means a shift of mind, even transcendence toward a higher purpose.[2]

This *metanoia* takes leading corporate citizens away from thinking that their actions—as individuals or as organizations—can be taken in isolation. It moves them toward more ecological or systems understanding of embeddedness, interconnectedness, and interdependence. It also asks them to think about the decisions they make as managers/leaders in an integrated way, that is, not only with their heads but also with their hearts and spirits. It asks leaders to think about the meaning their decisions and actions have and the meaning embedded in the work that they and others jointly do—and then to create and tell stories that help them to share the meanings with others.

The new perspective thus asks leaders of and within corporate citizens to think deeply about the meaning and implications of *all* of the decisions they are making and what their impact on the world around us is likely to be. Leading citizens can do this because they explicitly recognize that there will be impacts and consequences of decisions. They know that *all* decisions are embedded with a set of values that either honors the relationships and stakeholders they impact or not. They are *engaged* in ongoing *relationships* with stakeholders and understand their perspectives, even when they are radically different from the company's internal perspective. This *metanoia* asks leading citizens to seek meaning and meaningfulness in decisions so that everyone can bring his or her whole self—mind, heart, body, spirit—to work (as opposed to checking their brains or heart at the door). It demands mindful rather than mindless action, thought, and decisions from managers who are connected to their hearts as well as their pocketbooks.

The changes in organizations and societies today also demand that leadership be distributed throughout the enterprise rather than held closely in a few top managers' hands. Distributed leadership means taking responsibility for the consequences of one's actions (and thinking through what those consequences are likely to be). It also asks many—most—individuals to assume qualities more like entrepreneurs, self-initiators, and leaders than ever before, to be responsible for their own productive engagement with others and for the results that the decisions they make achieve. Leadership, in this sense, falls to everyone who takes part in bringing to reality the vision embodied in the higher purposes shared by individuals within the enterprise.

Ultimately, this *metanoia* asks leaders in corporate citizens to seek *wisdom* and *mindfulness* in their work as leaders of and within corporate citizens.[3] Mindful and wise leaders think through the consequences of their decisions to all of the stakeholders those decisions impact. Mindful leaders are aware that they do not and cannot know all that they need to know, but take seriously the responsibilities—all of them—attendant on their leadership. They continue to grow, learn, develop, and embed learning practices within their enterprises as part of the culture. They seek wisdom, knowing that, in the words of leading management thinker Russell Ackoff:

> *Wisdom is the ability to perceive and evaluate the long-run consequences of behavior.* It is normally associated with a willingness to make short-run sacrifices for the sake of long-run gains.[4]

Imaginization and the Leading Corporate Citizen

As difficult as the developmental task for achieving the emergent *metanoia* in real-world corporate citizens might be for some individuals and organizations, it is possible to begin to imagine what an individual working in a new-paradigm organization might experience. This task of what management thinker Gareth Morgan terms "imaginization" will be the subject of the next several sections.[5] Imaginization asks us to think in terms of metaphors and images of what might be, not necessarily what is. Imaginization is a technique for enhancing leadership and management creativity that helps leaders understand situations in new ways, find new images about organizing, create shared understandings, and link those capacities to both personal and organizational learning and continued development. Adapting the technique of imaginization for our purposes here, we will explore in this chapter the vision, values, leadership attributes, individual and organizational work shifts, and structures that might be able to provide leading corporate citizens with patterns for coping in the turbulent world of the future. We will explore emerging new values and logics, or ways of thinking, as well as societal implications of these logics in an imaginary trip into a true leading corporate citizen.

Vision Shifts

The first stop in our imaginary trip into the emerging-paradigm organization will be at some of the implications of the new *metanoia* for vision. (See Table 12.2 for the shifts that are likely to take place.)

Imagine living and working with passion for your work and the purposes of your employing organization, a leading corporate citizen! Imagine a company with a vision embedded with bigger meanings and purposes that draw people

TABLE 12.2 Vision Shifts Needed in Emerging Leading Corporate Citizens

Vision Shifts From . . .	To . . .
Maximizing shareholder wealth without regard for other stakeholders	Doing something important and useful for customers using the full resources of employees in a way that treats all stakeholders with dignity and respect resulting in success and profitability
General, nonspecific core purpose	Building a better world in some way, creating meaning and higher purpose generating passion and commitment to that purpose and vision among stakeholders, especially employees
Corporate vision and strategy available only to top managers	Corporate vision and strategy shared by all primary stakeholders, clearly articulated, and related to higher purposes
Business separate from society Discretionary responsibility	Business integral to society Responsibility integral to and implicit in all practices that impact human and natural ecologies
Stakeholder management	Stakeholder relationships
Authority from the top	Meaningful leadership that guides core purposes and enables others to act in their own and the enterprise's best interest

in so that they can bring mind, heart, body, and spirit to work, where leaders and managers learn and practice mindfulness in all their decisions and actions. Imagine that the vision is clearly enough articulated that all of the relevant stakeholders understand it, acknowledge it, share it, and value it. Understanding the vision, primary stakeholders can live it because it is not just articulated but also is fully implemented, a lived, live, living, and lively vision. Imagine that this enterprise treats all of its stakeholders, internal and external, primary and secondary, with dignity and respect and is rewarded with long-term success and profitability. This is what vision in the emerging paradigm for leading corporate citizens is.

Further, imagine that the organization is a business, a business that sees itself and its impacts as an integral part of the broader set of societies in which it operates so that it carefully acknowledges the inherent and unavoidable responsibility in all of its practices, decisions, and impacts. Imagine that top leadership is acknowledged as developing the core vision, a vision that demonstrates the enterprise's higher purpose and benefits stakeholders and societies, and guiding practices by enabling, truly empowering, others to act in their own and the enterprise's best interest. Imagine that everyone involved knows exactly what that vision is and what his or her contribution is to achieving it.

Imagine a company that understands—and acts on—the need for balancing its own power, resources, and strategies with those of other stakeholders. Imagine that all relationships with stakeholders are engaging, dialogue based, and mutually respectful. Imagine that rather than managing the stakeholders, which implies an unbalanced power relationship, this company develops and manages its relationships carefully by respecting the interests, needs, and dignity of other stakeholders. Now imagine that responsibility is integral to and implicit in all of the multifaceted day-to-day operating practices the company develops. No longer is responsibility considered discretionary or something that is done after business is taken care of. Instead, business is undertaken responsibly, in a "both/and" logic that accepts the inherent tension and paradoxes of such a stance. Such is the nature of vision in the emerging paradigm organization.

Values in the Emerging Paradigm

The second part of our imaginization takes us to the realm of values. What are the values that underpin the leading corporate citizens as compared to more traditional organizations? (See Table 12.3 for a summary of the shifts in values accompanying the shift to the emerging paradigm.)

Economizing and power-aggrandizing values underpin all business activity as we know it today. Even as the new paradigm emerges, we can imagine that these values are likely to sustain business enterprise, but that they will be supplemented and complemented by the values that help balance the other spheres of activity. Thus, imagine economizing and power-aggrandizing values complemented by values of civilizing, which helps to build community internally and externally, and ecologizing, which provides for community and ecological sustainability. Imagine that leaders of future corporate citizens are far more likely to operate with an understanding of the importance of community, relationships, civilizing than

TABLE 12.3 Value Shifts in the Emerging Paradigm

Values Shift From . . .	To . . .
Economizing and power aggrandizing	Inclusion of civilizing and ecologizing
Imbalance	Balance
No respect or dignity for stakeholders	Respect and dignity for all stakeholders
Hierarchy	Shared power, empowerment with *appropriate* hierarchy
Dominance	Partnership, equality
Authority	Democracy
Competition	Collaboration *and* competition
Control through systems	Control through goals and values
Exclusive	Inclusive
Value the objective, scientific, observable	Value the objective and subjective, interobjective and intersubjective
Disconnected, fragmented, autonomous	Connected, holistic, networked (linked)

do most present-day companies, to think relationally and systemically. In operationalizing this understanding, leaders create numerous means of engaging in mutually respectful conversations with stakeholders, some of which appropriately influence corporate practices. Simultaneously, imagine that current and future pressures from the resource constraints imposed by the natural environment may well heighten sensitivity to values of ecologizing, increasing attention to natural ecology and sustainable development.

Further, imagine that, pushed by communications technology and the ready availability of information, the trend toward democracy in societies continues unabated and even enters the workplace. Imagine that the workplace itself has structurally transformed so that many individuals, wherever they are in the company, are expected (as they largely are today) to exert more entrepreneurial qualities than they did in the past. The combination of entrepreneurial attitudes and the independence among stakeholders it is likely to foster may well move companies away from valuing hierarchy and dominance. Companies may move toward truly sharing power and empowering employees, but will likely sustain appropriate levels of hierarchy in the firm (some of which is likely to continue to be necessary as a structural element).

Along with this shift, imagine that companies move away from stakeholder management toward developing stakeholder relationships because they value the mutuality inherent in the relationship itself. Even more radically, perhaps, imagine that leading corporate citizens come to value the synthesis and generativity that is inherent in fostering collaborative as well as competitive relationships with stakeholders in all spheres of society. Values of collaboration and competition, rather than simple competition, might, in this world, meld in a tension of opposite and paradox that yet provides a basis for continual creativity and innovation.

In organizations with clearly articulated vision and core values, where leadership involves creating meaning rather than directing through authority and hierarchy, we can imagine that controls through organizational systems will be supplemented by controls provided by the glue of common goals and shared values. Organizations thereby respect and value employees (in particular) and the contributions they wish to and will make toward accomplishing the organization's vision. And such enterprises are, we might think, also likely to value the diversity of inclusive stakeholder relations in their primary relationships, whether with customers, suppliers, owners, or employees, rather than explicitly or implicitly generating exclusive tactics and policies.

Finally, we can imagine that there will be value for the holons (whole/parts) that corporate citizens recognize are always present in the connected, holistic, and networked system they call an organization. Individual stakeholders are holons that may form into groups that are themselves holons, which are part of larger organizations. All of these levels are respected as the wholes that they are, while recognizing that each is yet incomplete without the rest. Leaders in the emerging-paradigm organization recognize the interrelatedness of the parts of the whole system and are careful about developing operating practices so that the integrity of each holon is maintained and negative ripple effects are minimized.

TABLE 12.4   **Individuals and Work Shifts in the Emerging Paradigm**

Individual Mind-set Shifts From . . .	To . . .
Self-interest	Self- and other interests
Contributions using body or mind	Contributions using mind, body, heart, spirit
Conventional reasoning, awareness	Postconventional reasoning, awareness
Single perspective held	Multiple perspectives held simultaneously
Mindlessness, lack of awareness	Mindful, aware, fully conscious
Do the job as structured	Learn constantly; improve the job and its results
Instrument of the corporation, a tool	Purposeful, self-directed
Moral reasoning from society's demands	Principled, care-based moral reasoning
Emotionally immature	Emotional maturity
Developmental Perspectives Move From . . .	**To . . .**
Individualistic ideology	Individualistic *and* communitarian ideologies
Single-perspective stages of development	Multiple-perspective stages of development
Reactive, proactive stakeholder relations	Interactive stakeholder relations
One-way (top-down) communication	Dialogue and mutual conversation
Just do my job	Constant scanning the environment for trends, opportunities, challenges
Work Shifts From . . .	**To . . .**
Meaningless	Meaningful
Powerless	Empowered
Individual gain	Individual and community gain
Not visibly connected to larger purpose	Visibly connected to larger purpose

Individuals Leading Corporate Citizens

Individuals operating within leading corporate citizens will need skills tomorrow that they probably can get away without today. Table 12.4 lists a few of the more obvious attitudinal (or mind-set) attributes and developmental characteristics, as well as some implications for the nature of work in leading corporate citizens where, remember, we have argued that leadership needs to come from everyone at every level. Let us continue our imaginary trip into the leading corporate citizen of the future at the individual level. What would this organization be like for people and for working?

Imagine coming to work every day knowing that your best contribution is expected. That best contribution taps all of you. Of course your mind in this knowledge-based economy is a crucial part of doing your work. And for some employees, physical labor is still demanded. But your contribution also involves thinking about the ways in which what you do and how you do it affects others in an emotional and aesthetic sense. You are also called upon to consider the ways your activities, especially in working with others, develop a meaningful and important contribution to making the world around you a better place, contribute to the organization's achievement of its vision, and enhance your feeling of being in a worthwhile community.

In coming to your job every day, you know that the organization (and life itself) has high expectations of that type of learning that you will do. You are expected to always be pushing the edges of your own learning to enhance the organizational vision and community, and to push yourself toward the higher stages of individual development demanded by an increasingly complex and dynamic world. You work at mindfulness—awareness of the implications of each decision and presence here and now—so that you are aware of what you and others do and fully conscious of how others (other stakeholders) are affected by the decisions you make and the practices you develop.

Thus, developmentally you have moved toward the capacity to hold multiple perspectives simultaneously and are very skilled at taking the other's (whichever "other" is relevant in a given situation) perspective when necessary. This skill helps you develop good relationships with important stakeholders whom your daily activities and work affect (or whose activities affect your work!).

You personally and the company have moved away from simply reacting to external pressures, and have even moved beyond proactive strategies to forestall others' actions, toward more consistently interactive strategies of conversing, or being in dialogue with important stakeholders. This interactive posture helps you and the organization avoid nasty surprises from the external environment. In part you can do this because you are constantly alert to any concerns from the stakeholders you interact with. In part it happens almost naturally because your constant learning means that you pay attention to signals coming in from outside (or arising inside) the organization. And because your opinion is as respected as others, you know that when you voice an idea it will be listened to.

Your work has become meaningful and you have, in this transition to the emerging-paradigm organization, become truly empowered, not just in rhetoric, but in actuality. Power is shared and the need for power aggrandizement, whether by individuals or the company, has diminished (while still present) in favor of focusing on a combination of individual person and company gain combined with gains for the larger communities that are relevant. You handle this somewhat paradoxical "both/and" well because you see how what you do is connected to the larger purpose of the organization. You are connected to communities both within and outside your organization and know exactly how your contribution fits in to making these enterprises better.

TABLE 12.5 Structure and Practice in the Emerging Leading Corporate Citizen

Structures Shift From . . .	To . . .
Rigid boundaries	Overlapping, merging boundaries (boundary-less-ening)
Leadership through authority	Leadership through vision and values
High, relatively rigid structure	Emergent, flexible and adaptive structure
Single, simple financial bottom line, financial capital	Multiple bottom lines
One dominant stakeholder (shareholder)	Multiple primary/secondary stakeholders
Leadership at the top (top down)	Leadership is everywhere (top down and bottom up)
Practices Move From . . .	**To . . .**
Economizing, power aggrandizing	Inclusion of civilizing and ecologizing
Exploitative practices, disrespectful	Integrity in practices, respectful
Reactive, proactive strategies	Interactive strategies
Objective, unemotional, meaningless	Objective/subjective, emotional/meaningful
Discretionary corporate responsibility	Responsibility integral to operating practices
Managing stakeholders	Developing stakeholder relationships
Fragmented functions	Integral systems
Operating instrumentally	Operating with integrity
Valuing contributions from and to owners	Valuing contributions of all stakeholders
Lack of accountability and transparency	Necessary accountability and transparency
Externalizing costs	Internalizing costs
Wasteful, exploitive operations	Ecologizing, nature-based operations

Structure and Practice in the Emerging Leading Corporate Citizen

Accompanying the shifts in vision, values, and work in the new paradigm organization, leading corporate citizens will find themselves shifting both their structure and practices to accommodate improved relationships with stakeholders and more awareness of responsibilities. Table 12.5 lists some of the significant shifts in structure and practice that can be expected as we continue our imaginization.

Imagine an organization where there is consistent and regular interaction and dialogue between internal stakeholders and those who used to be outside, such as suppliers, customers, and community members. Because new-paradigm organizations will likely tend to structure themselves through collaborative alliances and partnerships of various kinds, the formerly clear and rather rigid boundaries separating different stakeholder groups have tended to blur. Overlapping and merging boundaries can be expected in areas such as customer relations where practices that tie one company's purchasing system directly to others can be expected to increase, or in community relations where social partnerships to solve community-based problems of mutual concern evolve.

Leadership through vision and values continues apace, creating the organizational glue and direction that provides structure, substituting emergent, flexible, and adaptive teams, ad hoc groupings, task forces, and project/process units for formerly readily identifiable (and permanent) structures and units. This adaptive structure, while complex and somewhat difficult to understand, allows the company to meet different stakeholders' needs as they arise in what might be called emergent structure or webs of connected groups that develop sustaining relationships over time.

The respectful and interactive stakeholder relationships point the company in the direction of being accountable for and to multiple rather than a single stakeholder. Indeed, the company has moved from managing stakeholders to a more respectful stance of managing stakeholder relationships and assuring their mutuality of interests. Thus, measurement systems and the relevant reward systems are geared to performance in the essential primary and secondary stakeholder domains of not only owners (financial performance and wealth generation), but also employee relations, customer relations, supplier relations, community relations, public and governmental affairs, and others as relevant. Multiple bottom lines are followed and reported on externally so that the company's responsibility and practices are transparent to and accountable for impacts on key external stakeholders.

Imagine that internal corporate practices have also shifted so that the dominant behaviors associated with economizing and power-aggrandizing values have expanded to also include values of civilizing (relationship building) and ecologizing, assuring ecological, community, and company sustainability over the long term. Because of the transparency of corporate actions to stakeholders, the company is clear that it operates in all respects with integrity in both of its definitions, honesty/straightforwardness and wholeness. Responsibility is considered integral to all operating practices; little is done without considering the stakeholder and ecological implications: thus, accountability is built into the operating practices.

The close link of the company's vision and articulated higher purposes helps generate meaning for stakeholders who interact with the firm. Clear attention is paid to the corporate environment aesthetically, as well as to assuring that stakeholders are satisfied, in the traditional sense of customer satisfaction and quality management. To cope with the complexity of knowing that stakeholders are whole individuals, care is taking in developing all relationships so that abuses and exploitation of stakeholders, wherever they are, are practically nonexistent. Stakeholder contributions are valued, wherever they come from.

Costs are fully internalized, with accounting systems incorporating the full product or service life cycle and all associated environmental costs. The company is an industry leader in advancing full-costing processes globally. Operations are based on ecologizing and natural principles that indicate no-waste practices.

TABLE 12.6 New Logics and New Values

Sources: This chart is adapted from Douglas R. Austrom and Lawrence J. Lad, "Issues Management Alliances: New Responses, New Values, and New Logics," in *Research in Corporate Social Performance and Policy*, vol. 2, ed. James E. Post (Greenwich, CT: JAI Press, 1989), pp. 233–355; Ken Wilber, *The Image of Sense and Soul: Integrating Science and Reason* (Boston: Shambala, 1998); plus author's additions.

Prevailing Paradigm	Emergent Paradigm
Basic World View	
Mechanistic, simple, linear	Organic, complexity, chaotic
Cartesian, Newtonian	Ecological, systemic
Atomistic, fragmented	Holistic (holons)
Objective	Objective, subjective, interobjective, intersubjective
Disengaged, passive	Engaged, active
"It" orientation	"I," "we," and "it" orientations
Implicit Logics: Perspectives	
Focus on distinctions and separations	Focus on interdependence and interrelatedness
Either/or oppositions	Both/and relations
Dualities as opposites and contradictions	Dualities as paradoxes
Top down	Top down/bottom up
Leading Values	
Self-contained individualism and agency	Communitarianism and community
Zero-sum-game mentality	Positive-sum-gain mentality
Win–lose orientation	Win–win orientation

New Logics across the Globe

Gaining the needed new perspective or *metanoia* involves incorporating into our thinking a new set of logics, or ways of thinking and new values that accompany those logics.[6] Some years ago scholars Douglas Austrom and Lawrence Lad neatly synthesized these new logics and values that appear to be emerging globally. (See Table 12.6, which has been supplemented with ideas from Ken Wilber and the present author.) As has been discussed throughout this book, even Western thinking is rapidly moving from the fragmentation and atomization of the mechanistic Western view of science, nature, and the world at large, in part because of the influence of the new chaos and complexity theories.

In many respects, progressive thinking about business in society is already generally moving toward a more integrated and holistic view that includes an ecological and systems perspective. It also is beginning to incorporate the nonobservable elements of emotions, aesthetic appreciation, and individual and collective meaning, sometimes characterized as creating meaningful work, other times as spirituality in work. These new logics and values are manifesting themselves in many of the companies, research, and ways of thinking cited earlier in this book, as well as many others omitted in the interests of space and time. The general movement is thus away from passive and toward engaged (interactive) behaviors, away from fragmentation and toward interdependence and interrelatedness, encompassing the logic of both/and rather than either/or. Paradoxes emerge in this both/and logic, necessitating a need for individuals and organizations to be able to cope with tensions of the opposites, such as in the top-down/bottom-up authority implied in the new logics.

Table 12.6 thus illuminates a decided shift away from mechanistic and inorganic perspectives on organizing and society, which foster dominance and rigidity along with a win–lose orientation. Movement is generally toward a more organic and holistic framing that incorporates a both/and rather than either/or logic, representing in some respects an integration of Western and Eastern philosophies. Although this emerging paradigm for leading corporate citizenship is fundamentally more complex than the older more linear and mechanistic approach, it can also be energizing and exciting because it asks leaders to think deeply about what they are doing and why they are doing it. The excitement comes in part because it based on a realistic assessment of the complexity of human life itself and becomes the emerging perspective as embedded in an understanding of the meaning of relationship, a fundamental aspect, as we have seen, of corporate citizenship.

Because the emerging paradigm is organic and holistic, it incorporates not only objective and scientifically observable phenomenon, but also the aesthetic, emotional, and appreciative, more subjective and intersubjective elements of living life within communities of various sorts, shapes, and sizes. Transformation in thinking—the *metanoia* we have been discussing—is thus needed in societies, too, a transformation that has implications for us all as human beings living in what we hope will be civil and democratic societies, with economies that are growing successfully, profitability, and sustainably.

Leading Corporate Citizens in Societies

The final stage of our imaginization is to assess what this metanoia might mean for the societies in which leading corporate citizens operate. Table 12.7 identifies just a few of the dominant social and political shifts that can be expected in our imaginary trip into the future.

Imagine that businesses act collaboratively with nongovernmental organizations, international nongovernmental organizations, and governmental organizations (NGOs, INGOs, and GOs), to ensure that the activities of each sphere are appropriately balanced with each other. Governments, tending toward democracy because of the power of information and its ready availability, rely on businesses to provide employment, economic development, and growth in the well-being and lifestyles of their citizens. All of this economic and social development is sensitively handled, keeping in mind the core cultural identity of each society and its

TABLE 12.7 Global Governance in the Emerging Paradigm

Social and Political Shifts From . . .	To . . .
Dominant economic sphere	Balance among economic, political, and civil society spheres of activity
Nonsustainable development	Sustainable development
Exploitive and abusive development	Respectful development
Uninformed, passive, voiceless stakeholders	Informed, active stakeholders with voice
Nation-state legal-regulatory framework	International legal-regulatory framework
Diminishing social capital	Enhancing constructive social capital
Few global standards, expectations	Global standards and expectations
Little enforcement capacity globally	Global enforcement mechanisms
Little stakeholder involvement in governance	Stakeholder engagement in governance

distinctiveness so that citizens can develop a sustained sense of local community, bolstered by appropriate local, regional, and national infrastructure.

Development in the new paradigm is handled with ecological sustainability clearly in mind. INGOs have evolved that demand accountability and transparency from the corporation, assuring responsible practice, and providing clear global standards to which all companies voluntarily adhere. Many stakeholders are now involved in assuring that companies are governed properly—and that they meet global standards, ethically, operationally, and strategically. When abuses in human rights, labor rights, or human and child welfare do occur, companies as well as organizations from the political and civil society spheres are quick to act and compel the abuser to either change its practices or drive it out of business. Independent observers regularly audit corporate practices with audits then released publicly because international standards have created high expectations that such reporting will be standard.

The wide availability of information about these practices online makes keeping abusive practices difficult, especially as governments are clear about educating all citizens to a high enough level that democracy and free markets based on the biological principles articulated by David Korten, The Natural Step, and others are followed rigorously. All market-based activities tend to support communities, rather than debilitate them, and citizens are encouraged to voice concerns so that they can be attended to by the appropriate corporate relations people, who are spread, in their leadership capacities, throughout companies.

An international legal and regulatory framework has been devised by all the nations of the world to foster sustainability, to provide opportunities for stakeholders to voice concerns, and to assure accountability in all corporate activities. Enforcement mechanisms are strong and sanctions, when necessary, are quickly imposed. Perhaps the most critical sanction is that of releasing negative reputational information about corporate abusers publicly, a type of sanction that tends to damage the company's reputation among its stakeholders sufficiently that it actually prevents abuses.

Leading Challenges: Leading Corporate Citizens in the New Paradigm

Throughout this book, we have been discussing the shift to an emerging paradigm for leading corporate citizens. Admittedly, the book takes an optimistic rather than pessimistic point of view in suggesting that such a shift is taking place and will continue to evolve in a constructive and positive direction. Clearly, power and resource inequities exist and not all corporations behave responsibly, pushed by intense competition and demands for shareholder value to economize in sometimes destructive ways.

Part of the agenda has been to look explicitly at what a new paradigm for leading corporate citizens would look like when it is more fully evolved. We have done this by using information, examples, and research that are already available as guides to what might be in a world where balance, collaboration, and respect guide operating practices and, in this chapter, by imagining the possibilities.

Why do I believe that this optimistic scenario makes sense? After all, problems abound in the economic, political, and civil society spheres of activity that constitute human civilization—as well as in the natural environment. Despite these problems and the inherent difficulties, dilemmas, and paradoxes in overcoming them, we have attempted to paint a picture of the way that companies can act if they hope to become leading corporate citizens. And there are signs that many leading corporate citizens, some of which have been cited in earlier chapters, are beginning to move in the directions articulated in this chapter.

Over the course of the book, we have looked at significant evidence that acting as a leading citizen not only results in effective behaviors—doing the right thing with respect to stakeholders and the natural environment—but also economizes, resulting in practices that are efficient and profitable. Leaders of leading corporate citizens today have begun to understand this truly bigger picture and to act accordingly. Slowly but surely, they are moving their companies along this path toward this emergent and progressive corporate paradigm.

It requires leadership and significant wisdom to take steps that others might view as against the mainstream in a time of turbulence and great performance pressures. It requires courage to take responsibility for one's (and one's company's) impacts. It demands mindfulness and true wisdom to operate with respect for stakeholders and to engage with them rather than making assumptions about them and their needs.

Is taking this path always easy? No. Is it always more profitable in the short run? No. Will competitors still act in aggressive and competitive dog-eat-dog ways trying to outstrip companies acting in the paradigm of leading corporate citizens, which is far more collaborative in its orientation? Yes. But are companies that act with respect for stakeholders, with consideration for the full impacts of their decisions, with integrity and wisdom, successful? The evidence strongly suggests that the answer is yes.

Endnotes

1. See David Korten, *The Post-Corporate World* (San Francisco: Berrett-Koehler, 1999). See also Fritjof Capra, *The Web of Life* (New York: Anchor Doubleday, 1995); and Stuart Kauffman, *At Home in the Universe: The Search for the Laws of Self-Organization and Complexity* (New York: Oxford University Press, 1995).

2. Peter M. Senge, *The Fifth Discipline* (New York: Currency Doubleday, 1990).

3. See Russell L. Ackoff, "On Learning and the Systems That Facilitate It," *Reflection* 1, no. 1 (1999), pp. 14–24, reprinted from the Center for Quality of Management, Cambridge, MA, 1996. See also Karl E. Weick, "Educating for the Unknowable: The Infamous Real World," presentation at the Academy of Management, Chicago, IL, 1999.

4. Ackoff, "On Learning," p. 16. Italics added.

5. The term *imaginization* was developed by Gareth Morgan in *Imaginization: The Art of Creative Management* (Newbury Park, CA: Sage, 1993).

6. See Douglas R. Austrom and Lawrence J. Lad, "Issues Management Alliances: New Responses, New Values, and New Logics," in *Research in Corporate Social Performance and Policy*, vol. 2, ed. James E. Post (Greenwich, CT: JAI Press, 1989), pp. 233–355.

Index